THEOLOGY IN THE RESPONSA

THE LITTMAN LIBRARY OF
JEWISH CIVILIZATION

*The Littman Library of Jewish Civilization is a registered UK charity
Registered charity no. 1000784*

Theology in the Responsa

◆

LOUIS JACOBS

London

The Littman Library of Jewish Civilization

in association with Liverpool University Press

The Littman Library of Jewish Civilization
Registered office: 4th floor, 7–10 Chandos Street, London W1G 9DQ

in association with Liverpool University Press
4 Cambridge Street, Liverpool L69 7ZU, UK
www.liverpooluniversitypress.co.uk/littman

Managing Editor: Connie Webber

Distributed in North America by
Oxford University Press Inc., 198 Madison Avenue,
New York, NY 10016, USA

First published 1975 by Routledge & Kegan Paul Ltd for
The Littman Library of Jewish Civilization
First issued in paperback 2005

Catalogue records for this book are available from the
British Library and the Library of Congress
ISBN 978–1–904113–27–0

Printed and bound in Great Britain by
CPI Group (UK) Ltd., Croydon, CR0 4YY

Contents

Preface

The Responsa literature extends for a period of over a thousand years down to the present day. The majority of the questions to which the authors addressed themselves concerned Jewish law in all its ramifications. New situations and circumstances, different in many ways from those which obtained in former ages, posed problems of conduct for which no direct guidance could have been expected in the classical sources. Yet it was believed that Judaism, if properly investigated, had an answer to every question, was capable of showing which way was right and which wrong in matters of ritual, social and family life, reaction to the Gentile community and communal endeavours. The central theme of the Responsa literature is the discovery of the right way for a Jew to behave; what it is that God would have him do. With their mastery of the sources, especially the Talmud (the major fount of wisdom for those who engaged in this task), the famous Respondents were able to give advice on all the practical problems that were the concern of their questioners; most of their replies came to enjoy authority in subsequent Jewish law.

Although most of the emphasis in the Responsa is undoubtedly on practice, there are to be found in nearly all the great Responsa collections discussions of a theological nature; naturally so since new conditions pose problems for belief as well as for practice. From time to time, questions were asked regarding fundamental principles of the Jewish faith, the answers being arrived at by more or less the same methods that were used to propound the law in a particular case.

The fact that theological problems found their way into Responsa collections, collections generally put together either by the authors themselves or by their disciples, gives them a special significance. It is almost as if these questions were treated with the full precision, seriousness and weight demanded when the masters of the law gave their legal decisions. A theologian might see no great harm in an occasional flight of fancy, he might feel encouraged to embark on a purely speculative exercise, he might be inclined to present some of his conclusions only very tentatively. But a Rabbi discussing theology in a Responsum would try to be as clear, unambiguous and decisive as when he was determining in a legal dispute whether A or B were in the right.

This book is a study of theological questions as they appear in the Responsa literature. To my knowledge, this kind of investigation has never hitherto been undertaken, perhaps because of the unpromising nature of the literature, at first glance, for this purpose. The study will reveal, it is hoped, that matters of belief occupied a prominent place in the writings even of those authors who won their reputation as distinguished academic lawyers rather than as metaphysicians.

The method adopted has been to examine, century by century, those Responsa collections in which theology is considered; theology here being interpreted as meaning any topic in which the chief preoccupation is with belief, even when, as is not infrequent in this literature, belief has practical consequences that can immediately be seen. Since there are several thousand collections of Responsa, it has not been possible to list every theological topic treated in the literature. None the less, an attempt at a fair degree of comprehensiveness has been attempted, at least in that the more noteworthy Respondents have all been studied, unless, of course, their collections contain no theological questions. One result of the investigation is to give the lie to the view that Jewish theology is un-Jewish and that the Halakhist concentrates solely on the deed, ignoring the beliefs that provide the deed with its sanction and infuse it with life.

My thanks are due to Dr David Goldstein for reading through the manuscript and offering a number of helpful suggestions. Mrs Camilla Raab has edited the book, taking great pains to bring order into a somewhat chaotic text, and I am most grateful to her.

Dates
Dates are given in the English version for the sake of convenience. The authors of the Responsa, it is hardly necessary to state, always use the Jewish reckoning.

CHAPTER I

The Gaonic Period (to 1050)

The Gaonim, the heads of the Babylonian schools of Sura and Pumbedita after the close of the Talmud down to the middle of the eleventh century, had questions addressed to them from many parts of the Jewish world. Their decisions came to enjoy the weightiest authority in Jewish law. The majority of Gaonic Responsa are those of Sherira Gaon (d. 1006), head of Pumbedita, and his son Hai (939–1038). Sherira retired at an advanced age in order to make way for Hai. It is reported that after Sherira's death there was read in the synagogue the narrative of Solomon's succession to the throne of David (I Kgs 2 : 10–12) adapted to the occasion: 'And Sherira slept with his fathers . . . And Hai sat upon the throne of Sherira his father; and his kingdom was established firmly.' Both these teachers were the acknowledged leaders not only of their own community but of Jews in North Africa and Europe. They were both active for an extremely long period, Sherira dying at the age of one hundred, and Hai writing Responsa in the month before he died at ninety-nine.

The Babylonian schools flourished during the Gaonic period under generally benevolent Islamic rulers. The two main challenges to Rabbinic Judaism in this period came from Islam from the outside, and from the Karaites from within. The challenge posed by Islam was not only that of a rival religion. Arabic culture and Greek philosophy in its Arabic garb won many adherents among Jews. There was much theological speculation, and the need to reconcile philosophical views with the Jewish tradition was keenly felt. The Karaites, rejecting Rabbinic interpretation in favour of their own understanding of the Bible, frequently poured ridicule on the Talmud, the depository of Rabbinic thought. More especially, the Karaites, divided among themselves in matters of law, were united in their scorn of the Aggadah (the non-legal part of the Talmud) for its anthropomorphism. The Karaite author Qirqisani, for example, some time before the year 937, wrote his work *The Book of Lights and the High Heavens*, in which he attacks the Rabbinic Aggadah as well as the Rabbinic work *Shiur Komah*, dealing with the 'measurements of God'.[1] The Responsa of the Babylonian Gaonim reflect this cultural and philosophical background. Saadiah Gaon (882–942) of Sura wrote his systematic defence of Rabbinic Judaism, *Book of Beliefs and Opinions*, devoting himself in this work entirely to the new theological problems with which the tradition was faced. But other Gaonim, too, were obliged to deal with this kind of question as is evident from their Responsa.

A topic much considered during the Gaonic period, obviously under the influence of Islamic thought, was the Jewish attitude to fatalism. One of the questions addressed to Hai Gaon by the sages of Gabès in Tunisia[2] concerns the verse: 'Go and say to Hezekiah: Thus saith the Lord, the God of David thy father: I have heard thy prayer, I have seen thy tears; behold, I will add unto thy days, fifteen years' (Isa. 38 : 5). This promise was made to Hezekiah when he prayed to be allowed to live, after Isaiah, at the command of God, had told him, 'Set thy house in order; for thou shalt die and not live' (Isa. 38 : 1). Does this mean that the original declaration, 'For thou shalt die and not live', was only conditional? Does it imply that even when God has set a limit to the number of a man's years they can later be added to or diminished? Is the meaning of it all that God is capable of changing His mind? This problem must have been acute for thoughtful Jews for some time, since

[1] See W. Bacher, 'Qirqisani, the Karaite, and his work on Jewish Sects', *Karaite Studies*, ed. P. Birnbaum, pp. 266–71
[2] S. A. Wertheimer, *Kohelet Shelomo*, no. 2, pp. 2–14

Saadiah discusses it in his *Beliefs and Opinions*.[3] Saadiah remarks that the verse does not imply that God abrogated His original decree. The decree was conditional on whether Hezekiah chose to be reprimanded and the same idea is behind every instance of God accepting the plea of a submissive penitent.

Hai gives his own understanding of the matter. When Isaiah said, 'thou shalt die and not live', he did not set, in God's name, any time limit for Hezekiah's death. Once it was seen that Hezekiah had recovered from that particular illness it became known retrospectively that God's decree for Hezekiah to die did not mean that he would die from that particular illness. Many of God's decrees are conditional, depending on the various possibilities present in God's thought. This idea is implied in the verse: 'At one instant, I may speak concerning a nation, and concerning a kingdom' (Jer. 18 : 7).

When it is said that God knows that certain conditions will produce certain effects and other conditions will result in different effects, it must not be understood to mean that there is any doubt in God's mind. The meaning is rather that God knows what the character of certain events would be like were they to happen, though, in fact, He knows that they will not happen. God knows beforehand with absolute certainty those events that will actually happen, but the other possibilities are also present in His mind *in potentia*. For instance, when David asked: 'Will the men of Keilah deliver me into his hand? will Saul come down, as Thy servant hath heard?', God replied: 'He will come down' (I Sam. 23 : 11). In fact, the men of Keilah did not deliver David into Saul's hand and Saul did not come down. There is no doubt that God knew beforehand what would actually happen, but He knew that if David were to remain in Keilah Saul would come down and the men of Keilah would deliver David into Saul's hand. In the same way, God knew that if Hezekiah failed to offer his supplications he would die from that illness; although God also knew beforehand that, in fact, Hezekiah would offer his prayers and that, as a result, years would be added to his life. Only God knows how that which did not actually happen would have happened if in fact it had happened.

---

[3] III, 9, trans. Samuel Rosenblatt, p. 170

3

God's foreknowledge of events, continues Hai, is not causative. Although God knows beforehand that a man will sin, the sin is not caused by God's foreknowledge. Therefore, it is preferable to say: 'God knows beforehand what will be', than to say: 'That which God knows beforehand will be', as if that which will be depends on God's foreknowledge. Furthermore, remarks Hai, there is no such thing as an allotted span to man's life. God does not determine beforehand how long a man will live, although the actual span of a man's life is present in God's foreknowledge. The verse: 'the number of thy days I will fulfil' (Exod. 23 : 26) means no more than that God will prolong life, and possibly refers to the promise of long life; i.e. not to the completion of a span allotted beforehand. Similarly, the verse, 'or his day shall come to die' (I Sam. 26 : 10), refers to the day on which he will die naturally as it is known beforehand to God. It does not imply that each individual is given beforehand a special term of life beyond whose span it is impossible for him to live. In this Responsum Hai expressly denies any fatalistic interpretation of the life-span as taught by some of the Arabian philosophers to whom he refers.

The question Hai now has to consider is: when a man is murdered does this mean that even had he not been murdered he would have died at that particular moment? Hai replies that we simply do not know. We can either suppose that he would have died at that time in any event, even if he had not perished at the hand of his murderer, or we can suppose that if he had not been murdered he would have lived on until a later date. But, it might be objected, supposing a murderer slew a large number of people on the same day, is it plausible to suggest that if they had not been murdered they would all have died in any event on the same day? Why not?, replies Hai. From our experience we know that many people do sometimes die in a short space of time as the result of a fatal accident, as when, for instance, a building collapses killing a crowd of people assembled there, or when a ship goes down with the loss of all passengers.

But, it can be argued, if the view is taken that the victim of a murder would have died in any event at that precise moment, why should the murderer be held guilty and why should he be punished? The answer Hai gives is that it is the act of murder which constitutes the offence even though the victim would have died in any event at the same time by other means. The murderer is deserving of punishment for the evil act which was his and his alone.

The same sages of Gabès put another theological question, founded on the doctrine of providence, to Hai.[4] Why did Jonah try to escape after God had commanded him to go to Nineveh? The difficulty is in God's choice as a prophet of one who refused to obey Him. Does it not look as if God made a poor choice and hence was mistaken? Hai notes that this is no new problem. It has long been discussed by a number of sages. Some have argued[5] that Jonah did go to Nineveh at God's behest. Jonah's flight took place after he had delivered his message, which went unheeded by the men of Nineveh. Jonah anticipated that God would send him a second time with even more dire threats and he felt sure that, were these to be delivered, they would have their effect. It was to avoid being sent a second time that Jonah fled. There was thus no actual disobedience on the part of Jonah. Other sages argue that Jonah did try to escape from fulfilling God's commands. But this was not an act of defiance or wilful refusal, so as to call into question God's poor choice. Jonah believed that even when God sends a man on His errands that man has a right to take steps to avoid his mission. Jonah knew quite well that once a prophet has accepted his mission he must not fail to carry it out, but he imagined that it is legitimate to refuse to accept the burden in the first place. To be sure, Jonah was mistaken in his belief, but even a prophet, being only human, is capable of error. Moreover, it is possible that God chose Jonah, knowing that he would refuse. God was prepared to choose an unreliable man precisely in order to bring about the miracles which happened to Jonah when he tried to escape from carrying out his mission.

The background of Islamic thought is evident in the whole of this discussion. Behind it all is the Muslim claim for Mohammed,

---

[4] Wertheimer, op. cit., pp. 7–10.
[5] Wertheimer, op. cit., p. 7 note 1, suggests that Hai refers here to Saadiah, *Book of Beliefs and Opinions*, III, 5, trans. Rosenblatt, pp. 153–4

reliable and infallible, as opposed to the claims made for the Hebrew prophets. Hai is anxious to defend the Biblical account in that it does not impute error to God, but in the process he states the view that it is no part of the Jewish religion to believe that a prophet must be a moral and intellectual superman. Even the prophet is subject to error and God can make use of His frail creatures to fulfil His own purposes.

The sages of Gabès also addressed a question to Hai[6] on the story of Eve and the serpent (Gen. 3). The problem is the obvious one of how a serpent could talk. Hai admits that in any event the story bristles with difficulties. Briefly, he says, from the plain meaning of the narrative it is clear that the serpent was able to converse with Eve, though we are unable to state with confidence whether or not the serpent used human speech. From the statement that the serpent was punished it is also clear that he was a moral creature capable of sinning. However, when Scripture says: 'Now the serpent was more subtle' (Gen. 3 : 1), this may only refer to that one particular serpent, not to the whole species; though, Hai adds, this is not conclusive.

A number of Hai's questioners were disturbed by the Karaite attack on the anthropomorphism of the Talmudic Aggadah. Hai was asked[7] to explain the Talmudic saying[8] that there are three watches in the night at each of which the Holy One, blessed be He, sits enthroned and roars like a lion over the destruction of the Temple. Hai first explains that the 'watches' are the fixed times in the night when the angels sing praises to God. The saying that God roars like a lion has to be understood figuratively, and the true significance of the passage is that Israel should offer supplication to God during the watches of the night for the Temple to be rebuilt.

This idea, that the Talmud really refers to man's obligations when it speaks of God doing this or that, is used by Hai in another Responsum[9] in dealing with the Talmudic sayings that God wears *tefillin*,[10] that He prays,[11] and that He wrapped Himself in a shawl

---

[6] Wertheimer, op. cit., pp. 13–14
[7] Lewin, *Otzar Ha-Gaonim*, vol. 1, *Berakhot*, Haifa, 1928, pp. 2–3
[8] Ber. 3a   [9] Lewin, *Berakhot*, p. 12   [10] Ber. 6a   [11] Ber. 7a

like a Prayer Leader.[12] The meaning is, according to Hai, that God taught Moses how to pray and how to use the *tefillin* in prayer. When the Talmud gives God's prayer as: 'May it be My will that My mercy may suppress My anger, and that My mercy may prevail over My attributes so that I may deal with My children in the attribute of mercy', the meaning is not that God prays to Himself but that He taught Moses how to recite the kind of prayer that will result in the flow of the divine mercy. In reality, this interpretation goes back to Saadiah.[13]

In another Responsum[14] Hai defends the Talmud by engaging in a demythologising process. In his reply to this questioner, Hai wishes to explain a passage, particularly offensive on the face of it, in such a way as to provide a key for the understanding of all such passages. The passage in question[15] concerns the rumblings of the earth. It is said here that R. Kattina was told by a necromancer that earth rumblings are caused when the Holy One, blessed be He, calls to mind His children plunged in suffering among the nations of the world. God lets fall two tears into the ocean, and the sound is heard from one end of the earth to the other, and that is the rumbling. R. Kattina appeared to reject the saying of the necromancer but, the Talmud continues, he only did so in order to prevent people relying on such a base person. R. Kattina added that the earth rumblings are caused by God clapping His hands, as it is said: 'I will also smite My hands together, and I will satisfy My fury' (Ezek. 21 : 22). R. Nathan said that the earth rumblings are caused by God emitting a sigh, as it is said: 'I will satisfy My fury upon them and I will be eased' (Ezek. 5 : 13). The Rabbis said: He treads upon the firmament, as it is said: 'He giveth a noise as they that tread grapes against all the inhabitants of the earth' (Jer. 25 : 30). R. Aha b. Jacob said: He presses His feet together beneath the throne of glory, as it is said: 'Thus saith the Lord, the heaven is My throne and the earth is My footstool' (Isa. 66 : 1).

Hai first observes that this passage belongs to the Aggadah and, with regard to such non-legal matters, the Talmudic sages

---

[12] RH 17b   [13] Lewin, *Berakhot*, pp. 14–15
[14] Ibid., pp. 130–2   [15] Ber. 59a

themselves say that one does not rely on the Aggadah: a statement that served as a guiding principle for teachers of the Talmud when confronted by particularly embarrassing passages.[16] This was known to the Karaites who took issue with this line of defence.[17] We must be convinced, says Hai, both by our commonsense and by the authority of our sages that God cannot be compared to any of His creatures. Laughing, weeping, sighing or tears cannot be applied to God. Once this is appreciated, it becomes obvious that any Talmudic reference to such things as applied to God must be understood figuratively. For that matter the prophets, too, speak of the eye of God, the hand of God and the like, because 'the Torah speaks in the language of men'.[18] The same principle is to be observed at work in the Talmudic statements about God. R. Kattina, in our passage, holds, as do the Rabbis generally, that Israel is especially significant to God. Even natural phenomena are therefore interpreted by the Rabbis as indications of God's love for Israel, serving Israel as reminders of its responsibilities, just as Scripture interprets the natural appearance of the rainbow as a sign of the covenant (Gen. 9 : 8–17). God is grieved at the destruction of the Temple and Israel's dispersion among the nations. He suffers, as it were, with Israel and it is to this that R. Kattina wishes to call attention. Thus rain pouring into the ocean is interpreted poetically as if God is dropping His tears in grief at Israel's troubles. After all, the poets do speak of the clouds as 'eyelids' and the rain dropping from them as 'tears'. Scripture says of Moses that God spoke to him 'mouth to mouth' (Num. 12 : 8). Obviously it was never intended to suggest that God had a mouth like that of Moses but that God, when He spoke to Moses, created a special sound resembling human speech and it is this sound that is said to be God's 'mouth'. By the same token the

[16] See the sources cited in *Encyclopedia Talmudit*, vol. I, p. 62. The Talmudic source is JT Peah 2: 6, 17a

[17] See Bacher, op. cit., p. 268

[18] This saying, originating in the Talmud (Ber. 31b and freq.) and denoting that no laws are to be derived from poetical expressions in Scripture, is applied here by Hai to the problem of anthropomorphism. Subsequent to Hai, the term was used in this sense by other thinkers, e.g. Bahya Ben Joseph Ibn Pakuda, *The Book of Direction to the Duties of the Heart*, chapter 1, 10; Maimonides, *Commentary to the Mishna*, Sanhedrin 10 (*Helek*), Principle 3. It would appear that Hai is the first to have used the term in this sense

Rabbis are justified in calling the rain God's 'tears'. The Talmud[19] tells us that when R. Abbahu died, the columns of Caesarea ran with tears. The meaning is that God caused moisture to run from the columns so that they appeared to be weeping. If such happened when a single great teacher died how much more so at the destruction of the Temple and the sorrows of Israel as a whole. The same interpretation must be given to the other descriptions in our Talmudic passage. The earth rumblings are compared to sounds resembling human sighs, the clapping of hands and the stamping of feet. In an interesting aside, Hai refers to Greek mythology which similarly endows natural phenomena with personality, a striking example of how an official Rabbinic leader was ready to acknowledge the mythological element in both Biblical and Rabbinic thought.

One of the great themes for discussion during the Middle Ages was the Jewish doctrine of creation. A Responsum on the theme is attributed in some sources to Hai, in others to Sherira.[20] The Talmud[21] reports R. Joshua b. Levi as saying: 'All creatures of the creation were brought into being with their full stature, their full capacities, and their full beauty.' This is explained by the earlier Gaonim to mean that God asked each creature, before He created it, how it wished to be created and He then brought it into being in the form it had chosen for itself. The questioner found this concept absurd. How could a creature have a form *before* it was created? The Gaon replies that the concept is, indeed, difficult. He personally had never heard of such an interpretation nor can he accept it now that he has heard it. True, remarks the Gaon, the philosophers have stated that an idea of each creature is present in the mind of God, but they do not say that a creature can have a form before it is created. In any event this notion of the philosophers (the reference is, of course, to the Platonic *idea*) is not found in Jewish sources. Consequently, the suggested interpretation is nonsense. Others, however, he goes on to say, do accept it but understand it as referring not to particular creatures but to the

---

[19] MK 25b
[20] Lewin, *Otzar Ha-Gaonim*, vol. 5, *Rosh Ha-Shanah*, Jerusalem, 1932, p. 22
[21] RH 11a

spiritual forces, the angels on high, appointed to be the guardians of particular species of animals. It was to these that God addressed His question as to the form each particular species was to assume when created. The Gaon himself, on the other hand, understands R. Joshua b. Levi's saying to mean that God created each creature in the form which, in His foreknowledge, He knew it would eventually possess.

The Gaonim, like the sages of the Talmud, never questioned the belief in angels. The Karaites were critical of the Rabbinic view that man can turn to the angels to bring his petitions before God. Qirqisani[22] finds fault with what he says is the Rabbinic interpretation of: 'For a bird of the air [lit. a winged creature] shall carry the voice' (Eccles. 10 : 20), namely, that the 'winged creature' is an angel (after Isa. 6 : 2) who brings prayers to God. A question addressed to the Gaon of Pumbedita by the sages of Kairouan in Tunisia in the year 992[23] concerns the role of the angels in this matter. The Talmud[24] tells of R. Eleazar who would say to a sick person: 'May God visit thee in peace', which he would say either in Hebrew or in Aramaic. The Talmud objects: R. Judah said that a man should never petition for his needs in Aramaic, and R. Johanan said: When a man petitions for his needs in Aramaic, the ministering angels do not heed him, for they do not understand Aramaic; i.e. they cannot, therefore, bring his prayers to God. To this the Talmud replies that the case of a sick person is different because the Shekhinah, the Divine Presence, is with him; i.e. he does not require the mediation of the angels. The Kairouan sages concluded that, with the exception of prayers for a sick person, prayers must not be recited in Aramaic. But, they asked, why are many of the prayers composed by the ancients and still recited at Sura and Pumbedita, from where they have spread to other parts of the world, in Aramaic? It might have been argued that during the Ten Days of Penitence the Shekhinah is near and it is akin to the instance of a sick person; but as a matter of fact Aramaic prayers are regularly recited on other days as well

---

[22] See Bacher, op. cit., p. 267
[23] Lewin, *Otzar Ha-Gaonim*, vol. 2, *Shabbat*, Haifa, 1930, pp. 4–6
[24] Sabb. 12b

as these—on public fast-days, for example. Moreover, the majority of the Gaonic compositions for both public and private worship are in Aramaic.

The Gaon first defends the practice of man's entreating angels to do his behest and sees no objection to it.[25] This does not constitute any worship of the angels. It is simply that the angels are permitted to carry out some of man's wishes without having first to obtain permission from God. An example of this is provided by the angel who did as Lot asked him (Gen. 19 : 21). It is only to this type of request, directed to the angels, that the Rabbis refer when they say that a man must not use Aramaic. This is obvious since the angels, to whom the prayer is addressed, do not understand the language. But when a man asks of God direct, he can pray in Aramaic. When the Talmud states that the sick person is different because the Shekhinah is with him, the meaning is that here the angels can do nothing without obtaining permission from God, and hence the prayer, directed to God and not to the angels, can be in Aramaic.

The Gaon is dissatisfied with this reply. Even in his day, he notes, Aramaic prayers are used even when it is the angels who are addressed. Furthermore, there are reports in the Talmud of Rabbis conversing with the angels in Aramaic, which shows that the angels do understand this language. It follows that the Talmudic sages themselves are divided on this question and it is not a unanimous view that the angels do not understand Aramaic. It is, indeed, hard to understand the view that the angels do not know Aramaic. The angels are put to service by God to record man's speech. How, then, can it be said that they do not know Aramaic? The Gaon concludes that since some of the Talmudic Rabbis themselves reject the view that the angels do not know Aramaic, we, too, are justified in rejecting it.

25 On the much-discussed question of the invocation of angels in prayer see Zunz-Albeck, *Ha-Derashah Be-Yisrael*, p. 546 n. 100, in which the Rabbinic sources opposing such invocation are cited. The more philosophically-minded teachers in later ages were strictly opposed to the invocation of angels. Jacob Anatoli, for instance, in his *Malmad Ha-Talmidim*, p. 68a, goes so far as to find the practice condemned by the second commandment. There is a full discussion of the attitudes of later Jewish teachers on the question in Hezekiah Medini's *Sede Hemed*, ed. Friedman, vol. 8, pp. 288–90 (*Rosh Ha-Shanah*, II)

It is worth noting that in this typical Gaonic response the Talmudic Rabbis are only accepted as infallible authorities on matters where there is complete unanimity among them. Where there is a debate among the Rabbis on non-legal topics it is permitted to favour one view against the other on the grounds of common-sense. In legal matters the position is different, because, in the Gaonic period, there were precise rules for deciding the law when it was debated by the Talmudic Rabbis. The question of actual practice is also involved. Since the schools in Babylon had long accepted the practice of reciting Aramaic prayers, the established custom is to be followed unless it is based on a view that is rejected by all the Talmudic Rabbis. The process of accepting the whole of the Talmud as a corpus of revealed truth, in which even the contradictions somehow have a place in the entire pattern, had not yet emerged in the Gaonic period, though, as we shall see, the Gaonim differed among themselves on how far this attitude was to be advocated.

In their determined effort to defend the Talmud, the Gaonim rebuke questioners who fall into the trap of taking Talmudic hyperbole in a literal fashion. Sherira and Hai, for example, reply in this way to a questioner from Egypt[26] bothered by the extremely harsh statements in the Talmud regarding the ignorant Jew, the Am Ha-Aretz. In one passage[27] it is said that an Am Ha-Aretz may not eat meat; that a man must not marry the daughter of an Am Ha-Aretz; that it is permissible to stab an Am Ha-Aretz to death even on the Day of Atonement which falls on the sabbath; and that it is permitted to tear an Am Ha-Aretz like a fish. The questioner, puzzled by these statements, wished to know the reasoning behind them and whether they contained a rule of practice. He was particularly concerned because he had heard that some of the students in his native Egypt, taking these statements quite literally, had no qualms about cheating the ignorant.

The two Gaonim reply that passages such as this were never intended to convey a rule of practice. They are examples of

[26] Lewin, *Otzar Ha-Gaonim*, vol. 3, *Pesahim*, Jerusalem, 1930, pp. 67–70
[27] Pes. 49b

scholarly hyperbole whose purpose it was to decry ignorance of the Torah. Ironically, the Gaonim remark that if the students referred to really understand this passage literally as conveying a rule of practice, then poetic justice would demand that they, too, should be stabbed to death and their goods confiscated since, by giving their false interpretation, they are, on their own admission, total ignoramuses. Were they true disciples, they would know that it is forbidden to rob even a heathen,[28] let alone a fellow-Jew. The statement that an Am Ha-Aretz may not eat meat refers to the meat of an animal he had slaughtered himself without supervision. Ignorant as he is of the ritual laws, he may easily render the animal unfit for consumption. As for the statement that it is permitted to stab an Am Ha-Aretz to death, only a complete imbecile will imagine that it was intended to apply this in practice. It is forbidden to execute even the worst criminal on the sabbath. The statement refers to an Am Ha-Aretz who has designs on the life of another and is observed as he is about to carry out an act of murder. The life of the intended victim must be saved even if it means that the Am Ha-Aretz will be slain on the sabbath. The same rule would apply if the intended murderer were a scholar but, the passage wishes to imply, it is extremely unlikely that a scholar will ever be found in such a situation, whereas it is not so remote for an Am Ha-Aretz, without the discipline of the Torah, to be a potential murderer. When the passage goes on, however, to list six things that were said in connection with an Am Ha-Aretz, these do convey a rule of practice. The six things are: we do not commit testimony to an Am Ha-Aretz; we do not accept testimony from him; we do not reveal any secret to him; we do not appoint him a guardian of orphans; we do not appoint him to be a steward of charity funds; and we must not join his company on the road. But even here the testimony of an Am Ha-Aretz should be accepted if he is a God-fearing man, though with regard to ritual matters one should never rely on his testimony.

The most rationalistic of the Gaonim was undoubtedly Samuel b. Hophni (d. 1013), Gaon of Sura and father-in-law of Hai. A question regarding the strange Biblical story of the Witch of

[28] BK 113a

Endor (I Sam. 28) was put to Samuel b. Hophni. The questioner wished to know whether the story was to be taken literally, and whether the woman actually succeeded in raising Samuel from the dead. The Gaon replies that he finds it impossible to believe that God would have made a witch the instrument of raising Samuel. The true meaning of the story is that the witch, by trickery, persuaded Saul that she had succeeded in bringing up Samuel. The words attributed to Samuel in the narrative are the words the witch put into Samuel's mouth in order to convince Saul that she had succeeded. In that case, it can be asked, how is it that she forecast so accurately that Saul would die in battle? To this the Gaon replies that she knew it either because Samuel had so prophesied while he was still alive or that it was pure guesswork which by coincidence happened to come true. If God had really desired to inform Saul of his impending death in battle, He would have done so through a prophet, not through a witch. The Gaon adds that while he is aware that earlier teachers did understand the story literally, we are not obliged to follow them when what they say is quite contrary to reason. Both Saadiah Gaon and Hai Gaon, on the other hand, refuse to accept the rationalistic interpretation as stated by Samuel b. Hophni.[29] According to both these Gaonim, God really did bring up Samuel from the dead. The witch, not having enjoyed such miraculous powers hitherto, was consequently astonished, as Scripture implies, that she had been successful. The Talmudic Rabbis clearly understood the story to mean that it was Samuel who spoke to Saul, not the witch in Samuel's name. Scripture states that Samuel said: 'to-morrow shalt thou and thy sons be with me' (I Sam. 28 : 19), upon which the Rabbis comment:[30] ' "with me"—in my section of Paradise.' If it was the witch who said it, how could she possibly have known such a mystery?

Reading between the lines of the debate between Samuel b. Hophni and the other Gaonim, one sees that important theological issues were at stake. The first concerns the authority of the Talmudic Rabbis. It is one thing to be guided by commonsense, as Hai was ready to be guided in the matter of the angels, where the Talmudic Rabbis are in disagreement among themselves. It is quite another to reject, in the name of reason, what appears to be the unanimous view of the Rabbis, even though the matter does not concern law. Samuel b. Hophni is prepared to go to the lengths of preferring his rationalistic interpretation to the views of the Rabbis. The other Gaonim could not agree to go so far. The second point at issue, and this is stated explicitly by Samuel b. Hophni and the other Gaonim, is the attitude the Jew should adopt to Scripture as a whole. What was at stake was not simply the correct interpretation of a single chapter. If, as Samuel b. Hophni has argued, the Scriptural references to Samuel 'saying' this or that mean no more than that someone imagined him as saying it, what guarantee have we that other Scriptural references to someone 'saying' something are authentic; for example, when Moses 'said' something or when God 'spoke' to Moses?

A number of Gaonic Responsa deal with mystical or esoteric subjects. A famous Responsum of Sherira and Hai to the sages of Fez[31] concerns the *Shiur Komah* which, as we have seen, the Karaites attacked for its anthropomorphism and which was a constant source of embarrassment to later Jewish thinkers like Maimonides, who declared the book to be spurious.[32] The Mishnah[33] expressly forbids the exposition of the divine mysteries, declaring: 'Whoever takes no thought for the honour of his Maker, it were a mercy if he had not been born.' And yet the *Shiur Komah*[34] proceeds to give the detailed measurements of the Deity. Furthermore, R. Ishmael says: 'When I presented this to R. Akiba he said to me: Whoever knows these measurements of the Creator, and the praise of the Holy One, blessed be He, is assured of a share in the World to Come.' The sages of Fez took it for granted that

---

[31] Lewin, *Hagigah*, pp. 10–12
[32] See *Responsa of Maimonides*, ed. Joshua Blau, no. 117   [33] Hag. 2: 1
[34] See Lewin, *Hagigah*, p. 11 n. 1 for the source of this Midrash. Cf. *Merkavah Shelemah*, ed. S. Mussajov; G. Scholem, *Jewish Gnosticism, Merkabah Mysticism and Talmudic Tradition*, pp. 36–42; A. Altmann, *Studies in Religious Philosophy and Mysticism*, pp. 180 ff; and especially G. Scholem, 'Shiur Komah', *Encyclopedia Judaica*, vol. 14, pp. 1417–19

R. Ishmael really said what he is reported to have said but wished to know whether he was giving expression to an authentic tradition reaching back to Moses at Sinai or whether it was a purely personal opinion. If, in fact, R. Ishmael invented it himself, how could his view be reconciled with the stern injunction of the Mishnah?

In their joint reply, Sherira and his son state that it is not possible for them to explain fully this esoteric topic. Yet it can be stated categorically that R. Ishmael could not have invented such a thing. God has neither limbs nor measurement so that the references in the *Shiur Komah* are to the mystical measurements of God. The truth is that the *Shiur Komah* deals with the most recondite matters regarding the divine nature. These tremendous themes can be revealed only to initiates, and even then it is permitted to uncover only some of the basic principles and no more. As for the rest, the true disciple will be shown it from Heaven 'in the secret recesses of his heart'. Sherira and Hai remark further that even this they have only been permitted to reveal to the sages of Fez because they acknowledge their worth. They are not allowed to say anything more than this in writing. Even from mouth to mouth they can convey these mysteries only to students worthy of being initiated into them, and then only in the strictest privacy. They can only conclude with the prayer: 'May it be God's will that those who are worthy will receive illumination from Heaven.'

Another Responsum of Hai[35] dealing with esoteric subjects concerns the Talmudic account[36] of the four who entered the 'orchard' (*Pardes*). The passage reads:

Four entered an orchard: Ben Azzai, Ben Zoma, Aher and R. Akiba. R. Akiba said to them: When you reach the stones of pure marble, do not say: Water, water! For it is said: 'He that speaketh falsehood shall not be established before mine eyes' (Ps. 101 : 7). Ben Azzai gazed and died. Of him Scripture says: 'Precious in the sight of the Lord is the death of his saints' (Ps. 116 : 15). Ben Zoma gazed and

[35] Lewin, *Hagigah*, pp. 13–15
[36] Hag. 14b. On this passage, about which so much has been written, see now the acute analysis of E. E. Urbach in *Studies in Mysticism and Religion Presented to G. Scholem*, Heb. section, pp. 1–28

was stricken. Of him Scripture says: 'Hast thou found honey? Eat as much as is sufficient for thee, lest thou be filled therewith, and vomit it' (Prov. 25 : 16). Aher cut down the shoots. R. Akiba departed in peace.

Hai's questioner asked: What is the orchard? At what did Ben Zoma gaze that he became stricken and what precisely does 'stricken' mean in this context? What is the meaning of 'cutting down the shoots' and what are the 'shoots'? Where did Akiba go, that it is said of him that he emerged in peace? And why was it that Akiba alone emerged in safety? The reason for the latter cannot be that he was righteous, since the others, too, were righteous men.

After protesting that he always endeavours to be completely honest in his interpretation of Talmudic passages, Hai proceeds to give his interpretation of the orchard narrative. He first refers to the mystical circle of those who gaze at the Heavenly Chariot seen by the prophet Ezekiel (Ezek. 1), and the halls of the angels.[37] It is to this mystical ascent of the soul that our passage alludes, the ascent being described figuratively as 'entering an orchard'. That this is the correct meaning can be seen from two considerations. First, the narrative is appended, in the Talmud, to the Mishnah which speaks of the Heavenly Chariot. Second, in the *Hekhalot* literature (discussing the heavenly halls—the *hekhalot*) it is stated that at the entrance to the sixth hall there is an appearance of myriads of darting waves, though, in reality, there is not a single drop of water there, only the sparkle given off by pure shining marble. This is the meaning of Ben Azzai gazing and dying, for his time had come. When it is said that Ben Zoma gazed and was stricken, the meaning is that the terrifying visions he had seen

---

[37] On this theme see especially G. Scholem, *Major Trends in Jewish Mysticism*, pp. 40–79. Hai's very interesting description (Lewin, *Hagigah*, p. 14) is: 'You may perhaps know that many of the sages held that when a man is worthy and blessed with certain qualities and he wishes to gaze at the Heavenly Chariot and the halls of the angels on high, he must follow certain procedures: he must fast for a certain number of days; he must place his head between his knees and whisper softly certain praises of God with his face turned towards the ground. As a result he will gaze in the most hidden recesses of his heart and it will be as if he sees seven halls with his own eyes, moving from hall to hall to see that which is there contained'

drove him out of his mind. Aher, as a result of his mystical experience, became a heretic, believing (like the Zoroastrians, says Hai, who believe in Ormuzd and Ahriman) that there are two divine powers, one a source of good, the other of evil; one all light, the other all darkness. Since the experience is described as entering an orchard, this abuse of the experience is described as cutting down the shoots which grow in the orchard, of not having sufficient regard for the owner of the orchard. R. Akiba was sufficiently mature to undergo the experience without coming to harm. He had learned the art of seeing visions without their frightening him out of his mind or leading him to entertain heretical thoughts.

It is well known, continues Hai, that God vouchsafes to the righteous in every age such splendid visions. The opinion of Samuel b. Hophni that only a prophet can ever be the recipient of a vision must be rejected. Samuel b. Hophni and those who think like him have been unduly influenced by the Gentile literature they have read. This leads them to deny narratives such as this, even though in the Talmud, by holding that only in legal matters must the words of the Talmudic sages be accepted as true. Hai concludes: 'We hold that the Holy One, blessed be He, performs miracles and great wonders for the righteous and it is not implausible to suggest that He shows to them in their innermost heart the vision of His halls and the place wherein stand His angels.'

On the same theme of esoteric knowledge there is a lengthy Responsum in which Hai replies to the query, put to him by a number of questioners,[38] concerning the use of various divine names for the performance of white magic. The questioners wish to know whether there is any truth in the reports that the saints can use divine names in order to perform such marvels as making themselves invisible. When they first put this question to him, Hai had replied that it was all nonsense and that these things could not possibly happen. The questioners were surprised to receive such a curt dismissal, which contradicts the testimony of many reliable reporters who claim themselves to have witnessed the

[38] Lewin, *Hagigah*, pp. 16–17

saints performing such miracles. There are reliable reports of sages writing a divine name on an olive leaf and then throwing it at robbers, causing them to become rooted to the ground unable to move. There are also many tales of men travelling great distances in the twinkling of an eye. These 'masters of the name' (*baale shem*) have been observed by trustworthy witnesses in one place on the eve of the sabbath and in another place, many days distant, the same day. There is a tradition among Spanish Jews that Natronai Gaon of Sura (853–8) travelled in just such a miraculous fashion from Babylon to teach the Spanish Jews the Torah and then returned the way he had come. Furthermore, we have in our possession numerous books of divine names together with detailed instructions for their use. People have been known to practise this kind of magic, though admittedly some of them lost their lives in the process. Can all this be sheer delusion? Moreover, the Talmud contains references to the use of divine names for magical purposes, as in the story of Solomon and Ashmodai,[39] and in many other instances. And what of those holy men, some of whom we know personally, who fasted and recited certain verses so that they saw visions? There is even a report that Hai himself has a family tradition regarding a certain divine name effective in prayer! Will he consent to share this knowledge? Finally, the questioners wish to know which kind of magic is forbidden and which permitted and what is the difference between miraculous acts performed by witchcraft and acts of the same nature performed through the prophetic gift? In this question is all the tension inherent in a situation in which credulous Jews, accepting the Talmudic accounts at their face value, are puzzled by the apparent contradiction between the strict injunctions against witchcraft and the resort to magic by the Rabbinic heroes. We know, furthermore, that the Karaites ridiculed their Rabbinic opponents for their belief in magic and superstition.[40]

In his reply, Hai seeks to preserve the balance between extreme rationalism and sheer credulity. He first remarks that he remains

[39] Gitt. 68a
[40] See Jacob Mann, *Texts and Studies in Jewish History and Literature*, vol. 2, pp. 82 ff.

convinced that all reports of men making themselves invisible by the divine names are false. God is not a divine conjurer and He exercises a strict economy in performing His miracles. God has ordained the natural order, from which miracles are a radical departure. The force of a miracle consists in its infrequency. If miracles were diffuse they would be self defeating, for they would then themselves be part of the natural order. That is why miracles must be rare. They are performed chiefly by a prophet in order to substantiate his claim that his message is from God. Supposing you were told, argues Hai, that an elephant and a camel were locked in mortal combat before your eyes but that you cannot see them and are looking straight through them. Would you believe it for one moment? Or supposing someone told you that there was an invisible man in front of you, only God had not given you the ability to see him. Would you not treat the one who made such an assertion as insane? True, Scripture does speak of God opening men's eyes to see angels, but that is because angels are refined spiritual beings normally invisible to the human eye but there all the same. With invisible men, however, the matter is quite different. If a man is invisible he does not exist at all, and that is an end of the matter. As for the report of Natronai Gaon's miraculous journeys through space, if they really happened it must have been a man masquerading as Natronai, but, in fact, after the most careful investigation into the report, says Hai, we have been unable to discover the slightest trace of evidence that it is true. In all such matters Scripture has laid down for us the great principle: 'The fool believes everything' (Prov. 14 : 15). Credulity is evidence of stupidity. Hai does, however, believe in the power of amulets, since these are mentioned in the Talmud, but their efficacy depends on the worth of the person who writes them and they are not always effective even when written by one skilled in the art. Nor does Hai deny the power of the divine name to work miracles, but he points to the many strong injunctions against such use except by the very greatest of saints. Hai continues at length in this vein, proceeding to discuss the whole question of the divine names and how, in the main, we are ignorant of both their nature and their use.

Two of Hai's Responsa deal with the subject of vicarious merit. In one,[41] Hai replies to the question whether merit is added to the spiritual stock of a deceased person when his son, other relatives or friends perform good deeds on his behalf, paying his debts, for instance, or giving alms for the repose of his soul. Hai replies that there are two aspects to a man's failure to pay his debts. The man owes the money and he sins by failing to pay. The demand that the debt be paid can be satisfied when others pay since, after all, the creditor has received his due. But such payment cannot absolve him from the punishment he deserves for failing to pay in the first place. Yet even here, if a good man gives alms for the repose of the soul of the deceased, it can free him from the punishment that is due, not in his own merit but for the sake of that good man who has become personally involved. All this concerns punishment alone. The reward of enjoying the radiance of the Divine Presence in the Hereafter can be attained only through deeds a man performs himself while alive on earth. For a man to attain to this sublime bliss it can avail him nothing even if all the good men on earth carry out virtuous deeds on his behalf.

In the other Responsum[42] on this theme, Hai replies to the question—one much discussed in a number of later Responsa by famous Rabbis—of whether a man can donate to another the reward he has acquired for himself through the performance of virtuous deeds. Supposing a man gives to another the reward of his fasting, or he sells this to him, drawing up a proper deed of sale, or supposing a man gives another a gold coin to study the Torah on his behalf—is the transaction valid? Hai says it is sheer nonsense to imagine that a contract of this nature can enjoy any validity. Just as it is axiomatic in Judaism that no man is ever punished for another's misdeeds, it is equally certain that no man can receive reward for another's good deeds. What reward can there be, in any event, for a man who traffics in good deeds? The seller, by his very act, demonstrates that he has nothing to sell. In such instances the good deeds are not performed as acts of worship but as part of a business transaction. This is quite different from the reward promised to the patron of scholars. Here there is

[41] Lewin, *Hagigah*, pp. 27–8   [42] Ibid., pp. 28–30

reward, but it is the reward for the patron's own good deed in seeing to it that the Torah is studied. But it is the height of absurdity to think that good deeds can be sold or their reward transferred to others.

Eschatology was much discussed during the Gaonic period. The Jews of this age were heirs to the apocalyptic speculations of former times as well as to theological formulations of the doctrine of the Messiah. Many of the more thoughtful Jews of the time appear to have been in a considerable state of confusion as to what they were expected to believe with regard to the events that would herald the coming of the Messiah, the Messianic age and the resurrection of the dead that would follow the advent of the Messiah. How were the inconsistencies and the downright contradictions in the sources to be reconciled, if reconciled they could be? Was it possible to obtain a sufficiently clear picture of the world of the future, the realisation of which was the constant theme of so many of their prayers? It is not surprising, therefore, to find Hai Gaon replying at great length[43] to a questioner who had asked him to describe in detail the advent of the Messiah, the resurrection of the dead and the new heavens and earth that were to be created. Hai's scheme draws on all the statements in the earlier sources. If his scheme is too neat, if it allows too little room for mystery and borders on the crude, if it accepts legend as fact, this is because for Hai the Talmudic and Midrashic passages dealing with the Messiah are seen as revealed truth. Hai does remark that to describe it all in full detail would require a far longer treatment than he is able or willing to provide, but he will attempt, he says, a broad outline.

First, says Hai, the Messiah son of Joseph, together with a number of his followers, will conquer Jerusalem and proclaim himself king of Israel. The majority of the Jews in the Diaspora will remain unconvinced, however, that the end of days is nigh. When the nations of the world hear that the Jews now have a king, they will drive the Jews out of their cities, questioning the Jews' loyalty to their own realm now that they have a kingdom of their own. Many Jews will be compelled to flee for safety to the desert

[43] Lewin, *Otzar Ha-Gaonim*, vol. 6, *Sukkah*, Jerusalem, 1934, pp. 72–5

surrounding their former places of residence. There they will
dwell in tents and suffer severe deprivations. So great will be
their sufferings that many will abandon the Jewish faith. The anti-
Messiah Armilus will then attract a great following by means of
the magical powers that are his and he will succeed in his plan to
murder the Messiah son of Joseph. From this, further acts of
apostasy will result, only the most faithful Jews remaining loyal
to Judaism. These will suffer from 'the pangs of the Messiah' of
which the Rabbis speak. But they will cry out to God in their
trouble and He will heed their cry. Elijah will then appear to the
Jews in the desert. He will be followed by the Messiah son of
David who will bring back from the dead the Messiah son of
Joseph. This resurrection will be the first of the many miracles
the Messiah will perform. The Messiah will then reign in Jerusalem
where the Jews from the desert will come to live in safety and
tranquillity for many days, planting vineyards and building
houses. But Gog, hearing of the Messiah's fame, will raise a
mighty army for an attack on Jerusalem. Gog and his army will
be defeated, God visiting terrible calamities upon them. In order
to appease the Messiah, the nations will bring gifts to Israel. All
the Jews in the world will then come to Jerusalem, some of them
by miraculous means, until only the dead will remain behind in
the Diaspora.

The great trumpet will then be sounded and the dead will rise
from their graves. At first the risen dead will have the form that
was theirs at the time of their death. Those who died as old men
will rise again as old men. The cripples will rise as cripples. This
will be for the purpose of establishing their identity with their
previous existence. Afterwards God will heal them and they will
all become young and whole in body. Seven shepherds will lead
them—Adam, Seth, Methuselah, Abraham, Jacob, Moses and
David; and eight princes—Jesse, Saul, Samuel, Amos, Zephaniah,
Hezekiah, Elijah and the Messiah. Which of the dead will be
resurrected at the time of the Messiah? Only those Jews who were
either righteous all their lives or who repented of their sins before
their death. The resurrected dead will be shown how to rebuild
the Temple. Others say, however, that the new Temple will

drop down complete from Heaven. All Jews, as well as their male and female slaves, will then be prophets. All the nations still alive will be converted to Judaism and will go up to the house of the God of Jacob. 'For out of Zion shall go forth the Law and the word of the Lord from Jerusalem.' When these nations come to the Messiah, he will order them to cease making war one with the other. All the wild beasts will be banished from the holy land.

As for people still alive when the Messiah comes, and who thus never suffer the death decreed for all mankind, they will live on to a ripe old age but will eventually die. No one will die young, however, in that blessed age. Death will ultimately be destroyed for ever. Those who have died during the Messianic age will be resurrected to live for ever in the World to Come. The Divine Presence will come down to rest on the Temple, appearing as a great column of fire reaching from earth to heaven and so bright that the light of the sun and the moon will be dimmed. The heavens and earth will then appear as if they were new, as if the old heaven and earth had been utterly transformed.

Some say that this state of affairs will last until seven thousand years have elapsed from the creation of the world, but others say that it will endure for many thousands of years. But eventually the heavens and earth will come to an end. The dead who have been resurrected will then enter the World to Come. God will then create a new heaven and a new earth. In the World to Come, the righteous will live for ever.

This astonishing picture leans heavily on the similar account in Saadiah's *Beliefs and Opinions*.[44] Maimonides' description[45] is in some measure a conscious reaction against the extreme supernaturalism of these Gaonim, as when Maimonides expressly ridicules the notion that the Messiah will revive the dead. In Hai's account, legends culled from various sources and accepted as authoritative, such as those regarding the Messiah son of Joseph and the anti-Messiah Armilus, have been combined to form a coherent, albeit highly artificial, picture.

Not strictly speaking a Responsum, and its author, though a candidate for the Gaonate of Pumbedita, not a Gaon, a statement

[44] VII–VIII, trans. Rosenblatt, pp. 264–322   [45] *Yad*, Melakhim, chapter 11

on the command to rebuke sinners belongs, none the less, to this account in which consideration is given to theological Responsa during the Gaonic period. This is the reply to a question in the *Sheiltot* of R. Ahai of Shabha (680–752).[46]

R. Ahai's statement (in Aramaic) reads in translation:

It is forbidden for Jews to indulge in quarrels since quarrelling leads to hatred and Scripture says: 'Thou shalt not hate thy brother in thy heart' (Lev. 19 : 17). It goes without saying that a lesser person should be submissive to a greater but even a greater person should be submissive to a lesser in order to avoid a quarrel. We find this of Moses our teacher, as it is written: 'And Moses rose up and went unto Dathan and Abiram' (Num. 16 : 25). R. Simeon b. Lakish commented on this: We can learn from it that it is forbidden to allow a quarrel to continue.[47] And R. Judah said in the name of Rab: Whoever allows a quarrel to continue transgresses a negative command, as it is said: 'And he shall not be like Korah and his company' (Num. 17 : 5).[48] R. Asi[49] said: He will become leprous . . . R. Hama b. Hanina said: Whoever quarrels with his teacher it is as if he had quarrelled with the Shekhinah . . . And R. Haninah b. Papa said: Whoever grumbles at his teacher it is as if he had grumbled at the Shekhinah . . . And R. Abbahu said: Whoever has base thoughts about his teacher it is as if he had had base thoughts about the Shekhinah . . . And R. Hisda said: Whoever disagrees with his teacher it is as if he had disagreed with the Shekhinah. This, however, is the problem. If a disciple sees his teacher doing wrong, is he obliged to rebuke him? Do we say that it is unfitting since the teacher's honour is compared to God's honour or do we rather say that God's honour comes first? We can solve this problem, since our Rabbis taught:[50] Scripture says: 'Thou shalt rebuke thy neighbour' (Lev. 19 : 17). We know that a teacher must rebuke his disciple. How do we know that a disciple must rebuke his teacher? Therefore Scripture says: 'Thou shalt *surely* rebuke thy neighbour', which means—in all circumstances.

It is not difficult to see behind this and numerous other formulations of R. Ahai in his *Sheiltot* a reflection of the tensions engendered among the Rabbinic teachers by the challenges to Rabbinic

---

46 In Lewin, *Otzar Ha-Gaonim*, vol. 13, *Baba Metzia* (n.p., n.d.), pp. 55–6, from a MS. in the possession of Saul Lieberman; *Sheiltot*, Korah, no. 131. On R. Ahai and the *Sheiltot* see *Encyclopedia Judaica*, vol. 2, pp. 449–51

47 Sanh. 110a   48 Sanh. 110a

49 Sanh. 110a, other reading *Ashi*   50 BM 31a

authority that were certainly not unknown even in his day. Problems of teacher–disciple relationships must have been especially acute in this period among the upholders of the Rabbinic tradition and must have become even more troublesome at a later period when the Karaites began to achieve some successes in their attacks on Rabbinic Judaism.

A theological question with the strongest practical implication, discussed by the Gaonim and in many a subsequent Responsa collection, was the status in Jewish law of a convert to another faith. During the earlier Rabbinic period, conversion by a Jew to another faith was unknown. The Rabbinic discussions, upon which the Gaonim based their arguments, concerned a Jew who worshipped idols. Such a Jew—a *mumar*—was treated generally as a heathen, so that, for example, according to the majority opinion in the Talmud, to slaughter an animal for food, even if the act had been carried out in the prescribed ritual fashion, would be forbidden as though it had been slaughtered by a heathen.[51] During the Gaonic period, when conversions to Islam were not too infrequent, the legal status of an apostate Jew had to be spelled out.

The general ruling[52] was that an apostate did not require formal reconversion (i.e. immersion in a ritual bath) when he returned to the Jewish fold. The accepted argument was: once a Jew always a Jew. In support it was pointed out that even a convert to Judaism who had relapsed did not require reconversion when he returned to the fold. A Responsum attributed to Moses Gaon of Sura (825–36)[53] rules that if an apostate reverts to Judaism in a place where his act of apostasy is not known, he can be assumed to be sincere. He is to be accepted forthwith as a Jew. He is not

[51] See e.g. the discussion in Hull. 5a

[52] Lewin, *Otzar Ha-Gaonim*, vol. 7, *Yevamot*, Jerusalem, 1936, p. 341. Cf. ibid., vol. 10, *Gittin*, Jerusalem, 1941, p. 207 that a bill of divorce given by an apostate is valid because he has the status of a Jew even when he has been converted to another faith. However (Lewin, *Gittin*, pp. 132–3) a *kohen* who had been converted to another faith must not be called first to the Torah and must not give the priestly blessing even after his return to Judaism. On the whole subject see Jacob Katz, 'Though he sinned, he remains an Israelite', *Tarbiz*, vol. 27, 1958, pp. 203–17

[53] Lewin, *Yevamot*, p. 111

obliged to return to the place where his apostasy is known and revert there in order to demonstrate his remorse. Other Gaonim rule, however, that while no immersion is required of the returning apostate he is to be flogged as a penance.[54]

Although, as we have seen, a major concern of the Gaonim was to defend the Talmudic Rabbis against the attacks of the Karaites, it was widely acknowledged that the defence would fail if everything in the Talmud was accepted as providing complete guidance for Jewish life. Thus a Responsum of Sherira Gaon[55] states that the Talmudic Rabbis were not infallible in their views on medicine and that the list of remedies for various diseases given in tractate Gittin[56] was not to be relied upon. The questioner wished to know the Arabic names of the roots and herbs mentioned in the passage. Sherira replies:

> We have to inform you that the Rabbis were not physicians. They simply recorded the remedies practised at that time. These matters do not belong to interpretation of law. Consequently, you must not rely on these remedies. None of these prescriptions should be adopted unless expert physicians declare that they are harmless and can in no way prove to be injurious to the health of the patient. Thus have we been taught by our ancestors and sages: No one may resort to these cures unless there is a guarantee that no harm will result from using them.

A famous Responsum of Hai Gaon[57] discusses another Talmudic rule. The Responsum is in reply to a question put by Nehemiah b. Obadiah of Gabès who wished to know the extent of the Talmudic prohibition of resort to music after the destruction of the Temple. The Talmudic passage in which the prohibition is recorded[58] reads:

> An inquiry was sent to Mar Ukba: Where does Scripture tell us that it is forbidden to sing? He sent back the verse, which he wrote on the lines: 'Rejoice not, O Israel, unto exultation like the peoples, for thou hast gone astray from thy God' (Hos. 9 : 1). Should he not have sent the following verse: 'Thou shalt not drink wine with music, strong drink shall be bitter to them that drink it' (Isa. 24 : 9)? From this verse I would have said that only musical instruments are

---

[54] Ibid., pp. 111–12   [55] Lewin, *Gittin*, p. 152   [56] Gitt. 68b–70b
[57] Lewin, *Gittin*, pp. 8–10   [58] Gitt. 7a

forbidden, but not song. Therefore, he informs us, from the other verse, that even songs are forbidden.

From this passage it would appear that it is not only forbidden for Jews to play musical instruments but that they may not even sing. The questioner was puzzled by this ruling which is disregarded by Jews everywhere. Is this the law, he asks, and, if it is, why do we play musical instruments at a wedding feast?

Hai remarks in the course of his reply:

We see that it is the universal Jewish practice at ordinary banquets, and it goes without saying at wedding feasts, that they make merry with joyful sounds, singing God's praises, recalling His mercies and wonders to Israel in the past, and hoping for His kingdom to be revealed and for the promises of the prophets to Israel to be fulfilled. There are numerous compositions on these and similar themes to the accompaniment of musical instruments. At wedding feasts the songs have as their theme the happiness and success of bride and bridegroom and no Jew anywhere abstains from such merriment.

He goes on to say that Mar Ukba refers only to secular songs at carousals. However, the questioner mentions the custom of women dancing and singing and playing musical instruments, and this is certainly wrong.[59]

---

[59] The Responsum attributed to Hai forbidding the study of secular sciences is not authentic; see S.W. Baron, *A Social and Religious History of the Jews*, vol. 8, p. 311 n. 22, who refers to H. Graetz's essay in *Monatsschrift für des Geschichte und Wissenschaft des Judentums*, vol. XI, pp. 37–40. Cf. *Teshuvot Ha-Gaonim*, no. 28

CHAPTER II

The Eleventh Century

From the eleventh century onwards we find teachers other than the Gaonim writing Responsa—in North Africa, Spain, France and Germany. Compared with the massive amount of material in later centuries, few eleventh-century Responsa are known to us and fewer still are those which deal with theological topics. Here we are able to consider the theological Responsa of Rabbenu Gershom of Mainz (960–1028) in Germany and the school of *Rashi*, a disciple of Gershom's disciples, in France. Like the Gaonim, these Respondents generally prefer short replies with little of the prolonged discussion of the sources typical of the subsequent literature.

Gershom b. Judah of Mainz is known as *Meor Ha-Golah*, 'Light of the Exile'.[1] He features prominently in the annals of Jewish law as the author of the ban on polygamy, though recent research suggests that this ban developed more gradually in Germany and was only later fathered on Gershom. Though legends abound, few details of Gershom's life are available. Gershom's teacher was Judah b. Meir of Leontin. There is a report that a son of Gershom was forcibly converted to Christianity. Gershom's importance in the history of Jewish law is conveyed in the description attributed to *Rashi*: 'Rabbenu Gershom, may the memory of the righteous

---

[1] On Gershom, see *Encyclopedia Le-Gedole Yisrael*, ed. M. Margalioth, pp. 322–9 and *Encyclopedia Judaica*, vol. 7, pp. 511–13

and holy be for a blessing, who enlightened the eyes of the exile, and upon whom we all depend and of whom all Ashkenazi Jewry are the disciples of his disciples.' Gershom's Responsa have been collected and edited by S. Eidelberg.

The status in Jewish law of the convert to Christianity was discussed by Gershom. A problem considered by the Gaonim and reappearing in the later Responsa was whether the law of levirate marriage (Deut. 25 : 5–10) applied to an apostate; i.e. whether his deceased brother's widow can remarry without having first to undergo the rite of loosing the shoe (Deut. 25 : 7–10), *halitzah*. Since it was obviously difficult to persuade the apostate to participate in a Jewish rite, this problem was particularly acute. Gershom[2] rules that the widow cannot be released to remarry without *halitzah*. His argument is that the apostate is still a Jew, though a sinner, and hence if he marries a Jewish woman she requires a *get*, a bill of divorce, from before she can remarry. By the same token, the brother's widow requires *halitzah*.

It is one thing, however, to treat the apostate as a Jew for the purpose of applying the strictness of the law as in the above cases. A further question considered was whether the apostate forfeits the privileges due to him in Jewish law. It is obvious that he does while he accepts another faith. But what is the position when he reverts to Judaism? This question was put to Gershom[3] with regard to a *kohen* (a priest descended in the male line from Aaron) who had converted to Christianity and then reverted to Judaism, a question discussed by the Gaonim.[4] A *kohen* is called first to read the Torah and it is his duty to recite the priestly blessing during the synagogue service. Can he still enjoy these privileges, if he had been converted, once he returns to the Jewish fold? The privileges of a *kohen* are based on the verse: 'And thou shalt sanctify him' (Lev. 21 : 8).[5] Although, Gershom argues, the apostate, by his conversion, profaned the sanctity that was his, he reverts to the state of sanctity when he returns to the fold. Gershom quotes the ruling of the Mishnah:[6]

The priests who ministered in the Temple of Onias may not minister

[2] Eidelberg, no. 48, p. 118   [3] Eidelberg, no. 4, pp. 57–60
[4] See chapter I, pp. 26–7   [5] Gitt. 59b   [6] Men. 13 : 10

in the Temple in Jerusalem; and needless to say another matter (i.e. priests who had served idols); for it is written: 'Nevertheless the priests of the high places came not up to the altar of the Lord in Jerusalem, but they did eat unleavened bread among their brethren' (II Kgs 23 : 9). Thus they are like those that had a blemish: they are entitled to share and eat of the holy things but they are not permitted to offer sacrifices.

Gershom argues that the only disqualification of priests who had served idols, according to this Mishnah, is that they are no longer allowed to serve in the Temple. For all other purposes they have the rights of priests, once they have repented, as have the priests with a blemish to whom they are compared in the Mishnah.

Against this it can be argued that of the priestly blessing Scripture says: 'So they shall put My name upon the children of Israel, and I will bless them' (Num. 6 : 27). The priest brings God's blessing to the people, but a priest who once forsakes his God is himself forsaken by God, as it is said: 'And will forsake Me, and break My covenant ... Then My anger shall be kindled against them in that day, and I will forsake them' (Deut. 31 : 16–17). But we are told by the prophets: 'Return unto Me, saith the Lord of hosts, and I will return unto you' (Zech. 1 : 3). Once the priest returns to God, God returns to him and concurs in his blessing. Does not the Talmud[7] warn us sternly never to taunt a former sinner with his sins? And is it not stated further in the Talmud:[8] He who asserts that King Manasseh, who repented, has no portion in the World to Come, weakens the hand of penitent sinners?

It is obvious that Gershom, in an age when conversions to Christianity by Jews were certainly not unknown, strives to be as severe as possible with apostates but to be lenient with them when they revert to Judaism. If, he argues, the repentant *kohen* is not allowed to enjoy the privileges that were his before his apostasy, he will be publicly branded all his life as a former apostate. Such a state of affairs would act as a serious obstacle to apostates who wished to revert to Judaism, but feared ostracism if they did. We are obliged to give these men every encouragement we can. Gershom clinches his argument by quoting the passage in the

---

[7] BM 58b   [8] Sanh. 103a

Talmud[9] in which it is said that even when a brother has sunk so low as to sell himself as a priest to idols, stones must not be cast at him and he must be redeemed.

Oddly enough, in another Responsum,[10] addressed to the scholars of Troyes, Gershom gives the opposite ruling: that the apostate must not enjoy the privileges of the priesthood. Eidelberg[11] is undoubtedly correct that this second Responsum deals with a *kohen* who, as stated in the Responsum, not only converted to Christianity but became a Christian priest. Moreover, in this second Responsum, there is no reference to the *kohen* having repented. In any event, it is the first ruling that is quoted in Gershom's name by the later authorities.[12]

From early Rabbinic times the profession of school-teacher was highly respected. In Jewish communities of any size there were schools in which the Torah was taught. The teachers were salaried employees of the community so that such matters as their financial obligations and manner of contract feature regularly in the Responsa dealing with civil law. But, in addition, the teacher was seen as engaging in doing God's work. There was a religious dimension to his activities. In a Responsum,[13] Gershom replies to the question: What are the obligations of a school-teacher? He discusses the details of contracts with teachers: e.g. unless it is specified otherwise in his contract, the teacher is entitled to assume that he is engaged according to the contractual obligations which obtain in that particular community. Gershom adds a note on the special obligations of the teacher:

> School-teachers and scholars are obliged to be reliable in carrying out their task and they must be virtuous in conduct. He who does his work faithfully has the merit of sitting in the Academy on High and he shall never be moved. For thus did David declare under the influence of the holy spirit: 'Lord, who shall sojourn in Thy tabernacle . . .' (Ps. 15).

Rabbi Solomon b. Isaac, called *Rashi* after the initial letters of his name, was born in the year 1040 and died in 1105. He is

---

[9] Arakh. 30b   [10] Eidelberg, no. 5, pp. 60–1   [11] Ibid., p. 60 n. 3
[12] E.g. in Tos. Sot. 39a and *Tur*, Orah Hayyim 128
[13] Eidelberg, no. 72, pp. 167–8

famed as the greatest Jew of the Middle Ages, with the exception of Maimonides, because of his marvellous commentaries to the Bible and the Talmud. The latter is still indispensable to any serious student of the Talmud. *Rashi* was the great teacher of Franco-German Jewry, a Jewry mainly indifferent to philosophical speculation and content with developing and furthering the thought patterns of the Talmudic Rabbis: in Solomon Schechter's felicitous phrase, neither understanding nor misunderstanding Aristotle.

Rashi is not among the more famous writers of Responsa; his genius was exercised in other fields. None the less, a number of *Rashi's* Responsa are extant, and have been collected and edited by I. Elfenbein. His theological Responsa are concerned chiefly with the question of the status of a Jew who had been converted to Christianity, the problem discussed by Rabbenu Gershom, *Rashi's* spiritual forebear.

Discussing the question of whether the apostate's deceased brother's widow requires *halitzah*,[14] *Rashi* argues that although an apostate is not to be trusted in religious matters he is still a Jew and his sister-in-law does, therefore, require *halitzah*. *Rashi* quotes in this connection the Talmudic saying:[15] 'Even though he has sinned he is still an Israelite.' Jacob Katz[16] has pointed out that none of the earlier authorities who discussed the status of the apostate thought of quoting this Talmudic saying, and for a very good reason. The saying is not a legal one and does not deal at all with the apostate Jew. The original meaning is simply that a Jew who sins does not thereby forfeit the high title of 'Israelite'— 'Even though he has sinned he is still an *Israelite*.' *Rashi*, however, understands it to mean that even though he has sinned by becoming a convert to another religion he is still a *Jew*. Katz surmises, and he may be right, that *Rashi* was moved to give this interpretation because it was intolerable to him that Judaism should allow conversion to another faith to have any standing in Jewish law, as it would have done if the law were that a Jew loses his Jewish status because of his apostasy. This application of the saying by

---

[14] Elfenbein, no. 173   [15] Sanh. 44a
[16] 'Though he sinned, he remains an Israelite', *Tarbiz*, vol. 27, 1958, pp. 203–17

Rashi became the standard text on the subject, so that later authorities quote the saying in *Rashi's* interpretation without the slightest degree of recognition that, in fact, a completely new idea has been read into the passage.

On the question of the repentant convert who is a *kohen*, *Rashi*[17] gives the same ruling as Rabbenu Gershom, though he does not quote him. He does quote the same Mishnaic passage as Gershom regarding the priests who may not serve in the Temple but can otherwise enjoy the privileges of the priesthood. Such a *kohen* is entitled to be called first to the reading of the Torah and give the priestly blessing.

The same attitude is evident in another Responsum of *Rashi*[18] on the same subject. Is wine prepared or handled by Jews who were once converts but have now repented permitted, or is it forbidden until they have proved their sincerity through a period of probation? God forbid, *Rashi* replies, that we should be guilty of causing any embarrassment to such folk. Once they have returned to the fold, they are to be treated like any other Jew.

In another Responsum[19] on conversion, *Rashi* considers the case of a Jew who had been forcibly converted and who married a Jewish girl in the presence of two witnesses who had also been forcibly converted. Is the marriage valid so that the woman requires a *get* before she can remarry? He replies that there is no doubt that the marriage is valid. Even the wife of an ordinary apostate requires a *get*, since the principle applies: 'Even though he has sinned he is still an Israelite.' This applies *a fortiori* to people who have been forcibly converted and in their hearts believe only in the Jewish faith.

A theological Responsum of *Rashi*,[20] dealing with a different topic, considers the Talmudic rule[21] that one should not rebuke sinners who offend unintentionally because it is better for them to remain ignorant that they are doing wrong than that they should be aware of it and continue to sin intentionally. In that case, what becomes of the Scriptural injunctions to rebuke sinners? *Rashi* replies that the Talmudic passage refers only to practices which

[17] Elfenbein, no. 170   [18] Elfenbein, no. 168   [19] Elfenbein, no. 171
[20] Elfenbein, no. 40   [21] Betz. 30a

the people have long held to be quite innocent. Even when they are told that these practices are wrong, they will continue in their ways out of habit. Here it is better to turn a blind eye. But where there is even a remote possibility that the sinners will acknowledge the error of their ways, it is a religious duty to rebuke them.

Responsa touching on theological questions from the school of *Rashi* are found in J. Mueller's collection of Responsa of the Rabbis of France[22] and in Irving A. Agus's edition of the Responsa of the Tosafists.

One of these, by an unnamed member of the *Rashi* school,[23] is in reply to the question whether a sick person is permitted to say his prayers. Since it is hard for him to concentrate, and adequate concentration (*kavvanah*) is demanded in prayer, it is possible that a sick person is not only exempted from prayer but is forbidden to pray. The reply given is that the sick person should recite only the declaration of faith, the *Shema*, but should not say the prayers. A Talmudic passage[24] is quoted which says that one who returns from a long journey must not offer his prayers until three days have elapsed, because he is unable to give proper attention to the prayers. Similarly, it is said that a drunken person may not recite the prayers. The conclusion to be drawn is that it is positively forbidden to pray if, for any reason, there is mental insecurity and a resulting incapacity to concentrate on the meaning of the prayers. This would apply to a sick person.

Another Responsum,[25] attributed to a disciple of *Rashi*, is in reply to a question concerning the ritual observed on Saturday night when the sabbath has departed. A benediction thanking God for the creation of light is recited, during which one gazes at the fingernails. This ancient custom was puzzling to the questioner and he turned to the Rabbi for an explanation. Finesinger[26] has shown that there are, in fact, superstitious overtones to the practice. But in this Responsum a completely rationalistic interpretation is given. The Talmud[27] rules that the benediction can only

[22] *Teshuvot Hakhme Tzarefat Ve-Loter*
[23] Mueller, no. 60, pp. 36b–37a
[24] Eruv. 65a
[25] Mueller, no. 19, pp. 10b–11a
[26] Sol Finesinger: 'The custom of looking at the fingernails at the outgoing of the sabbath', *HUCA*, vol. XII–XIII, 1938, pp. 347–65
[27] Ber. 53b

be recited over a light from which one has had use. By looking at the fingernails and so distinguishing by the aid of the light between the nails and the skin, one has made use of the light.

A Responsum on the status of the convert[28] is not, strictly speaking, of *Rashi's* school but by R. Eliezer b. Isaac the Great who lived in Mainz at the beginning of the eleventh century. A *kohen* became converted to Christianity of his own free will, eventually becoming a Christian priest. Later he repented and returned to the Jewish fold. Do he and his children have the privileges of a *kohen*? The reply is that there is no question whatever that the children are fit and cannot be disqualified because of their father's sin. As for the man himself, he is entitled to be called up to the Torah first, but he may not recite the priestly blessing. The reason for the latter ruling is that the priestly blessing is compared to ministering in the Temple,[29] from which he is disqualified. This ruling differs, then, from that given by Rabbenu Gershom.

A Responsum[30] of a teacher R. Judah, whose identity is uncertain[31] but who is of the school of *Rashi*, concerns a man who, during the synagogue service, cursed with the full Tetragrammaton anyone who would harm him. The questioner, Judah's disciple, aware of the Talmudic passage[32] which declares that one who hears another utter the divine name must place the ban on him, otherwise he himself will be under the ban, placed the ban on him but did so silently. The disciple observes that Maimonides[33] rules that the ban must be placed on such a person. The question is whether now publicity should be given to the ban and the man placed under it until he repents. Judah points out that the same Talmudic passage goes on to state that the ban is merely a token ban. There is no need for public remorse. If a man offends against his neighbour, it is necessary for him to make it up with him, but this does not apply to an offence against God.

[28] Agus, *Tosaphists*, no. 3   [29] Men. 109a–b   [30] Agus, *Tosaphists*, no. 46
[31] Since he refers to Maimonides he must have lived some time after or near the end of the twelfth century. Agus suggests either Judah Sir Leon of Paris or Judah b. Moses of Mainz
[32] Ned. 7b   [33] *Yad*, Talmud Torah 6: 14

The man must make his peace with his own conscience in private. Judah quotes: 'If one man sin against another; God shall judge him, but if a man sin against the Lord, who shall entreat for him?' (I Sam. 2 : 25).

Finally, there is the strange Responsum[34] of Isaac b. Elijah on whether it is permitted to conjure up demons to inform people where treasure has been hidden, or to tell of future events. Isaac refers to the Talmudic passage[35] in which certain conjurations of demons are permitted, with the implication that others are forbidden.[36]

The paucity of theological material during this period is to be explained by the fact that the writing of Responsa had not yet developed fully in any event. During the next century, when they were written more frequently by the famous teachers, the proportion of theological discussion also increased.

---

[34] Agus, *Tosaphists*, no. 121 [35] Sanh. 101a
[36] Agus, *Tosaphists*, refers to *Tur*, Yoreh Deah 179 and *Bet Yosef, ad loc.*

CHAPTER III

The Twelfth Century

During the twelfth century, the Jewish thinkers in Spain and Provence taught against a background of Arabic culture and philosophy. In this period, in particular, the problem of faith and reason loomed very large; so it is in no way surprising that in the Responsa of this century theological, as well as purely legal, problems are found.

Joseph Ibn Migash (1077–1141) was head of the community of Lucena for thirty-eight years. His Responsa were written in Arabic, significantly enough, but were translated into Hebrew. The following are the theological topics he considered.

During the long centuries of debate with the Karaites over the authority of the Talmud, it was natural for the Rabbinic teachers to elevate the Talmud to the rank of sacred writ. Since, according to the Rabbis, there are degrees of inspiration in Scripture, rules were laid down that a book containing a portion of Scripture with a lower degree of inspiration was not to be placed on top of a book containing a portion of Scripture with a higher degree of inspiration. For instance, a book containing the Pentateuch was not to be placed under a book containing the Prophets, or a book containing the Prophets under a book containing the Hagiographa.[1] The question addressed to Ibn Migash (no. 92) was whether a copy of the Talmud may be placed on top of a book

[1] Meg. 27a

38

containing the Prophets. It can be argued that the Talmud, as the depository of the teachings of the Oral Law, enjoys the same status as the Pentateuch itself, the Written Law. Ibn Migash replies that while it is undoubtedly true that the Talmud contains the correct interpretation of the Torah, it does not enjoy the sanctity of the Torah. There are, he says, formal laws on how the Biblical books have to be written—with ruled lines, for example— but these do not apply to the Talmud. Moreover, the status of a Scriptural book is, according to the Rabbis,[2] that it 'contaminates the hands', but this does not apply to the Talmud. It follows that a copy of the Talmud must not even be placed on top of a book of the Hagiographa and it goes without saying that it must not be placed on top of a book of the Prophets.

The need for the Reader in the synagogue to be a worthy man, free from sin, is stressed in the Talmudic sources. A Reader with a bad reputation was not acceptable for the purpose of leading the congregation in prayer. The question addressed to Ibn Migash (no. 95) concerns a Reader who was about to be elected to the position but was objected to by some members of the congregation on the grounds of a rumour that he had been a sinner in his youth and the Talmud[3] rules that a Reader is disqualified if 'an evil reputation had gone forth in his youth'. One sage argued that the Talmud refers only to a rumour subsequently established as correct, but in this case it was a mere rumour, which was insufficient to disqualify him. Another sage referred to a Responsum of the Gaonim in the *Siddur* of Amram Gaon in which the ruling was given that a Reader can be deposed on the strength of even a mere rumour. To this, the first sage retorted that the Gaonim refer to a Reader about whom there was at the time an evil report, not to a Reader reported to have sinned in his youth. What is the attitude to be adopted? Ibn Migash replies that if there is a rumour now that he is a sinner, he must not be appointed as Reader. There is no smoke without fire. But if it concerned sins which he had committed in his youth, he is not to be disqualified. Even if the rumour is true, he has now repented. The Talmudic statement which disqualifies even such a person refers only to a Reader on

[2] Mishnah Yadaim 4: 5–5; Meg. 7a   [3] Taan. 16a–b

a public fast-day, for which function special piety is required. Repentance is accepted by God, and a Reader must not be rejected for sins of which he has now repented.

An interesting question considered by Ibn Migash (no. 114) is whether a man ignorant of the Talmud but thoroughly familiar with the legal Responsa of the Gaonim can be appointed as a judge. And what if the man is not God-fearing? Ibn Migash replies that a man who is not God-fearing must not be given a permanent appointment as a judge but, if he knows the law, he can act as judge in an occasional capacity. As for the man's ignorance of the Talmud, significantly enough, Ibn Migash, far from considering this to be a disadvantage, holds it to be advantageous. The scholar who imagines that he knows the Talmud might be led into a misapplication of the Talmudic laws through his failure to grasp the correct meaning of a particular Talmudic passage, whereas the judge who relies on such great authorities as the Gaonim cannot go wrong. Ibn Migash writes:

> Know that it is far better for such a person to give decisions in law than for many others in our generation who possess neither knowledge of the Talmud nor any acquaintance with the decisions of the Gaonim. One should rather prevent from functioning as judges those who imagine that they are capable at arriving at a correct decision by studying the Talmud, since no one in our generation has attained to the degree of being able to decide on the basis of the Talmud without taking into account the opinions of the Gaonim of blessed memory. But one who renders decisions on the basis of the Gaonic Responsa and relies on these, even if he has no understanding of the Talmud, is more worthy than one who imagines that he knows the Talmud and is self-reliant. The former, even when his arguments are unsound, is not in error if he relies on the Gaonim of blessed memory, since he relies on the decisions of a competent court. But one who renders decisions on the basis of his own investigations into the Talmud imagines that his theorising demands that a particular decision be rendered where the opposite is true, since he can easily be mistaken in his understanding of the relevant Talmudic passage. In our age no one can be said to have reached the stage that he can be relied on when he bases his decisions solely on the Talmud. I have obtained the Responsa of some men in which they rendered legal decisions. They imagined that their rulings were as clear as day but were, in fact, quite wrong. They attributed the correctness of their decision to a

passage in the Talmud which was, in reality, quite irrelevant to the issue. The matter to be decided was quite different from the rule in the Talmud they quoted because of a subtle distinction that they failed to appreciate. They took the Talmudic rule in a general sense, without noticing the fine distinction which forbids an analogy between the two cases.

It is probable that Ibn Migash's attitude influenced Maimonides[4] in that the latter, in his great Code, gives only the actual decisions and not the Talmudic arguments at length. And Ibn Migash was, in all probability, himself influenced by his teacher R. Isaac Alfasi, the *Rif*, author of the celebrated digest of the Talmud in which only the final decisions are recorded.

In another Responsum (no. 202) Ibn Migash discusses the Talmudic saying:[5] 'Into the well from which you have once drunk water, do not throw clods.' If, says Ibn Migash, this applies to in-animate things, how much more should one's gratitude be shown to human beings. He tells of his teacher, the *Rif*, who was helped by the owner of a bath-house. When Alfasi fell ill this man looked after him in his house and saw to it that he was given medicinal baths until he recovered his strength. Later on the man fell heavily into debt and was obliged to have his bath-house evaluated in order to pay his creditors. Alfasi refused to be a judge in the case because of 'Into the well . . .' There are thus two reasons why a friend of one of the contestants in a lawsuit may not act as a judge. The first is the obvious one that he may be biased in his friend's favour. The second is that if honesty compels him to decide against his friend, he will be guilty of ingratitude. If, adds Ibn Migash, this applies to human beings, how much more should man ever be grateful to God, the source of his life, and never depart from obedience to His will.

Theological Responsa are found in the collections of two other twelfth-century Spanish teachers, Joseph Ibn Plat[6] and Abraham b. Isaac of Narbonne (d. 1179).[7] A Responsum of Joseph Ibn

---

4 In the Introduction to his *Commentary to the Mishnah*, Maimonides praises Joseph Ibn Migash in the most glowing terms
5 BK 92b, quoted as a popular proverb
6 Published in S. Asaf, *Sifran Shel Rishonim*, pp. 199–206
7 Published in ibid., pp. 1–50

Plat,[8] addressed, in fact, to Abraham b. Isaac of Narbonne, concerns a problem much discussed in the post-Talmudic literature. The Rabbis rule that a benediction, thanking God for sanctifying us with His commandments, is to be recited before carrying out a *mitzvah*, a precept of the Torah. Yet while the Talmud records the benedictions to be recited before the performance of some of the *mitzvot*, no benedictions were apparently ordained for recital before the performance of other *mitzvot* such as visiting the sick, comforting mourners, attending a funeral, sending away the mother bird when taking the young (Deut. 22 : 6–7) and many others. Is there any general principle according to which the Rabbis decided that a benediction is to be recited before the performance of some of the *mitzvot* and not before others? Ibn Plat replies in a Responsum worded in the classical Aramaic used by the Talmudic Rabbis. There is no general principle to cover all cases, he remarks, but some rules can be observed, of which the following are instances: 1. There is no benediction where the performance of the *mitzvah* depends on another—e.g. giving alms, since the recipient may be unwilling to be helped. 2. There is no benediction when what is enjoined is not a positive act—e.g. the cancellation of debts in the seventh year (Deut. 15). 3. There is no benediction if the *mitzvah* can come about only as the result of a sin—e.g. the duty of restoring stolen goods. 4. There is no benediction where the *mitzvah* is to give that which belongs to God— e.g. when one gives tithes to the priests. 5. No benediction is recited by the court when punishing criminals, even though this, too, is a *mitzvah*. This is because God has compassion on all His creatures and does not want to be thanked for a command which involves inflicting death or pain upon them. 6. No benediction is recited before carrying out the command to rebuke a sinner, because there is always doubt whether the one who administers the rebuke is sufficiently worthy to sit in judgment on another.

A Responsum of Abraham b. Isaac of Narbonne[9] deals with the question whether one has to recite the benediction, 'Blessed

---

[8] This Responsum is quoted by Solomon Ibn Adret, Responsum no. 18, see p. 75 below, and by Abudraham, *Seder Tefillot, Shel Hol, Shaar 3*, see Asaf's Introduction to *Sifran Shel Rishonim*

[9] No. 42 (p. 45)

art Thou O Lord Who makest diverse creatures', over a man with extra fingers. Abraham b. Isaac states that this matter requires some thought, since the question is not discussed explicitly in the Talmud. There are two Talmudic passages which seem to be connected. In one a list of deformities or unusual physical appearances is given[10] for the purpose of reciting the benediction, 'Who makest diverse creatures'; in the other, a list of deformities[11] which render a priest unfit to serve in the Temple. Some, but not all, of the items in the one list feature in the other. The man with extra fingers is in the list of disqualifications for the priesthood but not in the other, so it would seem that the benediction is not to be recited over him. But, remarks Abraham, the reasons for the omissions from the list which deals with the benediction are not clear.

In the Responsa literature many questions regarding the suitable penance for sin are found, especially Responsa which discuss the penance to be imposed on a man guilty of accidental homicide. In a Responsum of Abraham b. Isaac of Narbonne,[12] the teacher replies to the question: what penance is to be imposed on a man who, while drunk on the festival of Purim, stabbed another man to death. Abraham b. Isaac first notes that the Talmud[13] rules that one who is 'as drunk as Lot' (Gen. 19 : 30–8), who has no awareness of what he is doing, has diminished responsibility, so that if he murders another under the influence of drink he is not guilty of murder. On Purim, most of the ignorant folk do get drunk because they take too literally the Talmudic injunction[14] that a man is obliged to drink so much on Purim that he becomes unaware of whether he is blessing Mordecai or cursing Haman. Furthermore, in this particular case, the man was first attacked by his victim and was allowed in law to defend himself, though not, of course, to kill the attacker. The Talmud contains the curious tale[15] that Rabbah killed R. Zera when drunk on Purim and then brought him back to life again. Abraham evidently understands this quite literally. He argues that this man cannot be treated as a murderer merely because he did not possess Rabbah's holy

[10] Ber. 58b [11] Ber. 42a [12] No. 41 (pp. 42–6)
[13] Eruv. 65a [14] Meg. 7b [15] Meg. 7b

powers of reviving the dead. Nevertheless, he says, a severe penance must be imposed on this man guilty of manslaughter as a deterrent to others. Abraham quotes the Talmud[16] to the effect that the courts have emergency powers to impose severe penalties on criminals and sinners even though, after the destruction of the Temple, there can be no strictly legal recourse to capital or corporal punishment. This should be his punishment, says Abraham. For a whole year he should be flogged morning and evening. If the victim has left small children who are dependent on him, the guilty man must provide for their support and, if he refuses, the court must compel him to do so. He should shave his head and beard in mourning like Job (1 : 2). In support of the deterrent principle, Abraham quotes: 'And those that remain shall hear, and fear, and shall henceforth commit no more any such evil in the midst of thee' (Deut. 19 : 20). Abraham adds that his questioner should advise the guilty man to mortify himself further, for example by fasting, if he is willing to do so and is healthy enough. Once he has done penance, however, no one is allowed to call him a murderer or to insult his family. Abraham adds that his questioner can, if he so desires, either add to the penance or lessen it according to the circumstances as he knows them at first hand.

The figure of Maimonides (1135–1204) towers over his contemporaries in the twelfth century. He is the outstanding teacher in both law and philosophy, his Responsa containing replies to questions in both these subjects addressed to him in Egypt from the Jewries prominent in his time.

A Responsum of Maimonides (no. 173) concerns the question of divination. Although Maimonides is strictly opposed to magical and superstitious practices, he does permit Bibliomancy;[17] i.e. opening the Bible at random so that a verse or verses on the page opened offers guidance for a course of action, since this method of divination has Talmudic support.[18] In the particular case considered in Maimonides' Responsum, a teacher was in the habit of using this method when requested to do so by Christians and

[16] Sanh. 46a
[17] *Yad*, AZ 11: 5, arguing that it is only an 'indication' (*siman*) and there is no complete reliance on divination
[18] Hull. 95b

Muslims. Is this permitted? If it is not, should the man be removed from his post because of his offence? Maimonides replies that he should certainly be prevented from doing it in the future on behalf of non-Jews, but his having done so in the past is not a sufficient reason for him to be deposed.

Another Responsum (no. 215) concerns the Talmudic ruling[19] that when prayers are recited there should be no barrier between the worshipper and the wall. The questioner wished to know the reason for the rule and the definition of a 'barrier'. Would the curtain before the Ark in a synagogue act as a 'barrier', and what of a tapestry with figures depicted on it? Maimonides, in his reply, evidently wishes to reject the notion that there can be a spatial barrier to the ascent of prayer. He gives as the reason for the Talmudic ruling that it is in order to assist concentration in prayer by preventing distractions. It follows that the 'barrier' referred to is only one that affords a distraction, such as a cupboard or a heap of sacks or furniture. Maimonides adds that he personally closes his eyes when obliged to pray in front of a curtain or wall with figures on it.

In another Responsum (no. 216) on the same theme, Maimonides deals with the Talmudic saying[20] that prayers should only be offered in a house which has windows. The questioner wished to know the reason for the ruling and why many synagogues ignored it. Maimonides here, too, replies that the reason is that it assists concentration. The windows, open to the sky, fire the imagination of the worshipper so that he sees himself facing Jerusalem, the holy city, and this is a powerful aid to more profound concentration. But the Talmud refers only to private prayer. Public worship is itself the strongest aid to concentration and here no open windows are required. There is, therefore, no law that a synagogue must have windows.

The Ten Commandments occupy an especially honoured place in Judaism. But already in Talmudic times the tendency was discouraged of giving too much prominence to the Ten Commandments because this might give rise to the heretical opinion that only these were revealed by God and not the rest of the Torah.

[19] Ber. 5b   [20] Ber. 31a

The Talmud[21] observes that at one time the Ten Commandments were recited each day together with the *Shema*, but the custom was abolished 'because of the heretics'. In many synagogues in Maimonides' day it was the custom, as it now is universally, for the people to stand on their feet when the Ten Commandments are read from the Torah. In one town it had been the custom for the people to stand, but a great sage, following the implications of the Talmudic ruling, abolished the custom. Many years later another, inferior, sage wished to reintroduce the custom of standing, arguing that people should stand as their ancestors did when the Decalogue was given (Exod. 19 : 17). Moreover, it was the custom in Baghdad for the people to stand. Against this it was argued that the people in Baghdad did not stand in honour of the Ten Commandments, but rather to pay respect to the head of the school who was called to read this portion. What did Maimonides advise?

In his reply,[22] Maimonides rules in favour of the earlier sage, that the people should not stand while the Ten Commandments are read. Wherever it is the custom for the people to stand, the custom should be abolished, since it leads to the extremely dangerous opinion that some parts of the Torah are superior to others. As for the custom in Baghdad, if people are sick, healthy folk are not obliged to make themselves ill, too, for the sake of uniformity. On the theme of refusing to single out any particular passage in the Torah, Maimonides refers to his *Commentary to the Mishnah*[23] where he lists the thirteen principles of the Jewish religion, one of which is that the whole of the Torah was given by God. Here Maimonides states that there is no difference between verses like: 'Hear, O Israel, the Lord our God, the Lord is One' (Deut. 6 : 4) and verses like: 'And Timna was concubine to Eliphaz' (Gen. 36 : 12).

Maimonides' replies are generally very brief. He leaves it to the questioners to fill in the details. An example of this brevity is in his Responsum (no. 455) in reply to the question of two contradictory Talmudic passages. In one,[24] it is said that a man should

---

[21] Ber. 12a
[22] No. 263. On this subject see S. Sevin, *Ha-Moadim Ba-Halakhah*, p. 326
[23] Sanh., beginning of chapter *Helek*   [24] Pes. 50b

study the Torah and practise the precepts even if his motives are unworthy (*she-lo lishmah*) because it will eventually lead him to do it out of worthy motives. But, in another passage,[25] it is stated that whoever studies the Torah or practises the precepts out of unworthy motives, it were better for him that he had never been born. The standard commentators strive hard to reconcile the two passages.[26] Maimonides, however, refuses to recognise any contradiction. True, if he does it out of unworthy motives it were better for him not to have been born, yet it is, none the less, better that he should do it out of such motives than not at all. Clearly, Maimonides believes in the great value of the deed in itself. To practise the precepts is always to be preferred, whatever the motive. But this is not to suggest that motives are unimportant. The Talmudic Rabbis were concerned in the first instance that the Jew should keep the law. But they certainly expect him to be led on to observance that is out of only the purest of motives.

In chapter I we saw[27] how these teachers reacted to the *Shiur Komah*, dealing with the mystical measurements of God, treating it as a sacred work. Maimonides was asked (no. 117) whether the report was true that he considered it to be by a Karaite or was it, as Hai Gaon suggested, a secret work containing the most sublime mysteries? Maimonides replies that he has never considered for one moment that it is by one of the great sages. It was undoubtedly composed by someone influenced by Greek thinking, and it is a good thing to destroy the work and blot out its memory. Scripture says: 'make no mention of other gods' (Exod. 23 : 13). A god who can be measured belongs without doubt to 'other gods'.

In a famous Responsum,[28] Maimonides discusses whether Muslims are idolators. A convert to Judaism from Islam, Obadiah by name, had argued that Muslims worship only God and are not idolators. When he repeated this to his teacher, the teacher declared he was wrong and called him a fool. Obadiah turned to Maimonides for guidance. In a noble reply, Maimonides speaks eloquently of Obadiah's great heroism in leaving his ancestral

---

[25] Ber. 17a   [26] See e.g. Tos. Pes. 50b, *ve-khan*
[27] See pp. 15–16 above
[28] No. 448; for this Responsum in full with notes see L. Jacobs, *Jewish Law*, pp. 181–6

faith to become converted to Judaism because he is wise enough
to see the truth and follow it, wherever it leads. Such a man is no
fool but a great sage. In the particular matter of the Muslims,
Obadiah is quite right. The Arabs were idolators in former times
but, since the rise of Islam, are pure monotheists even though their
religion is false. It is wrong of us to defend our religion by telling
untruths about other religions. Scripture says: 'The remnant of
Israel shall not do iniquity, nor speak lies, neither shall a deceitful
tongue be found in their mouth' (Zeph. 3 : 13).

The question of divine providence was a key theme in medieval
Jewish philosophy, the Jewish thinkers generally opposing any
understanding influenced by Islamic fatalistic views. In another
Responsum to Obadiah (no. 436), Maimonides discusses providence. The Talmud[29] says that everything is in the hands of
Heaven except the fear of Heaven. Obadiah asked whether this
refers to all men's deeds, in which case there is a strong element
of determinism in the saying. Obadiah is inclined to interpret the
term 'the fear of Heaven' as covering all men's deeds. Maimonides approves. No deed of man is completely neutral so far as
religion is concerned. Any deed can lead either to virtue or to
vice, so that all are covered by the term 'the fear of Heaven' and
are not determined, but depend on man's free choice. The meaning of 'everything' in the passage is not intended to include man's
deeds but the natural order of things—i.e. it is determined by God
how nature is ordered, how creatures are distributed on earth,
how animals, birds and trees are to grow.[30] Any deterministic
view with regard to men's deeds is utterly false. Anyone relying
on Aggadic passages in the Talmud for the belief that man is not
entirely free to choose, even when a religious obligation is not
directly involved, commits spiritual suicide. True, there is a Talmudic saying[31] that forty days before a child is formed it is decreed whom he will eventually marry, but this obviously cannot
be taken to mean that in all instances a man's wife is fated to be his

---

[29] Ber. 33b

[30] Maimonides refers his questioner to his *Commentary to the Mishnah*, Avot 4: 22,
and to the beginning of his *Yad*, Deot

[31] Sot. 2a; MK 18b; see pp. 2–5 above for the treatment of this passage by the
Gaonim

before he and she were born. Scripture clearly implies the opposite when it exempts a soldier from battle during the first year of his marriage, because if he goes to fight he might perish and another man will marry her (Deut. 20 : 5). Maimonides gives a general rule of interpretation. Whenever one comes across a passage in the prophets or in the Rabbinic literature, it can be understood literally if it does not contradict the Torah. Otherwise, one must say: 'I do not understand the words of this prophet.' It must mean something other than it appears to mean. The meaning of the passage in question is that if the man and woman are worthy, God will match them so that their marriage will be happy. If they are unworthy, He will arrange for them to contract an unhappy marriage. The saying, implying that marriages are made in Heaven, does not mean to suggest that a man can take no steps of his own when acquiring a wife. He can decide freely to live a virtuous life and then God will arrange for him to marry a virtuous wife. Maimonides concludes by quoting the Rabbinic saying[32] that if there is a bastard male at one end of the earth and a bastard female at the other, God will bring them together and they will marry, since they are suited to one another.

Abraham Ibn David of Posquières, known as *Raabad* (d. 1198), son-in-law of Abraham b. Isaac of Narbonne, was a great Talmudic scholar and author of strictures on the Code of Maimonides, with whose methods and philosophical views he took strong issue. Abraham Ibn David, unlike many other Provençal scholars, limited his studies to the Bible and the Talmud and saw no value in the study of philosophy. It is as a Halakhist that Abraham Ibn David is known to posterity. His Responsa, published by Joseph Kapah, deal almost entirely with purely legal matters. Only two are of theological interest.

In the first of these,[33] Ibn David replies to a question on the Passover Haggadah. In the *Dayenu* ('It Would Have Been Sufficient') hymn, one of the phrases reads:

> If He had brought us near to
> Mount Sinai and had not given us the Torah
> it would have been sufficient.

[32] JT Kidd. 3: 12; Gen. R. 65: 2   [33] No. 11 (p. 55)

The obvious question that arises is: of what use could it have been for God to have brought Israel to Sinai if He had not given them the Torah? Of what value was the mere approach to Sinai? Ibn David replies by referring to the passage in the Talmud[34] that Eve copulated with the serpent and all her descendants became contaminated with its filth. But when Israel stood at Sinai they were cleansed of their filth. Hence, the mere approach to Sinai was highly significant in that it freed Israel from the taint of 'original sin'.[35]

A Responsum of Ibn David[36] deals with the status of the apostate Jew. Ibn David holds that the Jew converted to the Christian faith has the status of a *min* ('sectarian') of whom the Talmud[37] states that he is no longer 'thy brother' (Deut. 23 : 20), so that it is permitted to lend him money on interest, and there is no longer any obligation to restore to him property he has lost. Ibn David takes literally the ruling in this passage that the *min* can be 'lowered' (i.e. into a pit to die) and it goes without saying that he is not to be 'brought up' (i.e. if he is already in the pit he must be left there to die). Obviously, this is not a practical ruling. Apostates in Ibn David's day were not murdered by the community and, for that matter, there is no evidence that the original Talmudic ruling was anything but theoretical.[38] What Ibn David intends to derive from the passage is that the apostate has forfeited the privileges which belong to the members of the Jewish community. As for the argument that he might have children who are righteous,[39] Ibn David dismisses it on the grounds that the apostate will marry a non-Jewish woman and his children from her will in any event have the status of non-Jews. Ibn David adds the observation that there is no reason to be lenient towards apostates because, as some scholars of his day evidently held, the apostate is not sincere when he embraces Christianity in which he does not really believe and has appeared to embrace this faith only for financial reward. Ibn David refuses to accept such a point of view.

[34] Sabb. 146a; Yev. 103b; AZ 22b   [35] See E. E. Urbach, *Hazal*, pp. 378–9
[36] No. 126 (p. 173); see pp. 26–7 and 30–6 above   [37] AZ 26b
[38] See Louis M. Epstein, *Marriage Laws in the Bible and Talmud*, pp. 214–15. Cf. Maimonides, *Yad*, Edut 11 : 10
[39] See Tos. AZ 26b, *ani*

We judge the apostate for what he does, not for what may or may not be in his heart.

In the twelfth century, the subject of this chapter, theological questions are, as we have seen, beginning to be prominent in the Responsa literature. During the thirteenth century the storm over the works of Maimonides and the study of philosophy broke, dividing the scholarly world into Maimonists and anti-Maimonists. In this century, as was to be expected, echoes of the conflict are found in all the various types of literature produced by Jews and there are, consequently, many Responsa of a theological nature.

CHAPTER IV

The Thirteenth Century

Few Responsa have come down to us from the most distinguished Halakhist, Kabbalist and exegete of the thirteenth century, Nahmanides (1194–1270), known as *Ramban*, R. Moses b. Nahman. The Responsa collection attributed to Nahmanides is not his but contains mainly those of his disciple, Solomon Ibn Adret. We do have, however, one theological Responsum of Nahmanides.[1] It deals with the status of the apostate Jew. Like the vast majority of Respondents who have considered this question,[2] Nahmanides holds that he is still a Jew in that his wife requires a *get* before she can remarry, and the widow of his deceased brother requires *halitzah*. Nahmanides draws on the analogy of the Samaritans in Talmudic times.

Maimonides' son, Abraham (1186–1237), was a thinker and legal authority as well as a powerful defender of his father's philosophical views, which were severely attacked in this century. His Responsa contains a number of theological discussions.

As we have seen,[3] the problem of the Biblical story of the Witch of Endor in I Samuel 28 bothered the earlier teachers. Did the witch really succeed in bringing up Samuel from the dead? Abraham Maimoni replies (no. 27) that it is absurd to imagine that the witch really brought up Samuel. She had hypnotic

---

[1] In S. Asaf, *Sifran Shel Rishonim*, no. 2, pp. 56–8
[2] See pp. 30–6 above   [3] See pp. 13–15 above

powers which enabled her to persuade Saul that it was Samuel who was conversing with him. These powers have now been lost but were once possessed by witches as part of their idolatrous practices which the Torah so sternly forbids.

Abraham Maimoni (no. 34) gives a rationalistic explanation of why God was angry with David for counting the people (II Sam. 24). It was because of the denial, implied in counting, of God's promise (Gen. 32 : 12) that the Israelites would be so numerous that it would be impossible to count them.

Another difficult Biblical passage is that which says that King Solomon had a thousand wives (I Kgs 11 : 3). The questioner was puzzled by this, as it contradicts Solomon's own statement in the book of Proverbs: 'Give not thy strength unto women' (Prov. 31 : 3). Abraham replies (no. 45) that Scripture simply records Solomon's marriages but expresses no approval of his conduct. On the contrary, the Bible intends to suggest that Solomon was wrong in not living up to his own teaching in Proverbs. There is no suggestion in Scripture that its heroes are paragons of virtue; prominence is given to their faults and failings. The book of Job declares: 'Behold, He putteth no trust in His holy ones' (Job 15 : 15) and Solomon himself, in the other book he wrote, reminds us: 'For there is not a righteous man on earth, that doeth only good and sinneth not' (Eccles. 7 : 20).

Maimonides' views on the Hereafter were the subject of especially fierce controversy during the thirteenth century. His spiritual interpretation that the soul alone is immortal deeply offended the traditionalists.[4] Abraham Maimoni, in reply to a question on the nature of the Hereafter, gives his own views (no. 119). He observes that a student of philosophical works will appreciate that when the philosophers speak of matter being lost they do not mean that it is ever completely destroyed, only that it assumes a new form. Similarly, man's nature is not propelled into oblivion when his body dies. All that happens is that his form becomes separate from his material body. The fate of man's disembodied spirit in the Hereafter depends on his success in acquiring perfection for himself while in the body. If the spirit has acquired such

[4] See Maimonides, *Yad*, Teshuvah 8 and the Strictures of *Raabad*

perfection that it no longer requires the material body then, at the death of the body, it will live on as pure intelligence. But if the spirit has become so attached to the material body that it cannot enjoy an independent existence, then, indeed, at the death of the body, life itself is at an end. Abraham Maimoni adds that here on earth it is extremely difficult for us to grasp the nature of pure spirit, so that we can have no real understanding of the whole idea of a disembodied intelligence.

The greatest figure in the Franco-German Jewry of the thirteenth century was Meir b. Baruch of Rothenburg (d. 1293). This Jewry concentrated on Talmudic learning, with no interest in the philosophical questionings agitating their contemporaries in Spain and Provence. Meir's Responsa, edited by I. Z. Kahana,[5] are all of a strictly legal nature, but one or two have theological implications.

Meir was asked[6] whether a cripple can act as Reader in the synagogue. Meir replies that it is obvious that he can. Physical deformities are a disqualification only for priests who officiate in the Temple. On the contrary, he argues, it is all the better if the Reader is deformed! God is not like a king of flesh and blood who uses whole vessels and throws away those that are broken. God prefers broken vessels, as the Psalmist declares: 'A broken and a contrite heart, O God, Thou wilt not despise' (Ps. 51 : 19).

In another Responsum,[7] Meir replies to the question whether a scholar can recite his prayers in the privacy of his own home in order to save the time he would have to spend in attending services regularly in the synagogue. Meir roundly declares that for all the importance attached to the study of the Torah, there can be no question of any dispensation from attendance at public prayer in the synagogue. There are a number of reasons why the scholar must not absent himself from public worship. The Rabbis stress[8] the importance of a man having a fixed place in the synagogue where he recites his prayers regularly, and they also teach that a man's prayers are heard only when he recites them amid the con-

---

[5] *Teshuvot Pesakim U-Minhagim.* On R. Meir see Irving A. Agus, *Rabbi Meir of Rothenburg*
[6] Part I, no. 23, p. 53   [7] Part I, no. 30, pp. 57–8   [8] Ber. 6b

gregation. The prayer of an individual cannot be compared in worth to prayers offered by ten persons praying together, neither can the prayers of ten be compared to the prayers of twenty, nor of twenty to those of a hundred. This is because, as the Rabbis say,[9] God does not reject the prayers of a large congregation. Furthermore, if the scholar absents himself from the synagogue, it gives the impression that there is strife and contention in the community, it shows lack of respect for the congregation and it frustrates the aim of communal peace it should be the task of the scholar, in particular, to pursue.

Another question addressed to Meir[10] concerns the Rabbinic injunction[11] that a scholar should not participate in a banquet unless it is for the celebration of some religious event such as the marriage of a scholar to the daughter of a scholar. The questioner noted that this rule is totally disregarded and scholars do participate in banquets even where there is no specifically religious celebration. Meir defends the contemporary practice on the grounds that we do sing psalms and hymns at the table and this makes it a religious occasion.

In a poignant Responsum,[12] Meir discusses a case arising out of the tragic events which occurred in the city of Koblenz, where on 2 April 1265 some twenty Jews were slaughtered. At that time a man killed his wife and four children by his own hand in order to save them from torture and forcible conversion. He had intended to kill himself, but was saved by Gentiles before he could commit suicide. Meir was asked whether the unfortunate man was obliged to do penance for the murder of his family. Meir first observes that he has no doubt at all that suicide is permitted if the aim is to avoid forcible conversion to another faith. The Midrash[13] explicitly exempts from the sin of suicide instances such as that of King Saul who killed himself in order to avoid being tortured by the Philistines (I Sam. 31 : 3–5). And the Talmud[14] quotes with approval the tale of the young men and women being taken to Rome for immoral purposes, who threw themselves into the sea. All this, however, applies only to suicide. Meir is not at all sure

[9] Ber. 8a
[10] Part I, no. 58, pp. 72–3
[11] Pes. 49a
[12] Part II, no. 59, p. 54
[13] Gen. R. 34: 19
[14] Gitt. 57b

that it is permitted to murder others for the sake of the 'sanctification of God's name'—i.e. in order to prevent them being forcibly
converted. Meir, nevertheless, concludes that this, too, must be
permitted, since we know that many of the saints did kill themselves and their families when threatened with forcible conversion.
Consequently, no penance is required because no sin was committed. On the contrary, the man must not be allowed to undergo
any penance, for if he did penance it would imply that the saints
of old were wrong.

There is only one theological Responsum among those of the
Franco-German Talmudist Isaac b. Moses of Vienna (c. 1180–
1250), author of the work Or Zarua. He was asked to explain[15]
the puzzling passage in the book of Genesis (30 : 28–43) which
appears to suggest that Jacob tricked Laban. Isaac explains that the
narrative should not be understood as meaning that Jacob placed
the speckled sticks in front of Laban's sheep. A careful reading
shows that Jacob had been promised the speckled sheep and that
he separated these from the wholly white and wholly black sheep
which belonged to Laban. The purpose of this separation was in
order to avoid the slightest suspicion of trickery. It was only
in front of his own sheep that Jacob placed the sticks. Far from
the narrative suggesting that Jacob engaged in fraud, it suggests, in
fact, how scrupulous Jacob was in avoiding the slightest suspicion
of any underhand dealing. One does not require much imagination to hear in both the question and the reply strong echoes of
Christian–Jewish polemics in thirteenth-century France and
Germany.

Isaac's son Hayyim has a Responsum[16] on the question of
martyrdom. He relates that his friend and relation Nahman b.
Shemariah had shown him a letter of Moses b. Meir in which
reference was made to a ruling given by Shemariah b. Hayyim
that one should not mourn over the death of martyrs. The reason
behind this curious ruling was evidently that the martyrs enter
Paradise immediately at their death and are in a state of bliss. But
Hayyim remarks that whoever gave such a ruling requires to do

---

[15] Or Zarua, part I, no. 796
[16] Responsa Hayyim Or Zarua, no. 14, pp. 6–7

penance. On the contrary, the established ruling is that martyrs have to be mourned in all the synagogues and that the widow of a martyr, out of respect for the memory of her husband and for the sake of the glory of God, must not remarry.

Solomon Ibn Adret of Barcelona (1235–1310), known as *Rashba*, is the most famous Respondent in Jewish history, thousands of his Responsa being still available and quoted as authoritative in Jewish law.[17] *Rashba* was personally involved in the Maimonist dispute. A disciple of Nahmanides and a Kabbalist like his master, Adret was also the foremost Halakhic authority of his day. Together with numerous legal questions, Adret deals in his Responsa with many theological topics, reflecting the concerns of thirteenth-century Jewry in its attempt to grapple with the severe problems raised by philosophical thought.

The general view in the Middle Ages was that the prophetic experience was no longer possible. Yet the Kabbalist Abraham Abulafia[18] became convinced that he had been the recipient of prophetic visions. Abulafia won a number of adherents who spread his opinions far and wide, but many of the Spanish Rabbis viewed with strong suspicion his, to them, dubious activities. Abulafia's opponents eventually turned to Adret for advice. In his Responsum (no. 548), Adret first describes the report he had received of Abulafia's claims. Abulafia had boasted that the spirit of God had come upon him, at times during his sleep, at others while he was awake. An angel also appeared to him, under whose influence he wrote the book *Peliot Ha-Hokhmah* (*The Marvels of Wisdom*). It was rumoured that Adret had written in approval of Abulafia, but Adret strongly denies it and calls Abulafia a scoundrel, adding after his name the curse: 'May the name of the wicked rot.' He refers to the fact that Abulafia had proclaimed himself the Messiah in Sicily and had misled many into believing in him. It was widely reported that Abulafia was an ignoramus,

[17] See especially *The 'Responsa' of Rabbi Solomon ben Adreth of Barcelona (1235–1310)* by Isidore Epstein. The Bene Berak edition is used in this chapter

[18] On Abulafia see G. Scholem, *Major Trends in Jewish Mysticism*, pp. 119–55; Abraham Berger, 'The Messianic self-consciousness of Abraham Abulafia: a tentative evaluation', in *Essays on Jewish Life and Thought Presented in Honor of Salo Wittmayer Baron*, ed. J. L. Blau *et al.*, pp. 55–61

but in any event Adret refuses to believe that Abulafia is a prophet or that an angel had dictated a book to him. The Rabbis,[19] describing the basic qualifications of a true prophet, state that he must be wise, rich and physically very strong. Few, indeed, are men blessed with all these qualities and yet these are the preconditions for prophecy. It is extremely unlikely, therefore, that a prophet would rise overnight. Adret does not deny that even one lacking these qualifications, though such a man cannot be a prophet, can be inspired, since we find in the Bible that very ordinary men like Laban, Abimelech, Gideon and Manoah were inspired and even Balaam's ass saw the angel. But these were inspired only temporarily, and for some special purpose. They were not prophets. Why, even of the holy man Daniel, the Rabbis[20] say that he was not a prophet but possessed only the lower degree of inspiration known as the holy spirit. Moreover, personal qualifications apart, the generation must be worthy of having a prophet arise in its midst, which Adret's generation obviously is not. Even of the disciples of the great Hillel it was said[21] that while they personally were worthy of becoming prophets they could not attain to this state because their generation was unworthy. Add to this the tradition that a prophet can arise only in the holy land,[22] and it can readily be seen how devoid of all substance is Abulafia's claim.

Adret continues that he believes it possible for men gifted with a powerful imagination to see visions. There was an illiterate child in Laredo who sang sweet songs automatically and who prescribed an effective cure for a sick person. By means of a divine name, a certain preacher in Germany delivered marvellous sermons. Adret states that he knew personally a German Jew named Abraham of Cologne who changed his name to Nathan. When this man stood in the synagogue, a mysterious voice emerged from the Ark delivering marvellous sermons, the like of which had never been heard. Abulafia claimed, in fact, that it was the voice of Elijah that was heard. Adret admits that he is as puzzled as his questioner by the whole matter, into which a

---

[19] Ned. 38a
[21] Sukk. 28a; BB 134a
[20] Meg. 3a
[22] *Sifre*, Shofetim, 175

thorough investigation is required. Is the report true, for instance, that Abulafia had never sat at the feet of a great master of the law? It has always been to the credit of Jews that they prefer to endure the bitter yoke of exile than to entertain false hopes by uncritically accepting the claims of Messianic pretenders. They did not believe even in Moses until he had demonstrated the truth of his message by the miracles he performed. Adret concludes: 'May the God of truth show us a true sign through His true prophet Elijah, of whose coming we have been assured.'

One of the issues between the Maimonists and the anti-Maimonists was the question whether the world would ever have an end. Maimonides,[23] impressed by the Aristotelean view of the complete regularity of the natural order, held that the world would never come to an end and that the Biblical passages which appeared to suggest the opposite had to be understood in a non-literal fashion. But Adret, in his commentaries to the Talmud, observed that, according to the Rabbis, the world would have an end. Adret was asked (no. 9): what proof is there for the correctness of the Rabbinic view against that of Maimonides?

Adret observes that if we rely solely on human reasoning it must appear certain that, as Maimonides says, the world will have no end. This is because human reasoning is based on experience, and experience surely does demonstrate nature's complete regularity. But we Jews are not guided solely by reason. We have a more reliable guide in prophecy, so that wherever philosophy disagrees with either prophecy or the Jewish traditional view, the opinion based on philosophy must be rejected. No religious person denies that prophecy is superior to philosophy and it ill behoves the upholders of the true religion so to do, any more than we deny that God performed miracles for our ancestors, such as the parting of the Red Sea and the sun standing still at Joshua's behest. The philosophers have allowed their reasoning to persuade them that such things are quite impossible. They would say that the prophets who recorded these wonders were mistaken but we, the true believers, can have no truck with such unbelievers. Adret then puts forward the stock medieval argument against the

[23] *Guide of the Perplexed*, II, 27–9

rationalism of the philosophers. The philosophers are so impressed by reason, so ready to explain everything—but how do they explain rationally the magnet's attraction of iron? Had this not been confirmed, Aristotle would no doubt have argued that there could be no such thing as magnetic force. Adret expresses his particular astonishment at the Jewish philosophers who deny the supernatural and yet believe, at the same time, that God and His wisdom are identical.[24] They are guilty of self-contradiction in that they rely on reason to tell them what is and what is not possible in nature, and yet see nature as the manifestation of God's wisdom which, on their own premise, is as unfathomable as the very essence of God.

Adret now turns to the question of the authority of tradition. He sees tradition as the real basis for our beliefs as Jews. The Rabbis, for example, derive the doctrine of the resurrection from Scriptural verses,[25] but no one would ever have arrived at this doctrine solely on the strength of these verses, which, on any showing, can hardly be said to teach the doctrine unambiguously. It is rather that we believe in the resurrection because we rely on our tradition, the verses quoted by the Rabbis hinting at a truth we already know. To be sure, no blame is to be attached to a sage for interpreting Scripture figuratively when his reason tells him that the literal meaning is false. Indeed, verses like: 'And all the trees of the field shall clap their hands' (Isa. 55 : 12) make sense only if they are understood figuratively. It is quite different, however, when a firm tradition is at stake. No one is allowed to reject a tradition simply because the philosophers declare it false, any more than we would dream of denying the parting of the sea, the revelation at Sinai and the other miracles, even though the philosophers are in agreement that they were impossible. The philosophers, for that matter, hold it to be impossible for God to command man to refrain from eating the pig or to command that an animal be slaughtered in a particular way, yet we do believe that God commanded these things. 'For My thoughts are not your thoughts, neither are your ways My ways, saith the

[24] With reference to Maimonides' views, see *Yad*, Teshuvah 5 : 5
[25] Sanh. 90b

Lord' (Isa. 55 : 8), the prophet declares. Furthermore, a philosopher is by no means infallible even from the standpoint of human reason. Did not Plato confound the views of his predecessors and Aristotle those of Plato?

But, continues Adret, it might be asked: where does tradition say that the world will have an end? There is not much point in quoting Scripture since we have admitted the legitimacy of interpreting Scripture figuratively. The answer is that this tradition is to be found in the Talmud. In whatever way the well-known saying of R. Kattina[26] about the six thousand years of the world is to be understood, it is clear that he teaches that the world will have an end, and no other Rabbi disputes it anywhere in the Talmud. R. Ashi and Rabina, the editors of the Talmud, recorded R. Kattina's saying in their work and thus gave it the stamp of their approval. As for the ambiguity in R. Kattina's further statement that after the destruction of the world, it will be in a state of desolation for a thousand years, the meaning is that if the heavenly bodies had been in existence at that time, the period elapsed would have been a thousand years. The same applies to the saying that the Torah was in existence two thousand years before the creation of the world, although 'before' the creation of the world there cannot have been any 'years'.[27] Similarly with the verse: 'And Thy years shall have no end' (Ps. 102 : 28). Since God is beyond time, how can He have any 'years'? But it is all simply a manner of speaking. If the believer accepts the doctrine of *creatio ex nihilo* and thus follows the tradition that the world had a beginning, why should he find it hard to believe that the world will have an end? God will destroy His world at the end, only to create it anew. Adret then refers, but only by a hint, to the Kabbalistic doctrine of the cycles in which a new world is created after the old one has been destroyed.[28] He surmises that this doctrine is based on a tradition received by some of the sages.

The problem of anthropomorphism in the Bible and the

[26] RH 31a
[27] *ARN* 31, cf. the comment on this Midrash in Abraham Ibn Ezra's Introduction to his *Commentary on the Torah*
[28] On this, see I. Weinstock, *Be-Maagale Ha-Nigleh Ve-Ha Nistar*, pp. 153–241; with reference to this Responsum of Adret, see pp. 210–11

Talmud was especially keenly felt in the thirteenth century, when the philosophers increasingly advanced a theology of negation in an attempt to refine man's notion of the Deity, while the traditionalists tended to view the attempt as a desecration of true religion and found no difficulty in speaking of God in human terms. It is against this background that a Responsum of Adret (no. 60) on anthropomorphism has to be seen. The question concerns the verse: 'And the Lord God said: "It is not good that the man should be alone; I will make him a help meet for him" ' (Gen. 2 : 18). Does this mean that God changed His mind? Even more difficult is the Rabbinic comment[29] on the creation of Eve. The Rabbis say that at first God wanted to create two and then decided to create one, Adam. How can it be said of God that He eventually decided otherwise than He had at first intended?

It is important to appreciate, Adret replies, that the creation narrative is written so that a general statement is followed by a particular one: the main principle is stated first and is followed by the details. Thus, the first chapter of Genesis simply states that God created male and female, while the second chapter records the details of how God created them. The meaning of: 'It is not good that the man should be alone' is not 'alone without a female', but 'alone and apart from other creatures'. It is not a statement of God's change of mind but of His original intention. It is not good for man to be different from other creatures; to be on his own like disembodied spirits who do not propagate their kind. It is necessary for a man to have a wife and propagate his species. As for the Rabbinic statement, it certainly does not mean that at first God decided to create two, then decided to create one, and eventually reverted to His original intention. The Rabbis wish to describe God's purpose in creating man and, since human speech is the only language we have, they wish to convey by illustration that God had given much thought, as it were, to man's creation. It is as if to say that possibly man and woman might have been created as two separate creatures but that God ruled out this contingency by 'deciding' to create them as one, both in the sense of their complementing one another and in the sense that Eve was

[29] Ket. 8a

created from Adam. This interpretation, says Adret, is a key to many Rabbinic sayings on the theme of creation. When the Rabbis speak of God thinking of doing this or that, they intend to convey the idea that this is His plan and purpose in creation, as if He had chosen it after much deliberation. For example, the Rabbis[30] say that when the moon complained that two kings cannot wear the same crown, God told the moon to become smaller. This is a poetic way of saying that God's purpose in creation was to have a great light, the sun, and a lesser light, the moon. The moon is lesser in the sense that it receives its light from the sun and is subordinate to the sun. That is why, Adret explains, in Joseph's dream (Gen. 37 : 9–10) Jacob and Rachel are compared, respectively, to the sun and the moon, concluding: 'It is enough for someone like you that only the faintest of hints be given.' The meaning of this final cryptic observation is undoubtedly that there is a reference to the Kabbalistic doctrine of the Ten Sefirot, the powers or potencies in the Godhead. Of these there is a male principle—*Tiferet*—represented by Jacob, and a female principle—*Malkhut*—represented by Rachel. The male principle is symbolised by the sun; the female principle by the moon, whose light is from the sun. It is typical of Adret that he does refer to the Kabbalah, but always as an esoteric doctrine at which he can do no more than hint.

The doctrine of the immutability of the Torah occupied an important role both in Jewish life itself and in Jewish polemics against Christianity and Islam. The Jewish teachers were embarrassed by occasional statements in the Rabbinic literature which appear to deny the doctrine. A question addressed to Adret (no. 93) concerns the statement in the Midrash[31] that all the festivals will be abolished except the festival of Purim. But how can even a single letter of the Torah ever be abolished? The questioner remarks that he is aware of the answers that have been suggested, but has found none of them satisfactory.

Adret notes that in the same Midrash it is said that the Day of Atonement will never be abolished, since Scripture says: 'And this shall be an everlasting statute unto you' (Lev. 16 : 34). This

---

[30] Hull. 60b   [31] Midrash to Prov. 9: 2, *Yalkut* 844

presents an even greater problem, since of Passover it is also said: 'Ye shall keep it a feast by an ordinance for ever' (Exod. 12 : 14). The meaning of the Midrash is that in the future Israel may suffer so much that the people will forget how to rejoice on the festivals. It is in this sense that the festivals will be 'abolished'. But the Jews will never be so sunk in trouble as to forget the joyous message of Purim that God delivers. And, as the Midrash continues, the Day of Atonement will never be abolished since its atoning power will prevail even should Israel forget the day.

A hotly debated question in the thirteenth century was whether it is a legitimate pursuit to search for reasons for the precepts of the Torah. Maimonides and his followers believed that there is a reason, capable of being discovered by man, for every precept of the Torah. It is desirable to seek the reason because a man is better equipped to carry out an act if he knows why he is obliged to do so, and because God is no tyrant imposing arbitrary rules on man. There was also the apologetic motive. To defend Judaism one had to show the reasonableness of its laws. Maimonides devotes the major portion of the third section of his *Guide of the Perplexed* to a detailed statement of the reasons he has discovered even for the seemingly most unreasonable precepts. The traditionalists and opponents of philosophy, on the other hand, held the whole exercise to be fraught with danger. If reasons are given there are bound to be instances where the reason will not apply and the precept will then be set at naught. Moreover, the fallible human mind is incapable of grasping the immeasurable wisdom of the Creator, so that to search for the reason behind divine statements is sheer presumption. The devout should obey the laws because God commanded them. There need be no other motive, nor can any other be so satisfactory. No truly religious person should appear to question God's wisdom by asking why He commanded this or that.[32] Adret (no. 94) pursues a course of his own. The questioner asks Adret to explain the reasons for the precepts. He was especially concerned with the reason for the law that the mother bird be sent away when the young are taken (Deut. 22 : 6–7); a question discussed in the Talmud[33] and by Maimon-

---

[32] See the analysis of I. Heinemann, *Taame Ha-Mitzvot*, vol. 1   [33] Ber. 33b

ides,[34] and which became the *locus classicus* for the whole debate on the reasons for the precepts.[35]

Adret observes that the precepts are directed to the 'body' but contain hints for the 'soul'—i.e. over and above the acts enjoined there are deep spiritual aims for all the precepts. Even when the Torah gives a reason for a precept it is not the only one, but in reality: 'I have seen an end to every purpose; but Thy commandment is exceeding broad' (Ps. 119 : 96). The sabbath is a good example. The reason for sabbath observance given explicitly in the Torah is: 'for in six days the Lord made heaven and earth, and on the seventh day He ceased from work and rested' (Exod. 31 : 17). But this is only the plain meaning of the text. In reality, the institution of the sabbath 'contains a most exalted mystery'. And, even according to the plain meaning, there are numerous other ideas of the utmost significance such as God's providence and *creatio ex nihilo*. The same applies to the precept of tabernacles. The reason is stated in the Torah: 'That your generations may know that I made the children of Israel to dwell in booths, when I brought them out of the land of Egypt' (Lev. 23 : 42). But over and above this reason there are many others. Adret observes in this connection:

> You should know that with regard to all these matters the masters of the secrets of the Torah have exceedingly glorious reasons, even though, for our sins, the wells of wisdom have been stopped up. For our sins have caused the Temple to be destroyed from where there once proceeded the flow of prophecy and wisdom to the prophets and sages.

Adret then gives a general rule. There are three aspects to the precepts—mouth, heart and hand. The 'mouth' aspect is the study of the Torah so that one comes to appreciate its wisdom. The 'heart' aspect is the power of discernment, through which one obtains a knowledge of the secret things. The 'hand' aspect refers to the actual practice of the precepts.

As for the question regarding the sending away of the mother bird, Adret remarks that only one in his generation is permitted to reveal the tremendous mystery stated here by the Kabbalists.

[34] *Guide*, III, 48   [35] See e.g. Commentary of Nahmanides to Deut. 22: 6

Few are worthy to expound it and few to receive it. Adret says that he would be greatly astonished if anyone in his day could grasp these profundities. In general, he would say that the precept of sending away the mother bird hints at God's immeasurable wisdom, and our prayer is that we may be worthy of having it revealed to us in some small measure.[36]

Evidently the questioner had asked Adret another question regarding the precepts to which he now replies. Since the Patriarchs are said to have kept all the precepts of the Torah, how could the Patriarch Jacob have married two sisters, a practice forbidden by the Torah?[37] Furthermore, how could the Patriarchs have kept the precepts which had not yet been given at that time? Adret replies that each detail of the precepts contains a hint at some sublime mystery. The wisdom of God is expressed in every detail as manifested here on earth. Consequently, a perfect man, capable of reaching out to that wisdom, would know automatically which acts to perform without having to be commanded to do them. The Patriarchs knew God's wisdom and so were able to arrive by themselves at the performance of the precepts even before they had been given by God.

As for the question of how Jacob could have married two sisters, Adret gives the following Kabbalistic explanation:[38]

You must know that the Torah is based on three pillars—the first is *time*, the second *place*, the third *instruments*. *Time*—it is not forbidden to work on all the other days as it is on the sabbaths and festivals. It is not forbidden to eat leaven on other days as it is on Passover. There is no obligation to take the palm-branch and to sit in the tabernacle on other days as there is on the festival of Tabernacles. *Place*—in other places on earth there is no obligation to give the tithes as there is in the land of Israel. Sacrifices are not to be offered

---

[36] In all probability the reference here is to the Kabbalistic doctrine referred to by Adret's teacher, Nahmanides (end of comment on Deut. 22: 6, ed. B. Chavel, p. 491), that the 'mother' is the Sefirah *Binah*, which it is forbidden to contemplate because it is unfathomable, while the 'young' are the lower Sefirot which it is permitted to contemplate

[37] The question was widely discussed in the Middle Ages; see Ginzberg, *The Legends of the Jews*, vol. v, p. 295 n. 167

[38] Possibly a hint at the Kabbalistic doctrine that Jacob on earth is the counterpart of the Sefirah *Tiferet* and Rachel and Leah two aspects of *Malkhut*, the Shekhinah, see pp. 114–15 below on David Ibn Abi Zimra

in other places as they are in the Temple. *Instruments*—the precept of the palm-branch and the citron cannot be carried out with other plants. Other creatures cannot be offered on the altar as are cattle, sheep, turtle doves and young doves, and no other than a priest can offer the sacrifice. I am unable to explain more than this, but he who is intelligent will find what he has to find.

A Responsum (no. 132) of Adret deals with the subject of dreams. The Talmud refers to two methods of neutralising a bad dream. The first is fasting. The Talmud states[39] that fasting is as powerful in neutralising a bad dream as fire is to shavings and, in the same Talmudic passage, permission is given to one who has had a bad dream to fast even on the sabbath. In another passage,[40] the method of 'making good' the dream is recorded. The man who has a bad dream should bring together three persons and say to them: I have had a good dream, and they should reply: Good it is and good may it be. During the Middle Ages it was the custom to adopt both these methods.[41] The questioner asked Adret whether it is sufficient to rely on 'making good' the dream without fasting. Adret replies that there is no rule anywhere in the Talmud that one must fast after having had a bad dream. The Talmud only says that it helps 'like fire on shavings' and is therefore permitted even on the sabbath. But if one is not anxious about it, there is no need to fast. Adret remarks, somewhat laconically, that Samuel[42] would say, when he had had a bad dream: 'The dreams speak falsely' (Zech. 10 : 2), but when he had had a good dream he would say: 'Do the dreams speak falsely?'

One of the issues in the thirteenth century between the philosophers and the traditionalists concerned the Jewish religion as universalistic rather than particularistic. The philosophers generally tended to play down the particularistic elements in Judaism, such as the idea that the holy land is the special place of revelation.[43] There are echoes of the debate in a question addressed to Adret

[39] Sabb. 11a [40] Ber. 55b
[41] See J. Trachtenberg, *Jewish Magic and Superstition*, pp. 244–8 [42] Ber. 55b
[43] Judah Ha-Levi (*Kuzari*, I, 103 and 109; II, 14; IV, 17) holds that prophecy is confined to Jews and to the holy land. Maimonides (*Guide of the Perplexed*, II, 32 f.) has a more universalistic view. Cf. Alvin J. Reines, *Maimonides and Abravanel on Prophecy*

(no. 134): what is the meaning of the saying:[44] 'One who lives in the land of Israel is like one who has a God, but one who lives outside the land of Israel is like one who has no God'? Adret replies that the holy land is called God's inheritance: 'For they have drawn me out this day that I should not cleave to the inheritance of the Lord, saying: Go serve other gods' (I Sam. 26 : 19). This is because God's providence extends directly to this land and not through the heavenly princes. Scripture says: 'The eyes of the Lord are always upon it' (Deut. 11 : 12). Furthermore, the majority of the precepts can be carried out only in the holy land.

Belief in astrology, enjoying as it did the support of the Talmud, in which work there are numerous references to this science, was accepted by the majority of Jews in the Middle Ages.[45] But such a belief raised obvious problems in connection with God's providence. A questioner turned to Adret (no. 148) with the following problem. The Talmud[46] records the Babylonian teacher Raba as saying that whether a man enjoys long life, whether he has children or whether he earns an adequate living depends not on his merits but on the stars (*mazzal*, 'planet', 'destiny', 'luck'). But does not the whole of Scripture, in which these things are promised as the reward of virtue, teach the exact opposite? Adret first reminds the questioner that there is a debate in the Talmud[47] whether Israel is immune from the influence of the stars. Raba evidently held that Israel was not immune and that the fate of Jews as well as Gentiles was determined by the stars. But all this applied only to individuals. All the Rabbis agree that the stars have no influence over the destiny of the Jewish people as a whole. The fate of this nation depends not on the stars but on its own merit. The Scriptural passages all deal with the fate of the nation as a whole. The only objection that can be raised is from the instance of Hezekiah (Isa. 38) in which whether he lived or died was made to depend on his merits. But Hezekiah was a king and the fate of the king affects the nation as a whole, so that Hezekiah was not treated as an individual. According to the other Rabbinic opinion, however, that Israel is immune from the influence of the

---

[44] Ket. 110b
[45] See Trachtenberg, op. cit., chapter XVI, pp. 249–59
[46] MK 28a
[47] Sabb. 156b

stars, the Scriptural passages speak of individuals as well as of the people as a whole. Evidently, this is the view the Talmud eventually adopts, against Raba, since another Talmudic passage[48] states that 'nowadays' we do offer prayers for the recovery of the sick, which implies that their fate is not determined by the stars.

Another Responsum of Adret (no. 408) in which he considers the problem of dreams and providence is in reply to a question regarding the strange Talmudic tale[49] of Bar Hedya, the interpreter of dreams. Here it is said that Bar Hedya interpreted favourably the dreams of Abaye, who paid him a fee, and unfavourably those of Raba who did not pay him. In each instance the interpretation of Bar Hedya came true and Raba blamed him for the misfortunes which resulted from the baneful interpretation. The questioner was extremely puzzled by it all. How could God's providence be affected by Bar Hedya's interpretation? Adret, in reply, says that the question is 'philosophical', a term he uses here in a pejorative sense. Only a philosopher or one influenced by the ideas of the philosophers could have posed such a question. The trouble with the philosophers is that they are obsessed by the idea of 'nature', so that everything must have a reasonable cause. Our tradition teaches otherwise; that there are unknown forces at work in the universe: certain effects following on certain causes without our being able to see why it should so be. Thus, the Rabbis speak frequently of the beneficial effects of a blessing and the harmful effects of a curse. But, if nature is our sole guide, how can verbal utterances have any effect on material conditions? In some mysterious way it is true that the interpretation of a dream can bring about that which the interpreter says will happen. Once again, Adret refers to the magnet. Even the philosophers cannot help admitting that there is magnetic force in the universe though it is beyond their ability to offer any explanation for such an apparent contradiction to the laws of nature.

Adret takes up (no. 409) a further question regarding the Bar Hedya story. Raba accepted that Bar Hedya's interpretation was effective in such matters as prosperity in business and long life and yet, as above, it is Raba who says that these are determined by the stars. Adret draws on his previous distinction between the individual and the nation as a whole. Bar Hedya's interpretation was for Raba, whose fate, as a communal figure, affected the people as a whole. Though Raba as an individual ought to have been governed by the stars, he was immune from this influence because of his role in society.

In no. 220, Adret deals with the mysterious divine name of forty-two letters.[50] The old saying is that one who knows this name is beloved above and delightful below but, the questioner wished to be informed, does this refer to one who merely pronounces the name or to one who knows its meaning or, perhaps, to one who uses the name for magical purposes? Furthermore, the questioner wished to know how the name is to be read, in sets of three letters or of six letters? Adret replies that it is clear from a number of Talmudic passages that the divine names possess magical power.[51] Thus David is said to have stilled the waters of the deep by means of a divine name,[52] and the Talmud permits the carrying into the public domain on the sabbath of amulets containing the divine name.[53] However, the reference to the one who 'knows' the name is to one who understands its deeper spiritual meaning, the spiritual realities signified by the letters of the name. One who simply makes use of the name for magical purposes can hardly be said to be beloved above. Far from it. It is extremely dangerous spiritually to use divine names to work magic. As for the manner in which the name is to be formed, there are differing traditions. In some lands the tradition is that there are fourteen words each of three letters, in others there are seven words each of six letters. In these lands we follow the latter tradition which we have from Hai Gaon, but one hears that they have the other tradition in Germany. Adret finally refers to the famous prayer of R. Nehunia b. Ha-Kanah[54] which contains the forty-two-letter name in the initial letters of its words.

In another Responsum (no. 423), Adret considers two uncon-

---

[50] See pp. 18-20 above. For details of this name, see Trachtenberg, op. cit., pp. 94-5
[51] E.g. Yev. 49b   [52] Makk. 11a
[53] Sabb. 61a-b
[54] See Trachtenberg, op. cit., p. 95, and Singer's *Prayer Book*, p. 371

nected problems put to him by the same questioner. The first concerns the meaning of a Scriptural verse, the second, intention in prayer.

The first question is on the unusual syntactical form of the verse: 'For in six days the Lord made heaven and earth, and on the seventh day He ceased from work and rested' (Exod. 31 : 17). The Hebrew uses the word *sheshet*, meaning 'six', not *be-sheshet*, meaning '*in* six'. Why this peculiar form? The questioner had heard an interpretation, which he finds unsatisfactory, that the meaning is that God created six days—i.e. He created time. Adret states that according to the plain meaning there is no difficulty whatever. In Biblical Hebrew, *sheshet* is simply the same as *be-sheshet*. The plain meaning is that God created the world in six days and by resting on the seventh He created rest, which is itself a new creation. However, there is, in reality, a profound secret behind the omission of *be*, a mystery revealed to the sages of Israel. Here, too, Adret hints at the Kabbalistic doctrine of the Sefirot. He appears to be saying that God created 'six days', that is, the Six Sefirot, above *Malkhut*, the seventh.[55]

The same questioner also wished to be informed of the kind of intention one should have when offering prayers. Adret replies that *kavvanah* ('inwardness', 'intention', 'concentration') in prayer is the basis of everything, but the type of intention varies in accordance with the spiritual stage an individual has attained. Each individual, from Moses to the most inferior, has his own special type of intention. Adret remarks:

The first stage in the matter of intention, to which every Jew attains, is that all know and acknowledge that there is a God, blessed be He, whose existence is necessary. He created the world by His will and gave the Torah to His people Israel at Sinai, a Torah of truth with righteous judgments and statutes. To Him do we belong and Him we worship. He commanded us to offer ourselves up to Him when we call on His name. Him we recognise and to Him do we pray since everything is from Him. His providence extends over us all and He looks down upon our deeds to requite us for them and grant us our recompense. Every Jew should have this in mind when he prays,

55 See *Zohar*, I, 3b and 39b and Nahmanides' Commentary to Exod. 20: 11, ed. B. Chavel, p. 403, for the same explanation

even the women and the ignorant. They all receive reward for their worship. Even one who cannot pronounce the words accurately, substituting one word for another, receives reward for the general intention. As our Rabbis of blessed memory say:[56] 'And his skipping over me is love' (Cant. 2 : 4). God forbid that one unfamiliar with the intentions of the profound sages should abstain from prayer. For if you discourage such a person then women and ignorant folk will refrain from saying their prayers and from carrying out the precepts. Moreover, this applies to the whole body of Israel, with the exception of no more than one or two in a generation. As the true sages remark:[57] 'All Israel has a share in the World to Come.'

Adret attacks here by implication the aristocratic approach of the philosophers, which scorns the simple, unreflecting faith of ordinary Jews. He is saying that prayer is no esoteric exercise for the sophisticated alone, but an application of faith to life for all Jews.

Adret, in the same Responsum, says that the questioner had also asked him: why do we say in our prayers: 'The God of Abraham, the God of Isaac, and the God of Jacob', and not: 'The God who created heaven and earth'? (Again, the tension is to be observed between philosophical universalism and the particularism of the tradition.) Adret replies that a profound idea is here contained, one expressed in the saying: 'The Patriarchs are the Divine Chariot.'[58] But even if we follow the plain meaning, the reason we refer to the Patriarchs when we begin our prayers is because Moses did so in his prayers (Exod. 32 : 13), and God said to Moses: 'I am the God of thy father, the God of Abraham, the God of Isaac, and the God of Jacob' (Exod. 3 : 6). He did not say: 'I am the God who created heaven and earth.' Furthermore, we are human beings and our prayers are for the satisfaction of human needs; so it is right that we should begin our prayers by referring to the choicest examples of humanity, the Patriarchs. As for the meaning of 'God, the great, the mighty, the terrible',

---

[56] Cant. R. to Cant. 2: 4: 'If an ignoramus substitutes *evah* ['hatred'] for *ahavah* ['love'] and reads: "And thou shalt hate the Lord thy God", the Holy One, blessed be He, says: "His skipping [play on *ve-diglo*, 'his banner'] is beloved to Me" '

[57] Mishnah, Sanh. 10: 1

[58] Gen. R., ed. Theodor and Albeck, 82: 6, p. 983

with which we also begin our prayers, Adret remarks: 'Who can know the great secret, still less express it or write it down.'[59]

Finally, Adret replies to another question put to him by the same enquirer. Benedictions all begin with the word *Barukh*, 'Blessed [art Thou, O Lord].' But how can we humans 'bless' God? The questioner suggests an answer of his own. *Barukh* refers to the divine attributes. The meaning is not 'God *be* blessed', but 'God *is* blessed'. By a transposition of letters, the word *barukh* can, moreover, be read as three other words: 1. *rokhev*—'rider', the Governor of the universe; 2. *bekhor*—'first-born', the Powerful; 3. *kerubh*—'cherub', the Wise, since the wings of the cherubim soar aloft. Adret approves of this interpretation but adds that a further subtle idea is contained in *Barukh*. 'Blessed art Thou' is, in fact, a prayer for God to be blessed by all mankind, that all men should acknowledge His sovereignty.

A question was put to Adret (no. 480) concerning the saying of R. Kruspedai in the Talmud[60] that three books are opened at the New Year. The wholly righteous are inscribed forthwith in the book of life; the wholly wicked in the book of death; while average people are left in a state of suspension until the Day of Atonement. It was the statement about the fate of the average that caused the concern. Do not the Rabbis[61] interpret the words 'abundant in goodness' (Exod. 34 : 6) to mean that God tips the scales in favour of mercy where the balance is equal? The questioner suggested his own answer: that this latter Rabbinic saying refers to the final judgment in the World to Come. Adret approves. The distinction is clearly correct, since R. Kruspedai speaks explicitly of the time between the New Year and the Day of Atonement.

We have seen how very circumspect Adret is in the matter of dreams. In another Responsum (no. 483), he replies to a man who sought his advice regarding a constantly recurring dream in which his deceased father appeared to him giving him dire warnings. The man was disturbed because some of the evil tidings he received

---

[59] Undoubtedly referring to the Sefirot of *Hesed*, *Gevurah* and *Tiferet*, see Bahya Ibn Asher's Commentary to Deut. 10: 17, ed. B. Chavel, p. 309
[60] RH 16b   [61] RH 17a

in the dream had actually come to pass. Should he fast? Adret replies that although he is normally convinced that there is no truth in dreams and that fasting to ward off the effects of a bad dream is not obligatory, in such a frightening case he is reluctant to take a lenient decision and he advises the man to fast.

Superstitious practices were prevalent in the Middle Ages, though the Talmud [62] sternly forbids copying 'the ways of the Amorites'. The demarcation line between magical practices that are permitted and those forbidden in Jewish law being finely drawn, there was considerable discussion about certain practices. Jacob b. Machir Ibn Tibbon (d. 1307) of Montpellier wrote to Adret (no. 395) to say that he approved of Adret's stand in the matter of 'atonements' (*kapparot*) for infants. Adret notes that when he first came to Barcelona as its Rabbi he found there the custom of slaughtering a cockerel as an atonement when an infant was born. 'They used to suspend from the house the entrails, head and feathers of the slaughtered cockerel, together with some garlic, and did other such stupidities which seemed to smack of the ways of the Amorites.' Adret states that he was eventually successful in abolishing the custom, even though he has heard that they do this in Germany on the eve of the Day of Atonement. [63] He had also heard that they had asked Hai Gaon about it, and Hai simply replied: It is the custom.

We have noted above that among the questions addressed to Adret were some concerning providence and others concerning Rabbinic statements which appear to contradict the teachings of the Bible. In a Responsum (no. 19), Adret addresses himself to a problem which concerns both these themes. The Talmud [64] advises a man who is badly off in one town to go to live in another where his fortunes may change for the better. The implication is that a man can improve his lot by changing his place of residence. But Scripture says: 'O Lord, I know that man's way is not his own; it is not in man to direct his steps as he walketh' (Jer. 10 : 23),

---

[62] Sabb. 67a–b

[63] See *Tur* and *Shulhan Arukh*, Orah Hayyim 605. In reality, the German custom did not involve the whole procedure mentioned by Adret

[64] BM 75b

implying that there is nothing a man can do to avoid God's decree. Adret replies that the verse in Jeremiah refers to God's final decree. Once this has been made there is no way in which man can avoid it. But man can take steps to prevent the decree being made. One of these is to change his place of residence. There are two reasons why such a step can be effective. It may be that a man's sins act as a barrier to the flow of God's mercy, and by going into exile from his home town he will find atonement for his sins in the suffering involved. Or it may be that his bad luck is due to the influence of the stars in that particular place. When a man sins he removes himself from God's providential care and is at the mercy of the fate determined by the stars. Otherwise, we follow the opinion that Israel is immune from the influence of the stars.[65] This is the meaning of 'I will hide My face from them, I will see what their end will be' (Deut. 32 : 20). This means that God will remove His providential care from them and they will then be at the mercy of the stars. But of the righteous it is said: 'Yea, though I walk through the valley of the shadow of death, I will fear no evil' (Ps. 23 : 4).

We noted[66] Joseph Ibn Plat's Aramaic Responsum on the question why there is a benediction before the performance of some of the precepts and not before others. Adret (no. 18) replies to the same question in Hebrew by simply paraphrasing Ibn Plat with due acknowledgments to the earlier teacher. There is also a Responsum of Adret (no. 256) in shorter form on the same theme.

The ever-recurring problem of the status of the apostate Jew is considered by Adret (nos 194 and 242). The question put was whether the corpse of an apostate brings ritual contamination to the house in which it lies, so that a priest may not enter that house (Num. 19; Lev. 21 : 1). Do we argue that 'even though he has sinned he is still an Israelite'[67] or that, since we do not restore to him something he has lost and since we are allowed to lend him money on interest, he is not treated as a Jew for this purpose? Adret replies that it is true that the Jerusalem Talmud[68] says that

---

[65] Sabb. 156b   [66] See pp. 41–2 above   [67] See pp. 33–4 above
[68] AZ 5: 4, 44b, speaking of the Samaritans, see Tos. AZ 26b, *ani*

we are allowed to lend him money on interest because he is not 'thy brother'. But in connection with the law of contamination, Scripture says: 'This is the law: when a man dieth in a tent' (Num. 19 : 14). There, the reference is not to a 'brother' but to a 'man', and the apostate is a human being. If he marries a Jewish woman, his marriage is valid in Jewish law and his wife cannot remarry without a *get*. Adret concludes with an interesting observation, indicative of his concern not to reject entirely the apostate Jew.[69] He refers to the discussion at the end of tractate Kiddushin.[70] There a debate is recorded on the verse: 'Ye are sons of the Lord your God' (Deut. 14 : 1). R. Judah comments: 'When you behave as sons you are called "sons"; when you do not behave as sons you are not called "sons".' But R. Meir said that in both cases they are called 'sons' since Scripture says: 'they are sottish sons' (Jer. 4 : 22); 'they are sons in whom is no faith' (Deut. 32 : 20); 'sons that deal corruptly' (Isa. 1 : 4). Even though, says Adret, the general rule is that when R. Meir and R. Judah engage in debate, the opinion of R. Judah is followed, here it is an exceptional case since the Scriptural verses support R. Meir's view. Even a convert who has reverted to his former religion is treated as a Jew for this purpose; so it is certainly the rule for one born a Jew.

Adret's Responsum[71] on the use of a lion engraving as a talisman became one of the main items in the collection of anti-philosophical letters entitled *Minhat Kenaot* by Adret's contemporary, Abba Mari Astruc of Montpellier. This and another Responsum on the same theme is addressed, in fact, to Astruc. It was the practice to engrave the figure of a lion on a plate of gold or silver as a talisman to cure a sickness of the loins or kidneys. Adret was asked whether the practice is allowed in law. There are two possible objections: 1. it is forbidden to make an image of 'those who minister on high',[72] and a lion's face is one of the four faces of the beasts which carry the heavenly Throne (Ezek. 1 : 10); 2. it is forbidden to follow the ways of the Amorites[73]—i.e. superstitious

---

[69] See pp. 31–2 above   [70] Kidd. 36a

[71] No. 167. On this subject see H. J. Zimmels, *Magicians, Theologians and Doctors*, pp. 137–9 and nn.

[72] RH 24a–b   [73] Sabb. 67a–b

practices which have no evident natural cause (perhaps, too, cures which have no rational basis). Adret defends resort to the talisman. So far as the first objection is concerned, the prohibition applies only when all four faces on the Throne are depicted.[74] As for the second objection, the Talmud[75] states that any practice that is for the purpose of healing the sick is not forbidden by the rule regarding the 'ways of the Amorites'. Adret observes that this permission extends not only to natural remedies but also to magical practices, since we are so ignorant of what is 'natural' that, for all we know, magic may work in a 'natural' way. The Talmudic sages, for instance, permit incantations and magical spells.[76] Adret concludes that his master Nahmanides, so he has heard, permitted resort to this very talisman.

In his second Responsum (no. 413) on the subject, Adret remarks that when he gave his approval he was unaware that the subject was keenly debated in Montpellier. Now that he has been informed of the debate there, he is reluctant to take sides in an internal quarrel which is none of his business. However, there is a rumour that in some places they practise fumigation when the talisman is made, and that is certainly forbidden. But it is clearly permitted to make the talisman. Adret quotes Maimonides[77] in support. The Talmud[78] permits a nail from a gallows to be used as a cure, and Maimonides argues that it is permitted since, 'at that time', they thought this was a natural cure. It follows that even Maimonides, rationalist though he was, permits magical cures. In reality, of course, Maimonides seems rather to mean that the Rabbis permitted it because they mistakenly imagined it to be a natural cure. Adret is, however, aware that Maimonides[79] does not permit the use of amulets but here takes issue with him since the Talmud, in many instances, of which Adret quotes examples,[80] does permit resort to magical practices, but not those forbidden because of their idolatrous associations. The truth is, says Adret,

---

[74] RH 24b   [75] Sabb. 67a
[76] Adret refers to Hull. 105b; Sanh. 67b; Gitt. 69; AZ 12b
[77] *Guide*, III, 37   [78] Sabb. 67a   [79] *Guide*, III, 37
[80] As above, concerning a nail from a gallows and the avoidance of even numbers (*zuggot*)—i.e. eating or drinking two things at a time (Pes. 110a). The Talmud also contains many references to demons

that some of the magical practices recorded in the books of magic are forbidden but others are permitted. We must be discriminating in our use of these books. If we were to be so intolerant of books of magic as to ban any reading of them because of the bad things they contain, we should ban the reading of philosophical works which contain such heretical notions as the denial of miracles and express the opinion that matter is eternal. All books should be treated like pomegranates where we throw away the rind and enjoy the beneficial seeds.[81] Adret admits that he is confused in the matter and only wishes to learn, since the Torah does forbid certain magical practices. All he knows is that the Talmudic Rabbis did permit certain practices that are clearly of a magical nature.

Adret then delivers himself of his own theory on this complicated subject. It appears, he says, that when God created the world He created at the same time various means of replenishing the forces of nature when these began to run down. Some of these we now call 'natural' because we can see how they work. Others are 'magical' because there is no evident association between cause and effect and yet these, too, are permitted. As for the argument that to resort to magic is to betray a lack of faith in God, why not say the same about resorting to natural cures? And, indeed, if one relies solely on the natural cure, it is forbidden. King Asa was condemned for resorting to the physicians,[82] and yet the Rabbis say[83] that permission is given to the physician to practise his art. We are obliged to make a distinction between relying solely on the medicine and relying on God who created the medicine. Once such a distinction is accepted as valid, there is no logic in refusing to make it with regard to magical cures. Trust in God does not mean that all human effort is pointless. It is only forbidden to trust in men or events if in the process the heart is turned away from God. As Jeremiah puts it: 'Cursed is the man that trusteth in man, and maketh flesh his arm, and whose heart departeth from the Lord' (Jer. 17 : 5). In fact, apart from a few

[81] A reference to Hag. 15b, which mentions that R. Meir studied at the feet of the apostate Aher

[82] II Chr. 16: 12   [83] BK 85a

rare saints,[84] men are forbidden to rely on miracles.[85] Human effort is normally the precondition for success, and God helps those who help themselves. Adret records his puzzlement regarding Maimonides' principles in these matters. Maimonides only permits 'natural' cures and forbids resort to magic. But what precisely does Maimonides mean by 'natural'? Does he mean to suggest that only the cures found in Aristotle and Galen are permitted and that all others are forbidden because of the 'ways of the Amorites'? The philosophers did not know everything. Magical practices are also 'natural'. What of the magnet which is 'natural', but for which there is no rational explanation!

Finally, reference must be made to Adret's Responsa[86] on the study of philosophy. As we have seen, he became closely involved in the Maimonist controversy. In these Responsa he quotes in full the exchange of letters between him and Astruc culminating in the ban pronounced in the Barcelona synagogue, in July 1305, on anyone studying philosophy before reaching the age of twenty-five. The ban is also quoted in full, but together with the famous defence of philosophy by Jediah Bedersi (d. 1340).

From his theological Responsa, Adret emerges as a profound believer in the Talmudic tradition, with an acute awareness of the dangers to the Jewish faith inherent in the philosophical approach of his contemporaries. But he is a fair-minded opponent, seeking wherever possible to understand the views of those attracted to the study of philosophy, respectful of Maimonides, ready to admit his perplexities and uncertainties, and generally striving to provide a rational defence of the tradition. It is also worth noting how this distinguished Halakhist applies this type of reasoning to theological questions, always using precise logic and skilful analysis so that in method and presentation there is no difference between Adret's Halakhic and his theological Responsa.

---

[84] Adret quotes Ber. 33a   [85] Pes. 64b
[86] Nos 614–18. On the whole subject see Joseph Sarachek, *Faith and Reason*, and D. J. Silver, *Maimonidean Criticism and the Maimonidean Controversy*

CHAPTER V

The Fourteenth Century

R. Asher b. Jehiel (d. 1327), known as the *Rosh*, was a disciple of Meir of Rothenburg and a member of his Bet Din. Asher was the leading figure in German Jewry in his day but he left Germany for Spain in 1303, where he was elected to the position of Rabbi of Toledo. When Adret proclaimed the ban on the study of philosophy by persons under twenty-five, Asher encouraged the community of Toledo to support the ban. Asher discovered to his astonishment that the Spanish Jewish authorities occasionally punished offenders with death, especially informers who posed a serious threat to the safety of the community. The Talmudic rule is that no court, after the destruction of the Temple, has the legal right to inflict either capital or corporal punishment, although in cases of emergency, where the well-being of the community is at stake, emergency powers are given to the courts. On these grounds Asher came to accept the procedure in Spain. He is best known in the history of Jewish law for his compendium on the Talmud, *Piske Ha-Rosh*, in which he summarises all the opinions of the earlier authorities and states the actual ruling in each case. Asher's son, Jacob, basing himself on his father's work, compiled the *Tur*, a standard Code of Jewish law. Asher's Responsa are chiefly of a purely legal nature. He had little interest in philosophical questions and was a determined opponent of philosophical speculation, considering it to be harmful to faith. None the less, a few of Asher's Responsa do deal with theological questions.

One of these[1] considers changes in the standard prayer, the Amidah. Asher refuses to countenance a change that would add some words to the benediction against unbelievers because, he remarks, he has in his possession a manuscript from ancient times in which the number of words in each benediction of the Amidah is carefully recorded and in which this benediction has twenty-nine words, no more and no less. The reason is, says Asher, because there are twenty-two letters in the Hebrew alphabet and five final letters, making twenty-seven. Add to this number a further two, representing the Written and Oral Torah, and we have a total of twenty-nine. The unbeliever denies the letters of the Hebrew alphabet in which the Torah is written and he denies the Torah itself. It is right and proper, therefore, for the benediction against unbelievers to contain twenty-nine words for, when unbelievers are no more, the Torah will come into its own.

Another suggested change in the prayers was the omission, in the morning benediction praising God for creating the morning light, of the prayer for a new light to shine upon Zion. Asher remarks that the French Jews do not, in fact, recite this prayer, which has no apparent connection with the morning light. He himself, however, favours the retention of the prayer here as entirely appropriate. The light referred to in this benediction is the primordial light, which, the Rabbis say,[2] God stored up for the righteous in the World to Come, the present state of existence being unworthy of receiving it. Since the righteous in the Messianic Age will enjoy this light, it is only proper that the prayer for a new light to shine upon Zion be inserted in this benediction.

It was the custom of the aristocratic Spanish Jews to appoint to communal positions only men with a good family background. A community leader complained to Asher[3] that in some towns they appointed men of low birth to serve as Readers in the synagogues. Would they appoint such base persons to positions of trust in their own business? By treating the matter so lightly they despise

[1] IV, no. 20   [2] Hag. 12a   [3] IV, no. 23

the Torah. Asher says that he, too, complains of the disgraceful manner in which the Torah is treated, but for reasons quite other than the questioner mentions.

> You say that it depends on an aristocratic background, but it is not so in God's eyes. If a man is an aristocrat but wicked, what advantage is there to God in his family background? If, on the other hand, a man's family are aliens, a welcome is extended to him if he is righteous. What I do complain about is that in these lands the Readers sing for their own enjoyment so that others should hear how sweet their voice is. As long as a Reader has a pleasant voice, that is all they care about, no matter how wicked he may be. But the Holy One, blessed be He, declares: 'She hath uttered her voice against Me; therefore, have I hated her' (Jer. 12 : 8).

From this Responsum we learn that the office of Reader in the synagogue was highly prized. In another Responsum[4] Asher is asked: if a community can afford to appoint only one official, should he be a Reader or a Rabbi? Asher replies that they should appoint a Rabbi if he is an expert in Jewish law but, if not, it is better to appoint a Reader.

Should a man rebuke sinners if he knows full well that they will pay no attention to his rebuke? Asher[5] replies that if he is quite certain that they will pay no attention he should not rebuke them since, as the Talmud[6] remarks in this connection, it is better that they should sin unwittingly than intentionally. But if he is in doubt whether or not they will pay heed, then he should rebuke them and save his own soul.

Finally, in a Responsum[7] on the legality of a bond drawn up in Arabic, Asher attacks those who prefer the reasoning of the philosophers to the wisdom of the Torah, and he thanks God for making him ignorant of philosophy.

R. Isaac b. Sheshet Perfet[8] (1326–1408), known as *Ribash*, was born in Barcelona where his teachers were Peretz Ha-Kohen and Nissim b. Reuben, the *Ran*. He served as Rabbi in his native town, in Saragossa and in Valencia, and in 1391 left Spain for North Africa, where he settled in Algiers. Perfet's Responsa collection is

---

[4] VI, no. 1   [5] VI, no. 3
[6] Betz. 30a; cf. *Rashi*'s reply, pp. 34–5 above   [7] IV, no. 9
[8] See Abraham M. Hershman, *Rabbi Isaac ben Sheshet Perfet and His Times*. The edition of **Perfet**'s Responsa used is that of Israel Hayyim Daiches

among the most influential in Jewish law. The compiler of the *Shulkhan Arukh*, the standard Code of Jewish law, relies heavily on Perfet's decisions in these Responsa. A number of the Responsa deal with theological topics.

A famous Responsum (no. 157) of Perfet has to do with the Kabbalistic doctrine of the Sefirot. The questioner wished to know whether it is proper to believe in the doctrine and to pray to the Sefirot. Perfet refers to his teacher Peretz Ha-Kohen who never referred to the Sefirot and never had them in mind when he offered his prayers. Peretz spoke of R. Samson of Chinon, 'the greatest in his generation', who used to declare that he prayed 'like a child'; that is to say he had in mind only the simple meaning, not the intentions, of the Kabbalists who now have this Sefirah in mind, now the other. The Kabbalists interpret the Rabbinic saying:[9] 'One who desires wealth while praying should face north, one who desires wisdom should face south' as referring to the requisite Sefirot. All this, observes Perfet, is strange to the non-Kabbalist, who cannot be blamed if he suspects the Kabbalists of entertaining dualistic notions. He says that he once heard someone influenced by philosophy attack the Kabbalists on the grounds that while the Christians believe in 'three', the Kabbalists are worse in that they believe in 'ten'. Perfet describes a meeting he had with the venerable sage, Don Joseph Ibn Shoshan, whom he describes as a Talmudic scholar, familiar with philosophy and a famous Kabbalist and saint. Perfet asked him: how can the Kabbalists have one Sefirah in mind when reciting one benediction and a different Sefirah in mind when reciting another benediction? Is it not forbidden for a Jew to suggest that the Sefirot are deities, by praying to them? Ibn Shoshan replied that, of course, the prayers of the Kabbalists are directed to the Cause of causes but their concentration on the different Sefirot can be compared with supplication to a king, in which the monarch is entreated to command that the suppliant's wish be carried out through the prince appointed for that particular purpose. When the Kabbalist thinks of the Sefirah *Hesed*, 'Lovingkindness', as he prays for the righteous, and the Sefirah *Gevurah*, 'Power', as he

9 BB 25b

prays for the downfall of the wicked, his true intention is to pray to God to draw down His influence into the particular Sefirah. Perfet praises the ingenuity of the reply but expresses his dissatisfaction with it. Surely, he argues, it is better to pray to God with simple intention rather than appear to advise Him how to grant the bequest. He concludes that he does not reject the Kabbalistic system but, since he had not studied this subject at the feet of a master, he is ignorant of it and fails to grasp its meaning. Consequently he prefers simple, unsophisticated intention in prayer. This Responsum should be compared with that of Adret[10] on simple intention in prayer.

Perfet's Responsum[11] on the study of philosophy expresses moderate approval of this study. He was asked the meaning of 'Greek wisdom', which the Rabbis say[12] should be avoided. Does it refer to Aristotelian physics and metaphysics? Perfet gives a novel interpretation of the term, 'Greek wisdom'. This means a kind of secret language, a jargon invented by the philosophers so that their discussions should be unintelligible to the masses. There is no objection to studying the famous Greek works on natural science unless these express views contrary to the main principles of the Jewish faith—belief in *creatio ex nihilo*, for instance, or individual providence. Some of these works argue that the eternity of matter has been demonstrated and that God cannot change the natural order. The world, in its relation to God, can be compared, according to their view, to the light which proceeds from the sun or to the shadow cast by a tree. God can no more change nature than the sun can prevent its light from shining or the tree the casting of its shadow. God cannot make the wings of a fly longer than they are or the legs of an ant shorter. Furthermore, they hold that God's providence cannot extend to the sublunary world. And they hold that true knowledge can be attained only through philosophy, not by tradition. But we, the recipients of

---

[10] See pp. 71–2 above

[11] No. 45. This Responsum is quoted in Solomon B. Freehof's anthology *A Treasury of Responsa*, pp. 72–177

[12] BK 83a (given incorrectly by Freehof, p. 74, as 82a). On this topic see E. Wiesenberg, 'Related prohibitions: swine breeding and the study of Greek', in *HUCA*, vol. XXVII, 1956, pp. 213–33

the truth, believe that the Torah is of divine origin and all the wisdom of the philosophers can in no way be compared to it. The Rabbis forbid the reading of 'external books'.[13] It is to be noted, observes Perfet, that the prohibition extends even to the reading of heretical works, and not only to the acceptance of the heresies they contain.

Perfet refers to various scholars of former times who took the same line; Hai Gaon, for instance,[14] and Adret.[15] As for Maimonides, who did study these works, he was in an entirely different category since he first studied the whole of the Torah, including the two Talmuds, as can be seen from a perusal of the great Code he compiled. Only after he had gained all his tremendous knowledge of Judaism did he permit himself to study the philosophical works and he did so only in order to refute the heretical views he found there. He acted like R. Meir,[16] who permitted himself to sit at the feet of the heretic Aher, throwing away the rind of the pomegranate and retaining the wholesome seeds.[17] The Talmud, in this passage concerning R. Meir, expressly allows this only to a great man who is capable of discrimination between the true and the false. And even so great a sage as Maimonides did not emerge unscathed. He was influenced by those books he had studied to deny that Elijah really brought back the child from the dead (I Kgs 17 : 17-24).[18] He also expressed curious views on the nature of the revelation at Sinai,[19] and he treated the incident of the angels appearing to Abraham (Gen.

[13] Mishnah, Sanh. 10: 1
[14] See p. 28 n. 59 above where the Responsum on the study of the secular sciences is incorrectly attributed to Hai Gaon but was accepted as authentic in Perfet's day. See Hershman, op. cit., p. 90 n. 4 for Perfet's quotation of Hai here as saying that the fear of Heaven is only acquired by those who study the Mishnah and Talmud, *not* by those who study philosophy; Nahmanides ('Iggeret Ha-Hitznatzlut', in *Iggerot Ha-Ramban*, p. 41), however, quotes Hai as saying that the fear of Heaven is only acquired by those who are engaged in the study of the Mishnah, the Talmud *and* philosophy, not by those who study philosophy *alone*. Hershman refers to I. H. Weiss *Dor*, vol. IV, p. 160 n. 9
[15] See pp. 76-9 above   [16] Hag. 15b
[17] See p. 78 above for Adret's use of the same quotation in connection with books of magic
[18] *Guide of the Perplexed*, I, 42
[19] In *Guide*, II, 33, Maimonides states that Israel at Sinai only heard the sound of an inarticulate voice and only Moses heard the words in their proper articulation

18 : 1–15) as a dream,[20] for which he was severely and rightly attacked by Nahmanides.[21]

Gersonides, too, says Perfet, was a famous scholar and author of an admirable book on Scripture. He followed Maimonides in being attracted to the study of philosophy. But he, too, was misled in expressing the opinion that God's foreknowledge does not embrace particular events[22] and denying that the sun stopped for Joshua (Josh. 10 : 12–14).[23] On these topics he wrote things it is positively forbidden to hear.

If, then, concludes Perfet, two giants of the calibre of Maimonides and Gersonides did not escape serious error because of their philosophical studies, how can we have any confidence that we will emerge from such studies without suffering great harm? We have witnessed all too many victims who have cast off the yoke of the Torah as a direct result of their philosophical studies.

Another theological Responsum of Perfet (no. 439) concerns Maimonides' statement[24] that God does not know with a knowledge external to Him. What does this mean? Perfet replies that man and his knowledge are not identical. When a man knows, it is something external to himself. Man can be said to *have* knowledge but it cannot be said that he *is* his knowledge. But with regard to God, Maimonides intends to say that His being and His knowledge are one and the same, since God does not acquire any knowledge external to Himself.

Perfet, in his Responsum on the study of philosophy, was critical of Gersonides' views on God's foreknowledge. As a solution to the vexed problem as to how God's foreknowledge can be reconciled with the doctrine that man is free to choose, Gersonides advances the startling thesis, which Perfet vehemently rejects, that God's foreknowledge does not embrace the particular choices of man. Thus God knows all that can be known. He does know beforehand all the possible choices open to man. But God does not know beforehand which particular choice a man will actually make. Man's freedom of choice is thus defended by placing

[20] *Guide*, II, 42   [21] Commentary to Gen. 18: 1, ed. B. Chavel, pp. 103–7
[22] *Milhamot*, III, 6   [23] Commentary to Joshua 10
[24] *Yad*, Teshuvah, 5: 5

limitations on God's foreknowledge. Maimonides discusses the problem in his Code,[25] arguing that God has complete foreknowledge and that man is free to choose, but that it is beyond the scope of the human mind to grasp how this can be. To this Abraham Ibn David, Maimonides' critic, objects that it were better for Maimonides not to have raised the question at all since he has no solution to offer. Ibn David gives a very tentative solution of his own. This is that although God does know beforehand how a man will choose, that knowledge is not determinative. Man does not choose as he does *because* God knows it beforehand.

Perfet's questioner (no. 118), R. Amram of Oran, wishes to know how this opinion of Ibn David differs from that of Gersonides, which Perfet has attacked. Perfet replies that the distinction is obvious. Gersonides holds that God does not, in fact, know beforehand the particular choices of man. Ibn David, on the other hand, does not impose any limits on God's foreknowledge. All that Ibn David says is that God's foreknowledge is not determinative. However, remarks Perfet, Ibn David's solution is very unsatisfactory, as he himself is aware. (Although Perfet does not say this, the fatal objection to Ibn David's view is: how can God's certain foreknowledge fail to be determinative?) Perfet proceeds to offer his own solution to the problem. It is axiomatic in Judaism that God has complete foreknowledge and that man is free. If God were to know beforehand simply the bare act that man will later perform, then, indeed, God's foreknowledge would be determinative. But what God knows beforehand is not only the act itself but the act as performed by man out of his own free choice. Thus man is completely free to choose, but God knows how he *will* choose. This foreknowledge of God is not determinative, since what is present in God's foreknowledge is man's choice, of his own free will, to behave as he does.

[25] Ibid., and Stricture of *Raabad, ad loc.*

CHAPTER VI

The Fifteenth Century

R. Simeon b. Zemah Duran (1361–1444)[1] was known as *Tashbetz*, after the initial letters of his name preceded by the initial letter of the word *Teshuvot* (Responsa). He was born in Majorca, where he practised as a physician after study there and in Aragon in Spain. In addition to his vast Talmudic knowledge, Duran was thoroughly versed in philosophy and in the Kabbalah. He left Majorca for North Africa, eventually serving as a Rabbi in Algiers. In his Responsa he defends the right of a Rabbi to accept a salary, of which he availed himself.[2] To some extent Duran and Perfet were rivals, but Duran succeeded Perfet when the latter retired from the position of Rabbi of Algiers. He was the author of a number of philosophical works, and it is not surprising that theological topics are dealt with in his Responsa.

Duran has a lengthy Responsum[3] on a Kabbalistic theme. The *Zohar*[4] observes that in the first portion of the *Shema* (Deut. 6 : 4–9) there are sixty letters. The questioner, Isaac b. Saadiah of Tenes, was puzzled by this statement, since there are far more than sixty letters in this portion. Duran replies that the 'Midrash' (the term he uses here for the *Zohar*) means that there are sixty *words* in the portion. Actually there are only forty-eight words,

---

[1] See Isidore Epstein, *The Responsa of Simon b. Zemah Duran*
[2] Part I, nos 142–5   [3] Part II, no. 236
[4] Quoted as *Zohar Lekh Lekha*, but is not in our versions

but the verse: 'Blessed be His name, whose glorious kingdom is for ever and ever'[5] (which the Rabbis say should be added after the first verse of the *Shema*) has six words in the Hebrew. It was evidently the custom, in the time of the *Zohar*, to repeat this verse when reciting the evening *Shema* so as to make a total of sixty words. The purpose of this was for the soul to ascend at night to the Throne of Glory, there to become attached to the sixty princes surrounding the Throne. These are referred to in the verse: 'Behold, it is the litter of Solomon; threescore mighty men are about it' (Cant. 3 : 7).

Duran then discusses 'Blessed be His name . . .'. The Talmud[6] tells us that Moses did not say this verse but that Jacob did (because he had heard the angels singing it when he had his dream of the ladder reaching to Heaven). Since Moses did not say it, there was a danger that it would be treated lightly. Consequently, in the time of the *Zohar*, they repeated the verse. We say it in a whisper because we do not wish the angels to overhear and be envious of us for using their verse. But on the Day of Atonement, when we are like the angels, we say it aloud.

Not happy with this explanation, Duran concludes that, after all, the *Zohar* might possibly mean letters, not words. The sixty letters are to be found in the first verse of the *Shema*, if each letter (except the *he*, which is spelled without the silent *alef*) is spelled out in full—i.e. *shin*, *mem*, *ayin* and so forth.

Duran returns to the problem in another Responsum.[7] Here he remarks that his previous reply regarding the sixty *words* will not do, since the Aramaic word used in the Zoharic passage can only mean *letters*. He admits the force of the objection, but still feels that the word can occasionally mean *words*. However, the better explanation is the other he has given, namely, that the reference is to the sixty letters in the first verse spelled out in full.

A question put to Duran[8] concerned the Jewish calendar. Although it is a lunar calendar, the lunar months, by the addition of an extra month in some years, are made to tally with the solar year. Or, as the questioner puts it, so far as the months are concerned we reckon by the moon, but so far as the years are concerned we reckon by the sun. Why is this? Duran replies that it is Biblically ordained, since the Biblical word for 'month' is *hodesh*, meaning 'renewal' and referring to the phases of the moon, yet Passover is said to be a spring festival, falling always in 'the month of Abib' (Deut. 16 : 1). Duran observes that far from our having to apologise for our calendar, we ought to appreciate how superior it is to that of the Christians and the Muslims. The Christians, who have a solar calendar, are obliged to fix the months in a purely arbitrary fashion, some months having thirty days, others thirty-one. The beginning of each month is decided purely by convention and is not based on Nature, as in a lunar calendar. The Muslims, who do have a lunar calendar, pay the price of having a movable feast. We Jews have the best of both worlds, a natural series of months and a fixed spring festival. Duran concludes: 'You find a difficulty here but, in reality, it is a source of pride to us and a demonstration of the superiority of our holy Torah. Would you have wished us to be like them? They walk in darkness but to all the children of Israel there is light.'

Another Responsum[9] on the Kabbalah is addressed to the same Isaac b. Saadiah. On the verse: 'And Aaron shall cast lots upon the two goats' (Lev. 16 : 9) the *Zohar*[10] comments: 'in order to sweeten it from *terufina*'. Isaac b. Saadiah wished to know the meaning of this comment and, especially, the meaning of the last word. Duran replies that there is a scribal error in the text of the *Zohar* and it should read: 'in order to sweeten it from the filth' (*tinufa*). He then proceeds to give the Kabbalistic meaning of the passage. The two goats represent the Sefirot of *Hesed* ('Lovingkindness') and *Gevurah* ('Power'). The goats were placed in front of the High Priest, one on his right, the other on his left, to represent the 'right side' of mercy and the 'left side' of judgment: Abraham, the 'pillar of mercy', on the right, Isaac, the 'pillar of judgment', on the left. Aaron the High Priest belonged to the right and, by casting the lots, succeeded in harmonising the two sides, causing the harmonising Sefirah *Tiferet* ('Beauty') to emerge from *Hesed* and *Gevurah*. This is represented by the third

9 Part II, no. 237   10 *Zohar* III, 62b

Patriarch, Jacob. Satan belongs to the 'left side', but his powers are nullified. The operation of the harmonising Sefirah prevents Satan from prosecuting. This is the meaning of the 'bribe' to Satan of which the Rabbis speak.[11] Were it not for the harmony that is produced, were it not that *Hesed* softens the rigours of *Gevurah*, the latter would become so strong that mercy could not come into operation and the 'left side' would prevail. As it is, the power of *Gevurah* has been 'sweetened' and Satan is incapable of bringing before God the filth of Israel's sins. This is what the *Zohar* means when it says: 'in order to sweeten it from the filth'.

The problem of the apostate Jew comes up in the Responsa of Duran.[12] Supposing a father left the Jewish fold and then had a son who was brought up as a Gentile. If this son dies, is his Jewish brother obliged to mourn for him as he would be obliged to do for his Jewish brother? Duran replies that if the brother died while he was a child, there is to be mourning for him, since it was in no way his fault that he had not been introduced to Judaism. But if the brother died when he had grown to manhood, there is to be no mourning for him. However, he remarks, Maimonides[13] rules otherwise. According to Maimonides no blame is to be attached to the son of an apostate, because his parents brought him up as a Gentile so that, according to this opinion, there would have to be mourning, even if the brother died after he had grown to manhood.

A Responsum of Duran[14] concerns the significance of dreams. The following question was put to him by Amram Merevas Ehprati of Oran. A man had a dream in which he was informed that unless the whole community fasted it would be under the ban. Is the community obliged to fast on the strength of the dream? We have seen how Adret[15] deals with similar questions regarding the efficacy of dreams. Duran refers to a Talmudic discussion.[16] A man felt uneasy about a sum of money left to him by his father. The 'master of dreams' appeared to him to inform him that it was tithe money, but the Rabbis ruled that dreams have no

---

[11] *Pirke DRE*, 46; see Nahmanides' Commentary to Lev. 16: 8, ed. B. Chavel, p. 88
[12] Part II, no. 139   [13] *Yad*, Mamrim, 3: 3   [14] Part II, no. 128
[15] See p. 67 above   [16] Sanh. 30a

significance. Duran adds that some dreams are true none the less. A man's imaginative powers can become strong enough to reach the Active Intellect. When this happens, precognition can take place in a dream as part of divine providence, serving as a warning for man to take precautions against the fate foretold in the dream. Duran refers to a passage in the *Zohar*[17] 'by Rabbi Simeon b. Yohai'. But other dreams have no truth in them whatsoever. He relates an incident in which Isaac b. Sheshet Perfet was involved.[18] A man named Solomon of Tish (or Solomon Matish?) urged Perfet to proclaim a fast because he had dreamed that a fire would break out in the Rabbi's house. Perfet laughed it off, but the dream came true. Years later, Hakun b. Abu came to Perfet and told him that he had dreamed it was imperative for the community to fast on Monday, Thursday and the following Monday. Perfet, impressed by his earlier experience, proclaimed the fast but so few turned up on the day that it was only with great difficulty that a quorum was obtained for the prayers. Duran is, therefore, sceptical and does not advise the fast to be proclaimed.

We have seen that both Hai Gaon[19] and Maimonides[20] discuss the Talmudic saying[21] that a man's wife is destined for him forty days before he is formed. Moses Gabbai b. Shem Tov, puzzled by the saying, turned to Duran for help.[22] Moses points out that in the science of astrology there are two opinions as to the time at which a man's fate is determined by the stars. Some say that it is determined at the moment of birth, others at the moment of conception. Both these opinions make sense. But how can a man's fate be determined forty days before conception, which is what seems to be implied in the Talmudic saying? Forty days before conception there is no entity upon which the stars can have an effect.

Duran first notes that the earlier teachers found another difficulty in the Talmudic passage. How can it be fated at all whom a man will marry, since 'everything is in the hands of Heaven except the fear of Heaven'[23] and marriage, as a religious obliga-

---

[17] *Zohar* III, 92a

[18] See Abraham M. Hershman, *Rabbi Isaac ben Sheshet Perfet*, p. 92, who discusses this incident

[19] See pp. 2–5 above   [20] See pp. 48–9 above   [21] Sot. 2a

[22] Part II, no. 1   [23] Ber. 33b

tion, belongs to the 'fear of Heaven', the area in which free will operates and where there is no determinism? Maimonides, therefore, understands it all in moral terms. The saying does not mean that it is determined categorically beforehand whom a man will marry, only that it is determined that a virtuous man will be helped to find a suitable mate. It depends on the man himself to be the kind of person suitable for a particular wife and she for him. Man is free to propose to whichever woman takes his fancy, but it depends on God's decree whether she will accept him. Duran believes in astrology and argues that, even according to the opinion in the Talmud[24] that Israel is immune from the influence of the stars, this does not apply to marriage, where, as the Talmudic saying with which we are concerned has it, it is fated who shall marry whom. As for the difficulty raised by the questioner, the answer can be given either according to the Kabbalah or according to philosophy.

According to the Kabbalah, all souls were created at the beginning when the world was created, and the Talmudic reference, that forty days before the formation of a child it is proclaimed 'the daughter of So-and-so to So-and-so', is to the souls in Heaven. According to philosophy, the passage has to be understood as referring not to forty days before conception but before the full formation of the child in its mother's womb. It is worth noting how Duran, while accepting the truth of the Kabbalah, is prepared to advance a solution, 'according to philosophy', which, in fact, contradicts the Kabbalistic doctrine.

Duran is, none the less, suspicious of the extremes to which the adherents of philosophy can be led. In a Responsum[25] on a reported allegorical interpretation of the story of Noah's ark, he warns against the kind of allegory that leads people to deny the historicity of the Deluge. For all that, Duran admires Maimonides' philosophical works and vehemently attacks the view that Maimonides leans towards an acceptance of the Aristotelian notion of the eternity of matter. All this in no way affects Duran's complete adherence to the Kabbalah. In another Responsum[26] he explains the Kabbalistic idea of combining letters to form divine

[24] Sabb. 156b   [25] Part III, no. 53   [26] Part III, no. 54

names and concludes: 'I am not allowed to explain more of the Kabbalistic mysteries than they allowed me . . . The combination of letters is a great mystery. Bezalel knew how to combine the letters by means of which the world was created.[27] These matters must not be recorded in writing. They can only be conveyed verbally to one who is worthy.'

Duran deals[28] with the question considered by Adret[29] and other thinkers. The Rabbis say[30] that the Torah was created two thousand years before the creation of the world. But how could there have been any 'years' *before* the world was created? Duran replies that the meaning is that if there had been heavenly bodies before the creation of the world, impossible though this is, the time that the Torah preceded the creation would have been two thousand years. This is, in fact, the reply given by Adret.

Finally, like Adret,[31] Duran deals with the duty of residing in the holy land. His questioner[32] asks whether it is true that one who goes to live in the holy land has all his sins pardoned as soon as he enters its borders, provided he repents of them. Furthermore, if a man sets out on a journey to the holy land in order to live there but dies on the journey, is it counted as if he had actually lived there? Duran quotes the passage at the end of tractate Ketubot[33] on the supreme religious advantages in living in the holy land. Those who are buried there will be spared, at the time of the resurrection, from having to roll through underground tunnels[34] in order to reach it, the place where the resurrection will take place. (It is noteworthy that Duran, for all his philosophical interests, can take this quite literally.) Consequently, says Duran, the answer to the first question is in the affirmative; a man who resides in the holy land does have his sins pardoned. As for the second question, yes, even if he did not actually arrive in the holy land but had the intention of so doing, his sins are forgiven. The Rabbis say[35] that a good intention is counted as actual performance of a good deed and so said the King of the Khazars when the Haver departed to journey to the holy land.[36]

[27] Ber. 55a [28] Part III, no. 245 [29] See p. 61 above [30] *ARN* 31
[31] See pp. 67–8 above [32] Part III, no. 285 [33] Ket. 110b-112b
[34] Ket. 111a; cf. Montefiore and Loewe, *A Rabbinic Anthology*, pp. 660–3
[35] Kidd. 40a [36] Judah Ha-Levi, *Kuzari*, V, 24–8

R. Solomon b. Simeon Duran (d. 1467), known as *Rashbash* after the initial letters of his name, succeeded his father, *Tashbetz*, as Rabbi of Algiers. There are a number of theological Responsa in *Rashbash*'s collection, though, unlike his father, he was more a pure Halakhist than a philosopher and he declared that he was completely ignorant of the Kabbalah. It is curious that of the three Rabbis of Algiers in our period—Perfet and the Durans, father and son—the first and the third are openly indifferent to the Kabbalah while the second was fully committed to the secret lore. The explanation is to be found, probably, in the belief that one had to be initiated into the Kabbalistic mysteries by a master who imparted the secrets verbally. Neither Perfet nor the younger Duran had such a master. No doubt the elder Duran held it to be wrong to initiate his young son into the Kabbalah, but it is still somewhat puzzling that the younger Duran, when discussing the Kabbalah, makes no mention of his father's complete allegiance to it.

A Responsum of *Rashbash* (no. 3) addressed to Haggai b. Alzuk of Mostaganem deals with the same question considered above by the elder Duran, of the merit of residing in the holy land. *Rashbash* first takes his questioner to task for daring to suggest that perfection of soul is to be attained only through metaphysical contemplation so that it is irrelevant where one lives. If perfection is to be attained only thus, of what use are the practical precepts of Judaism? The truth is, according to Jewish teaching, that the attainment of perfection depends on two factors; a man must hold correct opinions and he must carry out the precepts of the Torah. His status in Paradise will depend on the degree to which he realised both these aims during his life on earth. But correct beliefs—that God exists, that He is the Governor of the world, that He rewards and punishes—avail nothing without good deeds. Where is the advantage in a man believing in God if he does not recite the *Shema* morning and evening, and so forth? Now the duty of residing in the holy land is one of the precepts of Judaism, as Nahmanides records in his Commentary to the Torah.[37] Consequently, the answer to the question is that it is a clear duty to live in the holy land. However, continues *Rashbash*, where the

[37] Nahmanides' Commentary to Deut. 19: 8, ed. B. Chavel, p. 431 and *passim*

journey is fraught with danger, the Rabbis exempted a man from this obligation.[38] That is why we must never compel a husband or wife to go to live there at the request of the other spouse. Yet, if one wishes to take the risk, one should go. Otherwise, one can remain where one is without detriment to one's faith.

Rashbash does not deny that there are Kabbalistic mysteries though he, personally, is ignorant of them. A questioner[39] asks him why we find the word *he* ('she') spelled sometimes in the Bible with a *vav* and sometimes with a *yod* in the middle? And why is the word *ha-naarah* ('the maiden') sometimes spelled with a final *he* and sometimes without? *Rashbash* replies: 'This matter has been delivered to the masters of the Kabbalah. Until the Messiah comes, I cannot claim to belong to their company.'

We saw[40] that Perfet was critical of Maimonides for holding that the episode of the angels appearing to Abraham (Gen. 18) happened only in a dream, and that Nahmanides disagrees with Maimonides. The debate concerns every reference to angels in Scripture and it is evident from a Responsum of *Rashbash* (no. 44) that the debate continued in the fifteenth century. The question put to *Rashbash* is: did the episodes of Balaam's ass (Num. 22 : 28), Jacob's wrestling with the angel (Gen. 32 : 25) and the angels appearing to Abraham take place only in a dream or while the persons concerned were awake? *Rashbash* replies curtly: 'Know that these events took place while the persons concerned were awake. This is the opinion of Nahmanides, of blessed memory. This is the opinion one should believe in and follow.'

Another question put to *Rashbash* (no. 52) is whether the statement that whoever studies two laws each day is assured of a portion in the World to Come applies even to one who studies two laws, not from the Talmud but in legal compendiums such as that of Maimonides. The saying is based on a Talmudic passage.[41] There the reference is to the study of 'laws' and, since the plural is used, it means at least two. There is no reason, says *Rashbash*, for excluding the Code of Maimonides. The Mishnah was also ar-

[38] See Tos. Ket. 110b, *hu amar*
[39] No. 36. On this subject see R. Gordis, *The Biblical Text in the Making*
[40] Pp. 85–6 above   [41] Nidd. 73a

ranged by R. Judah the Prince on the basis of earlier collections of laws. *Rashbash* concludes: 'May my portion be among those who study these laws for their own sake, not in order to be able to taunt others for their ignorance or to flaunt one's learning before the unlearned.'

A questioner asks *Rashbash* (no. 188) to explain the meaning of the book of Job. *Rashbash* offers a novel interpretation. Job was no saint. He avoided sin but was in no way conspicuous for his good deeds, despite his boast that he was. His 'comforters' did declare that Job was a sinner but, in all probability, they were as wrong in their assessment as he was in his self-assessment. Job was a neutral character, neither saint nor sinner. Even if it be admitted that Job did perform good deeds, these were done out of motives of self-interest and were ethical, not religious, duties. Job's attitude towards the obligations a man has to his God left much to be desired. This helps us to understand why the initial description of Job's piety is worded somewhat negatively: 'That man was whole, and upright, and one that feared God, and shunned evil' (Job 1 : 1). Of a great saint it would hardly have been said simply that he shunned evil. The implication is that Job successfully avoided doing evil but was not outstanding in his pursuit of good. Job did not complain when his wealth was taken away, but only when he was stricken with bodily afflictions. He was willing to accept the doctrine that a failure to do positive good deeds should result in loss of wealth, but he believed that bodily suffering should only be visited upon a sinner, which he knew himself not to be, despite the protestations of his friends. But Elihu (32 : 1 f.) explained to Job that while it is true that God does not punish a man directly with bodily sufferings unless he is a sinner, yet God does allow him to become the victim of natural calamities unless he has good deeds to his credit to act as a shield. Job should turn to God and perform good deeds sincerely. He will then be saved if he prays, since God hears the cry of the afflicted.

Although, as we noted in a previous Responsum, *Rashbash* declares his ignorance of the Kabbalah but implies that he believes in its truth, from another Responsum (no. 189, no. omitted) we learn that he was more than a little sceptical whether the doctrines taught by the Kabbalists of his day belonged to the true Kabbalah. His attitude appears to have been, and it is one shared by other thinkers,[42] that there is *a* Kabbalah, a secret doctrine going back to Moses at Sinai, but that contemporary Kabbalists, especially in their views of the Sefirot, are in error when they identify what they call Kabbalah with the true Kabbalah.

Rashbash was asked what attitude one ought to adopt towards the Kabbalah. He first defines the word 'Kabbalah', which comes from a root meaning 'to receive'. The Kabbalah is, then, a doctrine conveyed by word of mouth from master to disciple. The disciple must be given only the bare outlines and must be capable of understanding the rest for himself, as the Rabbis say.[43] It follows that the true Kabbalah must never be committed to writing. Since this is the case, then, if the Kabbalistic books contain the true Kabbalah which the authors have received from masters who were adepts, how could they have allowed themselves to offend against the fundamental principle of secrecy by writing it down? If, on the other hand, the authors did not have their doctrines from a master but invented them out of their own heads, that which they teach does not deserve to be dignified by the term 'Kabbalah', which means 'tradition'. So much for the general objection. As for the particular doctrine of the Sefirot, there is an insoluble difficulty.[44] Either the Sefirot are God Himself or they are attributes of God. If they are God Himself, then the Kabbalists are guilty of attributing multiplicity to the Godhead. They offend more than the Christians who believe in the Trinity.[45] If, on the other hand, the Sefirot are only attributes of God, in what way are they more significant than the other attributes of God? The Rabbis[46] tell us that there are thirteen attributes. Why do the Kabbalists omit three of them? If the Ten Sefirot are different from the thirteen attributes of which the Rabbis speak, then they must either be superior to the thirteen, or inferior. If they are inferior, why not be content with the thirteen? If they are superior, is it

[42] See e.g. the attack on this view in Joseph Ergas, *Shomer Emunim*, beginning of part I, 1–13
[43] See Mishnah Hag. 2: 1
[44] See Moses Cordovero, *Pardes Rimmonim, Shaar* IV
[45] See pp. 83–4 above   [46] RH 17b

not strange that Moses was told only of the inferior thirteen and not of the superior ten? If it be held that the Sefirot are neither deities nor attributes, but influences, how can one be allowed to pray to them? Even one who prays to an angel is a heretic.[47]

The Kabbalists, continue *Rashbash*, claim to teach the secrets of the Torah. But if what they teach is truly a secret, how can they be guilty of revealing it, and if what they teach does not belong to the secrets of the Torah, it is mere human speculation. When R. Akiba[48] identified the man gathering sticks (Num. 15 : 32–6) with Zelophehad (Num. 27 : 1–3), his colleague rebuked him. If the identification is correct, the Torah evidently wished to keep it secret, so why does Akiba reveal it; if the identification is incorrect, a good man has been slandered. We can say to the Kabbalists in the same vein: if they are the true secrets of the Torah, why do you reveal that which the Torah wishes to remain a secret; if they are not the true secrets, then you slander the Torah by pretending that it teaches the doctrine of the Sefirot. Either way you will be called upon to give account before the Judgment Seat of God. *Rashbash* concludes:

> It is right and proper to rebuke these persons and those who boast of their knowledge of such matters. Immature students, who cannot be bothered to master the legal passages in the Talmud, choose the easier way of reading these works in order to pride themselves that they know the Kabbalah. Their ambition is to acquire fame in the eyes of the women and the ignorant, to acquire a reputation in such an effortless manner; whereas, in reality, they are entirely empty of wisdom. It is of such matters that it is said:[49] Whoever wants to tell lies, let him make sure that there are no witnesses to the truth, and whoever wishes to commit suicide should hang himself on a high tree. He who values his soul should keep far away from them.

In another Responsum on the Kabbalah (no. 267), *Rashbash* dismisses the view propounded by Nahmanides,[50] if taken literally, that the whole of the Torah is composed of various and numerous divine names in combination.

[47] See pp. 10–11 above   [48] Sabb. 96b
[49] These sayings are often quoted as Talmudic but the first is not in the Talmud at all (*Rashbash* appears to be the first to use it) and the second is based on Pes. 112a
[50] Introduction to *Commentary to the Pentateuch*, pp. 1–8

We saw above that Adret defends the Rabbinic view that the world will have an end, against the view of Maimonides. In a Responsum (no. 436) on the subject, *Rashbash* rebukes his questioner for thinking that the world will never be destroyed and, especially, for calling stupid anyone who believes in an unenduring world. The Talmudic Rabbis[51] hold this opinion, so how dare one call it stupid? Maimonides, it is true, considers that the world will never have an end and he interprets the Biblical verses which appear to say the opposite in a non-literal fashion. But thinkers like Nahmanides have ably defended the Rabbinic view. For all that, *Rashbash* continues, no basic principle of the Jewish faith is here involved. One who argues that the world never had a beginning and who denies *creatio ex nihilo* is a heretic, but it is an optional belief that the world will come to an end. There is no harm to faith in the opposite belief provided, of course, that one asserts that God's power to bring the world to an end, if He so desires, is not limited in any way. However, the Psalmist does say: 'They shall perish, but Thou shalt endure' (Ps. 102 : 27). The plain meaning of this verse is 'they shall perish' in a literal sense, not 'they shall perish' if God so wishes (but that, in fact, He will not so wish). Consequently, the plain meaning of the verse supports the Rabbinic view that the world will have an end. But, says *Rashbash* to his questioner, 'you believe whatever you want to believe.'

Finally, *Rashbash* deals (no. 525) with a question put to him concerning Gersonides' commentary to the Deuteronomic passage regarding the total destruction of the city that has gone astray after idolatry (Deut. 13 : 13–19). Why must the little children be slaughtered? Why must the city never be rebuilt? Gersonides' explanation is that the influence of the stars in that particular place may be the reason for the propensity of its inhabitants for idolatry. Since the children born there will grow up to be idolators, they have to be destroyed and, since the very atmosphere is a threat to the true religion, the city must never be rebuilt. No one must ever again reside in that baneful place. The questioner asked: does this not contradict the Rabbinic teaching

[51] RH 31a

that Israel is immune from the influence of the stars?[52] More seriously, does it not appear to deny the truth that man is free? *Rashbash* replies that there is nothing in this comment of Gersonides to contradict Jewish teaching. Even when the Rabbis say that Israel is immune from the influence of the stars it does not mean that the Jews are automatically immune,[53] but that they can rise above that influence if they pursue virtue. Man has to take every natural step to avoid harm, just as his trust in God does not permit him to walk through fire hoping not to be burned. Consequently, Gersonides rightly says that if the effect of the stars in that particular place might be to encourage idolatry, all necessary steps must be taken to prevent this from happening. Furthermore, a careful reading of Gersonides' actual words shows that he only says that it *may* happen, not that it certainly *will* happen.

Jacob b. Judah Weil (d. *c.* 1450) served as Rabbi of Nuremberg and from 1444 as Rabbi of Erfurt. Weil's collection of Responsa contains a few of theological interest, mainly on the theme of the penance to be imposed by the Rabbis for various types of sin.

In a Responsum (no. 12) addressed to a R. Seligmann, Weil discusses the penance to be imposed on a young married woman who had been unfaithful. The *Rokeah* by Eleazar b. Judah of Worms (*c.* 1165–*c.* 1230), in the second chapter, describes at length penances for various sins. *Rokeah*'s *teshuvat ha-mishkal*, 'the penance of balance', has as its aim the self-torment of the sinner to the degree when the pain experienced outweighs any pleasure there may have been in the sin. The name of each sin in Hebrew is given its numerical value, and fasts have to be observed corresponding to this number. Weil notes how rigorous *Rokeah*'s penances are, involving severe mortification of the flesh. If this young woman is informed all at once what is demanded of her, she will refuse to repent. Therefore, she should first be instructed to confess her sin. Although public confession is not normally advised, the Talmud[54] does advocate it where the sin is known to the public. The woman should proceed to the women's compartment in the synagogue and there confess her sins in German. She should remove all her jewels and wear only black garments and

---

[52] Sabb. 156b   [53] Cf. Adret, pp. 68–9 above   [54] Yom. 86b

she should not sleep in a bed, only on the ground or on a hard board. This she should do for a whole year. During this year, except on the sabbaths and festivals, she should fast every day, and she should sit twice a week for a quarter of an hour in snow in winter and be stung by bees in summer. For the rest of her life she should keep herself away from men as much as she possibly can. She should spend all her days in repentance and mortification, to the limits of her strength.

Another Responsum (no. 123) describes the penance to be imposed on Phoebus of Munich who had taken a false oath. The *Rokeah* treats one guilty of swearing falsely as if he had denied the Jewish religion. Phoebus should be flogged on a Monday, Thursday and the following Monday in the synagogue, confessing the while in German. He should fast for forty consecutive days and then every Monday and Thursday for a whole year. If he lacks the strength to do this, he should give alms very liberally and accept another penance imposed on him by the Rabbis of his town.

A Responsum (no. 125) of Weil on penance was to become influential in later Responsa on the same theme. Jekuthiel sent Ezra to perform an errand for him and Ezra was killed on the way. Does Jekuthiel have to do penance? Weil quotes a Talmudic passage[55] which says that David was punished because, through him, Nob the city of priests was destroyed, Doeg the Edomite was banished and Saul and his sons slain. Now David was in no way directly responsible for any of these but, indirectly, he was involved. If David had been other than he was, none of these would have happened. It follows that *a fortiori* Jekuthiel, who sent Ezra on the errand that resulted in his death, must do penance. If he is able to do so he should fast for forty days. If Ezra had left little children, Jekuthiel should do all he can to see that they are adequately looked after, as they would have been had their father remained alive.

In another Responsum (no. 178) Weil considers the case of Rabbi Solomon whose court had imposed a penance on a cantankerous person, a trouble-maker in his community. The man now protests his remorse and Rabbi Solomon is inclined to relax

55 Sanh. 95a

the full demands he had previously made. Weil, however, suspects the offender's sincerity. His remorse is probably only a pretext to escape the rigours of the penance. Weil strongly advises that there should be no relaxation. He quotes his teacher Jacob b. Moses Moellin (d. 1427), the *Maharil*, who gave the same ruling.

In an interesting Responsum (no. 157), Weil replies to a questioner who wished to know why, nowadays, Rabbis often fail to rebuke the people, even though the Talmudic Rabbis say[56] that whoever can prevent his townsfolk from sinning and does not do so has a share in their guilt. Weil replies that the reason is that it is often dangerous to rebuke those who scoff at the Torah and its teachers, no doubt thinking of informers who could threaten the future of the Jewish community.

Israel Isserlein (1390–1460) was the most prominent German Rabbi of his day, and his legal decisions enjoyed great authority among the later Codifiers. From 1445 to his death Isserlein was Rabbi of Wiener-Neustadt (i.e. the new town near Vienna). His Responsa collection *Terumat Ha-Deshen*, published in Venice in 1519, contains 354 brief Responsa (the numerical value of *deshen* is 354). Isserlein does not give the names of his questioners but simply states the problem and provides the solution. In all probability, some of the questions were invented by him, but there is every reason to suppose that the majority were actual questions put to him by those seeking his guidance.

A theological Responsum (no. 40) of Isserlein deals with a question formulated as follows:

> A student wishes to leave his country in order to study the Torah at the feet of a Rabbi in whom he has confidence. He feels that if he studies there his efforts will be crowned with success and he will acquire expertise in the knowledge of the Talmud. The student's father protests vehemently, saying: 'My son, if you go to that country where the Rabbi resides you will cause me much grief, for I will worry all the time that, perhaps, God forbid, you will be put in prison or that they will libel you as they do in that country.' What should the student do? Should he obey his father or should he go to study the Torah in the place he desires?

[56] Sabb. 54b

Isserlein argues that the obligation to study the Torah takes precedence over honouring parents and since it is proper, as the Rabbis say, that a man should follow his instincts when choosing a teacher, the student is permitted to leave his home in order to study the Torah, even though his father objects.

Another Responsum of Isserlein (no. 196) concerns a priest or a nobleman who wears a cross. Is a Jew permitted to raise his hat to him or to bow to him out of respect? Isserlein states that if it is at all possible it should be avoided. He recalls that when he was a boy in Vienna there was a high dignitary of the Church who respected Jewish feeling and would cover his cross when he met Jews who were obliged to bow to him in respect. Isserlein quotes a Responsum of Isaac Oppenheim, however, who permits it, since the Jew bows to the priest, not to the cross, and the priest is not an object of worship; it is permitted to bow to a human being for precisely this reason. The Jew, however, should do his utmost not to gaze at the cross when he bows.

Isserlein also considers (no. 197) whether a Jew is allowed to pretend to be a Christian by wearing Gentile garb. Isserlein permits it only where there is danger to life. Then it is permitted, however, and martyrdom is not demanded. Here the Jew does not accept the Christian faith or make any direct statement that he accepts it. He simply allows the Christian to assume that he is a Christian and, for this, martyrdom is not required.

Isserlein, too, considers the case of the apostate Jew (no. 193). His formulation of the question is: 'An apostate Jew returned to the true religion. Is it necessary for him to engage in much penance and mortification of the flesh or is it unnecessary for him to torture himself to such a degree?' Isserlein replies that the court must not impose too severe a penance because such a man has become accustomed to Gentile ways, and if life as a Jew is made too hard for him he will be tempted to revert to Christianity. He will be tempted to argue that his life as a Christian was easy and comfortable and now, because of his return to Judaism, he has to suffer such heavy penances. Consequently, he should be welcomed back and not treated severely.

Again on the question of martyrdom Isserlein considers (no.

199) a question that must have arisen from time to time. The Talmudic rule is that, apart from the sins of idolatry, murder, adultery and incest, a Jew is not obliged to give his life if he is forced to sin. What is the position if a pious Jew wishes, none the less, to give his life rather than commit any sin? Supposing such a man came to the court and asked for a ruling; what should he be told? Isserlein points out that the great scholars debate this very question. Maimonides holds that wherever the Torah does not demand martyrdom it is sinful to undergo martyrdom. One who does, commits the sin of suicide. But others permit it, and still others argue that it is an act of special piety.[57] Consequently, Isserlein argues, the law applies that in cases of doubt one takes the more lenient view where life is at stake. However, it is possible that since the law does enjoin martyrdom in certain cases, a doubt whether martyrdom is allowed should not be treated as other cases of doubt. Isserlein concludes, therefore, that the court in each case should decide in accordance with the particular circumstances. Their decision should take into account the intention and motives of the man who comes to them to advise him in his terrible choice.

R. Elijah Mizrahi (d. 1526) was born and educated in Constantinople. As the foremost Rabbi in the Ottoman Empire at the end of the fifteenth century, questions were addressed to him from many Jewish communities. Mizrahi's fame also rests on his very popular super-commentary to *Rashi's* Commentary to the Pentateuch. A few of Mizrahi's Responsa deal with theological matters.

In two Responsa (nos 1 and 2) Mizrahi deals with the custom, now universal but not in Mizrahi's day, of the Reader repeating the last two words of the *Shema* and the first word of the next hymn, so as to make up a total of 248 words in the *Shema*. The custom is based on a passage of the *Zohar Hadash* to Ruth.[58] Mizrahi observes that the custom is not referred to in any of the Codes,[59] and even the Kabbalists did not seek to impose it on

[57] *Rosh*, Commentary to the first chapter of AZ
[58] *Zohar Hadash*, Ruth, ed. Ashleg, p. 31
[59] The *Shulhan Arukh*, however, does refer to the practice, Orah Hayyim 61: 3

others but kept it a secret. We follow the Talmud and the Codes, not the Kabbalah. Would that we could have the plain intentions in our prayers instead of trying to have in mind the extremely complicated intentions provided by the Kabbalists, which, in any event, they put forward only for the very few. It is incorrect to see Mizrahi, however, as an opponent of the Kabbalah. He quotes the passage from the *Zohar Hadash* in such a way as to suggest his familiarity with the work. All he says here is that the Kabbalistic mysteries are for the few initiates, not for the masses.

In a Responsum (no. 11) on the theme of divine judgment, Mizrahi replies to an acute problem which his questioner, Rabbi Solomon, had found in Rabbinic teaching. It is generally accepted that a man is judged immediately after his death. Speaking of this, the Rabbis say[60] that the wicked are judged in Hell for twelve months after their death. What then is the meaning of the great Judgment Day which is to be held after the resurrection of the dead? Surely, a man will not be judged twice? Mizrahi notes that Maimonides and Nahmanides are in conflict regarding the meaning of the term, 'the World to Come', used frequently by the Talmudic Rabbis. Maimonides holds[61] that 'the World to Come' refers to the state of the soul after death and is, in fact, identical with 'the Garden of Eden' where the souls repose. But Nahmanides[62] holds that the two terms are not synonymous. The 'Garden of Eden' refers to the state of the soul after death, but 'the World to Come' refers to the period after the resurrection. Thus, according to Maimonides, there are only two judgments: 1. at the beginning of each New Year to determine man's fate during the coming year in this world; 2. after death, to determine the fate of his soul in 'the World to Come'. According to this view of Maimonides, there is no further judgment after the resurrection. The wicked, whose doom was pronounced at their judgment when they died, will simply fail to be resurrected. The righteous will awake to enjoy the state already determined for them. Those who are neither wholly righteous nor wholly wicked will remain in a state of suspension until the resurrection. According to

---

[60] RH 17a   [61] *Yad*, Teshuvah 8
[62] *Torat Ha-Adam, Shaar Ha-Gemul*, ed. B. Chavel, pp. 291 ff.

Nahmanides, however, there are three separate judgments: 1. at the New Year; 2. for the fate of the soul after death; 3. at the resurrection, when it is determined who will enjoy bliss for ever and who will remain in Hell for ever.

A Responsum of Mizrahi (no. 81) concerns the sanctity of the synagogue. The beadle of a synagogue in Aragon had homosexual relations with a boy in the synagogue. Did his act pollute the synagogue so that it is forbidden thereafter to pray in that place? Mizrahi replies that since it is rumoured that it is forbidden to pray there or to keep a scroll of the Torah there, he feels obliged to proclaim that such an opinion is wrong. Indeed, it is wrong even to voice such a view. If it were correct, it would mean that it is forbidden to pray in any house once occupied by Christians, since they all have icons before which they burn incense. Even though idolatry has been practised in such houses, it is the universal Jewish practice to rent houses from Christians and to pray in them. The Rabbis say[63] that even the holy Temple did not become contaminated when they set up an idol there. In the Hanukkah prayer we declare that the Greeks 'contaminated the Temple',[64] yet when the Maccabees reconsecrated the Temple it was used as before. If a place possessing the great sanctity of the Temple does not lose its sanctity because of the severe sins committed there, a lesser sanctuary such as the synagogue obviously does not lose its sanctity even if grievous sins have been committed there.

Dealing with a similar theme (no. 88), Mizrahi considers whether a man who had been converted to another faith but who later returned to the Jewish fold, and is now a thoroughly pious Jew, can serve as a Reader in the synagogue.[65] Mizrahi has no doubts that he can serve as a Reader. According to one opinion in the Talmud,[66] a penitent is greater than a man who had never sinned and, according to another, he is not even disqualified from acting as a Reader. From Maimonides' statement[67] regarding a Reader's qualifications, it is clear that they all have to do with his present status. There is no suggestion that a man is disqualified from acting as Reader because he had sinned in his youth. As for

[63] AZ 52b [64] Singer's *Prayer Book*, p. 54 [65] See pp. 39–40 above
[66] Ber. 34b [67] *Yad*, Tefillah 8: 11

107

the statement in the Talmud[68] that a Reader must be a man regarding whom there had been no evil report in his youth, that statement refers only to a Reader who officiates on a public fast-day, not to an ordinary Reader in the synagogue. That this is so is borne out by this passage where it is also said that a Reader must have a field of his own and children to support. Obviously, these conditions apply only on a public fast-day when the one who leads the congregation in prayers for rain must be personally involved. It is true that the *Tur*[69] records the disqualification of an ordinary Reader about whom there had been an evil report in his youth. But Maimonides[70] records it only in connection with a public fast-day and not otherwise. We should follow Maimonides since the Talmud, in fact, records only a similar disqualification.

The status of the apostate Jew comes up for discussion in two other Responsa (nos 47 and 48). Here there is a lengthy debate between Mizrahi and Jacob Ibn Habib on the question, argued long before their day,[71] whether the widow of the apostate's brother requires *halitzah*.

Jacob Ibn Habib remarks that the matter has been widely discussed but, since the earlier authorities are in disagreement, we should apply the Rabbinic rule that in cases of doubt where Biblical law is involved the stricter view must be adopted. We cannot, therefore, permit the widow to remarry without *halitzah*. Ibn Habib surveys all the opinions on this question, among them that of Jehudai Gaon who permits the widow to remarry without *halitzah*. But, he argues, this opinion of Jehudai Gaon refers only to the case where the dead brother was also an apostate. The argument here is that the purpose of levirate marriage is: 'to raise up unto his brother a name in Israel' (Deut. 25 : 7). But the apostate had no desire to remain associated with Israel, so why should we refuse his widow the right to remarry? He took no steps himself to perpetuate his Jewish name during his lifetime, quite the contrary, so what obligation have we to see that his name be perpetuated after his death? We have a basic principle that only one who takes the trouble to prepare on the eve of the

68 Taan. 16a–b
70 *Yad*, Taanit 4 : 4
69 Orah Hayyim 53
71 See pp. 33–4 above

sabbath (i.e. in this world) can enjoy the sabbath bliss (in 'the World to Come').[72] Mizrahi takes exception to this and to some of the other arguments advanced by Ibn Habib, but eventually agrees that the widow does require *halitzah*.

[72] AZ 3a

CHAPTER VII

The Sixteenth Century

Next to Adret, the most prolific writer of Responsa in the history of that literature is R. David Ibn Abi Zimra (1479–1573), known, after the initial letters of his name, as *Radbaz*. *Radbaz* was born in Spain but went to Palestine in his early youth, settling in Jerusalem. From Jerusalem he journeyed to Egypt, where he served as a Rabbi for over forty years, eventually becoming both the spiritual and lay head of Egyptian Jewry. He ended his long life in Safed in Palestine. *Radbaz* was a man of great wealth, which enabled him to achieve a stern independence throughout his career. In addition to his profound mastery of the Talmud and the legal literature, he was a renowned Kabbalist. His Responsa,[1] totalling well over two thousand, contain many of a theological nature.

Radbaz was, naturally, a firm upholder of the Talmudic approach. The conflict between tradition and philosophy was still a live issue in sixteenth-century Jewry and he was opposed to any reductionist attempts by the adherents of the philosophical approach. In one of his Responsa (no. 344), *Radbaz* replies to a questioner who wished to be informed which formulation of the principles of the Jewish faith he should accept. Maimonides draws up thirteen principles, Joseph Albo three principles, and so forth. *Radbaz* replies:

[1] On *Radbaz* see Israel M. Goldman; *The Life and Times of Rabbi David Ibn Abi Zimra*

I do not agree that it is right to make any part of the perfect Torah into a 'principle', since the whole Torah is a 'principle' from the Mouth of the Almighty. Our Sages say that whoever states that the whole Torah, with the exception of one single verse, is from Heaven is a heretic. Consequently, each precept is a 'principle' and a fundamental idea. Even a light precept has a secret reason beyond our understanding. How, then, dare we suggest that this is inessential and that basic? In short, Rabbi Isaac Abravanel, of blessed memory, wrote correctly in his work *Rosh Amanah*. You should consult this work in which he develops the theme at length, criticising earlier scholars. My opinion is the same as his, that every detail and inference of the Torah is a 'principle', a foundation and a fundamental belief, and whoever denies it is an unbeliever who forfeits his share in the World to Come. For this reason, if a heathen forces a Jew to transgress any of the commands of the Torah, saying to him that God did not command it or that it was only given for a certain period of time and is no longer valid, he is obliged to suffer death rather than transgress. This only applies where he is urged to profane the sabbath in order to transgress against his religion. Rabbi Yom Tov b. Abraham, of blessed memory, writes accordingly, and derives from this that a Jew must be prepared to suffer death rather than become a Muslim, even though Muslims are not idolators. I have written that which seems to my puny intellect to be the correct view.

As a Kabbalist, *Radbaz* believed that behind the plain meaning of Scripture there are profound mystical meanings. A questioner asked *Radbaz* (no. 256) to explain to him the narrative of Adam's sin according to the plain meaning, not according to the Kabbalah, which, the questioner says, is not his concern. Adam was God's creation, the work of His hands. The Rabbis wax eloquent in describing Adam's lofty spiritual degree. All that God commanded him was to refrain from eating of the tree, a small matter surely. How, then, could he have yielded to the importunities of Eve and defy his God? *Radbaz* observes that the *Zohar* has tremendous things to say here but he is not permitted to divulge them and, in any event, the questioner had asked for the plain, not the mystical, meaning. *Radbaz* proceeds to expound the narrative in its plain meaning, as he sees it. Adam knew that he could become immortal only by eating the fruit of the tree of life. Unless he ate of this fruit he would be subject to the law of decay to which all creatures, by their very nature, are subject. But Adam wished to live for ever so as to be able to praise God for all eternity, attaining to the degree of the angels, nay, possibly, to an even higher degree. In pursuit of his aim of living for ever, Adam wished to discover where in the garden the tree of life was situated, for this information had not been imparted to him. When Adam saw that Eve's knowledge had been increased, as a result of eating the forbidden fruit of the tree of knowledge, he realised that if he ate of the forbidden tree his knowledge, too, would be increased, and that increase would endow him with the wisdom to discover the location of the tree of life. He knew that it was sinful of him to eat the forbidden fruit, but justified the sin on the grounds that it was, after all, for the realisation of the sublime aim of living for ever to praise God. And he believed, further, that once having attained his spiritual ambition he could erase the initial sin by repenting of it. Thus, Adam did sin, but it was out of the highest motives and so in no way unworthy of his elevated degree.

Another Responsum (no. 284), in which *Radbaz* offers his interpretation of a difficult Scriptural narrative, concerns the book of Esther. Mordecai placed the whole people in jeopardy because of his refusal to bow to Haman. Why did he do this? If he wished to avoid bowing to Haman, there was no need to provoke the tyrant unnecessarily. Mordecai could have left Shushan and gone to live elsewhere. It looks as if Mordecai was being consciously provocative, which was all very well so far as he himself was concerned, but not where the lives of a whole people were at stake. *Radbaz* notes that Abraham Ibn Ezra, grappling with this problem, suggests that Mordecai was an official at the court and could not leave. *Radbaz* finds this unsatisfactory. After all, Mordecai could have obtained leave of absence from the king. *Radbaz* suggests that Mordecai did not see his action as endangering all the Jews. He could not imagine that even Haman, in his chagrin, would wish to take such a terrible revenge or that, even in the remote possibility that he would, the king would acquiesce in the total destruction of all his Jewish subjects. Mordecai knew that by refusing to bow he was risking his own life, but of this he had no fears, wishing to suffer martyrdom, if necessary, for his principles. It is also possible, continues *Radbaz*, that Mordecai foresaw that God would not permit the destruction of His people. Mordecai deliberately set the dire process in motion confident that God would increase Israel's greatness by performing miracles on her behalf. In that case, why was Mordecai so distressed when he saw that Haman's plan might be realised? The answer is that he was afraid that the people might have sinned and so forfeited the right to God's deliverances. The Rabbis[2] say that, even where God has promised to deliver, the promise can be nullified through sin.

Another Responsum (no. 352) on a Biblical difficulty is in reply to the question why Scripture forbids a man to marry the mother of his mother-in-law but allows him to marry his own grandmother. Is it not an *a fortiori* argument that if he is forbidden to marry his wife's grandmother he should certainly be forbidden to marry his own grandmother? *Radbaz* replies that the *a fortiori* argument (*kal va-homer*) is based on human reasoning. But the forbidden degrees of marriage are a divine decree, so that human reasoning is incapable of operating here. All we can say is that God has so ordained. One degree of relationship is forbidden, the other permitted. If the questioner, for all that, desires a rational explanation, *Radbaz* retorts that he is under no obligation to provide one. Yet he is prepared to offer a tentative solution. Scripture only forbids that which a man is likely to do. Those affinities are proscribed for which man in his lust has some inclination. No man would ever want to marry his own grandmother, so there is no cause for Scripture to record a special law prohibiting it. But it is not beyond the bounds of possibility that a man should wish to marry his wife's grandmother. If, for example, a man marries a girl of thirteen and he is forty years of age, it is possible for his wife's grandmother to be younger than he, and so attractive to him. *Radbaz* concludes that Menahem Meiri of Perpignan (1249–1316) has, in fact, given this solution to the problem.

In another Responsum (no. 716) on a difficult Biblical verse, *Radbaz* considers: 'O Lord, I know that man's way is not his own; it is not in man to direct his steps as he walketh' (Jer. 10 : 23). This

[2] Ber. 4a

verse appears to be in flat contradiction to the basic Jewish belief that man is free to choose. *Radbaz* replies that the verse does not refer to man's ethical and religious life where he is, indeed, free to choose, but to such matters as the acquisition of riches. Here it does depend on God's decree, not on man's efforts. But then would it not be obvious? Not necessarily, for we might have supposed that just as in ethical and religious matters God's help is forthcoming only after man has himself made the effort so, too, God's blessing of wealth depends on the extent to which man himself initiates the steps. The verse, therefore, informs us that it is not so. In this area all depends on God, and human effort is futile.[3]

Radbaz also discusses (no. 696) the old problem of how Jacob could have married two sisters. The questioner is aware that this question has been dealt with by Adret,[4] but he is puzzled by Adret's cryptic reference to the fact that some of the precepts apply only at certain times and to certain persons. If all Adret is saying is that Jacob lived before the Torah had been given, why not say so instead of complicating the issue by referring to times, persons and places? Moreover, the Patriarchs kept the Torah before it was given.[5] *Radbaz* gives, by hint, a Kabbalistic interpretation. When Adret exempts Jacob from the prohibition of marrying two sisters, his reason is not because Jacob lived before the Torah had been given. The permission was given to Jacob and to Jacob alone. The reason for the prohibition is that man must not 'use the king's sceptre' but Jacob, whose countenance is engraved on the Celestial Throne, was allowed to use the sceptre. *Radbaz* is very circumspect and expresses his extreme reluctance to say too much here, but presumably he means that the two sisters represent two aspects of the Shekhinah, *Malkhut*. On high, the 'sacred marriage' of the Sefirot *Tiferet* and *Malkhut* takes place, and for a man to marry two sisters is to repeat on earth the Sefirotic process, which he is not permitted to do. Jacob, on the other hand, is, according to the Kabbalah, the counterpart on earth of the Sefirah *Tiferet*. He is, consequently, in a special category. That which is

---

[3] On this see pp. 48–9 above for the views of Maimonides
[4] See pp. 66–7 above   [5] Kidd. 82a and *passim*

forbidden to all others is permitted to him. *Radbaz* adds mysteriously: 'If you know why Leah was buried in the Cave of Machpelah (Gen. 49 : 31) and Rachel was buried on the way (Gen. 48 : 7) you will understand the secret of the two sisters.' What *Radbaz* intends to convey by this latter observation is far from clear. Perhaps he means to suggest that Jacob was only permitted to imitate *Tiferet* outside the holy land.[6] Finally, *Radbaz* says that 'according to the plain meaning' there is no problem in the first place since, although Jacob did keep the Torah before it had been given, his status and that of his wives was that of Gentiles (the Torah not having been given so that there were no 'Jews'), and the law of two sisters does not apply, in that the law does not recognise sibling relationships for Gentiles.

A further Biblical question considered by *Radbaz* (no. 769) is why the curses in Leviticus (26 : 14–43) are followed by verses affording consolation (26 : 44–5), while the curses in Deuteronomy (28 : 15–68) end abruptly without the note of consolation being sounded. *Radbaz* takes the Zoharic interpretation of *yaalem* in verse 61 to mean 'God will *hide* them [the curses] from thee', instead of 'God will bring them upon thee', so that a note of consolation is sounded. *Radbaz* also points out that the Tetragrammaton is used in this verse and that this name denotes God's mercy. Furthermore, the curses are followed by the description of the covenant God has made with Israel (Deut. 29 : 9–28), and there can be no greater consolation than this.

Radbaz and other Jewish leaders had to face the threat of apostasy. Even where the Jewish courts enjoyed autonomy, there were occasions when offenders, rather than submit to the punishments imposed by the courts, preferred to escape them by converting to another faith. *Radbaz* was asked (no. 187) whether a Jewish court should relax its demands when offenders threatened apostasy unless a relaxation was forthcoming.[7] *Radbaz* is aware of the seriousness of the problem: 'All my days I have been disturbed by the matter you have raised. The result of leniency will be a diminution of the Torah, and yet we have no power to coerce the wicked. Every day I offer the prayer that nothing untoward

[6] On the whole question see pp. 66–7 above   [7] See pp. 30–1 above

should happen through me, yet I shall share my thoughts with you.' He comes down on the side of a refusal to yield to threats. If the courts are to yield to blackmail, the wicked will be undeterred from robbery, plunder, rape and other crimes. Throughout Jewish history the courts wielded their authority and never desisted because of threats of apostasy. In any event, he says, a Jew who is prepared to make threats of this kind will sooner or later leave the Jewish fold whatever the court may or may not do. Yet *Radbaz* cannot bring himself to issue a categorical ruling on such a question. Theoretically he is certain that the law is as he has ruled, but he recoils from advising others to follow it. Each court should weigh the evidence carefully, since not all men are alike and not all sins are the same. It all depends on how the teachers assess each particular case. They should weigh it all up with the greatest care and then, provided they do it for the sake of Heaven, make their decision and act on it in confidence and without fear.

In another Responsum (no. 817), *Radbaz* deals with the nature of the revelation at Sinai. The Rabbis say[8] that at Sinai all the people heard the first two commandments 'from the Mouth of the Almighty'. This cannot mean that the people heard God speaking only to Moses, since of Moses it is said: 'And the Lord spoke unto Moses face to face' (Exod. 33 : 11) and exactly the same expression is used in describing God's speech to the people: 'The Lord spoke with you face to face in the mount out of the midst of the fire' (Deut. 5 : 4). It follows that God spoke these words directly to the people. In that case it must mean that the people had attained to the spiritual rank of Moses, so that God could speak to them as He spoke to Moses. But how can such a thing be possible? *Radbaz* replies that, of course, the ordinary people could never have attained Moses' rank permanently but, for the purpose of being addressed directly by God when the first two commandments were being given, the people were temporarily elevated to Moses' rank. There are instances in the Bible of men who were not prophets seeing angels when there was a special purpose in their having such a vision temporarily. The Kabbalists refer to this as the 'opening of the eyes'. For the purpose

[8] Makk. 24a

of 'hearing' the first two commandments, the people were temporarily elevated to the rank of prophets.

Again on the question of prophecy, *Radbaz* (no. 816) considers why it is that some prophets see their message or vision directly and others in terms of a parable, and this is sometimes true even of the same prophet. *Radbaz* states that he has seen in a book that the parable form is used whenever the prophet is given a vision of the future. He says that the answer is adequate, provided it can be shown to operate successfully in all instances. *Radbaz* offers a different explanation. It all depends on the degree of preparation the prophet has undergone. Where there is adequate preparation, the prophet receives his message directly, otherwise it is given to him in a parable. It can happen that, even when the parable has been given, the prophet, because of his inadequate preparation, has to ask how it is to be interpreted—as in the case of Zechariah (Zech. 4 : 1–6).

A questioner asked *Radbaz* (no. 824) the meaning of the Rabbinic saying:[9] 'There is no death without sin, and no suffering without iniquity.' The puzzling thing here is that the weaker term 'sin' (*het*) is used of death, and the stronger term 'iniquity' (*avon*) of suffering. Since we learn from a Talmudic passage[10] that death is a more severe punishment than suffering, the order should have been reversed. *Radbaz* replies that the meaning is: do not be astonished that even the righteous die, since, although these have never been guilty of 'iniquity', they, too, have committed 'sins'. He quotes: 'For there is not a righteous man upon earth that doeth only good, and *sinneth* not' (Eccles. 7 : 20).

Radbaz was asked (no. 828) to explain the statement, found in the Midrashim, that all festivals will be abolished except the festival of Purim. How can this be, since the Torah declares: 'All this word which I command you, that shall ye observe to do; thou shalt not add thereto, nor diminish from it' (Deut. 13 : 1)? *Radbaz* refers to Adret's discussion[11] of the problem and advances his own solution. The particular laws of each festival will never be abolished. The meaning of the Midrashic statement is that in the Messianic age every day will be as joyous as a festival so that

---

[9] Sabb. 55a   [10] Yom. 85b–86b   [11] See pp. 63–4 above

there will be nothing to distinguish the festivals from the ordinary days of the year and it will seem as if the festivals have been abolished. Yet the people will never forget Purim because they will always remember the sufferings from which they were delivered on Purim. He goes on to discuss another question of the same kind. A Midrash[12] states that the pig will be restored to Israel in the Messianic age. How can this be, since the Torah is immutable? *Radbaz* replies that here, too, the meaning is certainly not that the people will one day be allowed to eat pork but that they will enjoy such good food in the Messianic age that it will seem to them as if pork (a very tasty food) had been permitted. However, he also gives a mystical interpretation. There is a prince on high, the guardian angel of the pig species, called *Hazariel* (from *hazir*, 'the pig'). He is Israel's prosecutor but will be restored to Israel in the Messianic age to become Israel's defender.

Radbaz (no. 842) was requested for an explanation of the story of Jonah. A prophet who refuses to deliver his message, say the Rabbis,[13] is guilty of death. How, then, could Jonah have fled in order to escape his burden? Some say, observed *Radbaz*, that at first Jonah was not told to *prophesy* to Nineveh, only to *go* to Nineveh. Because of his love for his own people, Jonah thought that he was right to avoid going there.[14] Another possibility is that when Jonah fled to Tarshish he believed that the obligation to prophesy was cancelled when he left the holy land. Or, possibly, Jonah did not intend to avoid his mission, only to postpone it for a time.

A question (no. 839) was put to *Radbaz* concerning the resurrection of the dead: whether the dead who have been revived will die again. The questioner is aware of the differing opinions, but wishes to have *Radbaz*'s views. *Radbaz* refers to a tradition he has 'from the sages of old'[15] that there will be two resurrections. The first, taking place soon after the coming of the Messiah, will be of the righteous dead. The second will take place at the end of the Messianic age and will be for all mankind, as well as for the

---

[12] On this pseudo-Midrash and its interpretation in Jewish literature see H. Karlinsky, 'The pig and "permission" to eat it in the future', *Shanah Be-Shanah*, vol. II, pp. 243–54.

[13] Sanh. 89a   [14] See pp. 5–6 above   [15] See pp. 22–4 above

righteous Jews who were born during the Messianic age and died during that period. No one who has once been resurrected will ever die again. *Radbaz* concludes with the prayer: 'May God grant that our portion be among the righteous and may He show us wondrous things out of His Torah. I have written as it seemed right to me in my humble opinion.'

An interesting Responsum of *Radbaz* (no. 985) concerns a great scholar who lost a son but did not shed a single tear. Is such a stoical attitude reprehensible or is it to be commended? He replies:

> This is an evil trait demonstrating hard-heartedness and a bad character. This cruel attitude is that of the philosophers who say that this world is vanity, a huge joke . . . But we who have received the Torah must believe and appreciate that this world is very precious to those who use it properly and who conduct themselves in a fitting manner. It is through the way he behaves in this life that man attains to the World to Come and to immortality, for this world is called the world of deeds. Consequently, we must never treat it as vanity, attributing its sorrows to the poor way it is governed and complaining about the woes of temporal existence, as the majority of the poets have done. Man should rather mourn for his own bad deeds . . . One who weeps, mourns and sheds tears over the loss of his relatives, how much more over the death of the righteous, follows in the footsteps of the saints, the prophets and the men of good deeds. It points to purity of soul and submission to man's Maker. Man, when confronted with tragedy, should grieve for his sins that brought it upon him. It is not for nothing that the Rabbis, of blessed memory, rule that the first three days after the death of a relative are for weeping, seven days for mourning, and thirty days for abstaining from washing clothes and cutting the hair. If it were not a good thing, they would hardly have prescribed it for three days. Abraham, Jacob and David wept when they lost a relative. Consult the work *Torat Ha-Adam* by Nahmanides, of blessed memory, and you find enough to answer your question. Nevertheless, it is not proper to mourn too much over the death of a relative, as the Talmud says.

The traditional view held very strongly that the Masoretic text of the Bible was completely accurate in every respect. This opinion appeared to be challenged by the existence of variant readings.[16] *Radbaz* (no. 1,020) was asked the meaning of the Talmudic statement[17] that there are embellishments to the

[16] See p. 96 above   [17] Ned. 37b

Pentateuchal text introduced by the scribes and that there are words read differently from the way they are written. Does it not suggest that our present text is doubtful? *Radbaz* points out that the Talmudic statement refers to these things as being 'a law given to Moses at Sinai'. But, in that case, why refer to them as an introduction by the scribes? It cannot mean that the scribes were the recipients of the tradition going back to Moses, for this is the case with every law 'given to Moses at Sinai'. *Radbaz* is obliged to fall back on the exceedingly weak argument that even if these things had not been communicated to Moses the scribes would have understood them by themselves. They would have surmised that that was how the text had to be written. *Radbaz*'s tone here is particularly apologetic. Unless we affirm, he says, that every detail of the present text was given to Moses, we lay ourselves wide open to the accusation of the Muslims that we have tampered with the Biblical text. But, asks *Radbaz*, what of the *Keri* and *Ktiv* (a word being read in one way but written in another) in books compiled long after Moses; in Ruth, for example. How can these have been conveyed to Moses? Why not? he retorts. Do not the Rabbis say that whatever a diligent disciple may introduce has already been given to Moses at Sinai? *Radbaz* urges his questioner to accept no other theories on this matter.

In *Radbaz*'s day it was not too unusual for people to attempt to consult demons. A questioner (no. 848) has heard that there are permitted and forbidden ways of consulting demons. He has even heard of people offering incense to the demons, arguing that the Talmud does not forbid this since there is no actual demon worship. Moreover, it is reported that people did it in the presence of a great scholar, who was not moved to protest. *Radbaz* replies that he refuses to believe that a scholar would have acquiesced in a practice which the Talmud[18] expressly forbids. To offer incense is strictly forbidden, but the Codes differ about consulting demons.[19] *Radbaz* quotes Menahem Meiri as saying that it is forbidden to consult demons, assuming that these exist. But Maimonides holds that it is all nonsense in any event. There are no demons. Very revealing is *Radbaz*'s concluding observation:

[18] Sanh. 65a   [19] See Sanh. 67b and commentaries

Do not suspect me of denying the existence of demons because I have quoted Meiri. I believe in everything the Rabbis of blessed memory say, even their slightest remark. This is especially so since Scripture itself points to the belief in demons, i.e. 'And they shall no more sacrifice their sacrifices unto the satyrs' (Lev. 17 : 7); 'They sacrificed unto demons' (Deut. 32 : 17).

Radbaz discusses (no. 861) the famous Rabbinic saying[20] that one who fasts is a sinner. How can this be, since many of the saints used to fast? *Radbaz* refers to a report that R. Eliezer of Metz (*c.* 1115–*c.* 1198) argued that one who fasts is a sinner only if he does it out of bad temper or because he is disillusioned with the world, not if he fasts for the sake of Heaven. This is incorrect, and is contradicted by R. Eliezer of Metz's own comment to the Talmudic passage. There he says that one who fasts is, indeed, a sinner but the sin is sometimes worth while. Another solution is that he is a sinner only when he fasts without following the prophet's advice to deal out bread to the hungry on a true fast-day (Isa. 58 : 7). *Radbaz* himself refuses to see any problem here. There are, in fact, two opinions in the Talmud, not one. We do not follow the view that one who fasts is a sinner but the view that he is a holy man. However, this only applies if he has the strength to engage in fasting. Mortification of the flesh to an excessive degree is forbidden by all the authorities.

A source of embarrassment to the traditionalists who held the Masoretic text to be sacrosanct was the saying of the Rabbis[21] that Moses wrote the Torah in the old Hebrew script, and that, after the return from the Babylonian exile, this was changed to the square script (*ketav ashuri*) now in use. Apologetic reasons, as we have seen, caused the Jewish teachers to be hostile to any notion that there had been any change in either the text or the script since the days of Moses. *Radbaz* (no. 882) is aware of the Rabbinic saying[22] that the letters *mem* and *samekh*, which are circular in form, stood in the two tablets of stone by a miracle—i.e. the letters were said to have gone right through the tablets from one side to the other so that, being circular, they had no surrounds to support them. But in the original Hebrew script these two letters

---

[20] Ned. 10a   [21] Sanh. 21b–22a   [22] Meg. 2b–3a

are not circular. *Radbaz* replies that it is, in any event, hard to grasp the view that the Torah was originally written in the old script. All the Kabbalistic mysteries regarding the letters of the alphabet assume our present script. He offers a highly artificial solution to the whole problem. According to all the authorities, he says, the Ten Commandments on the two tablets of stone were carved in the square script. As for the rest of the Torah, certainly (according to one opinion) Moses wrote it in the old script, but this was not its original script. Moses knew the Torah in our present square script but, when he came to write it down for the people, he used the other script because he knew that it was this one with which they were familiar. Furthermore, the square script was so sacred that Moses was not allowed to use it. Ezra was allowed to use it (which is why we have it today) in order to substantiate his claim that if the Torah had not already been given to Moses it would have been given to him. However, the Jerusalem Talmud[23] states that it was the letter *ayin*—the letter that is circular in the old Hebrew script—that stood by a miracle.

Another Responsum on the Ten Commandments (no. 980) discusses the arrangement of the commandments on the two tablets of stone. *Radbaz* notes that the total number of letters in the Ten Commandments is 620. This corresponds to the 613 precepts of the Torah, together with the seven sounds heard when the Torah was given. There are five commandments on one tablet and five on the other, corresponding to the 'right' and the 'left', 'mercy' and 'judgment', the 'good inclination' and the 'evil inclination'. Why are seven of the commandments 'thou shalt not' and three 'thou shalt'? *Radbaz* states that he is not permitted to record the answer in writing but can only give it by word of mouth. No doubt he hints here at the Kabbalistic doctrine of the Sefirot, divided into groups of seven 'lower' and three 'higher'.

A question much discussed in later Responsa is which to follow in practice where the Kabbalah differs from the law as recorded in the Codes.[24] *Radbaz* (no. 1,111) discusses this. He was asked to explain the custom in his day of putting the *tefillin* on at home and

---

[23] JT Meg. 1: 11, 71c
[24] See *Encyclopedia Talmudit*, vol. IX, pp. 254–5, and p. 139 below

walking, with them on, to the synagogue. *Radbaz* explains that he has this in the name of R. Simeon b. Yohai, the reputed author of the *Zohar*: on entering the synagogue one says: 'As for me, in the abundance of Thy lovingkindness will I come into Thy house: I will worship toward Thy holy temple *in the fear of Thee*' (Ps. 5 : 8), and fear is represented by the *tefillin*. *Radbaz* then states the general rule:

> Whenever you find that the words of the Kabbalists disagree with the decision of the Talmud you must follow the Talmud and the Codes. But whenever, as in this instance, there is no actual disagreement, since the matter is referred to neither in the Talmud nor in the Codes, it seems right to rely on the Kabbalah.

Another Responsum (no. 1,203) on a Kabbalistic theme concerns the benediction over the moon. This is called in the Talmud[25] 'receiving the Shekhinah'. But the practice is to do this on weekdays, never on the sabbath. Why not on the sabbath, *Radbaz* was asked, since on this night it would seem to be especially appropriate to welcome the Shekhinah? *Radbaz* gives a Kabbalistic interpretation. The night of the sabbath is the time of the 'sacred marriage' between the King (*Tiferet*) and the Queen (*Malkhut*, the Shekhinah, symbolised by the moon). On such a night it is indelicate for humans to intrude by welcoming the Queen. But on Saturday night it is especially appropriate to recite the benediction over the moon, to offer homage to the Shekhinah and to pacify Her now that Her Beloved had departed. The mythological note sounded so strongly here is typical of Kabbalistic thought on this theme, though the Kabbalists always tried to avoid the slightest suspicion of any dualism or any real female element in the Deity.

A further Responsum (no. 1,328) on a Kabbalistic theme discusses how the palm-branch has to be waved on the feast of Tabernacles. *Radbaz* states that the palm-branch has to be waved in the six directions of north, south, east, west, above and below in order to proclaim God as King of all. It is waved three times in each of these directions, making a total of eighteen, the numerical value of the Hebrew *hay*, 'life', referring to God, the Life of all

[25] Sanh. 42a

worlds. There are four wavings in all during the service, making a total of seventy-two, representing the divine name of seventy-two letters, which governs rains for which we pray at this season. Since Satan wishes to prosecute, our wavings in the name of God have the effect of poking out Satan's baneful eyes.[26]

We noted at the beginning of this chapter that *Radbaz* quoted R. Yom Tov b. Abraham to the effect that a Jew must suffer martyrdom rather than embrace Islam. *Radbaz* quotes this authority in another Responsum (no. 1,163) in which he quotes this very question: whether martyrdom is demanded, since Islam is a monotheistic faith. *Radbaz* says that he feels obliged to go into the question at some length since many people do embrace Islam when compelled to do so and find a dispensation in that it is not as if one were being compelled to worship idols. He proceeds to elaborate on the laws governing martyrdom and refers to the standard Talmudic texts on the subject.[27] True, he says, Islam is monotheistic, but when a Jew is compelled to embrace Islam it involves his acknowledgment that Mohammed is greater than Moses, which involves 'the destruction of the whole of our religion'. Moreover, he is obliged to accept the view that our Torah is not true and that we have falsified it. However, *Radbaz* continues, if a Jew is compelled to desist from practising one of the positive commands—to refrain, for instance, from offering his prayers—he is not obliged to suffer martyrdom, since the tyrant can prevent it in any event if he so wishes. Daniel was prepared to be cast into the lion's den rather than refrain from offering his prayers, but he was exceptional; acting beyond the letter of the law in order to demonstrate to all the power of prayer.

Radbaz's reaction to the Islamic charge that the Jews had falsified the Torah is to be seen in another Responsum (no. 1,172). A scribe had altered certain words in the Pentateuchal text so as to make them accord with the explanation offered in the *Zohar*. Is this allowed? *Radbaz* replies that it is strictly forbidden. We must be absolutely scrupulous in following the accepted text in order to avoid conflict among Jews. This is especially important 'nowadays', when we reside among a people who declare that we have

[26] Based on the expression in Kidd. 81a   [27] Sanh. 74b

altered the text of the Torah. If they see that the Jews are divided among themselves as to how the Torah is to be written, they will be encouraged in their base claim. *Radbaz* concludes:

> I went myself to the house of this copyist and found there three scrolls that he had altered. I corrected them, restoring the Crown of the Torah to its former place as in all the scrolls we possess. I ordered him to desist from altering any scrolls in the future so as to accord with the Midrash, but only so as to accord with the majority of scrolls. In God I trust, for He knows the secrets of the human heart.

In another Responsum (no. 1,258), *Radbaz* is severe with a preacher who said in a sermon that the 'mixed multitude' held Moses to be divine. Moses, pleading on their behalf, entreated God to ignore their sin, arguing that no great harm had been done since Moses himself acknowledged God. *Radbaz* complains that the preachers in Christian lands have, unfortunately, been influenced by the views of their Christian neighbours. As to the question whether the preacher deserves to be punished for insulting Moses by implying that Moses tolerated the offence, the only reason *Radbaz* can find for leniency is that the preacher was not a wilful heretic but was misled by his own reasoning. That it is not culpable to hold heretical views, if one is sincerely led to these by reason, can be seen from the case of R. Hillel[28] who denied that there was a personal Messiah. Surely R. Hillel was not a heretic. If he were, the Talmud would not have recorded his view. Evidently the Talmudic Rabbis held that R. Hillel was compelled by his reason to entertain mistaken views and the general legal principle applied that a sin done under compulsion is not culpable.[29] Nevertheless, the preacher must be given a stern warning to desist from preaching this kind of nonsense and a copy of this Responsum should be sent to him.

Two Responsa defend the views of Maimonides. In one (no. 1,418), *Radbaz* replies to an apparent contradiction in Maimonides. The sage rules[30] that a heretic must never be received back into

---

[28] Sanh. 99a

[29] This idea, that there is no culpability for false beliefs sincerely entertained because one is 'compelled' to hold them by the force of reason, is found in the *Or Adonai* (II, 45) of Hasdai Crescas (1340–1416)

[30] *Yad*, AZ 2: 5

the fold. But this contradicts the basic principle that nothing can stand in the way of repentance. Moreover, Maimonides himself rules[31] that if a heretic repents on his deathbed he is pardoned. *Radbaz* replies that, of course, his repentance is accepted if it is sincere, but only God can know whether it is sincere. We, who do not know, must always be suspicious. Such a man can never again be trusted. Today his reason tells him to repent, tomorrow it may persuade him to entertain once again his heretical opinions.

In the other Responsum (no. 1,495), *Radbaz* considers Maimonides' apparent denial of Hell.[32] God forbid, says *Radbaz*, that Maimonides denies Hell. When Maimonides says that the greatest punishment is that the soul is utterly annihilated, he does not mean to suggest that Hell is to be identified with mere extinction. There is a Hell, but the greater punishment is annihilation of the soul. Surely Maimonides would not have disagreed with the Talmudic Rabbis who believed in Hell, describing the torments suffered there in great detail. Maimonides refers to annihilation as the fate due to the worst sinners, *after* they have been punished in Hell. In earthly courts, too, some criminals are tortured before they are executed! Nahmanides[33] has given this defence of Maimonides and it must be accepted.

Abraham Ibn David, in his Strictures to Maimonides' Code,[34] declares that Maimonides seems to suggest that there is no bodily resurrection. *Radbaz* was asked how this could follow from Maimonides' statements. He replies (no. 2,267) that Maimonides observes that the Rabbinic references to the 'banquet' enjoyed by the righteous in the World to Come are to be understood figuratively. But if there is a resurrection of the body, why cannot they be understood literally? *Radbaz* defends Maimonides. The sage's spiritual understanding of the concept refers only to the World to Come after death—i.e. to the fate of the soul in Heaven. But Maimonides does not deny that there will be a physical resurrection.[35]

[31] *Yad*, Teshuvah 7: 1   [32] Ibid., 8: 5
[33] *Torat Ha-Adam, Shaar Ha-Gemul*, ed. Chavel, pp. 291 ff.
[34] *Yad*, Teshuvah 8: 2
[35] For Maimonides' views on resurrection see L. Jacobs, *Principles of the Jewish Faith*, pp. 398 ff.

We have seen[36] the difficulties the medieval thinkers found in the saying of R. Kruspedai[37] that three books are opened on the New Year: the perfectly righteous are recorded forthwith in the book of life, the altogether wicked in the book of death, the average folk are kept in suspension until the Day of Atonement. Nahmanides[38] holds that the terms 'righteous' and 'wicked' do not refer to the true states but to whether or not a man is to be declared 'righteous' or 'wicked' in that particular assize. *Radbaz* (no. 2,263) was asked to comment. His understanding of the matter is that some precepts have the power of endowing a man with life for the coming year and some sins of depriving him of life, irrespective of whether, by general status, he is 'righteous' or 'wicked'. Thus the 'righteous' may be judged 'wicked' (i.e. guilty) so far as their fate in the coming year is concerned, and the 'wicked' declared 'righteous' (i.e. innocent) for this purpose. The assessment is not made on whether or not there is a preponderance of virtue over vice but in accordance with the type of deed and its life-giving or life-denying quality. This is known only to God and is the kind of assessment only He can make.

One of *Radbaz*'s questioners was puzzled (no. 2,154) by *Rashi's* comment[39] that God told Israel to keep the precepts even in exile so as to be ready to keep them on their return to the holy land. This strangely seems to imply that the precepts are to be kept only as a kind of reminder while the Jews are in exile, whereas they are eternally binding in themselves, wherever Jews reside. *Radbaz* replies that *Rashi* is not stating here his own opinion but is quoting from the *Sifre*.[40] The *Sifre* does not intend to imply that the precepts are to be kept only in exile as a reminder. The *Sifre* means that God has to issue a special warning to the Jews in exile to keep the precepts because they are in great danger of overlooking them in the bitterness of exile.

Radbaz (no. 2,003) was asked whether, according to the view that Elijah and Phinehas were the same person,[41] Elijah must have been a priest. In that case, how could he have revived the son of

[36] P. 73 above   [37] RH 16b   [38] *Shaar Ha-Gemul*, pp. 264 ff.
[39] To Deut. 11: 18   [40] Deut. 43, 82b
[41] For this identification in the later Midrashim see Ginzberg, *The Legends of the Jews*, vol. VI, pp. 316–17, n. 3

the woman of Zarephath (I Kgs 17 : 8–24), since a priest is not permitted to come into contact with a corpse? *Radbaz* replies that this question has often been raised and various solutions have been offered. Some say that the child was not really dead.[42] But the plain meaning of the text seems to suggest otherwise. Bahya Ibn Asher gives the curious reply that the child was a Gentile because his mother was a Gentile. Elijah did not actually touch the corpse. He was only in the same house as the corpse and this is permitted if the corpse is of a Gentile. But the Rabbis say[43] that the child grew up to be the prophet Jonah. Is it likely that the prophet Jonah was of Gentile birth? Even if it be argued that he was converted to the Jewish faith, he would not, then, have been called after his father, Jonah son of Amittai. And would God have performed such a miracle on behalf of a Gentile woman? And would the prophet have stayed in the house of a Gentile woman? The Tosafists[44] reply that Elijah was convinced that he would be able to bring the child back from the dead. In that case it was permitted for him to come into contact with the corpse, since the saving of life takes precedence. The objection to this is that one must never rely on a miracle. Furthermore, if Elijah was so confident that the child would be revived, because so he saw it in his prophetic vision, then his own act would have been irrelevant and could not then be construed as an act of life-saving. A possible solution is that Elijah only went near to the child. The Hebrew *alav* can have this meaning. Or it is possible that a special dispensation was given to Elijah as it was on Mount Carmel, where his act of offering sacrifices outside the Temple was similarly illegal. Or it can be said that in certain circumstances the law permits a priest to come into contact with a corpse —where there is no one else to bury it, for instance. But *Radbaz* prefers the solution that it was a special dispensation for the purpose of sanctifying the name of Heaven.

After stating all this, *Radbaz* adds that, according to the Kabbalah, there is no problem at all, for the statement that Elijah is identical with Phinehas means that Elijah was the reincarnation of Phinehas; the soul of Phinehas occupied the body of Elijah. In

---

[42] See p. 85 above   [43] JT Sukk. 5: 1, 55a   [44] BM 114b, *amar ley*

that case, why did Elijah not tell this to the Rabbi[45] who asked him what he was doing in a cemetery? Evidently, Elijah did not want to let the Rabbi into his secret and so allowed him to assume that he was actually Phinehas instead of the latter's reincarnation.

In another Responsum on Elijah (no. 2,294), *Radbaz* deals with the narrative in I Kings 19. God there makes Elijah journey for forty days and nights to Mount Horeb. But Horeb had sanctity only when the Divine Presence rested on it when the Decalogue was given. It possessed no sanctity at all in the days of Elijah. Why, then, did God not convey His message to Elijah in the holy land? *Radbaz* offers his own understanding of the narrative. Elijah was far too fond of accusing Israel. It is God's wish that the righteous should plead for Israel as Moses did, not accuse them, even if they are guilty. Horeb was the special place of Moses. The forty days and nights correspond to Moses' stay on the mount. It was all for the purpose of bringing home to Elijah the great lesson of Moses, to teach him the power of the 'still small voice' as opposed to the thundering denunciations to which he was so addicted. When God saw that in spite of it all Elijah had not learned the lesson, He resolved to take Elijah from earth because an accusing prophet was not the messenger He desired. But since Elijah, in his identity as Phinehas, had been promised that he would never die, God took Elijah to Heaven while he was still alive. As for the reason why Elijah, in fact, refused to pray for the people as Moses had, Elijah, in his zeal, thought that their sin was so great that no amount of prayer would avail, but in this he was greatly mistaken. God always hearkens to the prayers of those who intercede for His people.

In Jewish law, a minor has no responsibility. *Radbaz* (no. 2,314) was asked whether a man is obliged to do penance for sins committed as a child. *Radbaz* replies that, according to the letter of the law, no penance is required, and he quotes Maimonides[46] to this effect. However, the *Sefer Hasidim* states that he should confess his sins when he grows up. The reason is possibly that when a minor sins it is a sign that Satan dances there—i.e. he has a propensity for sin. When he grows to manhood he should confess

[45] BM 114b   [46] *Yad*, Hovel U-Mazzik, 4: 20

his sins in order to humble his heart and so free himself from his susceptibility.

In another Responsum (no. 198, printed at end of part IV), *Radbaz* discusses whether an apostate who returns to the Jewish fold should be made to undergo severe penance. He replies that such a person has become accustomed to a life outside the law and if he is treated too harshly he will be tempted to abandon the Jewish faith once again. He has suffered enough by being separated from the Jewish community and thus deprived of the great privilege of carrying out the precepts. *Radbaz* quotes this ruling in the name of R. Moses of Coucy (thirteenth century).[47]

Finally, there is the Responsum (no. 910) of *Radbaz* on prayer, used later by the Hasidim of the eighteenth century to justify their separate houses of prayer.[48] It deals with a group who separated themselves from the general community to pray, together with their teacher, in a synagogue of their own. *Radbaz* justifies their action. There are many indications in the Talmud that it is preferable for men to offer their prayers in an atmosphere conducive to prayer. *Radbaz* goes so far as to say that if he were not afraid to do so he would rule that it is better to pray in private than together with men with whom one cannot agree. When a man sees his friends, his soul is bestirred to concentrate and his heart is glad, so that the spirit of the Lord can rest upon him. Especially when a man is together with his teacher he acquires, as it were, an additional soul. The Kabbalists call this 'the mystery of impregnation while master and disciple are both still alive'.

A contemporary of *Radbaz* and, for a time, a member of his Bet Din, was the Talmudist and poet Moses Alashkar (1466–1552), who was born in Spain and served as a Rabbi in Tunisia, in Patras in Greece, and in Cairo. He eventually went to Jerusalem, where he died. Alashkar's Responsa contain a number dealing with theological topics.

In two Responsa (nos 53 and 54), Alashkar deals with the

[47] See the views of Isserlein, p. 104 above
[48] See my *Hasidic Prayer*, pp. 43–5. In Responsum no. 2,090, *Radbaz* gives two reasons why the eyes should be closed in prayer: 1. as an aid to concentration; 2. because the Shekhinah is facing the worshipper, who must hide his face as Moses did

question of authority in Jewish law. How does one decide the law in a case on which the authorities diverge? There is a rule[49] that from Raba onwards the ruling always follows that of the later authorities (because they know the arguments of the earlier scholars and yet disagree with them). But it has been suggested that this rule applies only up to the time of the close of the Talmud. Is this correct? Alashkar first examines the various opinions on this subject and comes to the conclusion that nowadays we must follow not the later but the greater authorities. Even though it is true that the Gaonim followed the later authorities, even in their day (after the close of the Talmud), the Gaonim, great though they were, were not prophets. If they had been they would never have given the final authority to the scholars of our day who, though 'later', are much inferior in every way to the giants of the past. It is forbidden to entertain for one moment the preposterous notion that in our generation we can dare to decide contrary to the decisions given by the great ones of the past, to whom we do not bear even the same comparison as a monkey to a man. Would that we of this generation could grasp properly the slightest matter taught by the earlier authorities! As for the generations still to come, they will be even more inferior, since there is steady degeneration through the ages. Alashkar quotes Sherira Gaon as saying that the wisdom of the Gaonim is that which the Lord commanded Moses, and also R. Abraham Ibn David, who writes that no scholar may disagree with the decision of a Gaon even if the latter fails to adduce any proof for his contention. Thus Alashkar adopts an extremely conservative stance. The later generations are necessarily inferior to the earlier ones and the legal decisions of the early authorities can never be countermanded. The idea of the progressive decline of the generations has become, for Alashkar, a dogma of the Jewish faith.

We saw above how concerned *Radbaz* was to defend the view that the square script we now have is the original script of the Torah. The same problem is discussed by Alashkar (no. 74) in an

---

[49] This rule is not found in the Talmud but in the Gaonic literature; see *Encyclopedia Talmudit*, vol. 9, pp. 341–5

interesting context. His questioner had obtained an ancient shekel bearing an inscription in the old Hebrew script. Does not the existence of such coins show that this was, indeed, the old and original Hebrew script in which the Torah was written? In that case, how do we explain the various Talmudic interpretations of the letters of the alphabet as they are in the square script we now use? Alashkar first remarks that there is no proof either way from the use of the old script on a shekel. It does not follow at all that because people used the old Hebrew script on coins that this was the original script in which the Torah was written. The Talmud debates whether the Torah was written in the old Hebrew script or in the square script we now use,[50] but even according to the opinion that it was written in the old script and that the square script was introduced by Ezra, the Midrashic explanations of the letters in Ezra's script should occasion no surprise. When, for instance, the explanation is given of why the point of the letter *bet* faces backwards,[51] the reference is clearly to Ezra's script. Mar Zutra, who holds that the square script is called the Assyrian script (*ketav ashuri*) because the Jews brought it with them from the Babylonian exile, does not mean that the Jews adopted during the exile a Gentile script. Far from it. Mar Zutra means that, as *Rashi* to the passage states, Ezra was shown this script by an angel. Consequently, even according to Mar Zutra, this script is of divine origin and Midrashic explanations of it are quite feasible. But, according to Mar Zutra, there is a difficulty. The Talmud states elsewhere[52] that the letters *mem* and *samekh* stood in the tablets of stone by a miracle,[53] but this cannot apply to the old Hebrew script, which, according to Mar Zutra, was the original script, since in that script these letters are not circular. Alashkar replies that R. Hisda, who makes the observation about the *mem* and *samekh* of the tablets, either must hold that the square script was the original script or, at least, his statement must be according to this opinion. I know, says Alashkar, that you have in mind the opinion of Joseph Albo in his *Sefer Ha-Ikkarim*,[54] but 'all his words on this topic have neither salt nor seasoning nor fragrance

---

[50] See pp. 121–2 above
[51] Gen. R., ed. Theodor and Albeck, 1: 10, p. 8
[52] Meg. 2b–3a
[53] See p. 121 above   [54] III, 16, pp. 143 f.

nor any taste whatsoever.' Incidentally, Alashkar refers to the Samaritans who have the old Hebrew script and to many ancient coins he has himself seen from ancient Palestine. One of these coins still in his possession has a palm-branch and citron on one side, together with a Greek inscription and an inscription in the old Hebrew script on the other.

In another Responsum (no. 76), Alashkar replies to a curious question. *Rashi*[55] remarks that Abraham asked the angels who visited him to wash their feet before they came into his tent (Gen. 18 : 3) because he did not know that they were angels but suspected them of being Arabs who worshipped the dust on their feet. In that case, how could Abraham have bowed down to them (Gen. 18 : 2)? Mordecai did not bow down to Haman because, while it is permitted to bow down to a human being as a token of respect, it is not permitted to bow down to anything or anyone worshipped as a god. Alashkar replies that it is only forbidden to bow down to the idol itself, and Abraham bowed to the Arabs, not to the dust they worshipped. He quotes earlier authorities[56] to the effect that it is permitted to bow in homage to a Christian priest, even if he is wearing a cross. Haman declared himself to be divine and that is why Mordecai refused to bow to him. In any event, the verse does not say that Abraham bowed to the men but that he bowed to the ground. He bowed, in fact, not to his visitors but to God.

Alashkar (no. 102) was asked by his son whether a man can sell to another the reward of his good deeds. Is such a sale valid and, if it is, does it mean that the purchaser acquires the reward and the seller loses it? Alashkar states that he has not found this question discussed by any of the authorities, except in a Responsum of Hai Gaon.[57] He quotes Hai Gaon in full to the effect that a man cannot sell his good deeds, and concludes that all that Hai says is based on a sound tradition from which one must not depart.

Finally, Alashkar added to his Responsa (no. 117) his defence of Maimonides' philosophical views against the severe attack of

[55] Commentary to Gen. 18: 4
[56] See Isserlein's opinion, p. 104 above   [57] See pp. 21–2 above

the Kabbalist Shem Tov Ibn Shem Tov (c. 1380–c. 1441) in *Sefer Ha-Emunot*. Ibn Shem Tov criticises Maimonides for allegedly denying the resurrection of the dead, for his denial of miracles, for his naturalism, and for his preference for reason over faith. Alashkar tries to show that Maimonides is a true believer in every respect, and has no difficulty in demonstrating this from a close examination of Maimonides' writings. Alashkar rejects what appears to be Ibn Shem Tov's basic contention—that Maimonides entertains esoteric views, at which he only hints—and that these are far less conventional than the views he states explicitly.

Benjamin Zeev b. Mattathias of Arta (early sixteenth century) published his Responsa in Venice in 1534. This collection, enjoying great authority, contains a number of theological questions.

In reply (no. 169) to the much-discussed question[58] of why there is no benediction before carrying out the obligation to honour parents and to respect elders and sages, Benjamin Zeev points to the standard form of the benediction recited before carrying out the precepts: 'Blessed art Thou Who hast sanctified us with Thy commandments.' We thank God for endowing Israel with special sanctity by giving us the precepts to carry out. But Gentiles also respect their parents, elders and sages so that Jews do not acquire any greater sanctity than the Gentiles who carry these duties out in as fitting a manner as Jews.

Benjamin Zeev (no. 194) was asked to explain the saying of R. Johanan[59] that one who wishes to take upon himself the full yoke of the Kingdom of Heaven should first evacuate his bowels, then wash his hands, don his *tefillin*, recite the *Shema* and offer his prayers. Benjamin Zeev explains that the head *tefillin* are worn over the brain in which the soul resides. When a man puts on the head *tefillin* he makes his soul subordinate to God. When he puts on the hand *tefillin* he subordinates to God both his deeds and his heart, the hand *tefillin* being worn on the upper arm opposite the heart. All man's thoughts and desires stem mainly from the heart, so that when he dons the hand *tefillin* man is reminded of his Maker and of the need to set limits to his indulgence in pleasure. If, after donning the *tefillin*, man recites the *Shema* and then offers

---

[58] See pp. 41–2 above   [59] Ber. 14b–15a

his prayers, he has, indeed, taken upon himself the yoke of the Kingdom of Heaven in the best manner possible.

In another Responsum (no. 200), Benjamin Zeev states the Kabbalistic understanding of the mystery of the *tefillin*. There are four sections in both the head and the hand *tefillin*. These are: 1. 'Sanctify unto Me all the first-born . . .' (Exod. 13 : 1–10); 2. 'And it shall be when the Lord shall bring thee . . .' (Exod. 13 : 11–16); 3. 'Hear O Israel . . .' (Deut. 6 : 4–9); 4. 'And it shall come to pass, if ye shall hearken . . .' (Deut. 11 : 13–21). The highest of the Ten Sefirot is *Keter* ('Crown') which is above the head. The four sections of the head *tefillin* correspond to the four Sefirot below *Keter*. Thus 1. referring to the 'first-born', represents *Hokhmah* ('Wisdom'), the beginning of God's creative processes; 2. represents *Binah* ('Understanding'), because through discernment they went out of Egypt—*Hokhmah* is to the right of *Keter* in the Sefirotic Tree and *Binah* to the left. 3., which speaks of loving God, represents *Hesed* ('Lovingkindness')—to the right of *Keter*. 4., which speaks of divine punishment, represents *Gevurah* ('Power')—to the left of *Keter*. These four, on the head, form a crown to the Sefirah *Tiferet* ('Beauty'). The four sections in the hand *tefillin* represent the four lower Sefirot: *Tiferet*, *Netzah* ('Victory'), *Hod* ('Splendour') and *Yesod* ('Foundation'). Thus the head and the hand *tefillin* together represent the eight Sefirot from *Hokhmah* to *Yesod*, with *Keter* above them and *Malkhut* ('Sovereignty') beneath them. It follows that the sanctity of the head *tefillin*, representing the higher Sefirot, is greater than that of the hand *tefillin*, representing the lower Sefirot. But both head and hand *tefillin* have to be worn, because only in this way is the whole Sefirotic Tree represented. Since the Sefirot form a unity and it is forbidden to separate any one from the others, it is forbidden to engage in conversation between putting on the head *tefillin* and putting on the hand *tefillin*.

In two further Responsa (nos 201 and 202), Benjamin Zeev expounds the idea of a son saying the Kaddish prayer after the death of a parent. According to the strict rule, it is only the son who recites the Kaddish for his father, not a father for his son; even though, generally speaking, a father loves his son more than

a son loves his father. The Kaddish is a prayer of sanctification.
The significance of the son reciting the Kaddish is that thereby
he brings further merit to his departed father. The merits of the
father are increased in that he has left behind a son who sanctifies
God's name. None the less, it is permitted for the Kaddish to
be recited by other relatives, just as it is recited by the Reader
in the synagogue on behalf of the dead of the community in
general.

In another Responsum on the Kaddish (no. 203), Benjamin
Zeev discusses the following problem. There were two apostates,
one murdered by bandits, the other dying in his bed and buried by
Christians. The son whose father had been killed by the bandits
recited the Kaddish for him, arguing that his father had intended
to repent but had been killed before he was able to do so. He
wished to reserve this privilege for himself, in spite of the claim
of the son of the other apostate that he, too, should be allowed to
recite the Kaddish. If the man who had died in his bed had
wished to repent there was nothing to have prevented him, since
other forced converts were present at the time. Benjamin Zeev
rules that the Kaddish is not to be recited for an apostate who dies
without repentance since, during his lifetime, he denied the whole
of the Torah.

In another Responsum (no. 204) on apostasy, Benjamin Zeev
states that it is forbidden to call up the son of an apostate to the
reading of the Torah by his father's name: A, son of B. He should
be called by his grandfather's name: A, son of C. In the same
Responsum, Benjamin Zeev explains the custom at the cemetery,
after the burial, of plucking up grass or pulling up clods of earth
and washing the hands. The purpose of plucking the grass is a
reminder of the resurrection when the dead will spring forth
from the earth like grass. Pulling up earth is to remind us that we
are dust. Washing the hands is to make us recall that the death of
the righteous atones for the sins of the generation, just as the heifer
whose neck was broken (Deut. 21 : 1–9) brought atonement. Of
the heifer it is said, 'they shall wash their hands' (Deut. 21 : 6).

There are only two theological Responsa in the collection of
R. Samuel b. Moses di Medina (1506–89), known after the initial

letters of his name, as *Maharashdam*. He was Rabbi in Salonika, where questions were addressed to him from many Jewish communities. His Responsa enjoy great authority.

Maharashdam discusses[60] whether it is permitted for a man under the age of forty to render decisions in Jewish law. Is there any difference in this matter between Talmudic times and our own day? Even if it is held that a man under forty cannot normally render decisions, what is the position if a community appoints him for the purpose?

Maharashdam first analyses the Talmudic passage[61] on which the ruling is said to be based. He acknowledges that such a rule is found in the passage, but notes that Maimonides does not record it. He comes to the conclusion that nowadays the books are our teachers and that we can, therefore, even though younger than forty, render decisions, since the decisions are not really our own but those we discover through our study of the books. He concludes, however, that in 'this generation' we must be exceedingly cautious since it frequently happens that immature scholars are appointed to positions of great authority while mature scholars are neglected.

In another Responsum,[62] he expounds the oft-quoted saying about the stages in the good life, as laid down by R. Phinehas b. Yair:[63] 'The knowledge of the Torah leads to watchfulness, watchfulness to zeal, zeal to cleanness, cleanness to abstinence, abstinence to purity, purity to saintliness, saintliness to humility, humility to the fear of sin, the fear of sin to holiness, holiness to the resurrection of the dead.'

Maharashdam explains the stages recorded as follows. The knowledge of the Torah enables a man to see which acts are sinful. He will avoid these and so be encouraged in the habit of *watchfulness*. This leads to special care, to *zeal*, in avoiding sin. This, in turn, leads to the avoidance of even thoughts of sin, to *cleanness*. *Cleanness* leads to the avoidance of that which is not even sinful but somewhat dubious—for example, eating the meat of an animal which had been declared fit by a sage but only after some

60 Hoshen Mishpat 1   61 AZ 19b
62 Orah Hayyim, no. 17   63 AZ 20b

deliberation. This trait is called *abstinence*. This leads to *purity*—i.e. special purity in deed so that, for example, food is eaten only when a man is in a state of ritual purity through immersion. This leads to *saintliness*, which means that man abstains even from permitted food, eating only enough to keep body and soul together. He leads an ascetic life, avoiding all luxuries. This leads to *humility*, since the ascetic, who looks upon the world as worthless, will never retaliate against those who insult or seek to deprive him of worldly goods or pleasures. This leads to the *fear of sin*. Such a man, high though his spiritual degree be, cannot avoid the fear, for all that, that he may sin, so that he will always be especially scrupulous. This will lead to *holiness*. At this stage, a man attains to complete separation from the world. He thinks only holy thoughts and has no other occupation than the study of the Torah. When it is further said that this leads to the resurrection of the dead, the meaning is either that he attains to supernatural powers —so that, like the prophet Elisha he can revive the dead—or the 'dead' may refer to the wicked, whom he can revive spiritually by setting them an example of holy living. *Maharashdam* adds that in all this he simply follows the comments of *Rashi* but spells it out more clearly. It is to be noted how a Halakhist like *Maharashdam* gives a legal turn even to a passage like this. It is worth comparing *Maharashdam*'s treatment with the work written on the same theme by Moses Hayyim Luzzatto (1707–47), the *Mesillat Yesharim*.

The two great Halakhic authorities and writers of Responsa in sixteenth-century Poland were Solomon Luria, known as *Rashal*, (d. 1574) of Ostrog and Lublin and Moses Isserles (*Rama*) (d. 1572) of Cracow, author of the celebrated notes to the *Shulhan Arukh* and chief authority for Ashkenazi Jewry.

Luria has a curious Responsum (no. 3) on witchcraft. Luria was asked whether a sick person may consult a wizard for a cure to his malady. Luria rules that it is permitted, even though witchcraft is nonsense and it is, therefore, better to avoid it. However, if the sickness is one that can be fatal, Luria tends to permit it categorically, especially if it is an illness brought on by the machinations of the wizards themselves. They will know how to cure it. But Luria cannot bring himself to give a man permission to resort to wizards where there is no danger to life.

The question of how far the Kabbalah should be followed in practice where the Halakhic norm is otherwise, is discussed by Luria in Responsum no. 98 to Mordecai b. Tanhum, who asked Luria whether he puts on his *tefillin* while sitting down, as the Kabbalists advise. Luria replies that there are many pseudo-Kabbalists who wish to pose as adepts, but who have no understanding of the *Zohar*. He informs his questioner that all the famous teachers followed in practice only the Talmud and the Codes. In a bold statement, Luria remarks that even should R. Simeon b. Yohai, author of the *Zohar*, come along in person and urge us to change any of our practices, we should pay no heed to him, since, in matters of Halakhah, R. Simeon's rulings are rejected. For instance, R. Simeon in the *Zohar* warns against reciting a separate benediction over the head and hand *tefillin*, and yet we do. R. Simeon also writes that one who puts on his *tefillin* on the intermediate days of festivals is deserving of death, yet our practice is to put them on. Joseph Karo was quite right when he recorded in his *Shulhan Arukh* many practices based on the Kabbalah but said nothing about putting on the hand *tefillin* while sitting down. R. Samson of Chinon used to pray like a child,[64] even after he had studied the Kabbalah (i.e. without having in mind the intentions of the Kabbalists). Luria quotes his father-in-law, R. Kalonymos, who received the tradition from the saintly R. Daniel, a pupil of Israel Isserlein, and he saw Isserlein put on his *tefillin* while standing, as we do. We must never change our customs because of what the Kabbalists say.[65]

Finally, there is Luria's lengthy Responsum[66] on the prayer-book. He was asked to supply details of the prayers as recited by his grandfather, the Saint, R. Isaac. Luria remarks that in his youth he concentrated on the study of the Talmud and paid little attention to the details of the liturgy, although he does recall some points. Among other matters reported in the name of his

[64] See pp. 83–4 above   [65] See pp. 122–3 above and 171 below
[66] No. 64. This Responsum has been translated into English by B. Berliner in *Jews' College Jubilee Volume*, pp. 123–39

grandfather, Luria refers to the recitation of the Ten Commandments morning and evening. His grandfather used only one of the two expressions *bore* ('Creator') and *yotzer* ('Former'). But Luria suggests that *bore* refers to God's creation of the soul and *yotzer* to His creation of matter, as in the verse: 'He *formeth* the mountains and *createth* the spirit' (Amos 4 : 13). Luria proceeds to give an account of his own practices in prayer—e.g. after the benediction over the Torah he recites three verses each from the Pentateuch (Lev. 19 : 16–18), the Prophets (Josh. 1 : 7–9) and the Hagiographa (Ps. 1 : 1–3). Before departing from the synagogue after the prayers, he sits down for a moment or two and says: 'Surely the righteous shall give thanks unto Thy name; the righteous shall dwell in Thy presence' (Ps. 140 : 13). When he rises to leave, he bows towards the Ark and says: 'For all the peoples walk every one in the name of his god, but we will walk in the name of the Lord our God for ever and ever' (Mic. 4 : 5). As he is about to pass through the door of the synagogue, he says: 'Lead me, O Lord, in Thy righteousness for the sake of my enemies; make straight Thy way before me' (Ps. 5 : 9). He observes the custom of repeating the three words at the end of the *Shema* in obedience to the Kabbalistic statement that the total number of words should be 248.[67] After stating that there are many other similar points, Luria concludes: 'These are my new ideas. Although they are modest, my soul may find life in them. I had no time to describe them at length, for I am overpowered by the busy time in which I live.'

A Responsum (no. 7) of Isserles is in reply to Luria who, in previous correspondence, had rebuked him for studying philosophy and for quoting Aristotle. Isserles protests that he is simply taking one side in an ancient debate and refers to the Responsa of Adret[68] in which the pros and cons are fairly stated. Even Adret's ban on the study of philosophy applies only to youths under twenty-five. Who is greater than Maimonides? Yet the whole of his *Guide of the Perplexed* is grounded on philosophical ideas. Although R. Isaac b. Sheshet, in his Responsum[69] on the subject, argued that Maimonides studied philosophy only in order to be able to refute the heretics in their own language, two things re-

[67] See p. 105 above   [68] See p. 79 above   [69] See p. 84 above

quire to be said. First, the prohibition refers only to the study of Greek metaphysics, and here those who issued the ban were right because of the heretical views in these metaphysical works. But there is no ban on the study of natural science. On the contrary, through this study man may come to learn more about the greatness of the Creator. The study of natural science is, in fact, to be identified with the *Shiur Komah*,[70] the value of which is described in the most glowing terms. He is aware that the Kabbalists identify the *Shiur Komah* with a mystical work, but both interpretations of the nature of the work are 'the words of the living God'. Even though the works on the natural sciences have been compiled by Gentile authors, the Rabbis[71] teach us that whoever gives expression to some matter of wisdom is a sage, even if he is a Gentile. Second, even if such innocent topics as the natural sciences are also proscribed, because their study might lead on to the study of metaphysics, yet surely there cannot possibly be any ban on the works of Maimonides. All Isserles' knowledge of philosophy is derived from the works of Jewish writers like Maimonides. Maimonides[72] writes that all the views of Aristotle on the sublunary world are true. If one is afraid that the study of philosophy may lead to heresy, one ought to have the same fears with regard to the Kabbalah. If Luria relies on R. Isaac b. Sheshet on the question of philosophy, why does he not heed the advice of this sage against the study of the Kabbalah?[73] In any event, Isserles protests, God is his witness that he studies philosophy only on the sabbaths and festivals, when other folk generally spend the time in taking a pleasant stroll. During the week, he occupies all his time, to the best of his ability, studying the Talmud, the Codes and the Commentaries. He has no desire to boast, but a scholar is allowed to declare that he is such when it is necessary for him to do so. As for Luria's further rebuke that he does not know Hebrew grammar and makes grammatical mistakes in his letters, Isserles admits his incompetence in this field but, then, his main interest has always been in ideas themselves rather in the manner in which the ideas are expressed.

[70] See p. 15 above   [71] Meg. 16a
[72] *Guide of the Perplexed*, II, 22   [73] See p. 83 above

In a Responsum (no. 37) on penance, Isserles considers the case of a man who inadvertently pressed the trigger of a gun he was holding, killing his servant. Isserles rules that it is an accident so that there can be no question of imposing the penance set forth in the work *Rokeah*[74] for the crime of murder. Nevertheless, the man should confess his sins and the following penance should be imposed. He should leave his home for a whole year to wander from place to place, staying no longer than a single day and night in any town. For a whole year he should fast during the day and confess his sin each night. The anniversary of the tragic event should be kept each year as a day of fasting and mourning. But no stricter penance should be imposed. Repentant sinners must not be treated too harshly. God accepts sincere repentance because He desires the life of the sinner, not his death. It is strictly forbidden for anyone to taunt him with the deed, and he himself should confess his sin to God alone and not dwell on it in public.

In another Responsum (no. 41), Isserles considers the question, discussed by Benjamin Zeev,[75] whether the son of an apostate should be called to the Torah by his father's name: A, son of B. Isserles agrees with his questioner that the man should be called to the Torah by his father's name in order to avoid public embarrassment. The Talmud[76] does say that a child should not be given the name of a wicked man but this does not mean that the wicked must never be referred to by name. The Talmud itself frequently mentions wicked persons by name. It is even permitted to refer to false gods by name, provided the name has already been used and is not a name praising the god. Furthermore, the Talmud cannot possibly refer to a name the wicked person shares with many others. Thus Isserles permits it in all circumstances and he disagrees with the view that where there is no public embarrassment—i.e. where the man is unknown—the name of the grandfather should be used.

There are a number of theological Responsa in the collection of Levi Ibn Habib (d. 1545). Ibn Habib was the Rabbi of Jerusalem. His controversy with Jacob Berab over the reintroduction of

---

[74] See p. 101 above   [75] See p. 136 above   [76] Yom. 40b

Semikhah ('ordination') is well known. The documents on this debate are printed at the end of Ibn Habib's collection.

Two of Ibn Habib's Responsa are on the subject of the Kabbalah. In one (no. 75), he writes:

> You are astonished at those who expound in the presence of the ignorant and in public the doctrine of the Sefirot and that of reincarnation, and other matters to do with the secrets of the Torah. I, too, am astonished. They will have to give a reckoning before the Judgment Seat. I have complained previously of this in a tract I sent you in which I adduced proof from the teachers of old who were truly versed in such topics belonging to the mysteries. I refer to Nahmanides and his commentators. They spoke of these matters only by hint and in riddles, and such is the way of those who came after him who know the Torah and preserve the testimony.

The tract referred to is evidently the other Responsum (no. 8) in the collection on the same subject of teaching the Kabbalah in public. Here Ibn Habib writes:

> With regard to the third question you asked me—whether belief in reincarnation is binding on all Jews and whether it is permitted to expound the doctrine in public—you should know that, for my sins, I have not as yet attained to knowledge of this science. [The reference is to the Kabbalah.] This is because permission has not been granted to any man to understand it or study it by his own efforts. As its name implies, the Kabbalah is a doctrine one must have from a master who had it himself from a master. But in our land, nowadays, few are found to be wholly versed in this knowledge. However, in connection with this particular doctrine, I have seen the books and studied them and note that there are two groups among our sages, of blessed memory, who lived after the close of the Talmud.
>
> The first group comprises the philosophers who investigate the basic principles of faith by the aid of reason alone and who engage, too, in the study of the natural sciences. These find it hard to accept belief in reincarnation since, if reason alone is to be the guide, there are many difficulties in the doctrine which reason is powerless to resolve.
>
> However, there is another group, enjoying great authority, comprising those Jews who rely on faith. All these write that the doctrine is true and is a basic principle of the Torah by means of which an answer is given to the problem of why the righteous suffer [i.e. because of their sins in a previous incarnation]. We are all obliged to

143

hearken to the words of these latter sages; to believe in the doctrine without any doubts or reservations. For all that, it seems to me to be very wrong to expound the doctrine in public. We are no better than our teachers, on whom be peace. I refer to those who wrote on the doctrine in the books they compiled. They never spoke of it except by hint and in riddles. And they wrote that it is a great mystery.

The language of Nahmanides in his Commentary to Job[77] testifies to the truth of what I have said. He writes there: 'If you wish to understand this great secret, set your ear to my opinion. Let your reins admonish you and mourn for the sin and let the cloud cover your face. Let your eyes see the king and the queen and hope for redemption. See the two fawns, twins of a gazelle, and the decree and the building.' In the word 'mourn' he hints at Onan (Gen. 38 : 9–10) [pun on this word]. The 'king' and the 'queen' are Judah and his bride Tamar (Gen. 38). 'Hope for redemption' refers to Boaz who was a 'redeemer' (Ruth 4). The 'twins of a gazelle' are Perez and Zerah (Gen. 38 : 27–30). The 'decree' is death, decreed for all. The 'building' is that of levirate marriage (Gen. 38; Deut. 25 : 5–10; Ruth 4) [i.e. Boaz was the reincarnation of Onan and Ruth of Tamar]. So you see that the Rabbi, of blessed memory, spoke of the matter as of a secret, referring to it only by hint and in riddles. How much more so should we of this age, whose minds in comparison with his are like those of unweaned infants.

In Responsum no. 73 Ibn Habib refers to the Zoharic teaching that there are 248 words in the *Shema*, corresponding to the number of limbs in the human body.[78]

Discussing the strange case of a man who donated a quarter of his body to the prophet Samuel, Ibn Habib (no. 3) remarks that if it was his intention to denote a quarter of his value if he were sold as a slave, there is no harm in it. But if his intention was to copy the practices of the Gentiles who give part of their body to the saints, not only is the vow invalid but penance is required for making it.

Ibn Habib writes in another Responsum (no. 74) that the hymn *Barukh She-Amar*, recited at the beginning of the morning service, is, according to a book he had read, a direct communication from Heaven, it having dropped from the skies on to a piece of parch-

[77] Chavel's version (p. 101) differs slightly from that given here by Ibn Habib
[78] See pp. 105–6 above

ment. Consequently, he refuses to countenance any alterations to the form of the hymn that one might be tempted to make on the basis of the Kabbalah. He writes: 'If you will pay heed to me, I advise you to ignore what such folk say. For this is their habit: in order to win a reputation among the masses they say startling things without reason or understanding. You must ignore their counsel to change anything in the liturgy and you must pay no heed to them.'

In Responsum no. 76 Ibn Habib discusses the question of visiting the sins of the fathers on the children. He rejects the view that this applies even where the children are righteous, because such a view imputes injustice to God. It only applies when the children are wicked like the parents. True, the Rabbis sometimes speak of infants dying as a result of their parents' sins, but that is because infants are classified as a man's property and may be taken from him as a result of his sins, just as his wealth may be taken from him for this reason. But no grown-up son is ever punished for the sins of his parents. When the Rabbis do speak of vicarious atonement, it does not mean that the righteous are punished for the sins of their generation but rather that the generation is punished by the departure of the righteous. It is the generation which does not deserve the righteous.

Ibn Habib deals again (no. 77) with the same topic. The Rabbis say[79] that all the people of Israel are sureties one for the other. This only applies when they can prevent others from sinning and fail to do so. The exception seems to be in the story of Achan (Josh. 7) where all Israel was punished for one man's sin. But there it was different. The meaning of the story is not that Israel was punished by defeat in battle because of Achan's sin. God would have performed miracles on their behalf, but miracles depend on God's providence. At that time all Israel were together and when even a single limb of the body is unhealthy, the whole body is sick. It was simply a case of God's special care failing to operate because there was no wholeness in Israel. But no man is ever punished for the sins of another if he was in no way responsible for them.

[79] Shev. 39a

Another Responsum (no. 79) of Ibn Habib deals with two theological topics:

1. A man tore up a prayer-book on the sabbath in a fit of temper because the book contained extra Psalms, and the man held this to be copying the practices of the Karaites. What penance should be imposed on him? Ibn Habib declares that the man should be placed under the ban, confined to his home for a week. He should fast, be flogged and give alms. He should then confess his sin before the Ark in the synagogue.

2. It is nonsense to describe the prayer-book as influenced by the Karaites. The Karaites recite only Psalms they have collected, but we say them in addition to the standard liturgy and in this there is no harm whatever. The man is guilty of slandering the community by calling them Karaites and must ask their pardon in public.

Finally, there is the Responsum (no. 126) on alleged obscenities in the Rabbinic literature—for example, the interpretation of Scripture in such a way as to suggest that heroes like David and Joseph intended to commit sexual offences. Ibn Habib replies that, on the contrary, the Rabbis wish to say that these heroes were so great that, although sorely tempted, they exercised the severest self-control and did not actually sin. As for the strange Talmudic passage regarding the huge sexual organs of some of the Rabbis, the Tosafists rightly comment[80] on this that these matters were recorded so that one should not speak ill of men who are made this way.

R. Menahem Azariah da Fano (1548-1620) was an Italian Talmudist of note and a famous Kabbalist, whose Responsa collection was published in Venice in 1600. Three of these are of theological interest.

In no. 3, da Fano discusses the Talmudic saying:[81] 'The Torah used hyperbole, the prophets used hyperbole, the sages used hyperbole.' The questioner was reluctant to accept this statement at its face value. Surely everything the Rabbis say contains a profound moral or religious lesson and is not simply a literary device? Da Fano agrees. By 'hyperbole' in this context is meant a surface

---

[80] BM 84a, *amar*   [81] Tamid 29a

exaggeration which, however, on deeper reflection is seen to contain literal truth. For instance, the illustration given for the Torah's use of hyperbole is the verse: 'The cities are great and fortified up to heaven' (Deut. 1 : 28). The meaning here is that the cities of the holy land are fortified 'up to heaven' because the heavenly princes, the guardian angels, have no access here, the land being entirely under the direct control of God Himself.

The second Responsum (no. 102 : 3) is on the subject of confession. Should confession of sin be recited silently or in a loud voice? Da Fano rules that in the case of an individual, who is obliged to state his sins explicitly in his confession and not rely on the general formulation, the confession should be in silence so as to avoid its being overheard by others. But where the general confession is recited by the Reader in the synagogue for the purpose of reminding the members of the congregation that they have sinned, there is no private confession and the whole point is lost unless the Reader recites the confession in a loud voice.

In a famous and oft-quoted Responsum (no. 113 : 1), da Fano rules that there should be no swaying of the body in prayer. The verse quoted in support of swaying: 'All my bones shall say: "Lord, who is like unto Thee"' (Ps. 35 : 10) applies only to the praises of God, not to prayer. The verse clearly speaks of praising God: 'Lord, who is like unto Thee.' The prototype of prayer is provided by Hannah, of whom it is said: 'only her lips moved' (I Sam. 1 : 13). Only Hannah's lips moved, not her body. External movements of the body prevent adequate concentration in prayer. Although the living creatures in Ezekiel's vision moved about, yet it is said: 'when they stood, they let down their wings' (Ezek. 1 : 25). We, too, when we stand in prayer, should make no movements at all, although some people do sway slightly at the beginning and end of each benediction, on the basis of the verse: 'And the posts of the door were moved at the voice of them that called' (Isa. 6 : 4).

CHAPTER VIII

The Seventeenth Century

Joseph b. Moses Trani (1568–1639), known as *Maharit*, was born in Safed and served there as Rabbi of the Sephardi community. In 1604 he became head of the Yeshivah in Constantinople and eventually Chief Rabbi of Turkey. Trani's Responsa are devoted almost entirely to legal subjects, but two are of theological interest.

In the first of these,[1] Trani deals with the case of a preacher who declared in a sermon that no charges of dishonest dealings may be brought against a student of the Torah. The preacher supported his opinion with a passage from the *Zohar* which says that one who studies the Torah will not be judged for his crimes.[2] On the verses: 'Wherefore is the land perished and laid waste like a wilderness, so that none passeth through? And the Lord saith: Because they have forsaken My law' (Jer. 9: 11–12), this preacher gave the following illustration. A gifted fiddler was pardoned by the king for the crimes he had committed because the king could not bear to be without his sweet melodies. But when the fiddler lost his hand and was therefore unable to perform before the king, the king allowed him to be punished for his crimes. The implication is that a scholar will be pardoned for whatever he has done, as long as he continues to study the Torah, because God has such

[1] Part I, no. 100

[2] The reference in Trani is said to be to the *Zohar* to Exod. 32: 16, but I have been unable to discover the words quoted by Trani in any passage of the *Zohar* in which this verse is quoted

delight in his studies. The questioner asked Trani whether this preacher should be silenced for causing a profanation of God's name.

Trani, in a noble reply, declares that this preacher has distorted the Torah. Did his teacher fail to tell him that the main thing is practice, not study alone?[3] The Talmud[4] says: 'The goal of wisdom is repentance and good deeds, so that a man should not study the Torah and Mishnah and then despise his father and mother and teacher and his superior in wisdom and rank, as it is said: "The fear of the Lord is the beginning of wisdom, a good understanding have all they that do thereafter" (Ps. 111 : 10). It does not say "that study" but "that do".' The Talmud also says[5] that even if a man has studied the whole of the Mishnah, it avails him not if he has no fear of God. In another Talmudic passage[6] it is said:

> If someone studies Scripture and Mishnah, and attends on the disciples of the wise, is honest in business, and speaks pleasantly to others, what do people say of him? 'Happy is the father who taught him Torah, happy is the teacher who taught him Torah; woe unto people who have not studied the Torah; for this man has studied the Torah—look how fine are his ways, how righteous his deeds.' But if someone studies Scripture and Mishnah, attends on the disciples of the wise, but is dishonest in business and discourteous in his relations with others, what do people say of him? 'Woe unto him who studied Torah, woe unto his father who taught him Torah, woe unto his teacher who taught him Torah. This man studied the Torah: Look how corrupt his deeds, how ugly his ways.'

The Rabbis say further[7] that one whose wisdom exceeds his deeds is like a tree whose branches are many but whose roots are few, while one whose deeds exceed his wisdom is like a tree whose branches are few but whose roots are many. This shows that the greater the man the more God-fearing he is expected to be. And the Rabbis tell us[8] that scholars are expected to behave in such a way that they do not give even the appearance of sinning, otherwise God's name is profaned. And they tell us elsewhere[9] that even the unintentional sins of scholars are counted as if they were intentional.

[3] Avot I: 17   [4] Ber. 17a   [5] Sabb. 31a   [6] Yom. 86a
[7] Avot 3: 17   [8] Yom. 86a   [9] BM 33b

It is true that the Talmud[10] says that Hellfire has no power over scholars. The meaning is that the Torah they study saves them from sinning and so from Hell. It certainly does not mean that if they do sin they will be unjustly saved from Hell. As for the Zohar, Trani says: 'they brought me a copy of the Zohar.' Trani consulted the passage in question, but finds it impossible to imagine that the Zohar intended it to be taken literally. The Zohar, like the Talmud, means that the Torah the scholars study will save them from sin. This Responsum of Trani should be compared with the Gaonic Responsum[11] on the same theme.

In another Responsum,[12] Trani considers the question of penance. A certain man enjoyed a good reputation in the community. One day he came to the court entirely of his own accord and confessed that he had been guilty of all three capital sins; he had been a highwayman and had killed his victims; he had seduced married women; and he had denied God. Trani was asked whether repentance is possible for such a severe sinner and, if it is, what penances should be imposed on him.

Trani answers that the criminal cannot bring back to life those he has murdered and he cannot rescue his children borne by the married women from the taint of bastardy. In this sense his repentance is of no avail. But so far as he himself is concerned, he is capable of repentance. His penance must consist in realising three separate ideas. He must repent sincerely, he must suffer much, and he must do good deeds. He must confess his sins publicly, except for the sins with the married women (which must be kept secret to avoid harming their reputation and that of their children). As for suffering, he should know that God will punish him, but, in addition, he himself must engage in self-torment. He should fast for many a day. Even though the Rabbis say[13] that one who fasts is a sinner, this does not apply to one who fasts as an atonement for sin. He should also go into exile from his home. As for the question whether he should fast even on the sabbaths and festivals, the answer is no. It will be even more painful for him if he has to revert to fasting after having enjoyed food on the

[10] Hag. 27a
[12] Part II, Orah Hayyim, no. 8
[11] See pp. 12–13 above
[13] Ned. 10a

sabbath. Even if, as a result of his fasts, he is forced to study less than he would were he to eat, he should still fast. Furthermore, the very fact that, as a scholar, he is unable to study will itself be a form of mortification.[14] At first he should study only passages of rebuke in Scripture and the like, just as a mourner does. But after thirty days he can study whatever passages in the Torah he so desires. As for exile, since he committed the three capital sins, he should go to three different towns, spending a year in each. After all this, he should devote as much of his time as possible to the study of the Torah and should not inflict ugly tortures on himself. But he should eat only bread and drink only water. On sabbaths and festivals he can eat a little meat. He should never attend a banquet. As for deeds, he should do 'heaps and heaps of good deeds'. He should help others, and buy books to lend to scholars. He should return unto the Lord and He will have mercy upon him, and to our God, for He will abundantly pardon.

R. Joel Sirkes (1561–1640), known, after the initial letters of his *magnum opus—Bayit Hadash*—as the *Bah*, was a leading Polish authority. He was born in Lublin and served as a Rabbi of a number of Polish communities, including Cracow. There are two Responsa of theological interest in his collection.

The first (no. 4) concerns a doctor in Amsterdam who is alleged to have scoffed at the Aggadah of the Talmud and at the Kabbalah, claiming that the only study worth pursuing was philosophy. Only philosophy should be studied, and nothing else. This doctor tried to persuade others to follow his evil way. Moreover, this man, in his role of community leader, had authorised a *shohet*, ignorant of the laws, to slaughter animals for food. When the Rabbis heard of this they proclaimed in the synagogue that it was forbidden to eat the meat of animals killed by that *shohet;* but the doctor retorted that he was prepared to accept full responsibility and no notice should be taken of the Rabbis. Sirkes was asked for his opinion. Does he agree that the doctor should be placed under the ban?

Sirkes replies that there is no doubt in his mind that the doctor should be placed under the ban. The Rabbis say that even a scholar

[14] Cf. the views of Ezekiel Landau, pp. 175–7 below

must be placed under the ban if his reputation is sullied.[15] Asher b. Jehiel understands this to mean: when he reads heretical works. How much more so when one scoffs at the Aggadah and the Kabbalah! The Kabbalah is the source and basis of the Torah and is full of the fear of God. Moreover, this doctor is attracted to philosophy, which is itself heresy and the false woman against whom Solomon warns us. It goes without saying that such a sinner who, not content with his own misdeeds, encourages others to sin, must be punished with the utmost severity. Sirkes has no hesitation in allowing his own name to go forward as a supporter of the ban, which should remain in operation until the doctor shows true remorse.

In another Responsum (no. 127, end) Sirkes discusses the use of church melodies in the synagogue service—on which matter he is lenient, with the exception of melodies especially associated with Christian hymns. Otherwise it is permitted. The prohibition of copying Gentile ways applies only to practices we learn from the Gentiles. Music is not specifically theirs, but is the common heritage of all mankind.

Another famous Polish Talmudist who flourished at the end of the sixteenth and the beginning of the seventeenth century was R. Meir b. Gedaliah of Lublin (1558–1618), known as the *Maharam* of Lublin. His Responsa collection has the title *Manhir Eine Hakhamin* (*Illuminating the Eyes of the Wise*).

Three of *Maharam*'s Responsa deal with penances. In one (no. 43), he discusses the case of a Jew who accidentally killed a man while practising shooting under government orders. The usual penance for accidental homicide is exile from home,[16] but the man is a cripple and cannot leave his home and has, moreover, a wife and children to support. *Maharam* rules that he should undertake a token exile to a neighbouring community each Monday and Thursday, there to be flogged, and he should prostrate himself at the threshold of the synagogue. This he should do for half a year and he should eat no meat and drink no wine during this period.

Another Responsum (no. 44) concerns the case of Rabbi Binash

---

[15] MK 17a   [16] See p. 142 above

of Brisk who gave a legal decision against a young man. A relative of the youth came to the Rabbi's house one night in order to plead for clemency, but the Rabbi, thinking that the man intended to attack him physically, dragged a heavy chest to the door to keep him out, suffering, as a result, a heart attack from which he died. What penance is to be imposed on the relative? *Maharam* replies that this man can in no way be considered to be a murderer since the Rabbi brought it on himself. Nevertheless, the man himself wishes to have a penance imposed on him for being instrumental in 'extinguishing the light of the Torah'. *Maharam*, therefore, suggests that the man should fast for forty consecutive days and then for three days a week. For a whole year he should sleep on the ground, not in his bed. He should prostrate himself at the threshold of the synagogue in Brisk, allowing the members of the congregation to trample on him. For a whole year he should take his seat in disgrace at the rear of the synagogue. Once a month he should take with him ten men to the Rabbi's grave, there to beg his forgiveness. For a whole year he should attend no banquets and he should fast on Mondays and Thursdays for three years. For a whole year he should allow himself to be flogged once a week by the beadle in private. But after he has undergone these penances, *Maharam* decrees, anyone who calls him a murderer will be cursed.

In a third Responsum (no. 45) on penance, *Maharam* discusses the case of a scholar who had sexual relations with a married woman while he was under the influence of drink. *Maharam* gives the following penance, but adds that whoever calls the man a sinner afterwards will be cursed. The man should confess his sin in public in the three communities of Lublin, Cracow and Lvov. The beadle should give him thirty-nine lashes each day. He should fast for a whole year, except on the sabbaths and festivals. He should sleep on the ground, not in his bed, for a whole year, during which time he should wear sackcloth. During this year he should sit, each Monday and Thursday, for an hour, in snow in the winter and to be stung by bees in the summer. After the year is over he should continue to fast on Mondays and Thursdays for three years. Throughout his life he should keep strictly away from any woman except his own wife. As a repentant sinner, his place in Paradise will then be greater than one who has never sinned.

In a Responsum addressed to a Rabbi Shabbetai (no. 83), *Maharam* discusses the correct pronunciation of the Tetragrammaton. Traditionally this is not pronounced as written, but the name *Adonay* ('Lord') is used instead. The usual pronunciation of this word is *Adonay* (with a *hataf-patah* under the letter *alef*). The questioner wished to know if the report is true that *Maharam* had ruled that it should be pronounced '*donay* (with a *sheva* under the *alef*). If the report is true, it is odd since grammatically the *alef* cannot take a *sheva*.

Maharam replies that he is extremely reluctant to treat of these mysteries in writing, but he has to inform his questioner that in such matters we do not follow the grammarians. Those who pronounce the name with a *patah* 'destroy the world', and are guilty of failing to pronounce the name correctly. *Maharam* refers to his grandfather Asher, Rabbi of Cracow, who compiled a work called *Emek Ha-Berakhah* dealing with the mysteries behind the liturgy, but did not have it published. Works of this nature, he argued, ought not to be printed lest they fall into the wrong hands. In that work, R. Asher wrote that the vowel under the *alef* is a *sheva*. There are tremendous mysteries here, conveyed as he saw it stated in a Kabbalistic book to Moses at the burning bush. R. Asher explains why there is no *patah* under the *alef*, but such secrets must never be communicated in writing. More than this, says *Maharam*, he dare not say. Indeed, he has to ask God to forgive him for revealing even this much. *Maharam* begs R. Shabbetai to keep the letter in a holy place and not allow it to be moved around. He signs the letter, as he does most of his correspondence, 'Meir, the preoccupied'.

Leon da Modena (1571–1648), Rabbi and preacher in Venice, man of many parts and contradictions, staunch traditionalist and equally fervent modernist, was quite different in type from the other Rabbis considered in this chapter. The influence of the Renaissance is clearly to be seen in all his writings. Da Modena is not conspicuous for his contribution to the Halakhic literature.

His Responsa collection *Zikne Yehudah* was published only as late as 1956 by Simonsohn.

A Responsum[17] of da Modena deals with the melodies composed by Salomone di Rossi for use in the synagogue service. The questioner asked da Modena whether it is laudable to use set pieces of music for hymns like *Adon Olam* and *Yigdal*. Traditional chanting in the synagogue is one thing, but here they wish to introduce complicated musical arrangements, compositions to be sung by a choir of assorted voices. There have been those who argued in its favour. But others have protested, quoting: 'Rejoice not, O Israel, unto exultation, like the people' (Hos. 9 : 1). What is da Modena's opinion?

Da Modena first notes the Talmudic objection[18] to music, based on the verse in Hosea, after the destruction of the Temple. But *Rashi* to the passage rightly understands it as referring only to musical performances at secular banquets.[19] No one ever intended to prohibit music on a festive religious occasion. The authorities[20] permit Gentile musicians to play at a wedding feast even on the sabbath. It follows that it is permitted to sing with a choir in the synagogue for this, too, is like a wedding feast since the sabbath is Israel's bride. The tradition advocates that the Reader must have a pleasant voice. How much more would it approve the assistance to the Reader of the vocal efforts of a gifted choir. If we prohibit this, the Gentiles will ridicule the Jews who, they will say, have no aesthetic appreciation, crying out to the God of their fathers in a way that is reminiscent only of the barking of dogs and the croaking of ravens. Appended to this Responsum is a certificate in which the Venetian Rabbis approve of da Modena's decision.

We have seen[21] that the medieval authorities discussed whether it is a belief of Judaism that the world will one day come to an end. Da Modena was asked[22] by a Rabbi of Amsterdam whether a preacher, who declared in a sermon that the world would never have an end, should be punished. Da Modena replies that there is no definite indication in Scripture of how this question regarding

---

[17] No. 5, pp. 15–20   [18] Gitt. 7a
[19] See pp. 27–8 above for the views of Hai Gaon
[20] *Tur*, Orah Hayyim 338 and Isserles, 560: 8
[21] See pp. 59–61 above   [22] No. 16, pp. 30–1

the world coming to an end is to be resolved. Anyone who wishes to affirm that the world will never have an end enjoys the weighty support of Maimonides[23] who was, in fact, anticipated by Philo.[24] However, the plain meaning of the words of the Talmudic Rabbis suggests that they held the opposite view, one that is, possibly, more advantageous to faith. It is not wise to preach in public on topics such as this. Ordinary people can become disturbed in their faith when mysterious questions, beyond the mind of man to grasp, are discussed without reserve. There are far more relevant and fascinating topics in Judaism for public exposition.

A Responsum of da Modena[25] concerns a Dr Farrar of Amsterdam.[26] Farrar, of Marrano descent, aroused the ire of Rabbi Isaac Uziel because of his free interpretations of the Bible. When Uziel wrote to the community of Salonika for support, they agreed to impose the ban on Farrar, but when Uziel turned for advice to da Modena he was severely rebuked for his pains. I am astonished, declares da Modena, that you saw fit to curse Farrar before making a full investigation into the affairs. You yielded to the entreaties of Farrar's enemies in the Amsterdam community without bothering to hear Farrar's own side of the case. He has been wrongly accused of denying the Oral Law and scoffing at Rabbinic teachings whereas, in fact, he is a fully observant Jew, keeping even such Rabbinic laws as the avoidance of Gentile wine, which even some of the teachers of the Torah in Italy treat lightly. The greater the man, the more enemies he makes, and it is these who have testified falsely against Farrar. Even if he did understand some Rabbinic sayings in a non-literal fashion and departed from *Rashi* and the other early commentators in his interpretations of the Bible, it is no offence. Preachers in the synagogue are fond of quoting in their sermons commentators who do precisely this and are, none the less, quite acceptable. And what guilt is there

---

[23] *Guide of the Perplexed*, II, 27–9
[24] See Simonsohn's note (p. 30 n. 1) that da Modena follows here the view of de Rossi, *Meor Einayyim, Maamar* 44 but, in fact, Philo holds the opposite view that the world will have an end
[25] No. 33, pp. 48–9
[26] This is presumably the doctor referred to by Joel Sirkes (pp. 151–2 above). On Farrar, see *Jewish Encyclopedia*, vol. V, p. 346, in which article he is called *Abraham* Farrar but da Modena refers to him as *David* Farrar

in the opinion Farrar expressed that there is none worthy, now-adays, of using the divine name for magical purposes?

There was, in fact, considerable tension between da Modena and this Isaac Uziel, Rabbi of the community of former Marranos in Amsterdam from 1607 to 1620. Isaac suspected da Modena of supporting the heretics, as when he defended Farrar; da Modena, in turn, suspected Isaac of being a reactionary. A Responsum of da Modena[27] to Isaac Uziel deals with a number of theological issues which evidently arose out of the Farrar case.

Da Modena first remarks that although the Kabbalists under-stand the Rabbinic term *maaseh bereshit*, 'the work of creation', as referring to mystical teaching, there is sound warrant for the identification of the term with natural science. Nature is from God, and the study of nature a religious duty. Da Modena quotes the saying that the Hebrew word for 'nature' (*ha-teva*) has the same numerical value as the Hebrew name for God (*elohim*). He notes that Albo, Abravanel and others have had a similar positive approach to the study of natural science.

On the question of free Biblical interpretation, da Modena admits that in matters of law it is forbidden to depart from Rab-binic teachings. But when it comes to Biblical interpretation one is allowed to expound the plain meaning even if, in the process, one departs from the Rabbinic Midrashim on the texts. The great commentators *Rashi* and *Kimhi*, and especially Abraham Ibn Ezra, do this frequently, as Azariah de Rossi[28] has pointed out.

As for the whole question of belief in the Kabbalah, da Modena remarks that much as he had tried to have the adepts enlighten him he is still very confused as to its nature. Da Modena does not deny that there is *a* Kabbalah, a traditional esoteric lore, but he is very uneasy about the claim made by the Kabbalists that their doctrines are to be identified with this tradition. Da Modena con-cludes that he writes all this because Isaac Uziel suspects him of supporting those who reject Rabbinic teaching. The truth is that, on the contrary, he devotes all his efforts to defending the Rabbis against the attacks of the Gentiles.

[27] No. 35, pp. 50–2   [28] *Meor Einayyim, Imre Binah*, chapter 15

Da Modena considers[29] the case of a notorious witch in the vicinity of Padua to whom a number of Jews have recourse. He observes that apart from the very severe prohibition of sorcery and the profanation of God's name, there is danger from the Gentile authorities who have outlawed the practising of witchcraft.

Saul Mortara of Amsterdam turned to da Modena[30] for advice regarding the mother of Uriel da Costa, who, like her son, was suspected of having rejected the Jewish religion. When she dies, should she be buried in the Jewish cemetery? Da Modena states that, according to the strict letter of the law, she should. However, the Rabbis say[31] that, where the generation needs the lesson, the court is allowed to act contrary to the strict law in imposing otherwise illegal punishments in order to protect the stability of Jewish life. Consequently, if on her deathbed she gives some indication that she wishes to return to the Jewish fold or, at least, to be buried in a Jewish grave, then she should be buried in the Jewish cemetery. Otherwise, as a warning to others, either she should be refused burial altogether in the Jewish cemetery or she should be buried in a corner away from the other graves and there should be a symbolical stoning of her coffin.

A Responsum[32] to Rabbi Melli of Urbino deals with whether a preacher who teaches the Kabbalah in public should be silenced. Da Modena writes:

> The truth is, if I am to state my opinions unreservedly, I would arrive at a view unlikely to prove acceptable to the pseudo-pious, namely, that before we can even begin to discuss whether it is permitted to teach in public that which is now called the Kabbalah, we must ask whether most of the Kabbalah we now have deserves to be called 'the secrets of the Torah' and whether it is permitted to study it even privately.

Da Modena refers to the Responsa on this subject by Isaac b. Sheshet[33] and Levi Ibn Habib.[34] Either the preacher made it all up out of his own head—in which case it is purely his own invention and it is certainly wrong to pass it off as Jewish teaching—

---

[29] No. 37, p. 53   [30] No. 54, pp. 75–6   [31] Sanh. 46a
[32] No. 55, pp. 76–8   [33] Pp. 83–4 above   [34] Pp. 143–4 above

or he claims that he has it by tradition—in which case one is entitled to ask whether he really understands that which he has received. In any event, the Kabbalists themselves hold that their teachings must be kept secret, so it is obviously forbidden to expound them in public. These topics are a cause of confusion even to the wise, to say nothing of the intellectually immature. This applies with even greater force when we reside among Christians who will either say that we intend to attack their religion or, on the contrary, will say that secretly we believe in their religion; for example, when they hear how much prominence is given in the Kabbalah to the Fall of Adam. Da Modena refers to his own experience. He has preached regularly in Venice and other Italian cities but has never quoted the Kabbalah, except for an occasional premise in which he may have just touched on the subject.

Da Modena deals with the Kabbalah in another Responsum.[35] A Reader in the synagogue, following the musical arrangement, used to repeat certain words of the prayers, including the divine names. Some object to the use of musical compositions as such in the synagogue but they object especially to the repetitions, in particular that of the word *Keter* ('Crown') in the Kedushah. Da Modena states that he is not personally familiar with the Kabbalah and has no desire to be, as he has explained in his anti-Kabbalistic work *Ari Nohem*. But he did consult two Kabbalists on whether there can be any objection to a repetition of the word *Keter*. One of these explained to him that the Sefirah *Keter* is 'the secret of all being' from which all the other Sefirot emerge, and no harm is done if one repeats the word. The other Kabbalist said that, in this particular hymn, *Keter* is not the Sefirah of that name but the 'Crown' provided by mortals who awaken the divine grace by their good deeds here on earth. If that is so, why not repeat the word? Indeed, the more good deeds one performs, the better. Da Modena quotes the ruling of Elijah Mizrahi[36] that we do not follow the Kabbalah unless the matter is found in the Talmud. Consequently, since there is no Talmudic objection to the repetition of divine names in prayer, we are justified in ignoring any Kabbalistic objections if such there be. It is true that the

[35] No. 131, pp. 177–8   [36] See pp. 105–6 above

Talmud[37] opposes the repetition of 'Hear O Israel', but that is because such a repetition might suggest a belief in dualism. But what objection can there possibly be to repeating the praises of God?

The German Rabbi Jair Hayyim Bacharach (1638–1702) was a great Talmudist, a Kabbalist, and widely read in the general literature of his day. His Responsa collection *Havvot Yair*[38] was first published by the author in Frankfort in 1699.

Bacharach has a lengthy Responsum (no. 210) on the study of the Kabbalah. A Talmudic scholar asked him whether, now that he had mastered the legal literature, he should devote some of his time to Kabbalistic studies. Bacharach first expresses his reluctance to offer any advice on such a matter. On the one hand, the Kabbalah is truly 'the soul of the Torah' but, on the other hand, its study is fraught with spiritual danger. Bacharach quotes: 'Love Socrates, love Plato, but love the truth more',[39] and urges his questioner not to rely on him but to make up his own mind. He gives an interesting illustration. Everyone knows that there are numerous Rabbinic sayings on the great advantage of residing in the holy land. Yet, for all that, where a journey to the holy land is attended by danger, one should remain in the Diaspora.[40] Similarly, while the advantages of Kabbalistic studies are immense, one should desist from them if there is any danger to the soul. Of the four who entered the Pardes,[41] only one, R. Akiba, emerged unscathed. The sages of the Talmud did not teach the Kabbalah. Bacharach remarks in parenthesis that he is aware of the Kabbalists' contention that the Mishnah does hint at the secrets of the Torah. He is only prepared to accept this, however, if it can be proved to be based on an authentic tradition. He rather suspects that it is a case of the Kabbalists reading their ideas into the Mishnah. Bacharach expresses his surprise that books are written by the Kabbalists with the aim of elucidating difficult passages

---

[37] Ber. 33b
[38] The title is based on Num. 32: 41 and contains a pun on the name of the author's grandmother, Eva (= Havvah)
[39] Cf. no. 9, where Bacharach quotes this maxim and refers to earlier Jewish authors who use it
[40] See pp. 95–6 above [41] See pp. 16–17 above

in the *Zohar* and trying to explain apparent contradictions in that work. But since the topics discussed are far beyond the grasp of the human mind, how can these authors apply their reasoning here? The *Zohar* itself states that there is a stage at which it is not even permitted to put a question.[42] The *Zohar* and Isaac Luria were divinely inspired, but how do the later Kabbalists justify the application of their own unaided reason to these unfathomable mysteries? Maimonides, in his *Guide of the Perplexed*,[43] tells us how difficult it is for the human mind to grasp the divine. How much more difficult is the task in connection with the Kabbalah.

Bacharach gives four reasons why Kabbalistic studies present especially severe difficulties. First, the very words of the *Zohar* are hard to understand. Second, the Zoharic syntax presents difficulties of its own. Third, the subject matter is so very profound. Finally, man's sins act as a barrier to the comprehension of this holy science. The student of the Kabbalah quickly becomes confused as he notices contradictions. For instance, sometimes the ten sayings in the creation narrative at the beginning of Genesis are said to represent the Ten Sefirot, and yet elsewhere it is said that the first six days of creation represent the six Sefirot from *Tiferet* to *Yesod*. The Ten Sefirot are sometimes formulated so as to include *Keter* and *Daat*, and at other times these are not counted among the Sefirot. The Sefirot are depicted sometimes as proceeding in a straight line, sometimes in circles. If understood literally, the Kabbalah is full of the grossest anthropomorphism. We human beings are constitutionally incapable of imagining that which is purely spiritual. We cannot even depict accurately to ourselves our own psychic nature, still less can we hope to depict the Limitless, *En Sof*. For people of our spiritual degree, simple faith is enough. It is quite sufficient if we accept the principles of the Jewish faith as laid down in the *Yigdal* hymn and avoid any further philosophical investigation into matters to be accepted in faith. If our reason ever tempts us to reject one or other of the basic principles of the Jewish faith, it is obvious that we must abandon our reason and rest securely in the truth as found in the tradition. Whoever studies the Kabbalah is bound to be puzzled

[42] *Zohar* I, 1b   [43] I, 34

by the numerous references to multiplicity and compositeness in the divine nature. Although the later Kabbalists do strive hard to remove all these difficulties, it is almost certain that their solutions will prove to be unsatisfactory and the student will be encouraged to entertain dualistic notions.

Furthermore, Bacharach continues, confusion is caused by numerous printing errors in the Kabbalistic books. And the Kabbalistic symbolism is especially bewildering, for instance, when the same Biblical verse is now made to represent this Sefirah, now the other. As for the identification of ideas by means of numerical values (*gematria*), such a method is so pliant that it can be made to yield anything one chooses.

Consequently, while Bacharach reiterates that he yields to none in acknowledging the great advantages to be derived from Kabbalistic studies, it remains true that the early Kabbalists did not study the sacred science out of books but received the knowledge directly by word of mouth from a master. We have only the books and so errors abound. Bacharach protests that it is not his aim to decry the works of the Kabbalists. The fault lies not in the inadequacies of the authors but in our inability to understand what they say. Therefore, he advises, by all means study the Kabbalah, but only accept as true those matters on which there are no debates among the Kabbalists and no contradictions. With regard to mystical 'intentions' (*kavvanot*) in prayer, it is far better to ignore these, having in mind only the simple intention: 'I offer my prayers to the Cause of causes, Creator of heaven and earth', which is enough in order to fulfil the obligation to pray.

Bacharach tells of a man who asked him the meaning of the Kabbalistic formula, recently introduced into the prayer-books:[44] 'For the sake of the unification of the Holy One, blessed be He, and his Shekhinah, through that Hidden and Concealed One.' Bacharach declared that it refers to a mystery incapable of being understood by all but the greatest sages. The man insisted, however, that the formula be explained to him, whereupon Bacharach said that he himself does not understand the meaning of these cryptic words. He remarks that this was not an exercise in false

44 See my *Hasidic Prayer*, pp. 140 ff. and pp. 177–8 below

modesty or a mere subterfuge in order to rid himself of the man's importunities. He really does not know the meaning of the formula and doubts whether any contemporary Kabbalist really understands it.

Bacharach appends to this Responsum an essay on the subject by his father, Moses Samson. Moses Samson argues that while it is exceedingly meritorious to study the Kabbalah, this is true only if the student is fortunate enough to have an expert teacher, not if he tries to gain his information from books. Therefore, he argues, it is better nowadays to refrain from studying the Kabbalah. Moses Samson, to illustrate the dangers, quotes the Responsum of Isaac b. Sheshet[45] who records that a philosopher once said to him that the Kabbalists are worse than the Christians, since the Christians believe in only three while the Kabbalists believe in ten.

Another Responsum of Bacharach (no. 125) begins with a very human touch. A friend in a neighbouring town invited Bacharach to be a guest at his son's Bar Mitzvah, hinting that he would make it financially worth his while, but Bacharach declined the invitation. The friend was annoyed and, after the celebrations, wrote to him to say that he will not forgive him unless he will consent to provide the boy, who shows much promise, with a programme of studies. Some scholars have advised that the boy study one or two pages of the Talmud each day. Others advise that he should study the *Tur*. But the father is prepared to adopt only the programme mapped out by Bacharach.

Bacharach willingly accepts the task, but says that he is not familiar with the boy's progress so far. Since the father mentions in his letter that the boy delivered himself of a fine *derashah* on the occasion of his Bar Mitzvah, it seems that he knows some Midrash and the *Ein Yaakov* of Jacob Ibn Habib. These are useful as appetisers and the boy can no doubt avail himself of them in order to parade his learning. There is no great harm in this, since through it he can win a reputation as a scholar and perhaps find a suitable match. Yet this is not the way for a man to become a real scholar, capable of rendering decisions in Jewish law and filled

[45] See pp. 83–4 above

with the meat and wine that are the main subjects of Torah study.

For the boy to study according to a set programme will be difficult, because the teachers are so inadequate. Even if the father is fortunate enough to obtain a good private tutor for his son, the boy will miss the sharpening of mind against mind that a school provides. The only solution is for a few householders to pool their resources and obtain a first-class teacher for their sons. It is hard to give preference among the many subjects to be mastered, but the current neglect of Orah Hayyim and Yoreh Deah (the parts of the *Shulhan Arukh* which deal with purely religious matters) in favour of Hoshen Mishpat (the part dealing with business law) together with the commentary *Sefer Meirat Einayyim*, lacks balance. Not that Bacharach denigrates the study of jurisprudence but, he says, the motives behind the conventional preference are hardly worthy. There are, on the whole, three reasons why teachers prefer to concentrate on this subject. First, the teachers already know other branches of the law and so teach civil law in order to extend the range of their own studies—a procedure hardly fair to their charges. Second, parents wish their sons to win fame in the commercial world for their expertise in this branch of learning. Third, there is great dialectical skill in the study of this branch of law. This is undoubtedly true, but it should not cause a neglect of Orah Hayyim and Yoreh Deah. After all, the main aim of study is that it should lead to practice. Bacharach remarks that he has heard how in former times they used to study the *Akedat Yitzhak* of Isaac Arama, the *Sefer Ha-Ikkarim* of Joseph Albo and the *Kuzari* of Judah Ha-Levi in order to learn the main principles of the faith from these philosophical works. But nowadays we do not teach these subjects to our youth and we are quite right, since it is far better for us and our sons to accept the beliefs of Judaism without philosophising about them. As for the argument that even if the study of Hoshen Mishpat does not lead to practice there is still the great virtue of Torah study for its own sake, this is undoubtedly so, but when it leads to a neglect of Orah Hayyim and Yoreh Deah, there is something very wrong.

Bacharach adds that it is very good to study the Mishnah,

especially now that we have Bertinoro's excellent commentary. The Codes of the *Rif* and the *Rosh* should also be studied because they provide fine summaries of the Talmudic deliberations. *Pilpul* (dialectic) should be avoided except for the purpose of comparing and contrasting different passages in the Talmud. Bacharach concludes with the hope that his advice will be followed. If father and son offer their prayers to God and the boy carries out this programme, his efforts will be crowned with success.

A questioner asked Bacharach (no. 152) how he would defend the many passages in the Talmud in which the Rabbis denigrate one another. The Mishnah[46] teaches that our neighbour's honour should be as dear to us as our own and yet we find in the Talmud such insulting remarks as: 'Rab must have been half asleep when he said this.'[47] Bacharach admits that the questioner has a point. Obviously reflected in both the question and the reply are the conditions of his own day, when bitter conflicts among scholars were by no means rare and the cantankerous were able to quote Talmudic precedent. True, replies Bacharach, the Talmud[48] describes scholars as 'enemies' to one another, but this has to be understood hyperbolically and refers only to the vehemence with which the Talmudic debates were conducted. It was not intended to encourage scholars almost to come to blows when arguing with one another. All violent physical movements should be avoided in debate, except for the spontaneous clapping of the hands when a particularly acute suggestion has been advanced, in joy at arriving at the truth. Dialectic is praiseworthy, to be sure. One of the questions a man is asked on Judgment Day is whether he engaged in *pilpul* while he was on earth.[49] But the debates should be conducted with decorum. As for the saying about Rab, Bacharach remarks that, if he dared to say it, he would suggest that Rab deserved the insult because he, himself, insulted his colleague Levi by declaring him to be brainless.[50] But one dare not say such a thing of such a holy man as Rab, the R. Abba who features in the *Zohar*. The Kabbalist Menahem Azariah da Fano

---

[46] Avot 2: 10
[47] Bacharach quotes Yev. 24b, 109b; BK 46b, 65a, 66b; Nidd. 60a; Bekh. 23b
[48] Kidd. 30b   [49] Sabb. 31a   [50] Yev. 9a

teaches that whenever the Talmud says of Rab that he was silent and did not reply to a problem presented to him, it means that he knew the answer according to the mystical lore but did not wish to divulge the secret. The saying about Rab being half asleep is not, in fact, derogatory. On the contrary, it intends to suggest that such a profound scholar as Rab was incapable of making a mistake while fully conscious and if he occasionally erred it could only be because he was half-asleep at the time. As for Rab rebuking Levi in such harsh terms, Rab was Levi's teacher and there are times when a teacher must reluctantly speak harshly to his disciples in order to keep them on their toes. All similar expressions in the Talmud are of this nature, or were uttered between colleagues who took no offence at playful taunts. When R. Zera was called a 'howling jackal' by R. Abbahu,[51] there is a deep reason behind it. We know that R. Zera was an ascetic. R. Abbahu believed that too much asceticism tends to rigidity in religion and he wished to hint at his disapproval of R. Zera's over-indulgence in self-mortification.

A questioner asked Bacharach (no. 233) to explain the Talmudic references to practices harmful to health, such as that one should not wipe oneself with a piece of potsherd,[52] for the harm of which there appears to be no rational explanation. Bacharach is surprised that anyone should find this difficult. If, he remarks, the questioner is bothered by Rabbinic belief in the supernatural, how does he understand the numerous references to magic, the efficacy of which the Rabbis accept?[53] And what of the Rabbinic belief in the salamander[54] which emerges out of the fire? There are many phenomena for which there is no rational explanation—the attraction of the magnet[55] for iron filings, for example, or why fire is produced when two sticks are rubbed together, or how worms can bore into wood, and how they appear in cheeses. If we cannot understand even the workings of Nature, how can we expect to understand the supernatural? Bacharach offers this explanation of magic: it is unnatural, so that it is plausible to suggest, on the principle that like attracts like, that it can have an

51 Sanh. 59b   52 Ber. 55a   53 See pp. 77–8 above
54 Hag. 27a   55 See pp. 60–1 above

effect on sinners, whose deeds are unnatural. There is a logical explanation, too, for the Rabbinic view that things in even numbers (*zuggot*) are harmful to persons who believe in this.[56] Odd numbers, based on the number one, represent unity, and, therefore, God, who is One; while even numbers represent division and multiplicity. The indivisible is protected by God, unlike that which lends itself to division. The reason why wiping with a piece of potsherd can be harmful is because it is an inadequate means of cleaning the body. The person remains soiled and hence more liable to become the victim of magic. Although the Rabbis warn us against following pagan customs, the magical practices for whose efficacy they had a tradition were recorded in the Talmud as true and tested.

In another Responsum (no. 141), Bacharach deals with the question (considered, as we have seen, by others) whether the court should be lenient in punishing sinners where there is the danger that strictness might encourage them to find safety outside the Jewish fold. The Kahal in a certain town wished to fine a man who was lax in the matter of drinking Gentile wine, and wished to proclaim the man a sinner, but the Rabbi of the town sought to dissuade them from this on the ground that severity might have the effect of encouraging the man, once branded as a sinner, to commit more serious offences. It might even lead to his apostasy, for which the community would then be responsible. Bacharach remarks that at first glance the Rabbi is right. In support of his attitude there are the rulings of the *Shulhan Arukh*,[57] the statement in the Talmud that the left hand should reject but the right hand bring near;[58] and the statement that it is better that people should sin unwittingly rather than that they should be rebuked and so continue to sin intentionally.[59] From all this it would appear that it is right and proper to be less than strict in the application of the religious norm if it is feared that otherwise people will be led into graver sin. Yet, on deeper reflection, continues

[56] Pes. 109b–110b
[57] Hoshen Mishpat 17: 3; Isserles, end of Yoreh Deah 344
[58] Sot. 47a. Bacharach states that in most editions this passage has been abbreviated 'because of the danger'—i.e. because of the references to Jesus
[59] Betz. 30a

Bacharach, it is clear that the Rabbi is wrong. On the contrary, as the Rabbi of the town, it should have been his responsibility to initiate the proceedings. If we are to be apprehensive of what might happen if the law is strictly applied, every criminal will threaten to leave the Jewish fold if he is punished, and who will then protect the innocent victims of oppression? In the examples quoted above the sin is not at all serious. Only in such instances should the court be circumspect. Bacharach quotes the retort of Rabban Simeon b. Gamaliel[60] to the suggestion of R. Akiba and R. Tarfon that had they been in the Sanhedrin they would have abolished capital punishment: 'They would have caused murders to increase in Israel.' Tradition has it that conversion to Judaism is to be made difficult on the ground that the converts frequently cause harm to Israel,[61] even though it is a great privilege to belong to the Jewish people; from which we learn that sometimes the interests of the individual have to be set aside in favour of those of the group as a whole. The main aim of punishment is as a deterrent, the individual being sacrificed on the altar of communal well-being. Why, the Talmud even rules[62] that where the community needs the warning, the court can even inflict otherwise illegal punishments on offenders.

A question from Amsterdam (no. 222) concerned a man who had no sons and who stipulated in his will that a quorum should be paid to meet in his house for a year after his death to study and pray so that his daughter can recite the Kaddish. Bacharach can see no legal objection since women, too, are obliged to honour their parents and are obliged to sanctify God's name, the Kaddish being a prayer of sanctification. Nevertheless, he finally rules that the wishes of the deceased should not be carried out because it is contrary to all custom for a daughter to recite the Kaddish.

Finally, Bacharach deals (no. 170) with the question of penance. Two horse-dealers were deadly enemies. One of them, riding to the fair with his friends, saw the other walking in front of them and remarked to his companions: 'Just watch! I shall scare the life out of him.' He took up his gun, which was unloaded, and pretended to fire at his enemy, who, in fact, died of

---

[60] Mishnah Makk. 1: 10   [61] Yev. 47b   [62] Sanh. 46a

fright. Does this man have to undergo a severe penance? Bacharach replies: indeed he does. Even if A sent B on an errand and B was killed while carrying it out, A requires to do penance;[63] how much more so in this case. Bacharach refers to a Gentile work he has read in which a similar case is recorded. A man frightened another to death, and the court ordered him to be executed. But the judge instructed the executioner to strike his neck with the flat of the sword instead of the blade. This was to be measure for measure, the criminal receiving the deadly fright he had inflicted on his victim. In fact, in that case, the criminal survived the ordeal and was pardoned. Thus it appears that according to the law of the Gentiles the criminal is to be punished in this way by the court, but no punishment is due to him from God. In Jewish law, remarks Bacharach, the exact opposite is true. The criminal cannot be punished by the court, since he did not actually murder his victim, but he is a murderer in the eyes of God, who will punish him. Therefore, concludes Bacharach, the court, when imposing a penance, must weigh up the matter most carefully. If they see that the circumstances were such that the man ought to have taken into account the possibility that his victim would die of fright, the severest penances should be imposed. But if the possibility seemed exceedingly remote, then it is a case of accidental homicide and the penance can be correspondingly lighter.

R. Zevi Ashkenazi (1660–1718) served as Rabbi in Amsterdam and was the chief opponent of the followers of the pseudo-Messiah Shabbetai Zevi. This famous Talmudist, though an Ashkenazi, became the acknowledged head not only of the Amsterdam Sephardi community but far beyond the confines of that city; hence the Sephardi title, Haham, by which he is known. His Responsa collection was published in Amsterdam in 1712.

His best-known Responsum[64] is in reply to a query from the Sephardi community in London. The Haham of London, David Nieto, preached an anti-Deist sermon on 20 November 1703 in which he expounded the view that God and Nature are the same.

---

[63] See p. 102 above

[64] No. 18, pp. 23a–d (given incorrectly in table of contents as no. 26). On this Responsum see especially Jakob J. Petuchowski, *The Theology of Haham David Nieto*

Nieto, refuting the Deists, declared that the view which sees Nature as an intermediary between God and the world is contrary to the Jewish faith. The word 'Nature' is a modern term for which the ancient Rabbis used the name 'God'. Nieto's congregation understood this to be a distinct leaning towards pantheism, as taught by Spinoza, and Haham Zevi was asked for his opinion. He sided with Nieto. For Spinoza, God is the name given to the totality of things, whereas in the Jewish view as stated by Nieto, God created Nature and He governs the world. He is transcendent as well as immanent. On the contrary, declares Haham Zevi, it is those who seek for the mediation of Nature who are likely to fall into error, whereas those who believe in the direct action of God's providence in all things are secure wherever they turn. Nieto rightly said that it is God who causes the winds to blow and who brings down the rain and the dew. All that Nieto is saying— and in this he is quite right—is that everything attributed by modern thinkers to Nature is due to the action of God.

A curious Responsum[65] of Haham Zevi is not in reply to a question put to him, but is a discussion of a problem he had set himself. There was a tradition in his family that by means of the divine name his grandfather, the Saint, Elijah of Chelm,[66] had created a Golem (a figure in human form) from clay. The Talmud[67] testifies to a Rabbi who created a man by means of the Book of Creation. Haham Zevi's problem is whether such a Golem can be counted in the quorum of ten required for public prayer. On the one hand, ten Jews are required, and the Golem is not a Jew. But, on the other, the Rabbis say that an adopted child is counted as a natural child[68] and also[69] that the offpsring of a righteous man are his deeds; so that the Golem, created by the act of Elijah, might be counted as his offspring. The Rabbi who created the man by means of the Book of Creation, we are told, later destroyed the man. This evidently was not considered to be an act of murder, which applies only to a man born of woman. But if the Golem could have served such a useful function as to

---

[65] No. 93, p. 81b
[66] See G. Scholem, *On the Kabbalah and its Symbolism*, pp. 158 f.
[67] Sanh. 65b   [68] Sanh. 19b   [69] Gen. R. 30: 6

help form the quorum for prayer, the Rabbi would surely not have destroyed him. He would have kept him alive to be counted when needed for this purpose. From which, Haham Zevi clinches the argument: it follows that the Golem cannot be counted.

In a Responsum[70] on the much-discussed problem of how to behave when the law as recorded in the Codes conflicts with the practice as advised by the Kabbalah, Haham Zevi considers whether it is better to skip parts of the service, when one has arrived late in the synagogue, so as to say the main prayer together with the congregation, as the Codes rule, or whether it is better to follow the *Zohar*, which sets great store by proceeding from stage to stage and not skipping over any of the prayers. Haham Zevi refers to the Responsum of *Radbaz*,[71] who rules that where the Kabbalah and the Codes disagree, we must follow the Codes. Haham Zevi is very conscious of the antinomianism of the Shabbateans influenced by the Kabbalah when he remarks that the *Zohar* is a very difficult book to decipher. If it is to be allowed to depart from the Codes in obedience to what one imagines to be the meaning of the *Zohar*, then 'the foundation of the Torah is destroyed'. We have seen, he concludes, how many have set the Torah at naught because of their claim to follow the *Zohar*.

[70] No. 36, p. 34   [71] See pp. 122–3 above

CHAPTER IX

The Eighteenth Century

Jacob Emden (1697–1776), son of Haham Zevi Ashkenazi, deals in his Responsa collection *Sheelat Yaavetz* with two questions of a theological nature, both also considered by his father.

The first[1] concerns the problem of which to follow when the Kabbalah is in conflict with the law as laid down in the Codes. The Talmud[2] states that the bed should be placed 'between north and south' and the Codes[3] understand this to mean that the head of the bed should face north and the foot south. But the Kabbalists say that the bed should lie from east to west. Rumour has it, observes the questioner, that Haham Zevi used to follow the Kabbalists in the matter of placing the bed, and yet he himself, in the above-mentioned Responsum,[4] rules that where there is conflict between the Codes and the Kabbalah one should follow the former. Emden's reply from Amsterdam, dated 1728, elaborates on the reason for the preference of the Codes to the Kabbalah. Emden was himself a Kabbalist of note, although critical of some of the Kabbalistic assumptions—e.g. that the whole of the *Zohar* was composed by R. Simeon b. Yohai. Like his father, he was extremely hostile to the way certain Kabbalistic ideas had been developed by the Shabbateans. Emden declares that both the

[1] Part I, no. 47   [2] Ber. 5b
[3] Maimonides, *Yad*, Bet Ha-Behirah 7: 9; *Shulhan Arukh*, OH 3: 6 and 240: 17
[4] P. 171 above

Codes and the Kabbalah are 'the words of the living God', but that the Codes, being later than the Kabbalah, knew of the Kabbalistic rulings and yet consciously departed from them at times. In all such instances the norm is to follow the later authorities, on the analogy of a Baraita which was not taught in the official schools of R. Hiyya and R. Hoshea in Talmudic times. Emden adds that where the Talmud disagrees with the Kabbalah it is not because the Talmud rejects all mystical reasons but rather because the Talmud has mystical reasons of its own, which it does not see fit to disclose. However, where the wording of a Talmudic passage is none too clear, one is justified in following the Kabbalah and in interpreting the Talmudic passage so as to accord with it. In this particular passage, the meaning is that the width, not the length, of the bed should be from north to south. The Talmud, in fact, agrees with the Kabbalah that the head of the bed should face east. The reason is so that when a man goes to bed he should bow to the Shekhinah, which is in the west. Emden then offers a novel Kabbalistic interpretation of his own. Abba Benjamin, in the Talmudic passage referred to, states that if a man places his bed in this way he will be blessed with male children. Now the term 'north' represents the 'female side', hinting at the 'female waters' which man's virtuous deeds provide for the Shekhinah, the Sefirah *Malkhut*, which She requires for the 'sacred marriage' in which She is united with *Tiferet*. The Rabbis say[5] that where the woman 'emits seed' before the man, the child will be a boy, hence Abba Benjamin's promise of this particular reward. The placing of the bed is really a euphemism for the marital act.

In the second Responsum,[6] Emden deals with the question of the Golem. He refers to his father's Responsum[7] on the subject and concludes that since a minor or an imbecile cannot be counted in the quorum for prayer, it goes without saying that a senseless Golem cannot be counted.

Ezekiel Landau (1713–93), Rabbi of Prague, was one of the most prolific writers of Responsa of all time. These cover every aspect of Jewish life. His Responsa were published in two series under the title *Noda Biyudah*. These still enjoy great authority, and many subsequent Rabbis wrote glosses to them.

One of Landau's Responsa[8] is addressed to the Haham Samuel Palaggi, head of the Sephardi congregation *Adat Yeshurun* in Hamburg. Palaggi had debated with another scholar whether the Tetragrammaton, pronounced *Adonay*, had the accent on the final or on the penultimate syllable. He turned to Landau for a ruling. Landau protests that questions of this kind are not for Rabbis or Hakhamim but for grammarians and Bible scholars.[9] Moreover, he is reluctant to become involved in the dispute since he has no information about the other scholar, and while he has heard of Palaggi, he does not know him personally. Although, Landau remarks, he is no grammarian, yet every schoolboy knows that in the majority of cases the accent is on the final syllable. It is only on the penultimate syllable when the final syllable, cannot, for some reason, take the accent. In the case of the divine name there is no such reason, so it is obvious that the accent should be on the final syllable (which is, in fact, how everyone does pronounce it). However, he adds, the matter is not worth quarrelling over. The Rabbis[10] note that the divine name can even be erased in order to promote peace between husband and wife. The other scholar quotes the practice of the Readers in the synagogue, but it is notorious that Readers, intent only on the melody, frequently adopt the wrong pronunciation of the words. Landau repeats that it is wrong to quarrel over such matters.

A Responsum[11] of Landau concerns the much-discussed question of the penance to be imposed where a fatal accident has occurred. The Responsum is addressed to Laib Lichtenstadt, whom an old man begged to be allowed to become his agent to sell goods on commission. Lichtenstadt warned the man that there was danger in the enterprise, but the man insisted on being sent. Lichtenstadt eventually gave in but, unfortunately, his fears were well founded and the old man lost his life. Lichtenstadt wishes to be advised how to do penance. The question, says Landau, has been

---

8 First series, Orah Hayyim, no. 2
9 Cf. the different approach of Meir of Lublin, p. 154 above
10 Makk. 11a, derived from Num. 5: 23
11 First series, Orah Hayyim, no. 34

discussed in the Responsa of Jacob Weil.[12] Weil's case concerns A who sent B on an errand, and B was killed by bandits, but here the old man virtually compelled Lichtenstadt to appoint him as his agent and he brought it on himself. It is the universal custom for agents to sell goods on commission at fairs. It has never been suggested that the owner of the goods should be held in any way responsible for fatal accidents that might befall the agents. However, since it appears that the Rabbi of Lichtenstadt's community has already imposed a penance, Landau does not wish to countermand the Rabbi's decision. Lichtenstad should fast on a Monday, Thursday, and the following Monday. If he wishes, in addition, to help the victim's heirs financially, so much the better.

Another Responsum on penance[13] is dated 1770 and addressed to a Rabbi whose name is not given, obviously so as to avoid any identification of the sinner. A scholar had sexual relations with a married woman for a period of three years and later he married the woman's daughter. Two questions were put to Landau. 1. What penance is required? 2. Since a married woman who is unfaithful is forbidden to her husband, should the husband be told? Landau discusses the second question at length and comes to the conclusion that the scholar should tell his father-in-law and ask his forgiveness, a decision which, incidentally, proved unacceptable to later authorities[14] who argue that the husband should not be told.

Landau is particularly interesting on the question of penance. He first observes that he has been asked a question it is hard for him to answer, since it is not his habit to render decisions on topics such as this, where the Talmud and Codes are silent. Nowhere in the Talmud do we find a specific number of fasts to be imposed for certain sins. True, fasting as an atonement for sin is found in Scripture, but there is no mention of a specific number of fasts. It is only in the moralistic literature produced in the Middle Ages that we find this notion and, so far as this literature

[12] See pp. 102–3 above   [13] First series, Orah Hayyim, no. 35
[14] See below, p. 237 for the views of Hayyim Halberstam and p. 264 for the views of Joseph Hayyim of Baghdad

is concerned, most of the ideas on penances are 'theories from the belly', one book simply copying what the other says without any foundation. The repentant sinner here is a scholar and he does not require Landau's advice. If he wishes to follow these books, he can read them for himself. Nevertheless, since he knows the man to be a most diligent scholar who is too weak to engage over-much in fasting, Landau is prepared to discuss the penance to be imposed.

The *Rokeah*[15] speaks of *teshuvat ha-mishkal*, 'balance repent-ance'—i.e. severe penances for each sin in order to cancel it out. The *Rokeah*'s words are 'words of tradition' and should ideally be followed, but the penances of *Rokeah* involve prolonged fasts for each individual sinful act. This man, who sinned for a period of three years, could not satisfy the requirements of the *Rokeah* even should he live as long as Methuselah. Various Kabbalistic books, which, says Landau, he has read in his youth, have different schemes, but, in any event, fasting is only secondary. Repentance chiefly involves giving up the sin, confessing it with a broken heart and turning to the love of God. The *Rokeah*'s prescriptions are not an end in themselves. They are no more than a means of bringing home to the sinner how grievous was his offence. Therefore, says Landau, he is always lenient with regard to fasting as a penance where a scholar, who can 'slaughter his evil inclina-tion with the sword of the Torah', is concerned. For all that, this man cannot be let off scot free. The study of the Torah is the best means for finding atonement, but he should study solid subjects; for instance, the Mishnah together with the Commentary *Tosafot Yom Tov*, which should be studied in depth, and the Talmud, the Codes and the Bible. He should also study the following moral-istic works: Bahya's *Duties of the Heart*, omitting the opening, purely philosophical chapter; the *Shelah* of Isaiah Horowitz, where he does not speak of the Kabbalah; and the section on repentance in Maimonides' Code. He should recite Psalms regu-larly, for there is no better way of setting the heart aflame with the love of God. The more recent prayers should be avoided. One cannot improve on David. The man should rise at midnight to

[15] See pp. 101-2 above

mourn the destruction of the Temple. In midsummer, when it is so hot, he should not fast, but otherwise he should fast once a week. During the month of Elul he should fast two or three times a week and every day of the Ten Days of Penitence. After three years, he can relax a little, provided that he rises each night to study the Torah. He should avoid all frivolity and jesting, keeping his eyes on the ground and never gazing at women. During the three years he should not drink wine, except on the night when he intends to have marital relations. Landau says that he refuses to dictate as a penance any abstention from a normal sex life, since the scholar has obligations towards his wife and, in any event, this depends on individual temperament. He should work it out for himself, preserving a balance but never erring on the side of severity. The Rabbis say[16] in connection with sex, the left hand should reject but the right hand should bring near. The scholar is a wealthy man, so he should give much alms. A good way of doing this would be to work out the number of fasts demanded by the *Rokeah* and give a proportionate amount in charity—i.e. a number of coins for the number of fasts due. God will them forgive him and his sins will be no more.

A famous Responsum[17] contains a polemic against the Hasidic movement, which began to gain ground in Landau's day. Dated 1776, it is addressed to Rabbi Baer of Kojetein in Moravia. The Hasidim had adopted the practice, referred to by the Kabbalists, of reciting before the performance of a religious duty the mystical formula: 'For the sake of the unification of the Holy One, blessed be He, and His Shekhinah' (*le-shem yihud*). We have seen[18] how Jair Hayyim Bacharach admits his ignorance of the meaning of this formula.

The first part of Landau's Responsum reads:

With regard to the fourth question you have asked regarding the formula *le-shem yihud*, which has only recently become popular and has found its way into the prayer-books, behold, in this connection I say: Rather than ask me the correct formula to be recited, you should

[16] Sot. 47a
[17] First series, Yoreh Deah, no. 93. I have treated this Responsum at length in my *Hasidic Prayer*, pp. 140–53
[18] P. 162 above

have asked whether it should be recited at all. In my opinion this is the grievous evil of our generation. To the generations before ours, who knew not of this formula and never recited it but laboured all their day at the Torah and the precepts, all in accordance with the Talmud and the Codes, whose words flow from the spring of living waters, the verse can be applied: 'The integrity of the upright shall guide them' (Prov. 11 : 3). They are those who produced fruit on high and whose love was higher than the heavens. But in this generation they have forsaken the spring of living waters, namely, the two Talmuds, Babylonian and Palestinian, to hew out for themselves broken cisterns. They exalt themselves in their arrogant heart, each one saying: 'I am the seer. To me are the gates of Heaven open. Through my merit does the world endure.' These are the destroyers of the generation. To this orphaned generation I apply the verse: 'The ways of the Lord are right, and the just do walk in them: but the Hasidim (instead of "transgressors") do stumble therein' (Hos. 14 : 10). There is much for me to say in this connection, just as it is a duty to speak if the people will listen . . .[19] May God have mercy on us.

The Hasidic reply was not long in forthcoming in the work *Shaar Ha-Tefillah* by R. Hayyim of Tchernowitz,[20] who takes Landau to task and defends both the Hasidic masters and the formula they adopted. Behind the debate are strong echoes of the conflict between the Rabbinic authorities and the adherents of Shabbetai Zevi, who based many of their ideas on precisely those contained in the formula. Crypto-Shabbateans were particularly active in Prague in Landau's day.

A Responsum[21] dated 1778 is in reply to a query from London. A *kohen* married an Indian woman according to Hindu rites which, the report has it, involves entering a Hindu temple and bowing down there. The *kohen* later divorced his wife and did penance. He now wishes to avail himself of the rights of a *kohen* to give the priestly blessing in the synagogue. Can he be allowed to do so? Landau replies that the questioner has already quoted the ruling in the *Shulhan Arukh*[22] that a *kohen* who had served

[19] 'So it is a duty not to speak when people will not listen', Yev. 65b
[20] First ed., Sudlikov, 1813, Responsum printed at the beginning of the book, pp. 3–10
[21] Second series, Orah Hayyim, no. 10
[22] OH 128: 37, quoting two opinions

idols can deliver the priestly blessing once he has repented. And even according to Maimonides[23] who rules otherwise, this man did not change his religious affiliation. All he did was to commit the sin of mentioning the name of a pagan god. Even if, in fact, he acknowledged the Hindu gods during the marriage ceremony, it was not because he believed in them. He simply went through the motions in order to please his wife who would not otherwise have married him. The proof of this is that even after the marriage he continued to be a practising Jew. He can certainly be allowed to recite the priestly blessing and, like any other *kohen*, is entitled to be called up first to the reading of the Torah.

Dated 1787 and addressed to the community of Trieste, there is a Responsum[24] on whether it is permitted to build a synagogue with an octagonal shape. Landau replies that there are no rules regarding the shape a synagogue has to have. It can be built in any form one desires. But Landau concludes:

> All this I have said in accordance with the strict letter of the law. But I wonder why they should wish to do this. Perhaps they saw something like it in the palaces of princes or in some other houses and wished to copy it. But the truth is that it is not proper for us in our exile to copy princes and be envious of them. If this was the reason, then I apply the verse: 'And Israel hath forgotten his Maker, and builded palaces' (Hos. 8 : 14). It is better, therefore, not to change any of the old customs, especially in this generation. But if their reason was that there would be more room if the synagogue was built according to these specifications, there is not the slightest fear of an objection. I have to cut short this discussion because I am very busy.

Landau returns to the problem of the Kabbalah in a Responsum[25] in his second series, dated 1780. The questioner remarks that people recite the formula: 'For the sake of the unification of the Holy One, blessed be He, and His Shekhinah', and in the moralistic works we find references to mourning for the exile of the Shekhinah. What is the Shekhinah? Landau first takes his questioner to task for discussing the question at length and so

---

[23] *Yad*, Tefillah 15: 3, cf. p. 36 above
[24] Second series, Orah Hayyim, no. 18. I have treated this Responsum at length in *Jewish Law*, pp. 197–203
[25] Orah Hayyim, no. 107

offending against the Rabbinic injunction[26] not to inquire about things too marvellous for us. It is impossible, he says, adequately to reveal the mystery contained here. Nevertheless, he promises to say something acceptable. So far as the *le-shem yihud* formula is concerned, he refers to his earlier discussion of the question. The formula is found in neither the Babylonian nor the Palestinian Talmud. Who gave permission for this formula to be recited? The earlier generations who knew nothing of it were far better off. However, the term 'Shekhinah' is mentioned frequently in the Talmud and there are references there, too, to the exile of the Shekhinah. Some explanation is therefore required. Landau refers to Maimonides' discussion of the term in his *Guide of the Perplexed.*[27] According to Maimonides, the root *shakhan* means 'to dwell', not only in the literal sense but also figuratively in the sense of permanent attachment, so that the term can be used in non-spatial contexts. Therefore, the term 'Shekhinah' has to be understood either as special spiritual light, created to denote God's indwelling, or as God's special providence. When Israel does God's will, His special providence extends to them and, through them, to all mankind. This is the meaning of the Shekhinah resting upon Israel. But now, because of our sins, we have been exiled from our land so that God's providence is directed mainly to the nations. Instead of their receiving through us we now receive from them. Hence the Shekhinah is said to be in exile.

In another Responsum,[28] dated 1779, Landau replies to the question whether it is permitted, in times of great drought, to take a scroll of the Torah to the cemetery in order to pray there for rain. Opinions are divided. Some advocate the procedure, basing themselves on the *Zohar*,[29] since, as a result, the Patriarchs in Heaven are informed by the dead in the cemetery of the fate of their children on earth and they will pray for them. Those who oppose the practice point to the law against taking a scroll into the cemetery. Landau states that both sides are in error. The *Zohar* does not say what it is reported to say and the law, as found in the

[26] Hag. 13a, quoting Ben Sira
[28] Second series, Orah Hayyim no. 109
[27] I, 25
[29] *Zohar* III, 71a

Talmud, does not forbid the taking of a scroll to the cemetery. The Talmud[30] forbids *reading* the Torah in a cemetery only because it is an offence against the dead, who are mocked in that they are reminded that they can no longer read out of the Torah. Landau refers to the Codes on this matter,[31] and is uncertain whether or not they would forbid it. As for the *Zohar*, Landau states that he has no knowledge of the secret things. He would be perfectly content if he did his duty adequately in studying the Talmud and the Codes, 'for they are our life, and in them will we meditate day and night.' What the *Zohar* does say is that there is danger in the scroll being taken to the cemetery if the scroll is deficient in even a single letter. Since we are no longer certain that our scrolls are accurate with regard to all the letters,[32] God forbid that the practice should be followed. Prayers can be offered without a scroll. If they are offered with tears and a broken heart, God will not despise them, for it is the heart that He desires.

Finally, Landau has a Responsum[33] on hunting animals for sport. He declares that he cannot see how a Jew can permit himself to be cruel to animals purely for his own pleasure. We are allowed to kill animals only for food or for the satisfaction of other basic human needs, and it is also permitted to kill wild animals when they invade places inhabited by men. But to hunt them out in their lairs, where God has placed them, is categorically forbidden. It is a serious offence to cause any unnecessary pain to one of God's creatures.

Joseph Ergas (1685–1730), Talmudist and Kabbalist, Rabbi of Leghorn, is noted for his work on the Kabbalah *Shomer Emunim*. His disciple Malachi Ha-Kohen published Ergas's Responsa collection entitled *Divre Yosef*, which contains a number of theological interest, in 1742 in Leghorn.

A number of these[34] contain the discussion by Ergas and other

[30] Ber. 18a
[31] *Kesef Mishneh* to Evel 14: 13; and to *Yad*, Sefer Torah 10: 6; *Shulhan Arukh*, YD 367: 2 and 282: 4
[32] Landau quotes Isserles' note to Orah Hayyim 143: 4
[33] Second series, Yoreh Deah, no. 10. This Responsum has been treated at length by Solomon B. Freehof, *A Treasury of Responsa*, pp. 216–23
[34] Nos 1, 2, 3, 4 and 5

Rabbis on the custom at Leghorn on Rosh Ha-Shanah and Yom Kippur of reciting the words *el hai*, 'living God', after the words *elohim hayyim*, 'God of life', in the additional phrase: 'Remember us for life...' The ordinary people insisted on retaining the practice of saying these words, which had been printed in the prayer-books, but the scholars objected to it. In the year 1715, Ergas was asked for his opinion.

Ergas begins with the observation that both the Codes and the Kabbalists disagree among themselves as to whether 'living God' should be said. The *Tur*[35] rules that it should not be said, whereas Abudraham[36] rules that it should. Similarly, Joseph Ibn Gikatila[37] rules that it should be said, but Luria and the later Kabbalists rule that it should not.[38] Ergas finds the argument of the *Tur* more convincing and it is supported by Luria. Interestingly, Ergas applies to the Kabbalists the Halakhic rule that one follows the later authorities[39] especially, he says, since Luria is both later in time and greater in spiritual rank. Furthermore, even if the matter can be said to be in doubt, since the authorities do disagree, it should not be said for the following reason: 'God of life' implies that God gives life, whereas 'living God' refers only to God as living but says nothing about Him giving life to His creatures. Consequently, after having voiced the higher and more comprehensive form of praise, it is wrong to go on to voice the lower and less comprehensive. It is as if one praised a king by first calling him a king and then referring to him as a duke. As for the question of changing an established custom, Ergas observes that this only applies to a custom based on some sound religious principle. But where an ancient custom is unreasonable, it can and should be abolished. Jews are not obliged to follow every practice that has come down from the past, only those that were introduced on sound religious principles or were for the protection of the law.

Ergas also adds the objection that since the matter concerned the practice in Leghorn it might be argued that the sages of Leghorn, who did not say it themselves, were biased in their ruling. Consequently, he decided to consult the Rabbis of Smyrna,

---

[35] OH 582   [36] P. 53   [37] Quoted by *Bet Yosef, ad loc.*
[38] *Sefer Ha-Kavvanot*   [39] See pp. 130–1 above

Aleppo and Egypt. The second Responsum is that of Benjamin Levi, Rabbi of Smyrna.

Levi agrees entirely with Ergas. Samuel da Modena, quoted by Ergas, has rightly said[40] that a custom without a sound religious basis should not be followed. The custom of saying 'living God' was introduced before the teachings of Luria had been disseminated. But now that we do have them, who dare disagree with 'the great lion'? True, the ruling is that where the Talmud differs from the Kabbalah one must follow the Talmud, but here the Talmud is silent. Even if all the Codes ruled one way and the Kabbalists the other, one should follow the Kabbalah,[41] and certainly so here where the Codifiers disagree on the matter. Here Luria is great enough to have the decisive voice.

The Rabbi of Aleppo also agrees with Ergas (no. 3). It is reported that the ringleader of the opposition spoke slightingly of Luria. For this he deserves to be placed under the ban. Elijah appeared to Luria, and Luria's teachings, like those of the son of Amram, are the very word of God.

Joseph Ha-Levi, Rabbi of Egypt, argues (no. 4) that since the members of the community decided to ask the scholars for their opinion they should abide by this decision. But on the basic question Ha-Levi disagrees with Ergas. Luria intended his rules only for the elite. He had no intention of changing the established customs of the masses, especially in this case where Abudraham and Ibn Gikatila do rule that 'living God' should be said. As for the illustration of the king who is called a duke, the truth is that *elohim hayyim* does not mean 'God who gives life' but 'God of life', and there is thus no decrease of God's praises.

Ergas, in his reply to Ha-Levi (no. 5), says that, of course, we must not compel a congregation to depart from its customs. Ergas agrees that the members of the congregation, in their silent prayers, should continue to say 'living God'. His question concerns the Reader, whose custom was not to say it, and they have no right to compel him to depart from his habit. Ergas is surprised that Ha-Levi did not see this clear distinction. He repeats his contention that a custom has no inherent binding force, and if

[40] Responsa *Maharashdam*, Orah Hayyim, no. 34   [41] See pp. 122–3 above

there is good reason to suppose that its abolition will benefit the cause of religion and if it is based on unsound principles, it can be rejected and a better custom introduced in its stead.

Ergas wrote Responsa on the Kabbalah, published at the end of his *Shomer Emunim*. These deal with pure Kabbalistic theory. But the Responsum (no. 25) considered here was published as part of the general Responsa collection because, although of a Kabbalistic nature, it concerns practice. According to the Talmudic Rabbis, the prohibition of shaving the beard applies only if the beard is shaved with a razor, not if it is shaved with scissors. The Italian Jews generally did shave their beards with scissors and did not let them grow.[42] But the Kabbalists hold that the beard represents the thirteen attributes of mercy and since, according to the Kabbalah, man's body is a mirror of the upper worlds, to shave the beard, even with scissors, is to impede the flow of the divine grace. In the work *Beer Esek* (no. 70) by Shabbetai Beer of Jerusalem, the view is expressed, tentatively, that even the Kabbalists apply their rule only to the holy land. In the Diaspora, it is possible that the Kabbalists would have permitted the shaving of the beard. Ergas was asked for his opinion.

Ergas first observes that the whole question concerns only the practice of the Kabbalists. Anyone who declares that it is forbidden by law to shave the beard with scissors denies the Rabbinic tradition and is thereby guilty of heresy. The truth is that every *mitzvah* has a revealed and a secret aspect. The revealed aspect, the law as found in the Talmud and the Codes, is for those who have not been initiated into the mysteries. The Kabbalists dwell on the secret aspect, as found in the *Zohar* and other Kabbalistic works. Consequently, one who is not thoroughly familiar with the Kabbalah has no right to make such distinctions as that made by Shabbetai Beer, who, as we can judge from his writings, is obviously unfamiliar with the Kabbalistic profundities. Ergas continues:

> It is regarding this that I have been grieved all my life: that a few of the men of our generation leap to study the Kabbalah and anyone who has only a slight acquaintance with the subject boasts of his

42 See pp. 194–5 below on Morpurgo

knowledge, like a coin rattling in an empty jar. These men raise problems, advance solutions and make distinctions so that they frequently go beyonds the boundaries of truth. The cause is their unfamiliarity with this science, which is not accessible to all because there are so few books on the subject—especially those which penetrate to the heart of the matter, for they are only found in manuscript. It is well known that lack of acquaintance with the basic principles is one of the five obstacles to the study of theology, as Maimonides has said in his *Guide of the Perplexed* (I, 34). Therefore, my advice to the skilled in this science is to remain silent, refusing to introduce any novel idea, great or small, unless he is confident of his ability to engage in casuistic reasoning on the basis of established premises.

As for Shabbetai Beer's claim that he has heard a report that the famous Kabbalist R. Menahem Azariah da Fano used to follow the Italian custom of shaving the beard, Ergas says that he asked his teacher in the Kabbalah, Benjamin of Reggio, what he thought of this report. Benjamin replied that, leaving aside the notorious unreliability of Shabbetai Beer's work in matters of law, he, Benjamin, had seen a portrait of Menahem Azariah in Mantua and it shows him as having a full beard. As for the argument that this rule applies only to the holy land, if that were so the duty of eating in tabernacles on Sukkot should also apply only to the holy land, since this *mitzvah*, according to the Kabbalah, causes one to be surrounded by holy light. It is obvious that every *mitzvah*, which is in the nature of personal obligation, applies to all Jews wherever they reside, unlike a *mitzvah* which depends on the soil. Furthermore, the Kabbalists describe the purpose of a negative command to be the thrusting away of the unclean, demonic powers. In that case, there is even more need for this aim to be fulfilled outside the holy land.

Another Responsum (no. 59) of Ergas concerns the verse: 'Two men, one named Eldad and the other Medad, had remained in camp' (Num. 11 : 26). Jonathan b. Uziel's Targum states that these two men were Moses' half-brothers, the sons of Jochebed from a different father. But in that case how could they have been chosen as members of the Sanhedrin, since Maimonides rules[43]

[43] *Yad*, Edut 16

that near relatives cannot serve together on the Sanhedrin? Ergas replies that prophecy had decided that they should serve and, where prophecy ordains, there is an exception to the rule. A woman, for that matter, cannot serve as a judge, and yet Deborah did so because she was a prophetess.

Finally, there is the Responsum (no. 60) of Ergas on intention. The Talmud, at the end of the first chapter of Kiddushin, and the Zohar[44] both state that God does not punish a man merely because he has the intention of sinning. There is no punishment for intention, only for the sinful act. Yet the Rabbis frequently say that there is punishment for such things as lustful thoughts. Ergas says that the distinction is an obvious one. Where the sin is a sin of thought, it is punished like any other sin. But there is no punishment for a mere intention to sin. Of this, he comments, the verse says: 'If I had iniquity in my heart, the Lord will not hear it' (Ps. 66 : 18).

Meir Eisenstadt (d. 1744), so called because in 1714 he was appointed Rabbi of the town of that name, was a widely acknowledged Rabbinic authority and author of the Responsa collection *Panim Meirot*.

Eisenstadt was asked[45] why we say in our prayers: 'The God of Abraham, the God of Isaac, and the God of Jacob' and not simply: 'The God of Abraham, Isaac and Jacob'? Another question was: why is there an 'and' before 'Jacob' and no 'and' before 'Isaac'? He remarks that he will offer a non-esoteric explanation but, he implies, he is not prepared to disclose the Kabbalistic meaning. David instructed Solomon: 'Know the God of thy father and serve Him' (I Chr. 28 : 9). The 'plain meaning' is that a man should not believe in God merely because his father believed in Him, 'for such is the way of the nations'. Each man should rather investigate the matter thoroughly for himself and arrive at his own deep personal conviction that God is. That is why David urged Solomon to *know* the God of his father. Now Abraham, the pioneer of monotheism, arrived at a belief in the One God, although his father was an idolator, by his own personal examination of the evidence which led him to attain complete and utter

---

[44] *Zohar* II, 150b   [45] Part I, no. 39

conviction that there is only One God. If we were to say: 'The God of Abraham, Isaac and Jacob', it would suggest that Isaac and Jacob did not investigate it for themselves but simply relied on Abraham's efforts. As it is, we mean to suggest that each of the Patriarchs discovered God for himself, and this encourages us in our own efforts to acquire a profounder faith in God. As for the 'and' before 'Jacob' and not before 'Isaac', there is a powerful Kabbalistic reason but, says Eisenstadt, we have no concern with the mysteries. He concludes that his explanation of why the word 'God' is mentioned three times is adequate according to the non-esoteric meaning, so that the questioner will now be equipped to reply to the heretics. The significance of this last remark is no doubt that Christological ideas were being read into the threefold mention of 'God'. Eisenstadt turns the tables on these 'heretics' and remarks that, on the contrary, we Jews do not believe merely on the strength of the tradition, as do 'the nations of the world'. We reason it out for ourselves and, when we do, we see that any belief except pure monotheism is false.

In a Responsum[46] on superstitions, Eisenstadt quotes the Talmudic rule[47] that where the purpose is curative the prohibition of 'the ways of the Amorites' does not apply. The case he considers is that of the old wives' tale that as a cure for an infant's insomnia his nail-pairings and a lock of his hair should be placed in an eggshell and hung on a willow. Eisenstadt argues that the Talmud permits curative acts of this kind only when performed by the patient himself. For others to practise magic on a patient's behalf is strictly forbidden.

In another Responsum,[48] Eisenstadt considers the penance to be imposed on a man who fired a gun he was not aware was loaded and killed another. He refers to the Responsum of Isserles[49] on the same subject and rules that a suitable penance is that given in the *Rokeah* for a woman who accidentally smothered her child. The man should confess his sin to his Maker each morning and evening. The anniversary of the fatal accident should be set aside as a day of mourning for him and for his descendants. But no

---

[46] Part I, no. 36   [47] Sabb. 67a
[48] Part I, no. 85   [49] See p. 142 above

stricter penance should be imposed on him, so that sinners will be encouraged to repent. Eisenstadt refers to Isserles' condition that once the penance has been done it is strictly forbidden for anyone to remind the man of the crime that has been committed.

The Talmudic Rabbis frowned on acts of excessive piety performed in public, considering such to be examples of priggishness. Eisenstadt was asked[50] whether this applies to the custom of wearing white garments, the symbol of purity, on the sabbath. He replies that it is the Kabbalists who advocate that only white garments should be worn on the sabbath, but the majority of Jews wear black. Consequently, anyone who wishes to parade his piety by wearing white is to be placed under the ban, unless he is noted for his saintliness. Furthermore, even the Kabbalists only advocate the wearing of white in lands where it is not the norm to wear black. In our lands, for one to wear white when everyone else wears black is to be 'like a bridegroom among mourners',[51] especially 'nowadays' when everyone has the ambition of posing as a great saint. It is far better not to wear white at all; but if his questioner insists on following the Kabbalah, he should put on a white robe only in the privacy of his home, never in public.

Eisenstadt[52] deals with the question of public confession of sin.[53] Is it permitted to confess one's sins in public? He quotes the relevant Talmudic passages[54] from which it emerges that only when everyone already knows of his sin is it permitted for a man to confess in public. Otherwise, the ideal is for a man to be so embarrassed at having sinned that he does not have the effrontery to acquaint others of it. Eisenstadt concludes:

> It follows from what we have said that it is forbidden to confess one's sins in public. Confession should be private, to God alone. The only exception is when a sinner wishes to have imposed on him a suitable penance. In that case he is allowed to confess his sin to a sage, who can advise him which penance to undergo . . . Recently, new sages have come, and they say that a man must confess his sins in public. Their opinion must be allowed to sink into oblivion and must never

50 Part II, no. 152   51 Sabb. 114a
52 Part II, no. 178
53 On this, see A. A. Rapoport, 'Confession in the circle of R. Nahman of Braslav', *Bulletin of the Institute of Jewish Studies*, vol. I, 1973, pp. 65–96
54 Sot. 7b; 32b; Yom. 86b

be repeated. Such an opinion comes from those outside the Jewish faith. May the Lord lead us in the way of truth.

It is just possible that both here and in his Responsum on wearing white on the sabbath Eisenstadt is thinking of the incipient Hasidic movement or, more probably, may be referring to the pre-Hasidic groups of ascetics to be found in his day in many Polish towns.

Eisenstadt is generally lenient in the matter of penances. In the case of a man who for some years had failed to wear the *tefillin* in the proper manner, he rules[55] that remorse is sufficient and no special penance is required.

An interesting question discussed by Eisenstadt[56] is whether it is permitted to raffle a scroll of the Torah in order to raise money for a poor bride's dowry. Those who wished to forbid it argued that it is a disgrace to the Torah when a scroll is raffled. Eisenstadt rules that, on the contrary, it shows that the scroll is precious if people are prepared to spend their money on the tickets even though there is only a remote chance of their winning. Moreover, there is no greater *mitzvah* than to assist a poor girl to marry. He adds that it is the common practice of scribes to write the book of Esther and raffle the scroll, without anyone raising an objection, and they do it for personal gain.

A famous early eighteenth-century legal authority was Jacob Reischer (d. 1733). He was born and studied in Prague, later becoming a Dayyan in his home town, then Rabbi in Ansbach, Worms and Metz. His Responsa collection *Shevut Yaakov* is frequently quoted by later authorities, and he has the following questions of theological interest.

Reischer was asked (no. 4) about the legal status of Siamese twins. The questioner had himself witnessed the phenomenon and had recited the benediction: 'Blessed art Thou who createth diverse forms of creatures.' He wishes to know what the law would have to say if two Jewish children were born attached to one another in this way. Reischer quotes the Talmudic discussion[57] about a child born with two heads, but here the case is different,

---

[55] Part III, no. 9   [56] Part III, no. 43   [57] Men. 37a

since the Siamese twins are two complete human beings. He remarks that there is nothing new under the sun, since the Rabbis[58] tell us that Adam and Eve were at first joined together until God separated them. Therefore, he rules that each one has to put on his *tefillin* and that each inherits a share in his father's estate. They may not marry, however, for two reasons. The unmarried twin would be guilty of sleeping with a married woman and the married twin of performing the marital act in the presence of another. For this latter reason it would be forbidden for a man to marry a girl who was a Siamese twin. A man whose wife has given birth to Siamese twins has fulfilled the obligation to be fruitful and multiply (which obligation is fulfilled only when at least two children are born to him), since Adam and Eve, though originally joined together, were considered to be two separate persons. Reischer concludes with the prayer: 'But may God deliver us from all strange and ugly creatures.'

Reischer was friendly with the well-known Talmudist Moses Hagiz (1672–1751). A Responsum to Hagiz (no. 11) concerns a case that had presented itself to him when he was in Amsterdam in 1697 for the purpose of having his book *Leket Ha-Kemah* printed there. A congregation had placed a ban on anyone who raised his voice during the synagogue service. A heard B insulting the Talmudic sages during the service and A raised his voice in order to drown the offending words. B and the rest of the congregation wanted to impose a fine upon A, but Hagiz sided with A. What is Reischer's opinion? Reischer replies that a great scholar like Hagiz hardly requires the support of other Rabbis. But it is clear that the original intention of the congregational rule was only for the promotion of decorum in the service and was obviously not intended to cover an exceptional case such as this. But even if it were, it should be ignored, out of respect for the Talmudic sages. If the Talmud can say[59] that, where there is a profanation of God's name, respect for a Rabbi can be disregarded, it follows that where, as in this instance, there is a profanation of God's name, the respect due to a synagogue should be disregarded *a fortiori*, since, according to Judaism, a scholar possesses a greater degree of sanctity, and

[58] Ber. 61a   [59] Ber. 19b

should be treated with greater respect, than a synagogue. Reischer quotes in this connection the Talmudic saying:[60] 'How stupid are people who stand up when a scroll of the Torah is carried before them and yet fail to stand when a scholar passes by.'

Ben Zion b. Moses Wengroff asked Reischer (no. 91) a number of non-legal questions. One of these is on the law (Num. 19 : 12) that one who has been in contact with a corpse has to be sprinkled with the waters of purification on the third day and on the seventh day. The commentators ask why the sprinkling has to take place on two days and advance the following reason. For all we know to the contrary, the corpse may have been that of a saint. If that is the case, then the corpse does not contaminate, in which case the man who touched the corpse requires no purification. Now the rule is that if the sprinkling is done for a man who does not need it because he is clean, then he becomes unclean by virtue of the sprinkling itself. Consequently, the sprinkling on the seventh day is for the purpose of purifying him from the sprinkling on the third day—if the corpse was that of a saint, as it may have been, for all we know to the contrary. But Ben Zion asks Reischer: in that case, why not say that the corpse may have been that of a sinner and so does contaminate. Then the sprinkling on the third day is essential but that sprinkling of the seventh day is unnecessary and would therefore render the man unclean. Reischer replies that there is an obvious difference between one contaminated by a corpse and one contaminated by an unnecessary sprinkling. Contact with a corpse brings a seven-day period of contamination, while an unnecessary sprinkling brings only a one-day period of contamination. Consequently, if the corpse were that of a sinner, the persons coming into contact with it would become contaminated for seven days and this would be removed by the sprinkling on the seventh day. If, on the other hand, the corpse were that of a saint, the only contamination would be that caused by the unnecessary sprinkling on the third day. This would last for a day or until the next sprinkling took place, hence the sprinkling on the seventh day.

Another Aggadic question in the same Responsum concerns the

[60] Makk. 20b

reason given in the Midrash[61] for Moses not eating or drinking during the forty days he was on the mount. The Midrash asks: How can a human being exist without food for forty days? The answer given there is: When in a town, behave as its inhabitants do—i.e. Moses in Heaven behaved as the angels do. Ben Zion was puzzled. How can the idea of conforming to the practices of a place be relevant? If, as the Midrash accepts in the question, it is axiomatic that a human being cannot live for forty days without food and drink, how does it solve the problem by saying that Moses had to conform to the practice of the angels? This is precisely the question, how, as a human being, could he have conformed to them? Reischer says that the meaning of the Midrash is that a special miracle was performed for Moses for the sake of conformity. Or, suggests Reischer in what he calls a 'playful way', not to be taken too seriously, the Midrash means that a human being cannot live without food or drink for forty days, and yet Moses did so. It can only be that from the time of his ascent Moses was no longer a human being but an angel. In that case, the Midrash asks, why did Moses eat and drink *after he had returned to earth*? And to this the Midrash gives the reply that it was in order to conform to the custom on earth.

Finally, Reischer (no. 140) was asked about the law recorded in the *Shulhan Arukh*[62] that a sage under the age of forty should not render decisions in Jewish law. Does this apply only to religious law or also to judges in a civil case? Reischer points to the source of this ruling in the Talmud,[63] but notes that the *Tur* is contradictory, in one place[64] stating explicitly that the rule applies to civil cases as well, yet in another place[65] stating that a scholar can act as a judge in civil cases from the age of thirteen. Reischer rules that a scholar under forty can act as a judge, provided he acts together with two other judges.

The Italian Rabbi Samson Morpurgo (1681–1740) was a pupil of Samuel Aboab in Venice and studied medicine in Padua. He became Rabbi of Mantua in 1721, in which capacity he served

---

[61] Quoting *Yalkut*, Ki Tissa, 406; but here it is not in the form Reischer put it, but as in Exod. R. 47: 5

[62] YD 242: 31, Isserles' note
[63] AZ 19b, see p. 137 above
[64] Hoshen Mishpat 10, by implication
[65] Hoshen Mishpat 7

until his death, at the same time winning renown among both Jews and Gentiles as a physician. Morpurgo's Responsa collection *Shemesh Tzedakah* was published and annotated by his son Moses Hayyim in Venice in 1743.

Since the Middle Ages there had been a debate on whether the *tefillin* are to be worn on the intermediate days of festivals, *Hol Ha-Moed*. The *Zohar* is very strict against wearing them, and so treating *Hol Ha-Moed* as if it were an ordinary weekday when the *tefillin* are worn. But the Ashkenazi practice is to wear the *tefillin*[66] on *Hol Ha-Moed*. The question addressed to Morpurgo[67] is whether an Ashkenazi congregation is allowed to depart from the Ashkenazi custom in order to follow the *Zohar*. Morpurgo replies in the negative. He himself, he remarks, is of Ashkenazi stock and though he does not wear the *tefillin* in the synagogue on *Hol Ha-Moed*, since he serves in a congregation in which they are not worn on that day, yet he never departs from the Ashkenazi custom in the privacy of his home. As for the views of R. Simeon b. Yohai, the author of the *Zohar*, Solomon Luria in a Responsum[68] has declared that we must not follow this sage and depart from the Ashkenazi custom. Morpurgo adds that although he has no knowledge of the Kabbalah he has a profound respect for the Kabbalists. But they should carry out practices based on the Kabbalah in the privacy of their homes and not flaunt themselves by altering established customs. Morpurgo also quotes the Responsum of *Radbaz*[69] on the scribe who altered the scrolls so as to accord with the teachings of the Kabbalah. There is appended[70] a lengthy decision of other Italian Rabbis who agree with Morpurgo.

A question addressed to Morpurgo[71] from Trieste, dated 1722, concerns the prayer: 'O angels of mercy, bring our supplications for mercy before the Lord of mercy.' Two scholars in Trieste debated whether the prayer should be abolished, one suggesting that it is offensive to pray to angels, the other seeing no harm in it.[72] Morpurgo states that both views can find support among earlier authorities. As long as we believe that all power is God's,

[66] See *Shulhan Arukh*, OH 31: 2, and H. J. Zimmels, *Ashkenazim and Sephardim*, pp. 30–1, 113
[67] Orah Hayyim, no. 4   [68] See p. 139 above   [69] Pp. 124–5 above
[70] After no. 15, pp. 26–8   [71] Orah Hayyim, no. 23   [72] See pp. 10–11 above

what harm can there be in asking the angels to intercede for us? Morpurgo remarks, in the name of his teacher Samuel Aboab, that the heading to the section in the *Shulhan Arukh*[73] which declares that the Ashkenazi custom of *Kapparot* on the eve of Yom Kippur is 'stupid' was added by the publisher, and that Karo, the author of the *Shulhan Arukh*, was not responsible for it. True, Karo holds that the *Kapparot* custom should not be followed, but this great sage would never have called 'stupid' a custom practised by the Ashkenazim. The prayer: 'O angels of mercy' is also a long-established Ashkenazi custom and one must be very cautious in criticising it. For all that, adds Morpurgo, the motives of those who protest are worthy since, to them, the invocation appears to border on angel worship. In a further Responsum[74] on the same subject, dated 1736, Morpurgo comments that he has been a student of the Torah all his life, yet has never once questioned the customs of the giants of former ages. In matters higher than nature he is content to be one who knows that he does not know.

Another question[75] on local custom and the Kabbalah was addressed to Morpurgo from the Italian Jews who lived in Salonika. These Jews followed the general Italian custom of not wearing a beard even though the Kabbalah urges that a beard be worn. The Turkish Jews, however, led by the Rabbi of Salonika, threatened to expel the Italians from the community unless they let their beards grow. Morpurgo, in dealing with the question, remarks that he wishes, at the same time, to consider, speaking ironically, whether a man can go to Heaven even if he is unfamiliar with the Kabbalah. Morpurgo demonstrates that there is no legal objection to a Jew being clean shaven. He appeals to the Turkish Jews to be more tolerant. On the more general question of practices based on the Kabbalah, he is insistent that no one can be blamed for his ignorance of the Kabbalah. On the contrary, the real danger to faith lies in the study of the Kabbalah by the immature. He quotes the Responsa of Jair Hayyim Bacharach[76] and Levi Ibn Habib.[77] How dare anyone suggest that the All-

---

[73] OH 602   [74] Orah Hayyim, no. 24

[75] Yoreh Deah, no. 61. This Responsum has been treated at length by Freehof, op. cit., pp. 190–5

[76] Pp. 160–3 above   [77] Pp. 143–4 above

merciful will shut the doors of Heaven in the face of good, observant Jews merely because of their ignorance of the Kabbalah? According to sound Jewish teaching, the righteous Gentiles have a share in the World to Come and these obviously have no knowledge of the Kabbalah. Some of the greatest Jews of the past, who spent all their lives in the study of the Torah and in the practice of the precepts, knew no Kabbalah. Dare we suggest for one moment that God will condemn them for being modest enough not to explore realms too marvellous for them?

We saw above[78] that Ezekiel Landau deals with the question of hunting for sport. Morpurgo, too, has a Responsum[79] on the subject, dated 1735. He quotes Maimonides[80] to the effect that the reason for all the laws regarding how an animal is to be slaughtered for food—such as that the knife must not have a single notch—is to avoid causing the animal more pain than is absolutely necessary. What greater pain can there be to a bird than to be filled full of lead? If we are even instructed to execute criminals in as painless a manner as possible,[81] how can we be so cruel as to slay innocent creatures painfully and to no purpose? According to the opinion the Talmud accepts,[82] it is a Biblical prohibition to cause pain to animals. Even so great a saint as Rabbi Judah the Prince[83] was punished by having sufferings brought upon him because he said to a calf about to be slaughtered, 'Go! For this you were created.' Even if those who engage in this pastime argue that birds feel no pain when they are shot, and even if such a highly dubious position is accepted, they ought to consider the indignities imposed on God's creatures and the prohibition of wantonly destroying anything in nature. The Talmudic Rabbis[84] call attendance at the circus where wild beasts are tortured, sitting in 'the seat of the scornful' (Ps. 1 : 1). Morpurgo also quotes the teaching of the Kabbalah that an animal has to find its elevation through being killed by the act of *shehitah*, the ritual manner of killing birds and animals for food. Birds deprived of their lives in any other way are denied their 'elevation'. Why do these men forsake the way

---

[78] P. 181 above   [79] Yoreh Deah, no. 18   [80] *Guide of the Perplexed*, III, 48
[81] Ket. 37b   [82] BM 33a   [83] BM 85a
[84] AZ 18b

of their father Jacob to follow the way of his wicked brother Esau, the hunter?

In another Responsum,[85] Morpurgo deals with the old question of how far the Jewish courts should be lenient with offenders in fear that a strict attitude might tempt them to leave the Jewish fold. The particular question came from Venice and concerned a loose woman with four children. It is almost certain that if the Jewish court attempts to punish her and proclaim her immoral life to all, she will leave the Jewish fold, taking her innocent children with her. Should the court, none the less, place her under the ban, or should they turn a blind eye? Morpurgo states that he is lost for a reply. On the one hand, it is essential for the courts to take steps in order to prevent the rot from spreading, but, on the other, the danger of her leaving the fold is real and the fate of innocent children is involved. Morpurgo refers to the very strict attitude adopted by Jair Hayyim Bacharach,[86] and comments:

> To sum up. If the teachers, the judges of the town, notice that the abandoned behaviour of this loose woman causes others to follow her bad example and brings harm to the community as a whole, and there is no other way of preventing it than by placing her under the ban, they should do it forthwith and proclaim to all her sinful deeds. But they should do nothing further in the way of punishment. They must not reject her with both hands by summoning her before their [i.e. the Gentile] courts. For it is enough if we deliver the community from sin and save all we can. If she is stubborn and takes no heed of our rebuke, then let her wear black and cover herself with black and let her do what she desires in her wicked heart; and with the destruction of the wicked there is rejoicing.

Morpurgo concludes with the story of Hezekiah and Isaiah as told in the Talmud.[87] When Hezekiah was rebuked by Isaiah for failing to marry, he replied that he had seen in his prophetic vision that, if he married, the son he would have would be wicked. But Isaiah retorted that it was the duty of Hezekiah to do what he was obliged to do without going into the question of what the future would bring. A man has to do his present duty and not be concerned with 'the secret things of the All-merciful'. By the same

---

[85] Yoreh Deah, no. 48   [86] See pp. 167–8 above   [87] Ber. 10a

token, the court must carry out its present duty and not be deterred by fears of what might happen if they do.

There are two Responsa of a theological nature in the collection *Shav Yaakov* by Jacob Popers (d. 1740), Rabbi of Koblenz, Trier and, from 1718, Frankfort.

Popers[88] discusses the question considered by Jacob Emden[89] on the saying of Abba Benjamin[90] that the bed must be placed 'between north and south'. *Rashi* understands it to mean that the bed must not be placed with its head to the east and its foot to the west, but the Kabbalists hold that this is the position in which the bed should be placed. Popers follows the *Zohar* against *Rashi*. If, he says, *Rashi* (in whose day the *Zohar* was not known) had seen the *Zohar*, he would have interpreted Abba Benjamin's saying so as to accord with the *Zohar*.

In the other Responsum,[91] Popers discusses the practice of a scholar who used to rise very early in the morning to study the Torah for some hours before prayer. May such a man eat and drink before the prayers, since the Kabbalist R. Hayyim Vital calls one who eats or drinks before saying his prayers an idolator? Popers says that Vital's remark is based on the *Zohar*.[92] But the prayer-book of Vital's master, Isaac Luria, permits it to one who is weak. The *Zohar*, in fact, prohibits it only if it is done purely for pleasure, for then power is given to the serpent. The *Zohar* certainly does not prohibit eating and drinking before prayers, where the purpose is to gain strength in order to be able to recite the prayers in a proper frame of mind and with adequate concentration.

Judah Ayash (d. 1760) was head of the court of Algiers from 1728 to 1756, after which he retired to settle in Palestine. His Responsa collection *Bet Yehudah*, published in Leghorn in 1746, contains a number of theological Responsa.

In one of these,[93] Ayash considers the special benediction recited after a deliverance from harm (*ha-gomel*). A little boy of two fell into a well but escaped miraculously without a scratch. Should the boy's father recite the benediction or was it ordained only for

---

[88] Part I, no. 3   [89] Pp. 172–3 above   [90] Ber. 5b
[91] Part I, no. 8   [92] III, 215b   [93] Orah Hayyim, no. 6

personal deliverance from harm? Ayash refers to Abudraham who discusses a similar case and rules, in the name of Gershom b. Solomon, that it is wrong for the father to recite the benediction. But, after discussing the pros and cons, Ayash agrees with those authorities who hold that the benediction should be said, not solely in cases of personal deliverance but also where a man's family or friends have been saved from harm.

A Responsum of Ayash[94] discusses the Talmudic passage[95] in which it is said that the repetition of the Tetragrammaton denoting God's mercy, in Exodus 34 : 6, is to suggest that God is merciful before man sins and merciful even after man has sinned. Asher b. Jehiel asks why mercy is required before a man has sinned, and gives two possible solutions. The first is that although God knows that a man will sin, yet He exercises His attribute of mercy by treating him as innocent until he has actually sinned. Second, the meaning may be that even in connection with idolatry (where the mere intention to worship idols is sinful), God is merciful until the idol has actually been worshipped. True, when that happens there is punishment for the intention as well as for the act, but this punishment for intention is not visited upon a man until he has acted sinfully. Ayash is dissatisfied with all this. According to the first solution, it is still hard to see why mercy should be required, while according to the second solution it is hard to understand in this light the many Rabbinic sayings which suggest that in the case of idolatry there is punishment for the intention, irrespective of whether the act was carried out. Ayash explains it as follows. According to the first solution, the meaning is that God exercises His mercy to such an extent that not only is the man not punished but, until he actually sins, he is treated as a righteous man. According to the second solution, Asher does not mean that God's mercy is always exercised where there is the intention to worship idols, but that it is sometimes exercised.

In a curious Responsum,[96] Ayash takes issue with the well-known opinion of Moses Rivkes (d. *c.* 1671) in his *Beer Ha-Golah* that all the baneful things said about Gentiles in the Talmud and the Codes apply only to Gentiles of the Talmudic period, who

---

[94] Orah Hayyim, no. 56   [95] RH 17b   [96] Yoreh Deah, no. 4

were idolators, not to Christians and Muslims, who do believe in God. Ayash argues that even though these are not idolators, they cannot be considered among the righteous of the nations of the world since they do not keep all the seven precepts of the sons of Noah (1. not to worship idols; 2. not to murder; 3. not to commit adultery; 4. not to be cruel to animals; 5. not to blaspheme; 6. not to steal; 7. to have an adequate system of justice). No doubt this Responsum reflects conditions in Ayash's day in Algiers, when relations between Jews and Gentiles were strained.

In a Responsum on mourning,[97] Ayash takes issue with Samuel Hagiz, author of *Halakhot Ketanot,* on the question of *keria* (rending the garments when a near relative dies). According to Hagiz, *keria* is enjoined in order to provide the mourners with psychological relief. By giving this expression to their emotions, the mourners are prevented from stifling their grief and thus having the dreadful thought of loss constantly on their mind. Ayash disagrees. On the contrary, the purpose of the rite is to awaken the dormant feelings of grief in order to render them more acute. Ayash proves his case from the narrative of the death of Aaron's sons. Aaron and his two remaining sons were ordered not to mourn for the departed and not to rend their garments (Lev. 10 : 5). According to Hagiz, they should have been told to rend their garments. This clearly demonstrates that the purpose of *keria* is not in order to soften the blow but rather to increase the feelings of grief. Ayash concludes that this is the aim of all the rules governing mourning for near relatives. This Responsum should be compared with that of *Radbaz*[98] on the father who shed no tears when his son died.

Ayash disagrees with Samuel Hagiz in another Responsum.[99] Hagiz was doubtful whether the injunction to rise before the aged applies to an old woman. Ayash states that it seems obvious to him that it is age that is being honoured and there is no difference between an old man or an old woman. Furthermore, just as the Rabbis extended the rule to include rising for a scholar, even if he is a young man, the same rule would apply to a woman who is a scholar.

[97] Yoreh Deah, no. 26   [98] See p. 119 above   [99] Yoreh Deah, no. 28

In a Responsum[100] from Algiers dated 1745, Ayash discusses the case of a man whose dearly beloved brother died far from home in a small village. The brother arrived too late for the funeral and was grief-stricken that the burial had already taken place, since it had been his intention to take the corpse back home with him to be buried in the family plot. The brother became so distressed that he had the body removed from its grave and took it back home with him, which created a scandal. Now the brother expresses remorse and wishes to do penance. What penances should be imposed on him? Ayash first lists in detail the various offences of which the brother had been guilty in doing this terrible thing, among them the offence of causing disgrace to a corpse. He should be given eighty lashes, preferably in the presence of ten ordinary persons or three scholars, and he should fast. Then will his sin be forgiven and he will find pardon.

Ayash[101] was asked whether a poor, starving man is allowed to steal food in order to keep body and soul together. Ayash is reluctant to give an out-and-out dispensation but states, none the less, that a man may commit a sin or a crime in order to save his life, and there is no reason for supposing that the sin of stealing is any exception. However, it goes without saying that, when he is able to afford it, the thief must return the money he has stolen.

Ayash discusses[102] the case of a bachelor who took an oath that when he married and had a son, that son would be given to God— i.e. to be a permanent student of the Torah. The man eventually married and had a son, but when the boy reached the age of thirteen the father wished to remove him from the school since it had become evident that the boy was not gifted intellectually and would never master the subject. Is the vow binding? Ayash discusses the laws of vows and oaths and comes to the conclusion that for a variety of reasons (e.g. a man cannot commit his son to behave in a certain way and a vow cannot take effect on something that is not yet in existence at the time of the vow), the vow is invalid. But what of Hannah (I Sam. 1) who promised to give the son she would have to God for the whole of his life? Ayash suggests that the case of Hannah was different, since she was barren

[100] Ibid., no. 35   [101] Ibid., no. 47   [102] Ibid., no. 49

and made a bargain with God. There it was as if God had granted her prayer only on condition that her son should minister to Him all the days of his life.

Finally, there is a Responsum[103] dated 1723, concerning a scholar who wished to leave his aged parents in order to study the Torah in Safed in the holy land, but the parents objected and forbade him to leave them. Does the fifth commandment apply here? Ayash comes to the conclusion that since God's honour takes precedence over honouring parents, and since by going to Safed the scholar will fulfil two *mitzvot*, that of Torah study and of settling in the holy land, there is no obligation for him here to obey his parents.

Aryeh Laib Breslau (1741–1809) was Rabbi of Rotterdam from 1781 to his death. His Responsa collection *Pene Aryeh*, published in Amsterdam in 1790, is famed for the author's novel approach, clear logic and interest in philological and theological, as well as in purely Halakhic, questions.

Breslau, in a Responsum addressed to Rabbi Meir Weil (no. 16), discusses the strange saying in tractate Soferim[104] that Abraham was a giant as tall as seventy-four men and he ate and drank at one meal as much as seventy-four men. Abraham built a great city of iron for the sons of Keturah. Its walls were so high that the sun could never enter there. He gave them precious stones for illumination, to be used for that purpose when the sun and moon are ashamed. What is the meaning of this? Breslau refers to the passage in Exodus 24. The seventy-four men referred to in tractate Soferim are the seventy elders mentioned in the Exodus narrative, together with Moses, Aaron, Nadab and Abihu, of whom it is said: 'And they beheld God, and did eat and drink' (Exod. 24 : 11), which refers to their prophetic vision. The meaning is, then, that Abraham was as great in prophecy as these seventy-four, and his 'eating and drinking' was equal to theirs. But the difficulty, then, is how can he be said to have been greater than Moses? The answer to this is that Moses attained the highest degree of prophecy only after he had been on the mount for forty days and nights. The Kabbalists remark that Abraham gave the sons of the

[103] Ibid., no. 54   [104] 20 : 5

concubines 'the wisdom of the sons of the east'. This is the meaning of the great iron city Abraham built. It was an iron barrier to Heaven in that this wisdom is purely human and has nothing in it of the prophetic, divine gifts. But it was higher than the sun—i.e. there was no sun-worshipper among them. The precious stones Abraham gave them are the rules of conduct and the sciences they will use when the sun and moon are ashamed—i.e. when sun and moon worship are no more. Breslau adds: Behold, the majority of nations in our day use them.

In another Responsum (no. 51) to Meir Weil, Breslau discusses the Rabbinic understanding of the verse: 'therefore shall thy camp be holy; that He see no unseemly thing in thee' (Deut. 23 : 15) to mean that it is forbidden to recite the *Shema* when one can see the genitals. The Rabbis extend this to mean[105] that there must be a division between the heart and the genitals, otherwise 'the heart sees the genitals'. Weil asked: How can the heart be said to 'see'? Breslau replies that when two things are uncovered in relation to one another, with no division between them, the sages say, figuratively speaking, that they 'see' one another—for example, when they speak of jars of wine[106] 'seeing' the beams of the ceiling. In the Bible, too, the term 'sight' is used both of the eyes and the heart. Consequently, the genitals must be 'seen' neither by the eyes nor by the heart. When a man recites the *Shema*, his thoughts must be pure, and it is the eyes and the heart that are the main causes of impurity when they are led astray.

In a Responsum (no. 60) addressed to Simeon Boaz, Breslau discusses the various terms used in Scripture for casting lots. For instance Joshua (Josh. 18 : 6) first uses the term *yarah* for casting lots, but then he uses (Josh. 18 : 8) the term *shalakh*. Why the sudden change? Breslau first remarks that three terms are used in Scripture: *yarah*, *shalakh* and *nafal*. *Yarah* means to throw—i.e. at a particular target. *Shalakh* means to cast away—i.e. to get rid of something. That is why this term is used in the verse: 'And cast them into another land' (Deut. 29 : 28), where the meaning is that, because of their sins, God simply wishes to get rid of them, not caring, as it were, where they go as long as it is out of the holy

---

[105] Ber. 25b   [106] Pes. 8b

land. *Nafal* simply means 'to fall down', and this term can be used of falling even where there is no intention for something to fall. Now the lots in Scripture were not stones that were thrown but slips drawn out of a bag. Sometimes the term *nafal* is used of this because the lot takes effect; it 'falls' on something previously having no relation to it. That is why we say that a man's fortune is his 'lot'—i.e. it is the way his destiny 'falls'. It follows from this analysis that for casting lots either *shalakh* or *nafal* should be used, since in these terms there is no necessary suggestion of aiming towards a target. But the term *yarah* is inappropriate for casting lots since the whole purpose is to determine something by chance, without intention. However, the truth is that we Jews do not believe that anything is really by chance. We believe rather that God's providence operates through the casting of lots, as in the verse: 'The lot is cast into the lap; but the whole disposing thereof is of the Lord' (Prov. 16 : 33). In a sense, therefore, the term *yarah* can be used of casting lots since, if seen from the point of view of God, as it were, there is intention as to how the lot should fall. The division of the land by Joshua by means of lots was purely an instance of divine providence, God arranging how the lots should fall. In that case, it might be asked, why have lots at all? Why not simply give each family its share without lots? The answer is that otherwise the people might have suspected Joshua of acting by himself to divide the land unfairly. The purpose of the lots was to demonstrate that God had approved. The verse says: 'The lot causeth strife to cease' (Prov. 18 : 18). Therefore, when Joshua spoke to all the people, he used the term *yarah*, implying, at least for the elders, that divine providence was involved. But when he spoke only to the three men he used the term *shalakh*. There was no need for him here to hint at providence. He was not giving them a lesson in theology, but simply instructing them to get on with their task.

Another Responsum (no. 79) is on the Rabbinic interpretation[107] of the law of levirate marriage (Deut. 25 : 5–10). The Rabbis understand the reference to the 'first-born' as being to the eldest brother of the deceased, though according to the plain

[107] Yev. 20b

meaning the reference is to the first-born child of the levir and the widow. Breslau states that Scripture puts it all in an ambiguous way in order to hint at a topic which Scripture never states explicitly, because there are no explicit references in Scripture to anything having to do with the Hereafter. The mysterious topic hinted at here, when it says that the first-born child will be in the place of the dead brother, is the doctrine of reincarnation—*Gilgul*. The whole purpose of *Gilgul* is for the soul to make good in the new existence that which it failed to make good in its previous existence. But when a man leaves a child who is flesh of his flesh, there is no need for *Gilgul*, since the son can make good any faults of his father. Where the deceased brother left no heir, *Gilgul* is required, but the soul, at least, can enter the body of the child that will be born to his brother whose flesh is near to that of the deceased. Thus the purpose of levirate marriage is to provide a new and suitable body for the reincarnation of the dead brother's soul. Breslau writes:

> Behold, we see and hear that our early teachers, may their souls rest in peace, declare that the belief in *Gilgul* is a true belief. For God does not wish a single soul in Israel to perish and He planned it that no soul be lost but that every soul should enjoy the illumination of the eternal light. As our Rabbis say: 'All Israel has a share in the World to Come.' Apart from the fact that they had this belief by tradition from person to person reaching back to the holy Patriarchs, on whom be peace (and many of the ancient nations of the world shared this belief and, as I have heard, to this day many of the great Christian sages hold this belief) they found it in the divine Torah [in the narrative of Judah and Tamar, Gen. 38].

Breslau concludes, however, that we should not speak too much of such mysteries which are really beyond our understanding.

Finally, there is the Responsum (no. 98) of Breslau to his disciple who had asked him to explain the difference between the two Hebrew names for an enemy—*oyev* and *sone*. Breslau observes that both terms have in common the meaning of negation of love and friendship, but there is a vast difference between them. The *sone* is one who hates another but commits no physical act of harm to him. The *oyev* is the enemy who carries out acts of physical harm against the one he hates. One can therefore be a *sone* even to abstract ideas, one can hate certain ideas. But one cannot be an *oyev* to abstract ideas, since how can one cause these physical harm? That is why David says (Ps. 139 : 21-2):

> Do I not hate them, O Lord, that hate Thee?
> And do not I strive with those that rise
>   up against Thee?
> I hate [*sinah*] them with utmost hatred;
> They were enemies [*oyevim*] to me.

Note that while David hated sinners they were enemies to him, but not he to them. A perfect man like David could never be an *oyev*, wishing to do harm to any human being. That is why the book of Lamentations (2 : 5) says: 'The Lord is become as an enemy' (*oyev*). Note that it does not say that God *was* an enemy, but only *like* an enemy. Even to those who provoke Him, God only appears as an enemy because of the suffering in the universe as it appears to men, yet He can never be called an 'enemy' even to those who provoke Him.

CHAPTER X

The Nineteenth Century

<hr>

In the Responsa written during the nineteenth century are reflected the many tensions in Jewish life produced by the Emancipation. The traditional pattern of Jewish life, already under fire, though not eroded, by the Shabbatean and Frankist movements and by the Mendelssohn school and the rise of Hasidism, came under much heavier attack with the emergence of new movements—Haskalah, Reform and, in the last decades of the century, Zionism. It is not therefore surprising that many of the questions addressed to the foremost Respondents in this century, while concerned with the correct procedure to be adopted, also deal with the defence and interpretation of the Halakhah as a whole. This is why, perhaps more than at any other period, we find an abundance of theological material in these Responsa. The Respondents are not presented in any particular order in this chapter, except that preference is given to those who deal with large numbers of theological topics, Eleazar Fleckeles being considered first because he belongs, in part, to the eighteenth century.

Fleckeles (1754–1826) was born in Prague where he studied under Ezekiel Landau whom he acknowledged all his life as master. After serving for a time as Rabbi of Kojetein, Fleckeles became, in 1783, a member of Landau's Bet Din and eventually the head of the Prague Rabbinate. His collection *Teshuvah Me-Ahavah* contains 450 Responsa.

One of these (no. 8), from Prague in 1791, is addressed to Fleckeles' pupil Mordecai of Kojetein, who wished to know whether it is permitted to intermarry with the Shabbateans and the Frankists and, in the particular case he mentions, is inclined to allow it on the grounds that the girl is very young and has therefore not become accustomed to the ways of the sect. Fleckeles rebukes Mordecai for even entertaining the notion that it is permitted, in some circumstances, to intermarry with the Shabbateans. To allow one's children to marry any of the children of these heretics is to be guilty of giving one's children to Moloch, for all they desire is to convert others to their false beliefs. They are far worse than the Samaritans and the Karaites and, *a fortiori*, than the Gentiles. For the Gentiles among whom we reside are not idolators and commit no wrong. They are 'the saints of the nations' who have a share in the World to Come. Not so the Shabbateans and Frankists, who are idolators and notorious sinners. Fleckeles continues:

> It is not only the Jewish religion that they insult but they pour scorn on every religion and every nation, scoffing at every belief and every opinion that people have held until this day; as anyone who has studied the history of their destructive faith is fully aware. You must have heard that which our master, the true Gaon [Landau], may God protect him, wrote to the leaders of your community regarding the *kohen* who made the sign of the cross when he delivered the priestly blessing. These are his golden words: 'With regard to that base *kohen* who made the sign of the cross when he went up to deliver the priestly blessing, it is not only the Jewish religion which he mocked but the Christian religion as well. For no one has ever heard of a Christian delivering the priestly blessing in a synagogue, and this man scorned both religions.'

Fleckeles reminds Mordecai of the attitude adopted by Ezra. We, too, must be exclusive with regard to these sectarians. The Rabbis[1] tell us that, once a family has had three consecutive generations of scholars, God promises that the Torah will always remain in that family, and yet we see in many instances that the promise in unfulfilled. The reason is only because the scholars allow their children to marry the children of the ignorant so that

[1] BM 85a, based on Isa. 59: 21

they are brought up as ignoramuses. It appears from Fleckeles' reply that it was Mordecai himself who wished to marry the girl. Even if there is only a suspicion that the family belongs to the sect, says Fleckeles, Mordecai should give up the match (the Shabbateans followed their beliefs in secret while professing to be devout Jews). The only way he can see for Mordecai to marry the girl is if he is absolutely certain that the rumour of her family's adherence to Shabbateanism is entirely without foundation.

A Responsum (no. 13) from Prague dated 1792 is addressed to a Rabbi Nathaniel. The *Zohar*[2] seems to hold that the silent prayer should be recited so softly that even the worshipper himself does not hear it, while the Codes rule that others should not hear it but the worshipper himself should. Fleckeles argues that the Codes should be followed.[3] 'I have nothing to do with the secret things. I reflect on those matters where permission was given, but have never sought to inquire of things too marvellous for me.'

Another (no. 26) from Prague in 1806 is addressed to Carolus Fischer (1755–1844), the Christian-Hebraist, librarian of Prague University and government-appointed censor of Hebrew books. The query is with regard to a Jew's oath when given to a Gentile. Is it as binding as when he gives it to another Jew and, if not, should the Jew take an oath to a Gentile while lying in a coffin dressed in a shroud? It has even been suggested that the Jew should swear with a copy of the *Zohar* in his hand, since the *Zohar*, so the Hasidim say, is such a holy book that whoever touches it while telling an untruth will die within a few days. Fleckeles replies, first, that there is no difference whatsoever between the binding power of an oath to a Gentile and an oath to a Jew. To break either is to offend against taking God's name in vain. The world would totter unless men could rely on one another when an oath is taken. We find that the great Biblical heroes took oaths, even to idolators, which they clearly considered to be absolutely binding. Now in Jewish law an oath is binding in itself, and there is no need whatever for a Jew to hold a Bible in his hand while taking one. It is most inadvisable to adopt

[2] I, 114b   [3] See pp. 122–3 above

any special procedure when a Jew takes an oath to a Gentile because this would defeat its purpose by suggesting to the Jew, what is patently untrue, that his oath to a Gentile is not binding. To use the *Zohar* for the purpose can only invite ridicule. If a person is suspected of defying God's law by swearing falsely, is it likely that he will be deterred by swearing on a purely human work like the *Zohar*?

This gives Fleckeles an opportunity of stating his opinion of the *Zohar*. The work is mentioned neither in the Mishnah nor in the Talmud and was entirely unknown before Moses de Leon suddenly produced it at the end of the thirteenth century. It could not possibly have been written, as the Kabbalists claim, by R. Simeon b. Yohai of the second century, since it mentions the names of sages who lived centuries later. We know that the Shabbateans and the Frankists relied on the *Zohar* for their perverse views, but if such a great saint as R. Simeon b. Yohai had been the author, God would surely not have allowed his work to become the cause of such religious anarchy.

Again on the theme of Shabbateanism, Fleckeles has a Responsum (no. 69) dated 1794, addressed to his pupil Hayyim Hirsch, a Dayyan in Kojetein. The question was whether one should say 'Amen' after hearing a benediction recited by a Shabbatean. Fleckeles refers to the ruling of Maimonides[4] that one does not answer 'Amen' after the benediction of a heretic. The Shabbateans, when they recite their benedictions, have not God in mind but Shabbatai Zevi, whom they worship as a god. In each generation they have a different god (referring to the Shabbatean and Frankist doctrine of God's incarnation in the successive Messiahs of the sect), and are thus far worse than any heretic who has ever arisen among Jews. Fleckeles refers to the books written against the Shabbateans which demonstrate how these heretics despise all religions, including Judaism, Christianity and Islam. However, he advises his pupil to refrain from stirring up controversy among the masses, who are not well versed in the Torah.

Finally, reference should be made to the Responsum (no. 112,

4 *Yad*, Berakhot 1: 13

para. 3) of Landau, in Prague, to Fleckeles in 1780 when the latter was Rabbi of Kojetein. Fleckeles had asked him whether a scroll of the Torah written by a scribe suspected of being a crypto-Shabbatean may be used. Landau replies:

> If when he wrote the scroll he was already suspect—even though it was not revealed until later, when he 'put too much salt into his dish openly'[5]—it is right to be strict in the matter and to hide the scroll away. For with regard to this accursed sect we say that it operates retrospectively, so that when he was suspected we must not accuse those who did suspect him of being guilty of stigmatising the innocent. I have found very few so suspected to be completely innocent; if they were not total adherents of the sect, they accepted the heresy, at least in part. This man whose root was eventually uncovered was rotten from the outset, and the scroll he wrote should be hidden away. Do it, however, without stirring up controversy.

Hayyim Kittsee (d. 1850), prominent Hungarian Talmudist, was Rabbi of Albertisa near Budapest from 1824 until his death. The following are the theological Responsa in his collection *Otzar Hayyim*.

Kittsee has a fiery attack on the Brunswick Reform Conference held in June 1844, in the form of a letter of protest.[6] He first pours scorn on these men who, he says, claim to be Rabbis but who, in reality, are ignorant of Rabbinic law, deny the Oral Law and other basic principles of the Jewish faith, and are heretics whose intention it is to mislead the people. Scholars recognise the incompetence of these men at a glance, but it is necessary to warn simple, unsophisticated Jews of the danger to Judaism. Nothing must be done to suggest for one moment that these men, who deny the authority of the Talmud, can be in any way considered as representatives of Rabbinic Judaism. Maimonides, in his Introduction to his great Code, states that since the Babylonian Talmud has been accepted by the whole house of Israel, no one has the authority to depart from any of the Talmudic rules and regulations. We have heard that these men profane the sabbath and encourage others to profane it. Consequently, it is forbidden to

---

[5] Rabbinic idiom for the open teaching of heresy; Ber. 17b
[6] Orah Hayyim, no. 4

learn anything from them, even true doctrine, just as it is forbidden to use a scroll of the Torah written by a heretic. Solomon
Ibn Adret banned even those who studied philosophy, because it
might lead to heresy.[7] We can have no doubts as to what his
attitude would have been to heretics such as these.

These men have dared to argue that a Jew is permitted to
marry a Gentile woman, and that the children of such a marriage
are Jewish—both utter lies, as every student of the Talmud knows.
They wish to abolish the recital of *Kol Nidre*, a custom established
in Israel for hundreds of years, on the grounds that it tends to
suggest that the Jew's word is not to be relied upon. But everyone
knows that the *Kol Nidre* formula does not apply to oaths taken
in a court of law where the interests of others are involved, as the
Ran and others clearly state.[8] Kittsee continues:

> From this you can see how nonsensical are all their words and that
> they will be blown away by the wind. Furthermore, some of the
> more brazen among them have declared in print that a critical
> survey should be made of the *Shulhan Arukh* and a new *Shulhan
> Arukh* composed. Observe, how brazen they are and see them for
> what they are! They appear to be unaware that even if, God forbid,
> a declaration of this sort were made by a great sage, expert in the
> Talmud and the Codes, it would be sheer effrontery, how much
> greater an affront when it is made by rebellious ignoramuses, in-
> capable of discerning between their left hand and their right. May
> the soul and spirit of these brazen-faced folk expire. Perhaps they
> wished to render vermin clean, imagining that the prohibition is
> recorded in the *Shulhan Arukh*. Verily they themselves are vermin
> and will never be made clean by our Father in Heaven. Hell will
> come to an end, but not their punishment, for they are of those who
> cause the public to sin. Those who ordained them to render decisions
> in Jewish law will be brought to judgment. It is right to inform all
> the communities that henceforth it is forbidden to eat any food they
> have decided is fit. All the food over which they have given decisions
> is *terefa*, and the vessels in which it has been cooked have to be
> purified. It is possible that they had themselves appointed as Rabbis
> by bribery or through the influence of some government authority
> for, at first, they were only *Lehrer* (teachers), a name very suited to
> people empty (*leer*) of the Torah and full of impurity. Their whole
> boast is of the foreign languages they know, may their tongues drop

[7] See p. 79 above   [8] Ned. 23b

out and their bones be crushed. This bunch of unclean vermin do only as their heart desires. They are popular only among the ignorant, whereas the scholars are fully aware of how empty and utterly worthless are their words. If they do have any knowledge of the Torah, let them go to the place of the great scholars to argue it out with them, and then they will see whether any of their arguments can be substantiated. We have now no other alternative than to cry out to our king, the compassionate, may God exalt him, to inform him that wicked men have arisen, cursed ones who wish to invent a new religion and who are neither Jews nor Gentiles. Today they say this and tomorrow they will teach even more perverse things, even, God forbid, service to idols. Therefore, arise, now, O our brethren of the house of Israel. Gird your loins with strength and pour out your hearts to God who will help us. And cry out to the princes and the noblemen not to permit any changes whatever in our religion, for it is a new religion they preach. We will never permit the abolition of any law, great or small, or any custom which our forefathers, may their souls rest in peace, established these very many years.

The letter is also signed by Matthew Unger and Nathan Elijah Ehrmann, Kittsee's two Dayyanim.

Kittsee's stepson, Abraham Aaron, Rabbi of Jemerung, asked him[9] how to refute the argument of the Brunswick Reform Conference that *metzitzah* (sucking the blood from the wound after circumcision) can now be abolished. It is easy to see how the other arguments advanced at the Conference can be refuted, but *metzitzah* is demanded by the Talmud[10] only because it is said to be dangerous to the child if this is not done. According to the testimony of all the doctors, nowadays, there is no danger and, on the contrary, there is a possibility of infection where *metzitzah* is carried out. Kittsee replies that the doctors are not to be relied on in a matter clearly enjoined by the Talmud. He quotes the famous maxim of R. Moses Sofer:[11] 'Anything new is forbidden by the Torah.' Kittsee's son-in-law suggests, in the course of his question, that the practice of *metzitzah* can be defended according to the Kabbalah. The Kabbalists say that the blood of circumcision represents the stain of sin and evil and it is therefore essential to draw out all the blood, which can only be effectively accomplished by the method of *metzitzah*.

---

[9] Yoreh Deah, no. 18   [10] Sabb. 133b   [11] See p. 213 below

Spanning the whole of the nineteenth century, the famous Sofer family enjoyed the widest authority. Moses Sofer (1762–1839) was born in Frankfort, where his teachers were Phinehas Horowitz (d. 1801), who appears to have been at one time a disciple of the Hasidic master the Maggid of Meseritch, and Nathan Adler (1741–1800), Talmudist and Kabbalist. Moses, known as *Hatam Sofer*, was one of the most authoritative Respondents of all time and the acknowledged leader in the struggle against Reform, his maxim being, as above: 'Anything new is forbidden by the Torah.' In 1806 he was appointed to the Rabbinate of Pressburg, where he served until his death. He was succeeded by his son Abraham Samuel Benjamin Wolf (1815–71), known as *Ketav Sofer*, whose son Simhah Bunem (1842–1906), known as *Shevet Sofer*, in turn followed him. During the whole of the nineteenth century the Sofer family and their numerous disciples espoused with complete and utter conviction the traditional stand and are largely responsible for the attitude of separatism typical of Hungarian Orthodoxy. The following are the theological Responsa in the collections of *Hatam Sofer*, *Ketav Sofer* and *Shevet Sofer*.[12]

A Responsum[13] of *Hatam Sofer*, dated 1821, is addressed to Solomon Uhlmann, Rabbi of Lochenbach, who had disqualified a Reader in the synagogue on the strength of adverse letters written by a number of Rabbis. *Hatam Sofer* remarks that, after reading the letters, he can find no dispensation for the man to continue to act as a Reader. According to the testimonies given in the letters, he is a notorious fornicator and thief and has committed other offences, each of which would in itself suffice to earn him disqualification. Although a Reader cannot be dismissed on the strength of a mere rumour, if there is a widespread report that he is a persistent sinner, his resignation can be demanded by any individual of the congregation. However, if the man goes to a place where he is unknown and there repents sincerely of his sins, his repentance is accepted and he can again serve as a Reader.

[12] On *Hatam Sofer* see E. Katz, *Ha-Hatam Sofer*; S. Sofer, *Iggerot Soferim* and *Hut Ha-Meshulash*; Moses J. Burak, *The Hatam Sofer*
[13] Orah Hayyim, no. 11

Two Responsa[14] of *Hatam Sofer*, addressed to Abraham Zevi Katz, deal with the Hasidic practice of demanding that the Reader in the synagogue must wear garments other than those of wool. The Hasidic reason for the ban on wool was that since Hasidim use the especially sacred prayer-book of the great Kabbalist Isaac Luria, based on the Sephardi rite and replete with mystical significance, one who wears wool—with the remote implication that the garment may also contain linen, and so offend against the prohibition of *shaatnez*, wearing a garment of mixed wool and linen (Deut. 22 : 11)—is not worthy of leading the prayers. *Hatam Sofer* replies that he is aware that some especially pious folk never wear garments of wool at any time for this reason and he can see the point of it, but if people do wear garments of wool (as, by law, they are fully entitled to do), he cannot see any possible connection between it and the use of the Lurianic prayer-book. The alleged claim that there is a special 'mystery', according to which the Sephardi version cannot 'bear' wool, is utterly beyond him. His teachers R. Phinehas and R. Nathan both informed him that all versions of the prayer-book have the same effect. The Lurianic prayer-book was composed by a Sephardi. If a man of similar status had arisen among the Ashkenazim he would have made the necessary corrections and improvements to the Ashkenazi prayer-book. Both R. Phinehas and R. Nathan used the Lurianic version themselves, but discouraged its general use. *Hatam Sofer* concludes:

> It follows from what has been said that those who use the Sephardi version can be assumed to have been initiated into the secrets of the Lord. They know the secret and understand what they say and so are entitled to use this version. But those, like us, who have not reached this stage, use the Ashkenazi version of our prayers, and our prayers are heard. One must not say that one version of the prayers is different from another, so as to justify not tolerating garments of wool. Such an opinion is nonsense.

Hatam Sofer's second Responsum on the subject, dated 1833, is in reply to the criticism of the first Responsum by the Hasidic

---

[14] Ibid., nos 15 and 16; I have treated these Responsa at length in my *Hasidic Prayer*, pp. 154-9

master Moses Teitelbaum (d. 1841) of Ohelje in Hungary.[15] *Hatam Sofer* here observes that just as the prophetic message is expressed by each prophet in his own style so, too, prayer is for all but should be recited by each group in accordance with its own particular tradition. Prophecy, coming from 'above to below', is all one, yet an Isaiah speaks differently from an Amos. By the same token, prayer, which is 'from below to above', is all one, yet Ashkenazim should be true to their own version and should not try to supplant it by the Sephardi version. As for Moses Teitelbaum's contention that the Sephardim have taken it upon themselves to refrain from wearing wool during prayer, such an obligation would, indeed, be binding, were it true, but the Sephardim now residing in Amsterdam, London and Hamburg do not know of any such obligation. As for the Hasidic work *Likkute Amarim*, where it is stated that the Maggid of Meseritch argued that, nowadays, when no one is aware to which tribe he belongs, the Lurianic version is 'a gateway to Heaven for all', *Hatam Sofer* admits that he has never seen the book in question but fails to see the point. If the argument is correct, why do Kohanim and Levites use the Lurianic rite and not their own, since they do know to which tribe they belong? The famous German and French scholars in the Middle Ages used the Ashkenazi rite. Are we to imagine that the prayers of these renowned scholars never ascended to Heaven? But *Hatam Sofer*, nevertheless, advises strongly against strife in the community. It will become a source of contention if an Ashkenazi persists in wearing wool in a Hasidic synagogue, mistaken though they are that their version cannot tolerate wool.

A Responsum[16] of *Hatam Sofer* dated 1829 deals with the prayer: 'Angels of mercy, bring our supplications for mercy to the Lord of mercy', considered by Samsom Morpurgo, among others, as we have seen.[17] The questioner refers to the work *Netivot Olam, Netiv Avodah*, 12, by Judah Loew b. Bezalel (1529–1609) of Prague, known as *Maharal* of Prague. *Maharal* objects to the prayer on the grounds that we do not require the intercession

---

[15] See *Hasidic Prayer*, pp. 157–9 for Teitelbaum's views
[16] Orah Hayyim, no. 165   [17] Pp. 193–4 above

of the angels. But, the questioner asks, do we not find in Scripture the use of intercessors in prayer? *Maharal*, replies *Hatam Sofer*, would not offer any objections to human intercessors. His objection is only to angelic intercessors, his reason being that the people of Israel are higher than the angels and can accomplish for themselves far more than any angel can do. *Hatam Sofer* remarks that he personally takes a little longer over the prayer preceding this one, so as to avoid saying the questionable prayer when the congregation say it.

In a Responsum[18] dated 1812, *Hatam Sofer* considers the penance to be imposed on a man who had relations with his wife during her periods. He observes that the main thing is true remorse. The detailed penances laid down in the books are solely for the purpose of warding off punishment and are not essential to repentance. He remarks that he must confess his ignorance of the penance to be imposed and advises his questioner to consult the books. The *Rokeah*[19] says that a man who has intercourse with a menstruant should fast for forty days for each forbidden act. The words of the *Rokeah* are 'words of tradition'. The man should try to satisfy these requirements but, in addition, he should set aside one day each year for fasting and remorse—either the day on which he sinned or the day on which he resolved to repent of his sin. Since the law demands that a man keep the anniversary of a miracle by means of which he was saved from physical harm, how much more should he keep the anniversary of the miracle of repentance which saved his soul from harm. *Hatam Sofer* adds that he later discovered that in the Responsa of Meir Eisenstadt, *Panim Meirot*,[20] a repentant sinner is similarly advised to set aside one day each year that will be for him like Yom Kippur. He gives thanks to God for enabling him to arrive at the same decision as this famous authority.

Another Responsum[21] on penance, dated 1839, is addressed to Rabbi Baer of Eibushutz. A man was forced to eat forbidden food in prison and in his weakness could not help enjoying it. Is a penance required? *Hatam Sofer* states that since the man could not

[18] Orah Hayyim, no. 166

[20] See pp. 188-9 above

[19] See pp. 101-2 above

[21] Orah Hayyim, no. 202

help it, he is not culpable in law. Nevertheless, some penance is possibly required for having enjoyed the forbidden food. But since the man is poor and sick in health, he should be burdened neither with fasting nor with too much almsgiving. He should be told that some degree of sinfulness was involved, so that he should feel remorse and God will forgive him.

In *Hatam Sofer*'s day it was not too unusual for Jews, consciously or unconsciously, to model the synagogue they built on the patterns of church architecture. Many of the Responsa of the period discuss the question of 'copying the Gentiles' in this connection. In a Responsum[22] dated 1837, he replies to the question of a Rabbi Hirsch whether it was right for a certain community to build a synagogue having a window in which was depicted a circle containing the Tetragrammaton with light radiating from it in every direction. *Hatam Sofer* states categorically that such a thing is forbidden. It is the practice of the Gentiles but we Jews refuse to give the slightest credence to the view that 'rays' can proceed from God. He remarks that the Gentiles do this as we do in connection with the figure of Moses.

The question of superstition features in another of his Responsa,[23] dated 1813 and addressed to a Rabbi Joel. It is reported in the name of Judah the Saint of Regensburg (d. 1217) that it is dangerous to build a house on a site on which there had been no house previously. People say that if it is decided to build a house on such a site a cockerel and a hen should first be taken into the house and slaughtered there. Is this permitted? *Hatam Sofer* offers the rationale that since the cock is called *gever* (also meaning 'man') in Hebrew, the slaughter of the two means that *gevarim* ('men') have already died there so that the powers of destruction have spent their force. But, he argues, it is far better to ignore the whole thing since there is mention of it neither in the Talmud nor in the Codes and it is very probable that Judah the Saint never said it. As for the notion that it is dangerous to build a new house, he puts forward the idea that to build a new house tends to suggest that the builder is resigned to living permanently outside the holy land. The *mitzvah* of residing in the holy land cannot,

[22] Yoreh Deah, no. 129   [23] Ibid., no. 138

therefore, afford him protection and he may succumb to the natural dangers inherent in human existence. It follows, if this is the rationale, that it is only forbidden to build a new house unnecessarily. But our needs being manifold, it is permitted to us. There should be a ceremony of dedication of the house at which prayers are offered and some Torah studied. 'For these are our life and the length of our days.'

In a Responsum[24] dated 1835, *Hatam Sofer* considers the case of the community of Csaba who wished to compel their Rabbi, Jonathan Alexandersohn, to resign because, in their opinion, he was a heretic. The charges against him were: 1. He was lax in religious observance, having been observed eating without washing his hands and without reciting grace, speaking while putting on his *tefillin*, and eating meat after hard cheese. 2. He was too lenient in the decisions he rendered and declared that he did not believe in reward and punishment after death. 3. He arranged for bills of divorce to be given in a town which had no such tradition, despite the protests of prominent Rabbis. *Hatam Sofer* remarks that the fact that a Rabbi has sinned does not warrant his dismissal from his post if he has sincerely repented. But the Rabbi's denial of reward and punishment means that he is a heretic and it is forbidden to learn from a heretic. However, the witnesses to the offence must be reliable and not be from the Rabbi's town. The people of the Rabbi's town cannot be trusted, since they may wish to get rid of him for purely personal reasons and are, therefore, biased witnesses. The cause of offence for which he can and should be removed from his post is that he delivered the bills of divorce unlawfully. No further testimony is here required, since it is known to all that he did it. He must never again have the title 'Rabbi'. The Rabbis who ordained him would never have done so had they known his true nature. So must he remain until God sends down His spirit from above to bring near to Him those who were far away.

Another Responsum[25] on the same topic is dated 1837 and addressed to Eleazar Segal, Rabbi in Vienna. *Hatam Sofer* here remarks that Alexandersohn paid him a visit, but he had refused

---

[24] Hoshen Mishpat, no. 162   [25] Ibid., no. 207

to discuss the matter with him. Alexandersohn protested that the witnesses against him had not been sworn in, but *Hatam Sofer* pointed out that in Jewish law there is no need for witnesses to take an oath before their testimony can be accepted. Alexandersohn claimed further that *Hatam Sofer* knew only too well that there was no case in law against him and that his recommendation that he be deposed was purely as a deterrent to others. *Hatam Sofer* admits it, but argues that the Rabbis, in order to safeguard the tradition, are entitled to adopt the sternest emergency measures, even if these are otherwise illegal, as we find in the Talmud.[26]

The traditional custom was for marriages to be celebrated in the courtyard of the synagogue or in a hall, never in the synagogue itself. Under the influence of the Reform movement, many communities began to have the marriage service performed in the synagogue itself, a practice that aroused the ire of the traditionalists as a clear example of copying church weddings. There is a Responsum[27] on the subject by *Ketav Sofer*, son of *Hatam Sofer*, addressed to Israel Zeev Segal, Rabbi of Ohelje. The question concerns the attitude to be adopted by the Rabbis if their communities insist on having the marriage service in the synagogue. Are the Rabbis obliged to protest even if this may endanger their position? *Ketav Sofer*'s reply is very revealing. The Rabbi's obligation to rebuke his flock applies only in an age where there is respect for the Rabbinic office. There is no such obligation where it is unlikely that they will pay heed, as is the case nowadays, when so many people have little respect for the Rabbinate. Nevertheless, it all depends on the particular circumstances in each case and it is impossible to give a definite ruling where one is unfamiliar with these. A further question is: where there is no obligation for the Rabbi to issue a reproof, can he himself officiate at a wedding in the synagogue? The questioner suggested that the Rabbi should be allowed to officiate. It is not as if his refusal to officiate will result in the ceremony being held outside the synagogue. There are many lax people only too ready to officiate if they are paid for it. But *Ketav Sofer* disagrees. The Rabbi himself must refuse to officiate, especially since the whole

[26] Sanh. 46a [27] Even Ha-Ezer, no. 47

practice is obviously based on the wedding in church. That is why they want the wedding to take place in a house of worship with the 'priest' officiating. He concludes that, busy as he is, he writes in haste, relying on the questioner to draw his own conclusions.

A Responsum[28] dated 1866 and addressed to Laib Berger, a disciple of the author, reflects Jewish–Christian relations in Hungary at that time. When the priests lead the procession with their icons at Easter they demand that candles be lit in the homes in honour of the icons. When the mob sees that there are no lighted candles in a home they pass, they throw stones to break the windows. Since there can be danger to life, is it permitted for Jews to light candles in their homes? *Ketav Sofer* quotes his father's[29] ruling that candles must not be lit even where there is a possible danger to life and limb, but each Jew should say to his Christian neighbour: 'save me'—i.e. hinting that he should light the candles. *Ketav Sofer* suggests that they should say to the priest or the government authorities: 'Under no circumstances will we light candles even if it puts our lives in danger. You must, therefore, offer us your protection from the mob. But if your people force their way into our homes to light the candles there in order to avoid trouble, what can we do about it?' It is permitted to say this.

A Responsum[30] dated 1848 deals with whether it is permitted to sell a scroll of the Torah to a Jewish convert to Christianity who still keeps the dietary laws and attends synagogue on Rosh Ha-Shanah and Yom Kippur. *Ketav Sofer* holds that since one is obliged to purchase from an apostate any scrolls he may have, out of fear that he may desecrate them, how can it possibly be permitted to sell scrolls to him in the first instance? Even though this man still keeps some of the Jewish observances, he cannot be relied upon to treat the scrolls reverentially. Although some authorities permit a scroll to be purchased with money donated by an apostate, that is because the scroll will be kept in the synagogue. To sell him a scroll is forbidden by all the authorities.

Another Responsum[31] of *Ketav Sofer*, addressed to a Naftali

[28] Yoreh Deah, part I, no. 84   [29] *Hatam Sofer*, Yoreh Deah, no. 132
[30] Yoreh Deah, part II, no. 133   [31] Ibid., no. 171

Baneth, discusses the case of a notorious sinner who has died. Should the mourning rites be carried out and should the Kaddish be recited for the repose of his soul? The author notes that the question has been discussed by earlier authorities and, after further discussion on the legal side of the question, leaves it to his questioner to make the decision.

Finally, a Responsum[32] dated 1894 deals with the attitude to be adopted when a marriage contrary to Jewish law has been contracted. A man married the widow of his mother's brother, forbidden by Rabbinic law. Furthermore, he had lived with her while her husband was still alive so that, in addition, she is forbidden to him by Biblical law. But the couple refuse to be divorced. What is to be done? There is the possibility of resorting to coercion by the Gentile authorities (who will declare null and void a Jewish marriage that is not in accordance with Jewish law), and the questioner is inclined to resort to this form of coercion, even though the result may be that the couple will be tempted to embrace Christianity in order to legalise their union. *Ketav Sofer* replies that he is far from confident that the threat to abandon the Jewish fold can be ignored. He knows that Jair Hayyim Bacharach[33] rules that the court must do its duty irrespective of what may happen in the future, and that his father *Hatam Sofer*[34] agrees with Bacharach. But in our case there are children to the union and these innocents must be saved from apostasy.[35] The whole purpose of insisting that the strictness of the law must be applied is for it to act as a deterrent to others, but where is the justice in allowing innocent children to be cast out of the Jewish fold for the sake of promoting better standards of conduct among the people generally? It is unjust to introduce the kind of deterrent that is at the expense not of the offenders alone, but of their innocent children.

There are two Responsa of a theological nature in the Responsa collection of *Shevet Sofer*, son of *Ketav Sofer* and grandson of *Hatam Sofer*. In the first,[36] addressed to his disciple Jacob Isaac Weiss, the author discusses the legality of the Hasidic practice of

---

[32] Ibid., no. 168   [33] See pp. 167–8 above   [34] Yoreh Deah, no. 323
[35] See pp. 196–7 above   [36] Orah Hayyim, no. 17

being absent from home at the court of the Zaddik on the festivals. Since, according to tradition, a man is expected to rejoice together with his wife and family on the festivals, how can it be permitted to leave home on these occasions? *Shevet Sofer* points to the Rabbinic teaching[37] that a man is obliged to visit his teacher on the festivals. This cannot mean only for the purpose of studying the Torah, since, from the context, it appears that it applies also to women, who have no obligation to study the Torah. It can be argued that any man with a reputation for holiness in his generation is counted as a teacher for this purpose. Consequently, despite certain reservations one may have, the practice of so many good Jews can be defended.

The second Responsum,[38] dated 1881, is on whether the near relatives of an apostate must sit on the ground in mourning on the day he is converted. After quoting the authorities who deal with the question, *Shevet Sofer* notes that the references in the *Sefer Hasidim* are that the relatives should weep, but not that they should observe the laws of mourning as if their relative had died.

Samuel Ehrenfeld (1835–83), Rabbi of Mattersdorf from 1877 until his death, was a son of the son-in-law of *Hatam Sofer*, hence the title of his Responsa collection *Hatan Sofer* ('Son-in-law of Sofer'), with a sound similar to the title *Hatam Sofer*. The following are the theological Responsa in the collection.

A Responsum (no. 28) dated 1873 is addressed to Aaron Tennenbaum and concerns the status of a Jew who profanes the sabbath publicly. Ehrenfeld first quotes the sources[39] in which a public sabbath desecrator is declared to have the status of an idolator because the sabbath attests to God as Creator. It follows that such a man cannot help to form the quorum for prayer (*minyan*), neither can he be called to the reading of the Torah.

Responsum no. 36 concerns the law that before a man eats he must first feed his animals, but that he is allowed to drink before giving his animals to drink.[40] Why the distinction? Ehrenfeld says that the rule cannot be based solely on the prohibition of cruelty

---

[37] RH 16b   [38] Yoreh Deah, no. 108
[39] Hull. 5a; Maimonides, *Yad*, Sabbath 30: 15; *Shulhan Arukh*, OH 123: 2
[40] *Magen Avraham*, Orah Hayyim 168

to animals for, if this were the reason, the Rabbis would simply have said that a man is obliged to feed his animals regularly, whether or not he himself eats. Ehrenfeld suggests two reasons for the rule, neither of which applies to drinking. The first reason is that a man needs some special merit before he can be said to deserve his daily bread. Before eating, therefore, he is obliged to carry out an act of kindness and then, since he has compassion, God will have compassion on him. Water is, however, free for all and here no special merit is required. The second reason is that if a man sits down to his meal before feeding his animals, they may have to wait too long before they are fed. But it is unlikely that drinking will be so prolonged.

In the course of a Responsum (no. 44) dated 1873 and addressed to Isaac Aaron Blau, Ehrenfeld discusses which is better, for a man to perform a *mitzvah* himself or to have it performed on his behalf if his agent can carry it out in a more fitting manner? Ehrenfeld argues that the reason why the Rabbis prefer a man to perform a *mitzvah* himself rather than have it done for him is out of respect for God's commands. He should wish to carry out the command himself and not delegate it to another. But since the whole aim of this law is for him to demonstrate his high regard for the command, it follows that where the agent can carry it out in a more fitting manner than he can himself, he should delegate it. Here, far from his delegation demonstrating that he has little regard for the command, it demonstrates that so high is his regard that he wishes it to be carried out in the best possible way.

A Responsum (no. 51) dated 1880 is addressed to Akiba Klein, Ehrenfeld's brother-in-law. There was a proposal to erect an iron railing around the grave of a famous Rabbi, but some objected that the practice smacked of Reform. Ehrenfeld agrees with the objectors. We must always be on our guard, he says, against appearing to acquiesce in any way to innovations and thus give the impression that we condone Reformist leanings.

At the end of another Responsum (no. 54), Ehrenfeld states his opinion that although we keep ourselves apart from any groups which have little regard for Jewish observances, if an individual, unobservant Jew wishes to join an Orthodox congregation he should not be rejected, but encouraged. His intention to associate with the God-fearing is a good sign in itself and he may well come under their influence to lead a fully observant life.

A Responsum (no. 79) dated 1873 is addressed to Ehrenfeld's pupil, Jacob Freistadt of Vienna. Why is no benediction recited before carrying out the *mitzvah* of telling the Exodus story on Passover? Ehrenfeld refers to the Responsum of Solomon Ibn Adret[41] on the general question of benedictions before the precepts, and also to a Responsum of Asher b. Jehiel.[42] This latter Ehrenfeld understands as saying that it is not the telling of the story in itself that is really significant but rather the remembering of it. Since this is in the mind, no benediction is required. Ehrenfeld suggests an interesting reason of his own. That man forgets is a spiritual flaw in his make-up. Indeed, we ought not to have any need to remember God's kindness when He brought us out of Egypt. It is only because we are so far away from holiness that this particular *mitzvah* is enjoined on us. Consequently, great *mitzvah* though it now is, we cannot thank God for giving it to us since if we were ideal men there would have been no need for us to have been commanded to remember our Creator and Redeemer and all He has wrought on our behalf, for we would never have been in danger of forgetting it. Furthermore, the duty of remembering the Exodus is part of our general obligation to believe in God. This latter devolves on us at all times and seasons and there is no benediction for a permanent *mitzvah* of this kind, only for a *mitzvah* that arises from time to time.

Another Responsum (no. 85) discusses whether it is permitted to have a marriage service in a house instead of under the open sky, as is the practice among the majority of Orthodox Jews. Ehrenfeld can see no basic objection. The Orthodox Rabbis oppose a wedding in the synagogue itself because it is an aping of Christian worship, but this objection obviously does not apply to a wedding in a private house. However, any departure from the established Jewish customs should be avoided, because this is bound to lead to a clamour for further reforms. Once the marriage

[41] See p. 75 above   [42] *Kelal* 24

service is allowed to take place in a private house, people will argue sooner or later that, if it can be held in a house, why can it not be held in the synagogue?

Moses b. Joseph Schick (Maharam) (1807–79), pupil of Moses Sofer in Pressburg, and Rabbi of Huszt from 1861 until his death, was a foremost exponent of the attitudes of Hungarian Orthodoxy in the tradition of his master. His Responsa collection contains a number dealing with theological matters.

A Responsum[43] dated 1875 and addressed to Rabbi Aaron Wilheim answers a question previously discussed by Leon da Modena.[44] It is the habit of some Readers in the synagogue to repeat certain words of the prayers so as to fit the words to the melody. Wilheim suggests that the Rabbis should discourage the practice on the grounds that there are profound mysteries in the number of words and letters as laid down by the Men of the Great Synagogue who composed the prayers. Schick agrees, and adds further reasons. The Reader, by repeating words, offends against the injunction not to add to the Torah. He is also guilty of speaking untruths, since he begins to declaim the praises of God and, instead of continuing, repeats words he has already uttered. There are the further offences of interrupting the prayers and of treating the Torah as a song to be sung for pleasure. Finally, would a man dream of repeating words when he entreats an earthly ruler to grant his request?

One of the most acute problems the Orthodox had to face was the attitude they ought to adopt to the Reformers. Rabbi Hayyim Sofer of Munkacs had argued that Reformers, who deny the coming of the Messiah and the rebuilding of the Temple, should be placed under the ban (herem), even to the extent of refusing to allow their children to be circumcised. Schick, in his reply to Sofer[45] who asked his advice, disagrees. He notes that in any event the suggestion is academic, since the law of the land does not allow the ban to be imposed. But even if it were allowed, he cannot agree that it should be extended to a refusal to circumcise the children of the Reformers. If we refuse to allow their children

[43] Orah Hayyim, no. 31   [44] Pp. 159–60 above
[45] Orah Hayyim, no. 304

to be circumcised, it will in no way strengthen the Orthodox cause. On the contrary, such an attitude will seem heartless and extremely odd to the masses and will succeed only in adding fuel to the fire; people will point to it as further evidence of Rabbinic intolerance, which is their main complaint. Levi Ibn Habib states in a Responsum[46] that one should never state in public any belief which seems strange to the masses, such as belief in the transmigration of souls. Furthermore, it is not improbable that the Reformers do not really hold with circumcision but are afraid to declare this openly; so that if we refuse to allow their children to be circumcised we are, in fact, playing into their hands and guilty of assisting sinners in their sin. Hayyim Sofer had written, too, that in his opinion it is forbidden to have recourse to a doctor who enters a Reform Temple. How does he know this? And where is it stated that it is forbidden even to enter a Reform Temple? Sofer quotes the ruling in the Talmud[47] that it is forbidden even to take shelter in a house in which idols are worshipped, but that is because it is forbidden to have any benefit from an idolatrous temple; but there is no law against merely entering a house in which heresy is preached.

Yet while Schick avoids the absolute extremism of some of his colleagues, he is extreme enough in his attitude towards Reform. In a Responsum[48] addressed to *Ketav Sofer* in Pressburg, Schick begs that an official Rabbinic protest be organised against the Reformers to declare openly that if we were allowed by the law of the land to impose the ban on them we would do so. In any event, let it be said openly and unambiguously that the Reformers are not Jews, that there must be no intermarriage with them, and that it is forbidden to pray in their Temples. This was the attitude adopted by Israel's sages throughout Jewish history. Ezra refused to recognise the Samaritans, even though they posed as friends and offered to co-operate in rebuilding the Temple. Rabban Gamaliel composed the benediction against the sectarians when the Jewish Christians began to grow in numbers. And the famous Rabbis of the more recent past adopted the same attitude towards the Shabbateans. Schick continues:

[46] See pp. 143-4 above   [47] Sabb. 11b   [48] Orah Hayyim, no. 305

And now unbelievers have arisen, evil Rabbis who have assembled to libel the Torah instead of to adorn it, as they have published in their protocol. Not content with deriding Rabbinic teaching, they have stretched out their hand against the very Torah of Moses our teacher, on whom be peace, rejecting laws which carry the death penalty and that of excision. They have publicly declared that they have no part in the Torah. How, then, can we bear to see the fire that has broken out among the thorns endanger the vineyard of the remnant of Israel! The power of imposing the ban has been taken from us by the government, may it be exalted, yet I fail to see why we should refrain from publishing the truth regarding the status in Jewish law of these men who deny that the Torah is from Heaven, as is demonstrated by so many of their publications and heretical works. It follows that they are not Jews and are like Gentiles; nay, they are worse, as Maimonides rules in many a passage. It goes without saying that they are not to be trusted to teach, to act as Rabbis, or to train Jewish children.

The Orthodox Hungarian Rabbis were bitterly opposed to any innovations in the synagogue service. Among those which seemed to them to be especially offensive, because they were instances of 'copying the Gentiles', were having the Bimah (the raised platform) not in the centre but at the east end, as the altar in a church; the wearing of canonicals by Rabbi and Reader; and the Reader having a choir to assist him. In a Responsum[49] dated 1866 and addressed to Mordecai Laib of Miklocs, Schick offers advice to this scholar. Mordecai Laib teaches in the House of Study and depends on the salary he receives for this to support his wife and family. If he loses his job, he will have nowhere to turn. In the synagogue adjacent to the House of Study there is a Bimah next to the Ark at the east end, a choir, and ministers who wear canonicals. From time to time Mordecai Laib is obliged to enter the synagogue to pray with the congregation, and they insist that he does this. But he has heard that some Rabbis have ruled that to enter a 'choir-shul' is a worse offence than to eat pork, and that one must be ready to suffer martyrdom rather than commit such a sin! Mordecai Laib believes this to be sheer hyperbole but is still anxious as to what he should do. Schick replies that there is no doubt whatever that Mordecai Laib is forbidden to pray in that

49 Ibid., no. 71

synagogue. If the argument is to be accepted that it is permitted to sin in order to safeguard one's livelihood, then, by the very same argument, business can be done on the sabbath. Schick urges Mordecai Laib to be firm and God will help him. But, in reality, says Schick, he fails to understand the whole problem. He continues:

> If the congregation refuses to pay your salary because you will not pray with them, I am greatly astonished and it all seems most odd to me. How can people be so guilty of self-contradiction? For these folk are always protesting that the spirit of the age teaches us tolerance and freedom to worship as we please. No belief, they say, should have greater rights than another. This is always on their lips and such is their constant boast. It is on these grounds that they demand freedom of worship for the Jews. How, then, can they themselves behave in exactly the opposite way by refusing to pay a man the salary to which he is entitled merely because he disagrees with their opinion? This is especially puzzling since they are fully aware of the fact that your honour does not agree with their views and that you are opposed to offering prayer in a synagogue that has a choir. Do they want you to be a hypocrite and be guilty of insincerity? Furthermore, as I see it, Jews are not suspect of such unfeeling behaviour as to deprive a God-fearing man of his due because he refuses to walk in ways he considers to be sinful. True, they themselves do not hold that their conduct is sinful, since bribery blinds the eyes of the wise, but they must surely believe that one who behaves as did our forefathers commits no sin. How, then, can it be imagined that they will do you so cruel a wrong? Behold, Jews are compassionate. Consequently, I fail to understand the problem and am convinced that they will continue to pay you your salary.

Hillel Lichtenstein (1815–91), Rabbi of Kolomea in Galicia, was one of the most extreme of the Orthodox Rabbis. Like Schick, he was a pupil of *Hatam Sofer*. Lichtenstein published a list of rules to be observed by the Orthodox congregations, one of which was that no one must be allowed to preach in German in the synagogue. Wolf Sofer, Schick's pupil, asked his opinion, since the people do not understand any other language. In his reply,[50] Schick says that he agrees with some of Lichtenstein's suggestions, but not all of them. He proceeds to give reasons why,

[50] Ibid., no. 70

in theory, preaching in German should be banned. It is a historical fact that from the time our people began to learn foreign languages they began to forget the Torah. There is great spiritual danger in such studies, as Asher b. Jehiel[51] has said in connection with the study of philosophy. In Jewish law it is forbidden to make any use of the cloth with which a criminal has been executed by strangling. All the more reason for not using a language that has been responsible for so many spiritual deaths. For all that, it remains true that no law may be imposed on a community unless the majority can abide by it.[52] If there are nowhere to be found 'righteous' preachers who can speak to the people in a language they can understand, the 'wicked' preachers will succeed. If the preacher is God-fearing and learned in the Torah and his motive is to win souls for the Torah, it should be permitted for him to preach in German. None the less, Schick concludes, what can he do? The majority of his colleagues disagree with him and he must bow to their decision.

To understand the following Responsa of Schick, a brief sketch of the background in nineteenth-century Hungary is necessary. The Reformers in Hungary were known as the Neologs or Neologists. In 1868 the Hungarian government convened a General Jewish Congress in order to establish an autonomous basis for the affairs of the Jewish community. Of the 220 delegates to the Congress, 126 were Neologs and 94 Orthodox, Schick being one of the leaders of the Orthodox group. The Orthodox delegates left in protest when the majority of delegates refused to declare explicitly that all the rules and regulations would be drawn up in accordance with the laws of the *Shulhan Arukh*. Eventually the Orthodox successfully petitioned the Hungarian Parliament to permit them to form separatist congregations of their own. Some communities refused to take sides in the battle between the Orthodox and the Neologs, preferring to keep to the *status quo*—i.e. before the new regulations accepted by the Congress were adopted. There were thus in Schick's day three types of community: the Orthodox, the Neologs and the *Status Quo*, as the middle party was called.

[51] See pp. 80-2 above   [52] BB 60b

In two Responsa,[53] Schick discusses the legitimacy of the Orthodox forming themselves into separatist congregations. Two principles are involved. First, is it a breach of contract since originally all members were party to the formation of the general community? Second, if the Rabbi of the community forbids the formation of a separatist congregation in his community, are not the separatists guilty of defying Rabbinic authority? Schick replies that they need not fear a breach of contract since they do not form a separatist congregation for their own gain but solely in order to strengthen the Torah. Nor can the Rabbi's order be operative since the separatists, far from defying Rabbinic authority, are following the decision of the most famous Hungarian Rabbis.

In a Responsum[54] dated 1878, Schick replies to a Rabbi Schlesinger who wished to know whether it was permitted for an Orthodox separatist community to allow themselves to be reunited with the larger *Status Quo* community. Schick replies: Why ask me? What do you expect me to say? Even if it be admitted that the reunion will not prove harmful to the older members of the community, what of the young who will be brought up in a more or less indifferent atmosphere? Schick concludes, therefore, that he finds it impossible to advise an Orthodox community to join a community of lax people who desire innovations. As for the argument that they cannot carry on without the assistance of the larger community and will therefore have to be reunited sooner or later in any event, whatever they can do to postpone the evil day, they should do, and God will help them.

Schick deals with a similar question in another Responsum.[55] A community was divided into the Orthodox and the Neologs who accepted the resolutions of the Congress. Now the Neologs have seen the error of their ways and have abolished the choir in their synagogue. But they have left the Bimah at the end near the Ark, because to place it in the middle of the synagogue where it belongs would result in a loss of seats. Should the Orthodox in this instance agree to become reunited with the Neologs in order to avoid strife in the community, peace being among the highest of the Jewish ideals? Schick replies that, of course, repentance is acceptable to

[53] Orah Hayyim, nos 34 and 35   [54] Ibid., no. 36   [55] Ibid., no. 37

God. Heretics who repent have a share in the World to Come. But this is only so far as God is concerned. In His mercy He will forgive them if their repentance is sincere, as only He can know. But we frail human beings cannot see into the heart. The Orthodox are far too naive in accepting at its face value the desire of the Neologs to repent. In fact, it is pure expediency. Having seen that the Congress was a tactical error, they now marshal their forces for a different type of assault, hoping that this time victory will be theirs. Let not the Orthodox be misled. There must be no union with the Neologs, even when they pretend to feel remorse.

In a reply[56] to a pupil, whose name is not given for obvious reasons, Schick advises this Rabbi who was confronted with the following problem. It is the practice in traditional synagogues to have a grille between men and women in the synagogue so that the women can see but not be seen. In the Rabbi's community they wished to open up the women's compartment so that the women could see and be seen. They threaten that unless the Rabbi gives his assent to the innovation they will open their shops on the sabbath. The ultimatum they declared was: An open women's compartment or open shops on the sabbath! What should the Rabbi do? Schick replies that the Rabbi must do his duty by preventing them from opening up the women's compartment and he should disregard their threat. Isserles[57] rules that where a ban has to be imposed, the court should not refrain from imposing it out of fear that those who are punished may be tempted to leave the Jewish fold. We are not allowed by the law of the land to impose the ban, but the principle laid down by Isserles is clear. The questioner had remarked in passing that he was now sorry that he did not leave the community when he had the opportunity of obtaining a Rabbinic post elsewhere. No, says Schick. Had you left them, they would have blamed you for their laxness. As it is, you are able to prevent them from introducing the innovations they desire. Schick tells of Moses Sofer who wished to leave Pressburg when he was offered the Rabbinate of Fuerth. He was tempted to leave for Germany, where faith was becoming weaker and where his services were especially needed. The President of

[56] Ibid., no. 77   [57] YD 334: 1

the Pressburg community, Hirsch Jaffe, pleaded that if Sofer were to leave Pressburg the religious situation there would deteriorate. Jaffe asked Sofer: Is it right to turn 'Gentiles' into 'Jews' if, in the process, 'Jews' become 'Gentiles'? Sofer, acknowledging the force of the argument, remained in Pressburg.

On the same theme, Schick has a Responsum[58] on whether it is right for the separatist Orthodox community to purchase a new cemetery or should they use the old one together with the members of the general community? Separatism is normally to be advocated, but for them to bury their dead in a different cemetery can be seen as an insult to the righteous dead of old who are buried in the general cemetery. Schick declares his unwillingness to render a decision, since he is unaware of all the circumstances. But of this he is quite certain: if the Reformers wish to introduce innovations into the burial rites and ceremonies, and if there is any danger that through association with them the children of the Orthodox will be led into heresy, the righteous dead, far from considering it to be an insult to them, will be pleased that a new cemetery is to be used.

Schick was thoroughly opposed not only to the Neologs but also to the *Status Quo* people, whom he suspected of indifference. He argues in another Responsum[59] dated 1872 that by remaining neutral in the struggle, the Status-Quo communities are, in fact, assisting the Reformers.

In a lengthy Responsum,[60] Schick gives a full account of the events of the Congress which led to the secession of the Orthodox, and why the Orthodox opposition is well founded. He remarks that the Orthodox had many reservations about attending the Congress in the first place and only decided to attend in order to protect the Torah. They demanded that the *Shulhan Arukh* be the guide of the Congress and that no resolution be passed which contradicted any ruling of Isserles in his notes to the *Shulhan Arukh* which recorded the established Ashkenazi practice. When the Orthodox saw that it was all to no avail, about fifty Orthodox delegates left in protest. This, says Schick, was right and proper. Separatism is the only answer. In a revealing aside, he remarks that

[58] Orah Hayyim, no. 717 [59] Ibid., no. 307 [60] Ibid., no. 309

among the nations, too, each religious denomination functions in isolation from the others and there has never been anything like a Congress of all the Christian denominations.

Schick then proceeds to refute, paragraph by paragraph, the resolutions passed at the Congress:

1. *All the individual Jews in each town must form themselves into a single community.* This would be correct if they all belonged to the same denomination. But it cannot apply in a town where there is a Temple with a choir and an organ. To have an organ in the synagogue is an abomination, as is stated in the pamphlet *Elleh Divre Ha-Berit.* Schick's reference here is to a collection of rulings by Moses Sofer and other prominent Rabbis against the use of the organ and the other innovations introduced by the early Reformers in the Hamburg Temple. The Reformers, continues Schick, have become a different denomination. How, then, in justice, can they interfere with our freedom to worship in separation from them? The comparison of Orthodoxy and Reform to Catholicism and Protestantism, which is implied in all of Schick's argument here and, especially, in the use of the word *kat* ('denomination', 'sect') introduces an idea, hitherto unheard of in Judaism, in which traditionally even sinful or heretical Jews are still members of the Jewish people. The same argument was used to justify *Austritt* ('separatism') in Germany by Samson Raphael Hirsch (1808–88) in his polemic against Seligmann Baer Bamberger (1807–78), the German Orthodox leader who held secession from the general community to be contrary to the Jewish tradition.

2. *Any member of the community is entitled to be nominated as a candidate for the Presidency of the community.* But, according to Jewish law, it is forbidden to elect to any communal office those who offend against the Torah by eating forbidden food, profaning the sabbath and the like.

3. *The Council of the community has the right to give rulings against which there can be no appeal.* But, according to Jewish law, only God-fearing men can act as judges.

4. *The Rabbi, too, must accept the rulings of the Council.* This clause is an affront to the Torah.

5. *There should be established a single communal organisation to*

represent the whole of Hungarian Jewry. But again we cannot accept unity under the conditions they have laid down.

6. *A Seminary should be established for the training of Rabbis.* The establishment of such a Seminary is forbidden by experience, by reason, and by tradition. Experience forbids it because it is notorious that the students of such Seminaries are not God-fearing, and the training they receive in no way equips them to render decisions in Jewish law. This is to say nothing of the heresies they are taught there. Reason forbids it because secular subjects will be taught in the Seminary, and the more of these one studies the more difficult it is to be God-fearing. It is forbidden by tradition because the law permits the study of secular subjects only on occasion,[61] not as part of a regular programme as in a Seminary. Furthermore, it is forbidden to sit at the feet of a teacher who is not God-fearing and it is wrong to study with the motive of making a career out of the Torah.

Schick was so convinced of the need for separatist communities to be formed that he intervened in the dispute between Hirsch and Bamberger, siding with the former. He writes to Bamberger[62] to apologise for his effrontery in stating his opinion on a matter that is the concern of German Jewry, but feels obliged to protest at Bamberger's stand. We can learn from the Torah, the Hagiographa, Rabbinic teaching and experience that it is forbidden to associate with the Reformers. The Torah says in connection with Korah: 'Separate yourselves from this congregation' (Num. 16 : 21). Isaac Arama's *Akedat Yitzhak* states that it was on the basis of this verse that the Rabbis introduced the ban (*herem*) on sinners. Schick remarks that he is convinced that if the government permitted a ban to be imposed on the Reformers, and Bamberger were requested to add his signature to it, he would do so. How, then, can Bamberger bring himself to associate with them? The Hagiographa, in the book of Ezra, teaches the same lesson. We see how strict Ezra was with Jews who had married foreign women. We are not allowed even to use the same cemetery as the Reformers, since the law is clear that a righteous man must not be buried near a wicked man, and this is practically

---

[61] Isserles, Yoreh Deah 246: 4   [62] Orah Hayyim, no. 306

unavoidable if the Orthodox share the cemetery with the Reformers. We can learn the lesson from Rabbinic teaching, too, since the Rabbis say:[63] 'Keep thee far from a bad neighbour and associate not with the wicked.' As for experience, it demonstrates conclusively that even if the older people remain faithful to the tradition, the younger people are influenced to abandon the tradition wherever there is a mixed community of Orthodox and Reformers. Schick appeals to Bamberger to be big enough to acknowledge his error, and he will then be instrumental in sanctifying the name of Heaven.

In addition to the above on separatism, there are a number of other Responsa of Schick on theological themes.

A Rabbi Joseph Fisch asked him[64] to explain why there is no benediction before reciting the *Shema* and saying prayers. Schick refers to the Responsum of Ibn Adret on the subject,[65] but offers a novel interpretation of his own. A benediction was only ordained by the Rabbis before the performance of a *mitzvah* where it was certain that the *mitzvah* would be carried out. There can be no such certainty in the case of the *Shema* and prayer, since concentration on the meaning of the words is an essential ingredient in the performance of the *mitzvah* and we can never be sure beforehand that our powers of concentration will be adequate to the task.

Another Responsum[66] deals with the question of whether one may pray in a synagogue that was built on the sabbath by a Jewish contractor. Schick replies that it is forbidden to pray there. He is aware that a case can be made out to permit it, but is convinced that it ought to be forbidden in order to serve as a warning to offenders.

An interesting question discussed by Schick[67] is whether one may use the Hebrew Bible printed by the Christian missionaries in London, if one removes the New Testament. He remarks that it would seem to be forbidden to destroy the Old Testament printed by the missionaries, but no one who values his soul should ever use such a Bible. The same applies, he observes, to the Commentary known as the *Biur*, produced by the school of

---

[63] Avot 1: 7   [64] Orah Hayyim, no. 39   [65] P. 75 above
[66] Orah Hayyim, no. 41   [67] Ibid., no. 66

Moses Mendelssohn. Since it contains the sacred text and that of the standard commentaries it must not be destroyed, but no one must ever use it in his studies.

Finally, Schick discusses[68] the much-debated question of whether it is permitted to ask the dead to pray for us. Is it 'inquiring of the dead', or not? Schick notes that the prohibition on 'inquiring of the dead' does not apply, since the *Shulhan Arukh*[69] permits attempts to be made to contact the soul of the dead. But the practice is forbidden on other grounds: namely, it is wrong to approach God through intermediaries. Nevertheless, some authorities permit it, arguing that when we inform the dead of our needs they are moved to pray to God on our behalf. Even if we are ourselves unworthy of having our prayers answered, God may grant them in order not to cause distress to the righteous dead who pray for us. Consequently, while it is certainly forbidden to pray to angels,[70] because to do so might suggest that divine status is being given to them, it is permitted to recite prayers at the graves of the righteous.

Hayyim Halberstam (1793–1876), Rabbi of Zans in Galicia, was both a distinguished Talmudist and a Hasidic master with many thousands of followers. His Responsa collection *Divre Hayyim* contains, as we might have expected, a number of theological discussions.

Two of these deal with penances. In one,[71] he discusses the general question of penance for severe sins. We have seen more than once that in the literature on this subject the 'balance' (*teshuvat ha-mishkal*) of the *Rokeah* is the guide.[72] Halberstam begins by stating that repentance involves chiefly a sincere resolve not to repeat the sin and to feel remorse for having transgressed God's laws. He remarks that the repentant sinner should take great care not to eat meat from an animal killed by an unreliable *shohet* and not to drink wine unless he is sure beyond doubt that it is *kasher*. The sinner should fast for forty consecutive days, except for the sabbaths and festivals, and during the night he

---

[68] Ibid., no. 293   [69] YD 179: 10   [70] See pp. 10–11 above
[71] Part I, Orah Hayyim, no. 34, cf. part II, nos 70, 87 and 137; Even Ha-Ezer, nos 1 and 21; *Hashmatot*, nos 1 and 10.
[72] See pp. 101–2 above

should eat no meat and drink no wine. On nine different occasions he should roll naked in the snow in winter. But if he is too weak to fast he should 'redeem' each fast by giving alms. Nevertheless, he should still fast for a few hours each day and, when he does eat, he should stop short of eating his fill. He should always dress modestly. Halberstam concludes: 'May God have mercy on him to accept his repentance, together with the repentance of all Israel who return sincerely to Him.'

In the other Responsum[73] on penance, Halberstam discusses the question of a man who had sinned with a married woman who, as a result, is forbidden to her husband. Is the man himself, or the Rabbi to whom he confessed his sin, obliged to inform the husband that his wife is forbidden to him, or should they keep quiet because the Torah respects human dignity? Halberstam refers to the decision of Ezekiel Landau[74] that the husband should be informed, but, after an analysis of the legal principles involved, comes to a different conclusion. The husband should not be informed. Halberstam observes that this is the advice given by 'the great ones of the generation'—i.e. the Hasidic masters, when their Hasidim confessed to them that they had misbehaved with married women.

In a Responsum[75] dated 1856, Halberstam discusses the question whether cousins may marry. There is no doubt that Jewish law permits the marriage of first cousins but, in the Ethical Will of Judah the Saint of Regensburg,[76] there are many rules forbidding certain marriages permitted by law, such as this one. Halberstam notes that there are a number of ambiguities regarding the Will; for example, whether Judah the Saint intended his rules to apply to all Jews or only to his own descendants. Consequently, it is binding only in those matters which Jews everywhere have accepted, which is not the case in connection with the marriage of first cousins.

Halberstam returns to the question of Judah the Saint's will in a Responsum[77] dated 1858. He observes that it is futile to apply

[73] Part I, Orah Hayyim, no. 35
[74] See p. 175 above
[75] Part I, Even Ha-Ezer, no. 7
[76] See p. 217 above
[77] Part I, Even Ha-Ezer, no. 8

human reasoning to these mysterious matters, which stem from a source higher than the human mind. The fact, for instance, that the Talmud not only permits the marriage of an uncle to his niece but positively advocates it is no contradiction to the Saint's disapproval of such a marriage. The Saint saw that in his day people no longer had the pure motives for marriage they had in Talmudic times. All the evidence goes to show that the great medieval commentators and teachers (the *Rishonim*) did not dispute the Saint's rulings, and we must not depart from them. 'For we are as nothing in relation to their wisdom, learning, saintliness and piety! We must accept their words in love, even when they are contradicted by the Talmud.' Nevertheless, since we are aware that there are ambiguities about the Saint's will, we should follow the practice of people in these lands who object only to the marriage of a man to a woman with the same first name as his mother, also mentioned in the Saint's will. Halberstam refuses[78] to permit the marriage of a man to a woman with the same first name as his mother.

As a Hasidic master, Halberstam was naturally consulted on the problems connected with the Hasidic patterns of prayer.[79] One of his Responsa[80] dated 1870 is addressed to Abraham Isaac, Rabbi of Kleinwardein, and concerns the substitution by the Hasidim of the Lurianic prayer-book for the Ashkenazi version. He is aware that *Hatam Sofer* forbids the change,[81] but finds such a decision very odd. Far be it from him to disagree with such a tremendous authority as the *Hatam Sofer*, but he relies on the famous Hasidic masters who encouraged the change of version. Every follower of the Baal Shem Tov, the founder of the Hasidic movement, should use the Lurianic version.

In two Responsa,[82] Halberstam expresses his disapproval of prayers being conducted by the Reader and a choir instead of, as in the normal Hasidic practice, by a man with a pleasant voice but whose intention is more on the prayers themselves than on the melodies. Halberstam rebukes the President of a community for

---

[78] Ibid., end of no. 101
[79] For Halberstam's Responsum on this subject see *Hasidic Prayer*, pp. 159–64
[80] Part II, no. 8   [81] See pp. 214–15 above
[82] Part II, nos 17 and 18

allowing the people to appoint a Reader and his choir. This is an attempt to ape Christian worship and must be discouraged. As for the complaint that without a Cantor and choir the services will seem uncouth, no notice should be taken of this. Every religion, says Halberstam, has practices which seem bizarre to outsiders, yet the adherents of these religions never dream of changing their pattern of worship because it is ridiculed. It is all an attempt to follow the Reformers, with whom there is no point in arguing since they reject all Rabbinic authority and will remain unimpressed even when chapter and verse from Rabbinic sources are quoted against them.

Halberstam expresses[83] his strong disapproval of Reform by strictly forbidding a community to appoint a Rabbi with Reformist leanings.

In a Responsum[84] addressed to the Rabbi of Mosichisk, he discusses whether it is permitted for the Hasidim to divide themselves up into separate congregations. Halberstam sees no legal objection, but advises against it on the strength of advice given by Hasidic teachers of his that they should try their utmost to pray together in a single conventicle.

A Responsum[85] addressed to Rabbi Meir Rokeah considers three different questions. The first is on an edition of Maimonides' work on logic, *Millot Ha-Higgayon*, edited by a 'heretic'. Halberstam rules that it is forbidden to use such a book. No benefit whatever must be had from anything produced by these 'wicked men'. The second question concerns the statement in the Talmud[86] that one who eats of food from which a mouse has eaten forgets his learning. Does it apply to all the food or only to the part at which the mouse has nibbled? Halberstam says that it is obvious that the statement refers to all the food. The third question concerns the chapter divisions in the Bible. These are, in fact, of Christian origin. They are found in the Vulgate but not in any Hebrew manuscripts until the fourteenth century, while the numbering of verses dates from as late as the sixteenth century. Jews adopted the chapter and verse divisions in order to assist

[83] Part II, no. 13
[85] Part II, Yoreh Deah, no. 60
[84] Part II, Orah Hayyim, no. 21
[86] Hor. 13b

them in quoting verses when disputing with Christians.[87] The questioner had asked Halberstam whether Jews should continue to use this untraditional division into chapters and verses. Halberstam quotes the Talmudic saying[88] that if the Jews are not prophets, they are the children of prophets. Customs adopted by Jews everywhere are divinely inspired and, since all Jews have accepted this division, no one must think up 'belly theories' in order to depart from the established Jewish practice.

Another Responsum[89] concerns a school-teacher who had insulted the Kabbalist Hayyim Ibn Attar (1696–1743), whose work *Or Ha-Hayyim* on the Pentateuch was highly regarded by the Hasidim, by declaring that he did not believe that this work was inspired by the holy spirit. Halberstam observes that there is no doubt whatever that great men can be the recipients of the holy spirit even in our day. From a Talmudic passage[90] it emerges that there are two kinds of inspiration. There is 'the holy spirit attained by the prophets' and 'the holy spirit attained by the sages'. It is said that this 'scoundrel' has the support of 'the great ones of the generation', but Halberstam finds it impossible to believe that the report has any truth in it. Either the rumour is entirely false or else the man misled them. 'The truth is that even in our day the real sages who are not attracted by material things have the holy spirit.' Halberstam is convinced that the work *Or Ha-Hayyim* was composed under the influence of the holy spirit. But every author, even nowadays, can be the recipient of the holy spirit, that is to say, in that his teachings are in full accord with the truth of the Torah. It follows that the said school-teacher is a heretic, both because he refuses to believe in the great masters who testified that the work was written under the influence of the holy spirit and because he denies the whole idea of the holy spirit operating nowadays and so rejects Talmudic teaching. Children must not be delivered into the care of such a fellow, but no decision can be given in his absence to deprive him of his salary, since he may have sinned unintentionally.

---

[87] On this, see the article by S. Weingarten in *Sinai*, vol. XXI, February 1958, pp. 281 ff.

[88] Pes. 66a   [89] Part II, Yoreh Deah, no. 105   [90] BB 12a

Halberstam was asked:[91] since there is an opinion in the Talmud [92] that to have a formula in mind is equivalent to giving it verbal expression, how is it permitted to have the Tetragrammaton in mind, the Mishnah[93] holding it to be a most serious offence to utter the divine name as it written? Halberstam refers to his discussion with his pupils of the Talmudic maxim quoted. Obviously where the offence is stated explicitly to be the *uttering* of the name, there can be no objection to having it in mind. This leads him to consider the Kabbalistic practice of having the divine name in mind. He refers to Maimonides'[94] distinction between the Tetragrammaton, denoting God's essence, and all other divine names that are only attributes. We are allowed to offer our prayers only to God Himself, never to His attributes. This is the meaning of: 'I offer my prayers to the Master of the Nose',[95] that is to say, to God's essence, because the nose is the organ of breathing and God the life of the Universe. Consequently, the Kabbalists certainly do not mean that a man should pray to the actual letters of the divine name but that, when praying, he should have in mind the essence of God as denoted by the Tetragrammaton. But all this applies only to the world beneath that of Emanation. In the World of Emanation, God and His essence are One. However, remarks Halberstam, he is very suspicious of things recorded in the Kabbalistic works because it is notorious that the Shabbateans have tampered with the texts to introduce heretical ideas of their own. Therefore, the only Kabbalistic works that can be said to enjoy full authority for him are those which he was assured were reliable by his masters, the disciples of the Baal Shem Tov.

A Responsum[96] dated 1866 concerns the case of the *katlanit*, the woman whose husbands have died and whom it is forbidden to marry because she is cursed with bad luck.[97] But supposing the death of one of her husbands was caused by his sins? Halberstam remarks that the Talmudic references to bad luck or to good fortune—*mazzal*—are not to be understood as meaning that God

[91] Part II, Yoreh Deah, no. 130   [92] Ber. 20b   [93] Sanh. 10: 1
[94] *Guide of the Perplexed*, I, 61   [95] *Zohar* III, 130b
[96] Part II, Even Ha-Ezer, no. 26   [97] Yev. 64b

has abandoned in any way His management of the world. The 'stars' are like the axe in the hands of the woodcutter. They can neither redeem from death nor prevent reward being given to the righteous. God has so ordered His world that the stars can have some effect—to ward off death and the like—but ultimately it is God who governs the world. Thus when the Talmud remarks that it is the bad *mazzal* of the *katlanit* that brings about the death of her husbands, the meaning is that her *mazzal* prevents any suspension of the death sentence due to the husbands. However, in these matters, beyond the scope of the human mind, too close an inquiry must not be made. Since many of the authorities are in any event lenient with regard to these matters, we are justified in saying that God will protect the simple. Halberstam advises the questioner to consult the Hasidic masters of the generation and do as they advise. He reports in the name of his master that in such matters all depends on the decree of the Zaddik—i.e. if the Zaddik declares that no harm will result, there is safety in the marriage.

Finally, there is his Responsum[98] on whether people who do not believe in the words of the Talmudic Rabbis are disqualified thereby from acting as witnesses. They are heretics, says Halberstam, as Maimonides has ruled,[99] and a heretic is disqualified from acting as a witness. The Torah itself enjoins us to believe in the Rabbis, and one who does not believe in them denies the Torah itself.

Joel Ungar of Rechnitz (1800–85) was a pupil of *Hatam Sofer* and a faithful follower of his master's opposition to Reform and innovations in Jewish religious life. But, unlike Moses Schick, he was opposed to schism in the Hungarian community. As the Rabbi of Paks, Ungar taught many disciples and won fame for his Responsa collection *Teshuvat Riba* published posthumously by his son-in-law Sussman Sofer.

The first Responsum in the collection contains a letter dated 1844 from the Rabbis of Amsterdam addressed to other Rabbis, urging them to take steps against the Reform protocol issued following the Brunswick Conference in June 1844, together with

---

[98] *Hashmatot*, no. 33   [99] *Yad*, Teshuvah 3: 8

Ungar's reply. The Jewish community in Brunswick was won over to Reform. The Brunswick Conference was summoned by the Rabbi of the town, Levi Herzfeld.[100]

Both from the original letter and from Ungar's reply we learn that the following were the chief reasons advanced for treating the members of the Conference as heretics, with whom there was no point in debating but who must be declared as such in order to prevent the masses from accepting their perverse opinions.

1. They reject the authority of the Talmud.

2. They permit intermarriage with Gentiles, provided the couple agree that their children be brought up as Jews.

3. They deny the coming of the Messiah and the return of the Jews to the holy land.

4. They wish to abolish long established customs such as the recital of *Kol Nidre* on Yom Kippur.

Ungar, supported by his Dayyanim, agrees entirely with the authors of the original letter that these Reformers are complete heretics. Anyone who rejects the authority of the Talmud is a heretic, and it is forbidden for anyone to change an established custom. In this latter connection Ungar quotes the opinion of Solomon Luria[101] that even if the author of the *Zohar*, R. Simeon b. Yohai himself, asked us to change the established custom, we must pay no heed to him. In a lengthy legal discourse, Ungar proves that intermarriage is among the most serious offences. As for the denial of the Messiah, it is true that Joseph Albo, following R. Hillel in the Talmud,[102] regards one who denies the coming of a personal Messiah only as a sinner, not as a heretic, but this does not apply to the Reformers, who deny the entire doctrine of Israel's return to the holy land in the Messianic age.

A Responsum (no. 27) from Paks dated 1864, addressed to Ungar's disciple Joseph Ehrengrüber, concerns a Reader in the synagogue who, while taking the scroll from the Ark, clumsily caused another scroll to fall to the ground. Ungar notes that it is general custom to fast when a scroll falls to the ground. But, in

---

[100] See W. Gunther Plaut, *The Rise of Reform Judaism*, pp. 74-9
[101] See p. 139 above   [102] See p. 125 above

fact, as the authorities point out,[103] it is only the person directly responsible who is obliged to fast, not the whole congregation. The Reader should fast on Monday, Thursday and the following Monday. He should offer supplication to the Giver of the Torah to pardon him for his lack of care. Although, according to the law, there is no need for the rest of the congregation to fast, yet, if their heart grieves them, they should 'redeem' their penance by giving alms to poor students of the Torah who reside in the holy land. It may be that this terrible thing was allowed to happen because the congregation did not pay sufficient reverence to the Torah—talking, for example, during the reading of the Torah. From now on they should be more careful and they need fear no evil.

It was generally held to be meritorious to disinter a corpse for the purpose of burial in the holy land. A Rabbi wished to suggest that this applies only during the first year after death. After the year, the body has decayed and the soul has left the body to repose in Paradise, so that there is no purpose in the reburial. Ungar (no. 155) refutes this. There is still purpose in reburial in the holy land in order to avoid the need for the corpse to roll underground[104] at the time of the resurrection. Furthermore, even though the wicked are punished in Hell for a year only, there are other less severe punishments which are visited on the dead even after a year; so there is point in the atonement provided by burial in the holy land. Again, it is not the whole of the body which suffers decay. There is a small bone which never decays and it is from this that, at the time of the resurrection, the new body is reconstituted. According to the great Kabbalist Isaac Luria, the 'spirit' (ruah) ascends to the 'soul' (neshamah) and never returns to earth, except in the case of the saints. But the vital spirit (nefesh), with which a man is endowed at birth, hovers over the bones of the dead always, only ascending on the New Moon and the sabbath.

Jacob Ettlinger (1798–1871), Rabbi of Altona, was the first Orthodox Rabbi to study at a university. He was the teacher of Samson Raphael Hirsch, the famous Orthodox German leader, and his Responsa were published in two series.

[103] *Magen Avraham* to end of 44   [104] See p. 94 above

A question which came to Ettlinger[105] from New York was whether a man whose face was disfigured by a skin disease may officiate as a Reader in the synagogue. Solomon Luria,[106] says Ettlinger, quotes R. Meir of Rothenburg[107] who rules that a cripple can serve as a Reader since God actually prefers broken vessels. Joel Sirkes[108] agrees. But *Magen Avraham*[109] quotes the *Zohar* saying that a cripple is unfit, so how can he, Ettlinger, disagree with such weighty authority? The man should not be allowed to officiate as a Reader.

A Responsum[110] dated 1837 is addressed from Altona to David Meldola, the Haham in London. Can a *kohen*, married to a Gentile woman and with children from her, serve as a *kohen*? Ettlinger is hesitant, but states that 'possibly' he may continue to serve as a *kohen*.

Another Responsum[111] from Altona, dated 1846, discusses the question of *metzitzah*, the drawing out of the blood by suction after circumcision.[112] The Talmud demands that this be done because otherwise there is danger to the child, but nowadays the doctors say there is a likelihood of infection if *metzitzah* is performed. Ettlinger fails to see how a believer can rely on the doctors against the explicit words of the Talmudic Rabbis. Rabbah Tosfoah says that a woman can carry her child for twelve months,[113] but all the doctors deny that such a thing is possible. Ettlinger quotes Jonathan Eibushütz[114] regarding the possibility of conception through a woman bathing in a bath into which a man had ejected his semen, which the sages believe to be possible but which all doctors deny. In another Responsum,[115] Ettlinger returns to the subject. After he had given his earlier decision, a number of critics poured ridicule on him. He would ask them to ask the doctors if they agree with the Rabbis on diseases of the lungs which render an animal *terefa* because it cannot live. If we are to follow the doctors, the whole Torah will fall by the wayside.

Ettlinger addressed an interesting Responsum[116] to Amsterdam

[105] I, no. 5
[106] *Yam Shel Shelomo* to Hull. chapter I
[107] See p. 54 above
[108] *Bah* to Orah Hayyim 53
[109] *Magen Avraham* to ibid.
[110] I, no. 6   [111] I, no. 23
[112] See p. 212 above   [113] Yev. 80   [114] *Bene Ahuvah*, Ishut 15
[115] I, no. 24   [116] I, no. 67

from Altona in 1852. A pious Jew was advised to have resort to magnetism, a form of hypnotism, to cure himself of a disease. Is it permitted or does it smack of magic? Ettlinger says that he consulted the physicians, who declared that it is a natural thing and there is no magic involved. In any event, the authorities rule[117] that it is permitted to have a Gentile recite a magical incantation over a wound provided that he does not mention the name of a pagan god.

A Responsum[118] from Altona in 1859 discusses whether a penance is required for one obliged to eat on Yom Kippur on doctor's orders since, if he fasted, his life would be in danger. He must not do penance, declares Ettlinger. Indeed, by eating, far from committing a sin, he performs a *mitzvah*. The Torah enjoins us to take care of our health and ward off all danger to life. Ettlinger adds that the man who was forced to eat was in fact cured, and a sick person who has been cured is one of those whose sins are pardoned in any event.

The new conditions in Germany in the nineteenth century are reflected in a Responsum[119] declared to be 'a decision in theory but not in practice', and dated Altona, 1860, addressed to Shemaryahu Zuckermann, a pious Jew who refused to touch wine handled by Jews who openly profaned the sabbath. Zuckermann was severely criticised for treating such Jews as if they were Gentiles, and he turned to Ettlinger for his opinion. Ettlinger decides that although according to the strict letter of the law Zuckermann is right, yet this law is based on the fact that wilful and public desecration of the sabbath is an act of defiance of the Jewish religion and amounts to a declaration that its perpetrator no longer wishes to be identified with the Jewish community. This is no longer the case. Many people nowadays profane the sabbath, not out of defiance, but because they are unaware of the seriousness of the sin. They imagine that to keep the sabbath is no more than an act of special piety. The proof that they have no intention of denying the Jewish religion is that they continue to attend synagogue services whenever they can and are identified in many other ways with the Jewish community. This Responsum of Ettlinger was used by

[117] YD 155 and *Shakh* to YD 179   [118] II, no. 25   [119] II, no. 23

many later Halakhists who had to face the same situation. Very few Orthodox Rabbis were prepared to invoke the full strictness of the law which treats sabbath profaners as being completely outside the Jewish community. Their argument is generally based on that of Ettlinger, to whom they usually refer when considering cases of this nature.

Finally, there is Ettlinger's Responsum[120] dated Altona 1854, addressed to Gabriel Adler, concerning a formulation of Maimonides. Maimonides writes in his Code[121] that sins are weighed against sins and virtues against virtues in God's assessment, not only of the individual, but of the community as a whole and of mankind as a whole in each generation. If the sins of a generation outweigh its merits, that generation is destroyed. Maimonides quotes the verse: 'And the Lord saw that the wickedness of man was great in the earth' (Gen. 6 : 5). When He saw that the sins of that generation were far greater than their merits, He resolved to destroy them and brought the Deluge. But, Adler asked, does not this verse speak of the Deluge? After the Deluge, God promised Noah never again to destroy the whole of mankind; so how can Maimonides record it as a part of the divine government of the world even now? Ettlinger replies that God's promise to Noah was never to destroy the world by means of a Deluge. He gave no guarantee that He would never wipe out mankind if their sins deserved it. He would not then choose a Deluge but some other means. The Talmud[122] tells us that if Israel had not accepted the Torah, God would have caused the world to revert to chaos.

Zevi Hirsch Chajes[123] (1808–55), Rabbi of Zolkiew, was an outstanding Talmudist as well as one of the pioneers of the scientific study of Judaism which goes by the name of *Jüdische Wissenschaft*. Chajes' Responsa collection *Teshuvot Maharatz* contains three works: part I is a collection of Responsa in the conventional sense; part II, entitled *Imre Binah*, deals with historical questions regarding the Rabbinic literature; part III, *Minhat Kenaot*, is a sustained polemic against Reform.

[120] II, no. 145   [121] *Yad*, Teshuvah 3 : 2   [122] AZ 3a
[123] On Chajes see the fine biography of Meir Herskovitz, *Rabbi Zevi Hirsch Chajes*

There are two Responsa of theological interest in part I. One of these (no. 12) discusses whether it is permitted to read books dealing with general, secular knowledge on the sabbath. Chajes quotes the ruling of the *Shulhan Arukh*[124] that it is forbidden, and remarks: God forbid that we should depart from this ruling. Even though Isserles, in his notes to the passage, permits, it, he does so only when the works are written in Hebrew, not in other languages. Chajes refers, however, to a ruling by Jacob Emden which permits the reading of newspapers on the sabbath.

In another Responsum (no. 32), Chajes rules that it is permitted for the Lemberg community to accede to the request of the authorities to lend a Sefer Torah to the court for the purpose of oath-taking by Jews. Although, he says, it is forbidden to teach the Torah to Gentiles, here there is no teaching and it is certainly permitted in order to promote harmonious relations with the general community.

The first chapter of *Imre Binah* is a Responsum addressed to Hayyim Chajes, the author's son. Here Chajes justifies the principle that the Aggadic passages in the Talmud enjoy far less authority than the legal passages. This is because there are frequent contradictions between the views expressed in the Babylonian and those expressed in the Palestinian Talmud and, moreover, the text is frequently unsound. With regard to Halakhah, the difficulties have been removed by the diligent attention of the great sages throughout history, but the Aggadic passages have been neglected by them to some extent and so are in an unfinished state.

In chapter 6 of *Imre Binah*, Chajes discusses the various types of 'heavenly voice' (*bat kol*) referred to in the Talmud. In chapter 12 he engages in literary criticism of the Mishnah, demonstrating that additions were made to the work after its original compilation. This explains the strange phenomenon that Amoraim are sometimes the authors of sayings found in the Mishnah. The truth is that such sayings were added later to the original part of the Mishnah. The other chapters deal with such questions as the nature of the Targum and the Septuagint and the relation of *Avot De-Rabbi Nathan* to Avot.

[124] OH 307: 16

In *Minhat Kenaot* Chajes attacks the Reformers on the following points:

1. Even though it is lawful to recite prayers in any language, public prayers in the synagogue must be recited only in Hebrew.

2. It is forbidden to play musical instruments on the sabbath, and the use of an organ in the synagogue is strictly forbidden.

3. Intermarriage is strictly forbidden.

4. Kohanim ('priests') are to be treated as such on the strength of their family tradition, and the priestly laws still have binding force.

5. It is forbidden to travel by train on the sabbath.

6. Since the prohibition of pulse on Passover has been accepted by the Ashkenazim everywhere, no power on earth can now permit it.

7. Circumcision is the sign of the covenant, and no one dare contemplate for one moment the possibility of its abolition.

8. No Jewish court has the power to set any law aside, even though the motive be to prevent people leaving the Jewish fold.

9. An oath taken by a Jew in connection with his business dealings can never be annulled by a sage. The *Kol Nidre* formula which the Reformers wished to abolish refers only to purely religious vows.

10. The customs obtaining in the synagogue can never be changed.

Chajes calls for a conference of Rabbis loyal to the tradition to refute the claims of the Reformers who, he says, merely wish to copy their Gentile neighbours. Although the Reformers appear to attack only certain provisions of the Oral Law, the truth is that when the Oral Law is weakened, the Written Law also loses its authority. Chajes blames the Orthodox Rabbis for their indifference. Experience has shown that when the Orthodox fight back they are successful; they are able to retain the loyalty of their youth and win the respect of their Gentile neighbours. Chajes is impatient with the contention that Reform is only a temporary phenomenon not worth fighting, that the Orthodox are not sufficiently strong to take on the Reformers, and that it is undignified for Rabbis to engage in polemics. All these betoken weakness, when strength is required to fight the Lord's battles.

Joseph Saul Nathanson (1810–75), Rabbi of Lemberg from 1857 until his death, was as prolific a writer of Responsa as *Radbaz*. His famous collection *Shoel U-Meshiv* is composed of fifteen parts in six volumes, each part containing on average 200 Responsa. Nathanson's forte was practical law, but some of his Responsa are of theological interest.

A Responsum[125] is addressed to Jacob Solomon, Rabbi of Premiszlan. The parents of a nine-month-old infant were kept awake at night by his incessant crying. The mother changed the baby's napkins and placed him in his cot. The child appeared to be peaceful and sound asleep. The exhausted parents overslept and, when they awoke, found to their horror that the child had had a fit, dying after an hour or two. The poor parents now wish to undergo a penance, but the Rabbi argued that they were in no way responsible for what happened. Nathanson refers to the consideration of similar cases in the Responsa,[126] and quotes Abraham Gumbiner's references[127] to the authorities who deal with the question. Nathanson discusses whether a penance is required where an act, or a failure to act, results in death, even where there is no legal responsibility. The mother is too weak to fast and, even so far as the father is concerned, Nathanson observes that nowadays we are all weak in health so that severe penances must not be imposed. Nor can the couple afford to 'redeem' their fasts by giving much alms. The mother should wear no jewellery for a whole year. The father should give as much alms as he can afford and attend no banquet for a whole year. They should support a school in which poor children are taught the Torah. Each year they should fast on the anniversary of the child's death, but if they find this too hard they should 'redeem' it by giving alms. But the main thing is for them to confess their fault and beg God's pardon. Nathanson continues:

Their sins should be ever before them. With this, their sin will be forgiven since they did not do it intentionally and only because

[125] Vol. I, part I, no. 172   [126] See pp. 101–3 above
[127] *Magen Avraham* 603 (printer's error has 423)

sleep overcame them. However, they should see to it that the children they have, as well as those yet to be born to them, should be brought up in the way of the Torah and in the fear of God to the best of their ability, for this is the whole duty of man and the Holy One, blessed be He, in all His world, has only the four ells of the Halakhah. And the purpose of the Torah is repentance and good deeds. Through this will their sin be pardoned. If they will so behave they need have no anxiety. The Holy One, blessed be He, opens His hand to welcome even sinners who turn to Him: how much more so when, by accident and without intention, parents are responsible for the death of their own child.

In another Responsum[128] to the same Rabbi, Nathanson deals with a similar case, but where the mother was rather more to blame. Here Nathanson adopts basically the same approach, but is more severe on the mother.

A Responsum dated 1862[129] is addressed to Michael Hubner, Rabbi of Nizhnov, where a man had served as a teacher of children for fifteen years. During that time he had become so popular that he was appointed beadle in the synagogue and as a jester at weddings. This man refused to allow any other teacher to settle in the town because he feared competition. Hubner, however, as the town Rabbi, protested at the man's attempt to secure a monopoly, fearing that it would affect the children's progress. Further, as town Rabbi, he decreed in a sermon that no children should be given into the care of this man until there was at least one other teacher in the town. Teachers from the neighbouring villages, hearing of this, came to settle in the town, but owing to the great popularity of the first teacher, the townsfolk refused to give their children into the care of any other. So Hubner himself went around collecting a few children for one of the other teachers. Soon afterwards, the first teacher fell ill and shortly died, and everyone in the town blames Hubner for being instrumental in causing the man's death. Does he require to do penance? Nathanson refers to the previous Responsa that if a man had been indirectly responsible for another man's death a penance is required, since God would not allow such a thing to happen through a completely innocent man. True, Hubner did it all out of a high

128 Vol. I, part I, no. 173   129 Ibid., no. 174

sense of duty, but even if a good man curses a sinner and the sinner dies, a penance is required. Hubner should fast each Monday and Thursday for a whole year. He should also fast each year on the anniversary of the man's death. If he is too weak to engage in all these fasts he should 'redeem' them by giving alms. Then will his sin be pardoned and he need have no anxiety.

There are two Responsa[130] in reply to a question put to Nathanson in the year 1858 by Rabbi Judah Mittleman of New York. A private house had been used as a Lutheran chapel, with the inscription 'Welsh–Scotch Methodist Church' over the gate. It was a Protestant church and so contained no ikons or crosses. Is it permitted to use this building as a synagogue? Nathanson rules that it is not only permitted but meritorious to convert such a building into a synagogue.

Another Responsum[131] on the synagogue concerns a window that closely resembled those in a church, the frame being in the form of four squares so that it looked like a cross. Is it permitted to pray in such a synagogue? Strictly speaking, says Nathanson, it is permitted, since there was obviously no intention of having a cross in the synagogue. Yet it is right to remove the window. However, nowadays the Rabbis are not heeded and controversy should be avoided. If it can be changed without fuss, so much the better.

An interesting Responsum[132] discusses whether a Gentile, a 'son of Noah'—i.e. who is obliged to keep the 'seven precepts of the sons of Noah', one of which prohibits idolatry—may have another being besides God as the object of his worship. This is known technically as *shittuf* ('association') and is the question which engaged Jewish teachers when they considered the status of Christianity. What it really amounts to is, whether according to the Torah, a Gentile may practise the Christian religion. Nathanson refers to the ruling of Isserles[133] that nowadays Gentiles have God in mind when they take an oath. Nathanson quotes various authorities who differ on this question, but then seeks to prove

130 Vol. I, part 3, nos 72 and 73   131 Ibid., no. 74
132 Vol. II, part I, no. 51
133 OH 156. On the whole subject see J. Katz, *Exclusiveness and Tolerance*

it from the Bible. He states that when he first considered the question he came up with a passage in the Bible which seemed to clinch the issue. He remarks in passing that it is his practice to read the Bible through each year from end to end. The passage is in II Kings 17. Here, in verse 33, it is said of the Samaritans: 'They feared the Lord, and served their own gods.' A careful examination of the passages demonstrates that the fact that they served their own gods was not held against them, since they also served the Lord. This proves that a Gentile is not obliged to reject *shittuf*. However, at the end of this Responsum Nathanson adds that in 1857, years later, he came across a proof to the contrary. The Midrash[134] puns on the word *Madai* (Media) in Esther 1 : 3 and says that it is from *modim* ('they acknowledge'). The Medes acknowledged God. The Midrash continues: 'The kings of Media were righteous. The only complaint God had of them was that they worshipped the idols their forefathers had handed down to them.' But if a Gentile may have *shittuf*, God would have had no cause for complaint at all. In the course of his discussion Nathanson also mentions that *shittuf* in any event means that there is the belief and worship of other gods, but God is recognised as the Supreme Being. If Gentiles believe that God is no greater than the other gods it is not *shittuf*, and is certainly forbidden.

Finally, Nathanson considers[135] a statement in the Mishnah:[136] 'In the World to Come the Holy One, blessed be He, will make each righteous person inherit 310 worlds, for it is written: "That I may cause those that love Me to inherit substance [*yesh* = 310 in numerical value] and that I may fill their treasures" (Prov. 8 : 21).' What is the meaning of this? Nathanson explains that a man can only do his best when carrying out the precepts. He must begin, and then God in His great mercy will turn his poor efforts into great treasuries of substantial worth. The spiritual worlds man has acquired will be made substantial by God. As for the references to 'treasuries', the saying can be understood through an observation of the Gaon of Vilna. A king's treasure is unobtainable. For God, who made all, the only 'treasure' is that which He cannot obtain, as it were, without the efforts of human beings. He has given man

[134] Esther R. 1 : 18   [135] Vol. III, part 3, no. 53   [136] Uktzin 3 : 12

free will and, in this sense, man's fear of Heaven is God's precious treasure.

Naphtali Zevi Judah Berlin (1817–93) was head of the famous Yeshivah in Volozhyn for forty years. He belonged to the great Lithuanian tradition of sober Talmudic learning, aloof from Hasidic fervour and Kabbalistic speculation. His Responsa collection *Meshiv Davar* was published in four parts in Warsaw in 1894.

A lengthy Responsum[137] is entitled 'Right and Left'. The author of an article in the journal *Mahazike Ha-Dat*, published in Poland with the aim of strengthening Orthodoxy, raised the question whether there exists in Judaism a three-part division into right, left and centre. Berlin understands the article as postulating that from the earliest times there have been three distinct trends among Jews. Those on the right were the saints who separated themselves from all worldly things. Those on the left were the wicked who, whether out of ignorance or wilfully, threw off the yoke of religion. Those in the centre lived a normal life in the world but did not rebel against the Torah and its teachings. With respect, says Berlin, the author contradicts himself. He begins by asking whether there are three trends *within* Judaism and goes on to state that one of these trends is outside the faith. There are, in fact, three trends—right, left and centre—but they are to be observed within the faith.

Those on the right have a mystical love of God and are attached to Him. Since such an attitude involves complete separation from the world it is possible only for a very few rare individuals. Those on the left keep all the precepts of the Torah but have never tasted the true flavour of attachment to God and the love of Him. This was the way of the medieval Jewish philosophers who taught the people the greatness of God and His Torah, but knew nothing of the mystical love of God. These can be described as 'leftists' because they were remote from the Shekhinah and the holy spirit. Those of the centre are near to God when they offer their prayers and recite the *Shema*, while occupying themselves in worldly affairs the rest of the time. Though they follow the centre trend, they are capable of leading heroic, saintly lives. They can be

[137] Part I, no. 44

Hasidim ('saints') either because of their exceedingly strong social concern or because they carry out the precepts in an almost super-human way. Those on the right certainly deserve to be called Hasidim, but the term is also applicable to the saints of the centre party. There are thus three types of Hasidim: 1. the mystics of the right who spend all their time in contemplation of God; 2. the great social workers and servants of mankind; 3. those exceedingly pious in their religious acts.

No one can be a Hasid, continues Berlin, unless he is well versed in the Torah. A Hasid in deeds requires to be learned since, if he does not know how to preserve the correct balance, he is incapable of drawing the line between true piety and religious fanaticism. But even the mystical Hasid of the rightist type requires learning; otherwise his mystical fervour will encourage him to neglect the practical precepts of the Torah.

It follows from all this, Berlin adds, that those who belong to the centre party are not necessarily mediocre in their religious standards. Indeed, they can rise to the degree of a saint.

Now the author of the article had argued that in all Jewish history there has never been a generation so neglectful of the Torah as our own. Nonsense, declares Berlin. During the period of the prophets, for instance, there were numerous idolators, as anyone who takes the trouble of reading the Bible can see. It is not lack of observance that is typical of our age. What is peculiar to our day is the proliferation of unbelievers who entertain heretical ideas, rejecting the authority of the Talmud, for example.

Berlin also takes the author of the article to task for suggesting that the cure for the malady is separation from the sinners and unbelievers. God forbid, declares Berlin, that it should be our policy to introduce sectarianism into Jewish life. The Temple was destroyed because of the conflicts between the Sadducees and the Pharisees. Once any group in the Jewish community are dubbed 'outsiders', it becomes all too easy for one who hates his fellow to contemplate his enemy's destruction because he belongs to 'them', to the sect that has been outlawed. It is unfortunately true that if a member of the *Mahazike Ha-Dat* organisation notices that, as he understands it, someone is not too observant, he allows himself to become separate from him and to permit religious persecution under the guise of law. Especially in their exile, Jews must band together. Unless we are united, the nations will sweep us off the face of the earth. See how the Torah enjoins us to keep apart from the nations in order to preserve our heritage, and yet see how hard it is for us to be apart from our Gentile friends. How, then, can it be expected of us to keep apart from our fellow-Jews even if they are sinners? If we really want to strengthen the Torah there is only one way to do it, and that is to study the Torah constantly.

Clearly, Berlin is here putting forward the traditional Lithuanian, anti-Hasidic view that the study of the Torah takes precedence over everything, and that flight into mysticism is not the answer to the problems Judaism has to face. Nor can he agree with the Hungarian type of Orthodox separatism—a founder of the *Mahizike Ha-Dat* Movement was Simeon Sofer, Rabbi of Cracow, a son of the *Hatam Sofer*. Without mentioning explicitly the Hasidic disapproval of Torah study where the motives are less than pure, Berlin continues that the only way to encourage the study of the Torah is to engage in that study without excessive scruples as to whether the motives are of the highest. In any event, he notes, the average person who studies the Torah nowadays does so because he acknowledges this to be a supreme religious duty. Such a person's motives are adequate, even if he has no mystical fervour and no attachment to God. Even if a man studies the Torah in order to win fame as a great scholar, he is no sinner, though he will receive no spiritual reward for such study. The Rabbis tell us[138] that it is good to study the Torah even if our motives are unworthy, 'for out of the unworthy the worthy motives will emerge'—will emerge in the next generation, comments Berlin. Indeed, according to the Rabbis, to study the Torah out of unworthy motives is far better than to engage in pietistic practices even out of the highest motives. What is needed is for Jewish parents to create proper schools in which their children can receive a sound Jewish education. If the only way this important aim can be achieved is by introducing secular studies into the curriculum of these schools, there is no harm in it. However, adds Berlin, it is

[138] Pes. 50b

quite impossible for a man to become great in Torah learning unless he devotes all his time and efforts to the task. True, there have been famous Torah scholars who were conversant with secular learning as well, but they were only able to achieve it because they learned these subjects either after they had studied the Torah or beforehand. No man can be successful in his study of the Torah if, at the same time, he studies secular subjects.

Finally, some members of the *Mahazike Ha-Dat*, in their ignorance of the Torah, pursue their own way in God's service and, as a result, behave in a way contrary to the Torah. Berlin concludes:

> To sum up. If we truly and sincerely wish to strengthen our religion there is no other way than the study of the Torah, it being irrelevant whether the study is engaged in out of pure or unworthy motives. It is given to God alone to know how to assess the motives of those who study His Torah. It should not be our concern at all. If this is the attitude we adopt it will result in a great increase in the number of students of the Torah. Then even the 'enlightened' will be compelled to acknowledge that the Torah is Israel's protection.

The old problem[139] of whether a man can sell his share in Paradise appears in a Responsum[140] of Berlin dated 1887 and addressed to Tiberias. A man with a reputation for learning and piety sold a half-share in his merits to a wealthy buyer for the large sum of 22,000 roubles. The buyer, after paying half the sum, consulted a sage. The latter 'inquired of Heaven in a dream', and was informed that the seller did not amount to much up there. The buyer, thereupon, wished to cancel the sale and have his money back, but the seller argued that the sale was valid and demanded the payment of the other half. What is the law? Is such a sale valid?

Berlin observes that quite apart from the sage's information about the seller's status in Heaven, the seller demonstrated his own unworthiness. He behaved like Esau who sold his birthright, when he agreed to exchange spiritual bliss in the Hereafter for financial gain in this world. It can be compared to the base action of a soldier who sells the medals awarded to him by his king. True, the Talmud[141] applauds the action of Simeon who supported his

---

[139] See pp. 21–2 above   [140] Part III, no. 14   [141] Sot. 21a

brother Azariah so that the latter could study the Torah, and Simeon recieved half of the merit, but there the assistance was given beforehand and without it Azariah could not have studied. In that case it was Simeon's own action in supporting the Torah that was rewarded. But no man should wish to sell his spiritual bliss for gain.

As for the question of whether the sale is valid, Berlin first proceeds to make a distinction between reward for studying the Torah and reward for carrying out the precepts. Reward for the precepts can be compared to a king who rewards a soldier for his bravery in the field. But reward for Torah study can be compared to a king appointing a general to a post in his government. When the king rewards the soldier he gives something external, a medal or a purse, but when he wishes to promote the general, he can do so only if the general is capable of filling that post. Similarly, the reward for the study of the Torah in this life is that the student is admitted to the Yeshivah on High. Only one who has actually studied will gain from being admitted there. The man ignorant of the Torah will find no delight in being admitted to the Yeshivah on High because he will fail to understand what is being taught there. How, then, can the reward for Torah study be transferred? Since, in our case, the sale included the reward for Torah study, and, as we have said, this cannot be sold, the whole sale is invalid on the basis of the law that if part of a sale proves to be invalid the whole transaction is invalidated.

What would the law be, then, if a man sold only the reward of the precepts he had carried out? Since this can be transferred, the sale ought to be valid. No, says Berlin, even here the sale is invalid, and for two reasons. First, one cannot sell something not yet in one's possession. Second, one can only sell something tangible. Furthermore, on reflection, the sale of reward for carrying out the precepts is not to be compared to a soldier who sells his medals, where, though it is unworthy, the sale has meaning. It should rather be compared to a sick man selling his medicines. This is meaningless, since the medicines have been prescribed by the doctor for that particular patient and are of no use whatever to a buyer who suffers from a different ailment. Berlin introduces here a novel idea of the significance of reward for the precepts: God, he says, does not issue a decree that rewards are to be given for the performance of the precepts, and punishments for sin. Reward and punishment follow automatically. The precepts are like a powerful elixir of life and the sins like a deadly poison. To perform the *mitzvot* is to drink the elixir of eternal life, while to sin is to drink spiritual poison. That is why the Rabbis say[142] that God does not let a sinner off lightly. He cannot do so, any more than a doctor can do anything about his patient drinking poison once the poison has had its effect. To be sure, repentance is effective, but this is because repentance is the antidote to the poison of sin. Berlin concludes: 'May God illumine our eyes and give us the merit of beholding that which the eye hath not seen.'

The Respondents considered up to now in this chapter were all Ashkenazim, living in Europe. A different world is reflected in the Responsa of the head of the Sephardi community, the *Rishon Le-Tzion*, in Jerusalem, Jacob Saul Elyashar (1817–1906).

Elyashar was asked[143] by Moses Shapir whether it is permitted to teach a Gentile the Hebrew language and its grammar. Elyashar first quotes the Talmudic passage:[144] 'The teachings of the Torah are not to be transmitted to a Gentile.' From the Tosafists[145] it appears that the prohibition includes anything pertaining to the Torah except those laws the Gentile is obliged to keep. But the commentary of Samuel Edels, *Maharaha*, to the passage suggests that in the context the prohibition refers only to the mysteries and secrets of the Torah. The *Zohar*[146] is very strict about teaching the Torah to one not circumcised. The *Sefer Haredim* of Eleazar Azkiri (sixteenth-century) states[147] that it is forbidden to teach a Gentile even a single letter of the Torah. Alyashar then quotes other authorities who are strict, but notes that even those who forbid teaching a Gentile the Hebrew alphabet do so only because the Gentile will then be able to read the Bible in the original Hebrew. But nowadays the Bible is in any event accessible to all through the many existing translations. If the Gentile already knows Hebrew and merely wishes to perfect his knowledge of the

---

[142] BK 50a   [143] Yoreh Deah, no. 7   [144] Hag. 13a
[145] See *en moserin*   [146] II, 73a   [147] 'Rabbinic Laws', chapter 4, 37

grammar, it is obviously permitted to teach him. If, on the other hand, he is entirely ignorant of the language, the opinion of those authorities who forbid it should be taken into account.

There are two Responsa[148] on cremation: the first, dated 1889, addressed to Elyashar by Rabbi Zurmani of Bucharest, the second containing Elyashar's reply. Zurmani argues that cremation is strictly forbidden in that it involves a mutilation of the corpse and is degrading to the dead. At no time in Jewish history do we find that Jews practised cremation. True, there is the strange remark of the Tosafists[149] that on public fast-days they used to place the ashes of a corpse on the Ark, but the reference there is to the ashes of a man who had been accidentally burned, not to a corpse cremated for this purpose. From the Talmudic statement[150] that the corpse feels the pain of the worms, it appears that some kind of vitality persists even after death, so that to burn the corpse is to cause it to suffer. The Midrash[151] observes that the wood for the altar fire could not be taken from olives or vines because *mitzvot* are performed with these trees, olive oil for the meal-offerings and wine for the libations. If one must not degrade trees because they have been used for a *mitzvah*, how can one degrade by burning a corpse of a human being who performed *mitzvot* in his lifetime? Moreover, the corpse of a human being is compared to a scroll of the Torah, so that those present at a death must rend their garments as if a scroll of the Torah had been burned.[152] Just as it is forbidden to burn a scroll, which must be reverentially buried in the ground,[153] so is it forbidden to burn a corpse.

Elyashar agrees. He fails utterly to understand how anyone can do such a thing. Cremation, he says, involves a denial of the resurrection. The *Zohar*[154] tells us that there is a certain bone in the body which never suffers decay and, at the resurrection, the body is reconstituted from this bone. But, if the body is burned, how can it be reconstituted? Nothing is impossible for God and He can, of course, reconstitute even a body that has been cremated. But it is wrong to cause Him to change the order of nature as He has ordained, namely, that the resurrection should take place from

[148] Yoreh Deah, nos 5 and 6   [149] Taan. 15b, *ve-notenim*   [150] Sabb. 152a
[151] Lev. R. 7: 1   [152] MK 25a   [153] YD 282: 5   [154] III, 222a

this reconstituted bone. Moreover, He has decreed: 'For dust thou art, and unto dust shalt thou return' (Gen. 3 : 19). And what of the Talmudic passage[155] that when a scholar's teachings are repeated on earth his lips move in the grave? If he is cremated, there will be no lips to move. In the book of Daniel (12 : 2) it says: 'And many of them that sleep in the dust of earth, shall awake', which clearly shows that the dead are to be buried in the earth, not cremated. Elyashar concludes that he is convinced that those who wish to introduce cremation are motivated by heresy.

Another Sephardi Rabbi of note was Joseph Hayyim of Baghdad (1835–1909), Talmudist and Kabbalist, to whom questions were addressed by Sephardi communities throughout the world. His collection *Rav Pealim* contains many Responsa of a theological nature. In addition, at the end of each volume is printed a special collection of purely theological Responsa, entitled *Sod Yesharim*. We treat the theological Responsa here in the order in which they occur.

A questioner[156] describes himself as a very modest student of the Jewish classics with no knowledge of the Kabbalah. He is a believer in the truth of Rabbinic teaching but is puzzled by the following difficulties he has come across in his reading. 1. As a pious Jew, before carrying out the precepts he recites the formula: 'For the sake of the unification of the Holy One, blessed be He, and His Shekhinah.'[157] What is he expected to have in mind when he says this? And what is the meaning of this word 'Shekhinah' we use so frequently? 2. What is the meaning of the 'sacred marriage' which is said to take place on high, and how can terms like 'male' and 'female' be used when speaking of the divine realms? 3. The special midnight prayer—*tikkun hatzot*—is divided into the sections Rachel and Leah. What should we have in mind when reciting these prayers and what is the meaning of Rachel and Leah? 4. Since, in any event, we simply repeat the words of this midnight prayer mechanically, without understanding them at all and without 'pain and tears' as was ordained, what is the point of saying this and other Kabbalistic prayers at all?

---

[155] Yev. 97a
[156] Vol. I, Orah Hayyim, no. 1
[157] See pp. 162–3 above

Hayyim in reply first gives a brief summary of the Kabbalistic doctrine. God as He is in Himself is known as *En Sof*, the Limitless. En Sof becomes manifest through the Ten Sefirot. It is impossible for us to grasp the nature of the Sefirot since the human mind while in the body is utterly incapable of grasping pure spiritual entities. We cannot even comprehend our own soul. Thus symbols have to be used when speaking of the Sefirot, the symbol of light, for example. Light is a popular symbol for these entities, since it is the most refined object ever presented to our senses, but we must never fall into the trap of imagining that the Sefirot are really 'lights' in the sense in which we understand it. We are unable to understand how it happens, but the souls of Israel are formed from the 'light' of the Sefirot, especially from the combination of the Sefirot *Tiferet* and *Malkhut*. Since our souls result from this combination, our deeds are connected with these Sefirot and can have an effect on them for good and for ill. Again it is impossible for us to grasp the tremendous mystery contained here. We must always keep in mind that the Kabbalistic descriptions of these matters must not be taken literally but express extremely profound spiritual ideas. Now the Sefirah *Tiferet* is known as 'the Holy One, blessed be He', and the Sefirah *Malkhut* as the Shekhinah. The root of this latter word is *shakhan*, 'to dwell'. It is so called because a portion of the 'light' of *Malkhut* 'dwells' on earth to benefit God's creatures. Thus when we perform a *mitzvah* we assist, as it were, the combination of the 'lights' of *Tiferet* and *Malkhut*. Hence we recite the formula referred to. Hayyim quotes Ezekiel Landau's treatment of the term 'Shekhinah' and his quotation from Maimonides[158] but, he says, Maimonides could not have elaborated the matter fully, since 'there had not been revealed to him the holy *Zohar* and the teaching of our master, Isaac Luria, of blessed memory, who received it from the prophet Elijah, may he be remembered for good.' As for the symbols of 'male' and 'female', the Kabbalists explain that the term 'male' is used for the active element in the Sefirotic realm and the term 'female' for the passive element.

As for the terms 'Rachel' and 'Leah', these refer to two different

[158] See pp. 179–80 above

aspects of *Malkhut*, the Shekhinah, but one is not permitted to expound it further. It is not that these two are given the names of the matriarchs. The opposite is true. The two matriarchs were given these names because each possessed in her soul a portion of that particular element on high. The *tikkun hatzot* 'puts right' the flaws we have made by our sins in these two aspects of the Shekhinah. As for the objection that we do not understand this prayer, so why say it, R. Hayyim of Volozhyn in his *Nefesh Ha-Hayyim* has rightly explained that it is the deed God requires of us even where the meaning is hidden from us. To be sure, concentration on the meaning of our prayers is extremely valuable, but a failure to concentrate or understand must never be the cause of our abandoning the deed itself.

In another Responsum,[159] Hayyim deals with Kabbalistic ideas on time. Each festival falls on its particular date, each event in Jewish history took place at a given time, the 'intentions' in prayer one has in mind on the sabbath and the festivals are different from those of weekdays. But how can these distinctions in time be associated with the divine realm where there is no time and which is beyond time? After a lengthy discussion of the Kabbalistic ideas, Hayyim comes to the conclusion that, indeed, at the highest reaches of the Sefirotic realm there are no distinctions between past, present and future, no time at all. It is only in that aspect of the Sefirotic realm which concerns human beings, since it is the source of their souls, that time divisions have any application.

A Responsum[160] deals with a man in Bombay who translated into Arabic that section of the *Zohar* known as the *Idra*, containing many anthropomorphisms, and had the translation printed. The scholars of Bombay objected, but the man failed to see what harm was done since no one in any event takes these anthropomorphic terms literally. There is no explicit prohibition in the sources, says Hayyim, but that is because no one ever dreamed of such a thing being done. In the generation before this, when a German scholar wished to translate the Rabbinic Aggadah he was rebuked by R. Hayyim Halberstam of Zans because a translation into the vernacular is bound to convey the impression that it is all being

[159] Vol. I, Orah Hayyim, no. 2   [160] Vol. I, Yoreh Deah, no. 56

taken literally. Hayyim reports that three years before this a school-teacher had prided himself on translating the Song of Songs into Arabic for the benefit of his pupils. Hayyim rebuked him for his presumption. The Song of Songs is a mystical tract, hinting at the profoundest mysteries. If it is translated into the vernacular, and especially for the young, it will be understood as a collection of love poems. To translate the *Idra* into Arabic is harmful for a number of reasons. First, non-Jews may obtain a copy of the translation and will ridicule the Jewish religion, failing to appreciate that the matters discussed in the *Idra* are profound metaphysical speculations never intended to be taken literally. Second, Jews, too, will be misled, failing to understand that it is all by way of hint, and that the true meaning is far beyond the capacity of the average mind to grasp. Third, the very words of the original Aramaic of the *Idra* form various combinations of divine names and other recondite matters, all of which is lost entirely in translation. If it be argued that the same applies to the Bible and yet it is permitted to translate the Bible, the distinction is obvious. The Bible, too, to be sure, has a mystical meaning but it also has a plain, literal meaning and it is this latter that is captured in the translation. The *Idra*, on the other hand, has only the mystical meaning, while any literal understanding is sheer blasphemy. Hayyim refers in this connection to the Responsum on the Kabbalah[161] by Jair Hayyim Bacharach.

In another Responsum,[162] Hayyim rules that a repentant sinner who has misbehaved with a married woman should not inform her husband. This question was discussed by Ezekiel Landau,[163] to whom Hayyim refers, and by Hayyim Halberstam.[164]

An atheist[165] embarrassed the Jews of his town by quoting the difficult Biblical verses: 'And God created man in His own image' (Gen. 1 : 27); 'And God said: "Let us make man in our image after our likeness"' (Gen. 1 : 26). Moreover, he taunted them, saying: 'You Jews say that God has a wife called the Shekhinah.' What answers should they give? To the question regarding the

---

161 See pp. 160–3 above   162 Vol. I, Even Ha-Ezer, no. 1
163 See p. 175 above   164 P. 237 above
165 Vol. I, Sod Yesharim, no. 1

264

Biblical verses, Hayyim gives the stock answers, such as that of Maimonides.[166] As for the question that the Jews believe that God has a wife, Hayyim is astonished that they did not retort there and then that it is a sheer *canard*. Any Jew who believes such a perverse thing is a complete unbeliever, no better than an idolator. The meaning of the Shekhinah is the spiritual light of the Sefirot as manifested on earth. This 'light' is so refined and so spiritual that no human being can possibly grasp its essence. As above, Hayyim repeats that we cannot even comprehend our own spiritual nature. Who is greater than Moses? Yet Jews steadfastly refuse to accord him any divine status, the Torah recording explicitly that he was born of a woman, giving the names of his parents. From this, our atheist ought to have appreciated that a Jew who believes that God has a wife is a gross unbeliever, his sin too great to bear. The truth, as everyone knows, is that no people is more staunchly committed to a pure monotheism than the Jews. Nothing more requires to be said on a matter immediately obvious to all.

Another Responsum[167] deals with three separate questions: 1. A minor under the age of thirteen is exempt from carrying out the precepts. Why? It cannot be that the mind is undeveloped up to the age of thirteen since we observe that some children aged ten or eleven are far more intelligent than adults twice their age, and we do not observe any noticeable increase in intelligence, say from twelve to thirteen. 2. We find the Rabbis saying that even where the strict law offers exemptions, a man should still 'satisfy the requirements of Heaven'. What are 'the requirements of Heaven'? 3. It is said that when one sheds tears and weeps in prayer, his prayers are answered. What mystery is here contained and what intention should be in the mind?

On the first question, Hayyim replies that a minor is exempt not because he is lacking in intelligence but because man's soul is not fully developed until he reaches the age of thirteen. The purpose of the precepts is the perfection of the soul and there is, too, the cosmic effect of the precepts which depends on the soul's power to influence the worlds on high. Only the mature soul can have this effect. However, a minor's sins, though not culpable, do have the

---

[166] *Guide of the Perplexed*, I, 1   [167] Vol. I, Sod Yesharim, no. 3

effect of tainting his soul. That is why Isserles rules[168] that it is proper for an adult to do some penance for sins he had committed in childhood. As for the second question, after a man has been pardoned for sins he enters Paradise, but there are many stages and further punishment is required even for the failure to carry out obligations not strictly demanded in law. This is the meaning of 'to satisfy the requirements of Heaven'. As for the third question, the eyes of man correspond to certain spiritual entities in the Sefirotic realm. By shedding tears, man has an effect on this realm, causing the 'eyes' there again to pour out their grace. This is the meaning of Isaac Luria's statement that the aim of shedding tears in prayer is to 'sweeten the judgments'.

Hayyim observes[169] that it is well known that there is a special unification on high on the sabbath and festivals and all the worlds are elevated. All this is associated with Israel's prayers on these days. But since the times of the sabbaths and festivals differ from place to place, and when it is no longer sabbath in the holy land it is still sabbath in some distant lands, how can the prayers in those places have any effect on high? After discussing the matter at length with reference to the Kabbalistic writings, Hayyim comes to the conclusion that there are 'branches' of the Sefirotic tree, each of which is influenced by the prayers of Jews in different lands.

A Responsum[170] deals with the location of the Garden of Eden. From the writings of the Kabbalists, it would seem that this is situated on earth somewhere below the equator, but the geographers have made a close survey of the whole globe and have never come across the Garden of Eden. Furthermore, the Rabbis[171] say that the Garden of Eden is sixty times larger than the earth and Eden itself sixty times larger than the Garden. In that case, how can the Garden of Eden be situated on earth? Furthermore, the Talmud[172] tells how Alexander the Great came in his travels to the door of the Garden of Eden. When he knocked at the door he cried out: 'Open the door for me.' They replied: 'This is the gate of the Lord, the righteous shall enter into it' (Ps. 118 : 20). Is this

---

[168] OH 343: 1
[169] Vol. I, Sod Yesharim, no. 5
[170] Vol. II, Orah Hayyim, no. 1
[171] Pes. 94a   [172] Taan. 32b

to be taken literally? Hayyim first observes that there are large tracts of earth still unexplored. Every scientific opinion is only a guess and can be refuted. It is true that the scientists are able to forecast eclipses, which seems to show that scientific method is reliable, but this is because all science was given by God to Adam and preserved among the Jewish sages from whom the Gentiles derived it. Therefore, science is true and reliable on those matters delivered to Adam, not when it is based on theories concocted by the scientists themselves. The Garden of Eden is a place on earth. As for the passage regarding the size of Eden, the meaning can only be that the Garden of Eden is on earth, but by a miracle occupies no space on earth. Or perhaps the meaning is that the Garden of Eden is sixty times greater in spiritual refinement than the rest of the earth. In any event the Garden of Eden must be extraordinarily large, since it has to accommodate all the souls of the righteous from the days of Adam, clothed in refined spiritual garments. Nevertheless, it is only the lowest part of the soul, the *nefesh*, which inhabits the Garden of Eden on earth. The higher parts of the soul—*ruah* and *neshamah*—have their abode in the Gan Eden on High.

A question addressed to Hayyim[173] is whether a man who ate on Yom Kippur or profaned the sabbath in a dream has to do penance. Hayyim quotes a number of passages which, according to his reading of them, suggest that a dream may be a kind of message from Heaven. Thus there is no question whatever that no penance is required for the act itself, since this was committed only in the dream. But it may be that the man was visited with such a dream because he had, in fact, actually committed the sin he saw himself committing in the dream, albeit unintentionally. The dream may have been sent to him for the express purpose of calling his attention to the sin and so, in the absence of any more convincing explanation of why he should have had this particular dream, he should do penance.

A Responsum[174] deals with three Biblical verses. 1. In the book of Genesis (35 : 22) we read: 'And it came to pass, while Israel dwelt in that land, that Reuben went and lay with Bilhah his father's concubine; and Israel heard of it.' There is a tradition that the last part of this verse, 'Now the sons . . .', begins a new paragraph. Why should there be a new paragraph in the middle of a verse? 2. In the verse: 'Behold, I give unto him My covenant of peace' (Num. 25 : 12) the word for 'peace', *shalom*, is traditionally written with a broken *vav*. Why? 3. Traditionally, certain letters have to be written in the scroll larger than the other letters—e.g. the first letter of the Torah, *bet*, the *gimmel* of the word *ve-hitgalah*, 'then he shall be shaven' in Lev. 13 : 33, and the *dalet* of the word *ehad*, 'one', in the *Shema* (Deut. 6 : 4). Why?

In reply to the first question, Hayyim quotes Rabbinic answers, but suggests one of his own, based on Rabbinic views, that Reuben did not really sin with Bilhah. In reply to the second question, he similarly quotes a Rabbinic reply and then gives a Kabbalistic one of his own. As for the third, the Kabbalists explain that some letters are larger than others, some smaller and most of them the ordinary size, because the differing size of the letters represent different stages in the Sefirotic realms. However, the scroll can still be used if the letters to be written larger or smaller are written like the others.

Hayyim makes a number of observations[175] on questions raised in a work sent to him by Schneor Zalman of Kopys (1830–1900), the Hasidic master, author of *Magen Avot*. The letter is addressed to Vilna and dated 1887. Hayyim refers to the old question, discussed by this author, whether a widow who has remarried will be reunited at the resurrection with her first or with her second husband. From the *Zohar*[176] it would appear that she reverts to her first husband at the resurrection, but this contradicts the Deuteronomic law (Deut. 24 : 1–4) that once a woman has married another she may not return to her first husband. Hayyim replies that, once death has intervened, the body which arises at the resurrection is not the same body the woman occupied during her lifetime and hence the Deuteronomic law does not apply. Hayyim proceeds to discuss the general question of whether the precepts will be in force at the time of the resurrection. He quotes authorities who argue that there will be no *obligation* to keep the precepts

[175] Vol. II, *Sod Yesharim*, no. 2   [176] I, 21b

at that time, but many will be kept automatically, just as the patriarchs kept the precepts before they were given.[177]

Hayyim was asked[178] on the paragraph in the *Shulhan Arukh* dealing with marital relations[179]—why no benediction was ordained to be recited before the performance of the marital act as there are benedictions before the performance of other precepts. Hayyim notes that the question has been discussed, but suggests reasons of his own. First, the *mitzvah* does not depend on the husband alone, since the wife may not be willing. Second, he is naked and cannot recite a benediction. Third, the *mitzvah* is not performed until there is an emission and, if a benediction were required, there would be too long a pause. Fourth, if the wife forgoes her right, there is no *mitzvah*. Finally, the Rabbis have recorded laws regarding the frequency of intercourse and, since these differ according to different classes of person, it would result in absurdity, for each person would have to calculate whether the act is determined by law, and is a *mitzvah*, or by his own desire, and thus optional.

In a Responsum addressed to Shanghai,[180] Hayyim rules that Jews known to be profaners of the sabbath cannot help to form the quorum for public prayer and cannot be called to the reading of the Torah. However, tact must be exercised. To insult such people in public may result in their leaving the Jewish fold entirely. When they recite a benediction, it is permitted to answer 'Amen', since there is no doubt that it is God and no other whom they have in mind.

A questioner[181] wished to know if the practice of 'redeeming' fasts by alms-giving is correct. Hayyim quotes a number of authorities who do refer to the practice, and adds that we are obliged to rely on the great authorities of the past. If they permitted it, it is permitted.

In a Responsum on penance,[182] Hayyim deals with the case of a doctor who prescribed a drop of opium every morning and evening for an infant who seemed to be wasting away and was unable

---

[177] See pp. 66–7 above
[178] Vol. III, Orah Hayyim, no. 10
[179] OH 240
[180] Vol. III, Orah Hayyim, no. 12
[181] Vol. III, ibid., no. 35
[182] Vol. III, ibid., no. 36

to sleep. The drug was administered by the child's grandmother. After about eighteen days of this treatment, the child died, and the poor woman wished to know whether she has to do penance. Hayyim says that there can be no question of the grandmother having to do penance. She simply carried out the orders of the doctor. The doctor, too, must not do penance. He was a highly qualified man who had acted in the best of faith. If every time a patient died the doctor was required to do penance, physicians would be discouraged from practising their profession. In the same Responsum, Hayyim gives a penance for a woman who accidentally smothered her infant during sleep. She should fast every other day for forty-four days. She should also hire fifteen worthy men to fast with her on the forty-second, forty-third and forty-fourth days of her fast. On the eve of his fast each of these men should say:

> Sovereign of the universe! Behold, I intend to fast tomorrow from dawn to dusk in order to put right the sin of A daughter of B who sinned before Thee in bringing about the death of a human being. Let my fat and blood, diminished through fasting, be as acceptable as if I had offered before Thee a sacrifice on Thy holy altar to atone for the sin of A, daughter of B, who brought about the death of a human being. May it ascend to Thee as if I had had in mind all the correct intentions for this purpose.

On the third night they should study the *Zohar* together. If the woman does not have the strength to fast for forty-four days, she should fast, together with the men she hires, for three days. The significance of forty-four and fifteen is that the Hebrew word for 'blood', *dam*, has the numerical value of forty-four, while three times fifteen is forty-five, the numerical value of the word *adam*, 'man'.

In another Responsum,[183] Hayyim discusses a penance for a young man of nineteen who had marital relations with his wife while she was menstruating. Hayyim quotes sources which state that there is no punishment from on high for sins committed before one has reached the age of twenty. Nevertheless, a severe sin has been committed and he should fast as a penance. Hayyim

[183] Vol. III, ibid., no. 37

approves of the ruling of another sage that the young man should stay awake to study the Torah for one whole night for each act of intercourse.

A Responsum[184] on the Kabbalah is addressed to a sage whose name is not given in order to avoid causing him any embarrassment. This man, in a letter asking Hayyim's advice on a number of Kabbalistic problems, had boasted that he had studied Hayyim Vital's *Etz Hayyim* no less than five times and was expert in the Kabbalah. Hayyim rebukes him severely for his presumption. The Kabbalah is a most recondite science. Merely to repeat the words of the Kabbalistic books is not to attain any knowledge of these very profound matters. One who imagines that he knows merely demonstrates that he has not even begun to understand.

In another Kabbalistic Responsum,[185] Hayyim was asked for his opinion on the report that Elijah had appeared to the famous Kabbalist Shalom Sharabi (1720–77). He replies that there is a tradition that one must never dare to weigh up the merits of the great Kabbalists by the application of human reasoning. None the less, he is prepared to say that by 'the appearance of Elijah' two different things are intended. The first is the literal appearance of the prophet on earth to teach the sages. Such a vision is only vouchsafed to extremely rare individuals such as Isaac Luria. But lesser saints, too, can have a 'spark' of Elijah enter their soul. When this happens they imagine that they have attained to certain truths by their own reasoning powers but, in reality, they were inspired from on high by means of Elijah's 'spark'.

Hayyim considers[186] whether any purpose is served by a stranger reciting the Kaddish for a departed person. The particular case was of a spinster who died, and because her father had to be away on business, he arranged for Kaddish to be recited by a stranger on behalf of the girl. Hayyim quotes the old tradition that where relatives are unable to recite the Kaddish, strangers can be hired for the purpose and this, too, benefits the soul of the departed.

A Responsum[187] on penance considers the case of a man who

184 Vol. III, Sod Yesharim, no. 1   185 Vol. III, ibid., no. 4
186 Vol. IV, Orah Hayyim, no. 7   187 Vol. IV, ibid., no. 10

accidentally caused the flame of a lamp to waver on the sabbath. He should fast for two days but, if this is beyond his strength, he should fast for at least one day. In the same Responsum Hayyim gives the penance for an ignorant man who indulged in lewd conversation. He should fast for twenty-two days, corresponding to the twenty-two letters of the Hebrew alphabet against which he sinned in his coarse speech.

Another Responsum[188] deals with the permissibility of delivering a funeral oration in the synagogue over a man who was no scholar, but very pious. Hayyim refers to the ancient custom in Baghdad that it is permitted to deliver a *hesped* in the synagogue only for a great scholar, not for anyone else, no matter how pious. But, he adds, all depends on local custom.

A questioner asked Hayyim:[189] since we are instructed always to end our reading of the Torah on a good note, how is it that the *sidra, be-midbar*, ends with: 'But they shall not go in to see the holy things as they are being covered, lest they die' (Num. 4 : 20)? Hayyim remarks that the questioner could have quoted further examples of *sidrot* ending on a tragic or unpleasant note—e.g. 'and Terah died in Haran' (Gen. 11 : 32); 'and of him that lieth with her that is unclean' (Lev. 15 : 33). He adds that since the benediction is recited after the reading, this is held to be the true conclusion. It follows that when these portions are read privately and no benediction is recited, the first verse of the next *sidra* should be read as the conclusion.

Hayyim considers[190] the case of a man who accidentally swallowed a fly or ate meat registered as *kasher* though it was, in fact, *terefa*. Though no sin had been committed, would the *terefa* food still contaminate his soul? Hayyim advances the interesting theory that it is not the forbidden food itself which contaminates the soul. The sin of eating it is the source of the contamination. This sin allows the spirit of impurity which hovers over the forbidden food to enter the soul. But where there is not the slightest degree of negligence on the part of the man who ate the food, the spirit of impurity is powerless to affect his soul.

---

[188] Vol. IV, ibid., no. 39   [189] Vol. IV, ibid., no. 42
[190] Vol. IV, Sod Yesharim, no. 5

Hayyim was asked:[191] how could Rachel and Leah, brought up among idolators, have come to acknowledge God? Hayyim replies that they were endowed with two exceedingly lofty souls and were thus able to discover the truth for themselves, just as Abraham recognised God without the aid of a teacher.

Among the questions addressed to Hayyim from Bombay[192] were: why there is no mention of God's name in the book of Esther? why does the Tetragrammaton not appear in the books of Canticles and Ecclesiastes? As for Esther, Hayyim points out that one of the reasons given is that during the period of the book God saved His people from behind the scenes, as it were, with no open miracles. Even though the men of that generation were unworthy of seeing God's hand openly at work, yet He saved them because of His promise to the patriarchs. The Tetragrammaton is not mentioned in Canticles because, unlike the other Biblical books, this one cannot be taken literally at all. The book is not really a collection of love poems. Consequently, as the Rabbis say, the word *Shelomo*, 'Solomon', hints at God, but His name is only stated obliquely to remind us that the whole of this book has to be interpreted only by hint and homiletically. As for the absence of the Tetragrammaton from Ecclesiastes, this is because the book denigrates the things of this world. Its purpose is to strike fear into men's hearts when they see the vanity of the world. Consequently, only the divine name *Elohim* (denoting divine judgment), not the Tetragrammaton (denoting His mercy), is used. Furthermore, the book deals with nature and the way people behave naturally, and the name *Elohim* has the same numerical value as *ha-teva*, 'nature'.[193]

Hayyim considers[194] the custom of a son reciting the Kaddish, kindling a special light and giving alms on the anniversary of a parent's death. Does it still apply even twenty years after the parent has died? Hayyim replies that though the son lived for a hundred years after his parent's death, he would still be obliged to do these things for the repose of his parent's soul. The reason is

191 Vol. IV, ibid., no. 6   192 Vol. IV, ibid., no. 11
193 See pp. 169–70 above   194 Vol. IV, Sod Yesharim, no. 17

that even after the soul has entered Paradise it does not acquire its perfection all at once but has to progress from stage to stage. Isaac Luria's father was a great saint, and died when Luria was a little child, yet we know that for many years afterwards Luria kept the anniversary rites so as to enable his father's soul to ascend even higher. Furthermore, the soul is judged anew at each stage of its progress to higher realms.

In a psychological Responsum,[195] Hayyim considers the remedy available for a man inflicted by irrational phobias. Hayyim quotes the Talmudic passage:[196] 'If a man is seized with fright, though he see nothing, his star sees. What is his cure? He should recite the *Shema*. If he is in an unclean place, he should move away four cubits. If he cannot do this, he should say: "The goat at the butcher's is fatter than I."' Hence, Hayyim advised, this victim of irrational fear should read the *Shema* morning and evening with full concentration on its meaning. He should never place his hand on his nostrils or mouth.[197] He should wash his hands thoroughly in the morning, after he has been to the toilet, or after having had a haircut or pared his nails. Whenever fear strikes him, he should recite: 'The goat in the butcher's is fatter than I.' He should suspend the fang of a wolf around his neck. Each morning he should recite Psalm 91 and Psalm 121 three times, and once at night before going to sleep. He should wear daily the 'small garment' (*tallit katan*) with fringes. Hayyim finally advises him to suspend around his neck an amulet containing two divine names found in the Kabbalah.

A leading representative of Hungarian Orthodoxy was Jacob Tennenbaum (1832–97), Rabbi of Putnok and author of the Responsa collection *Nahare Afarsemon*. The following, in the order in which they appear in the book, are the Responsa of theological interest in this collection.

One of the judges[198] at a *halitzah* ceremony hyperbolically stated that he would disregard the ban of Rabbenu Gershom and commit polygamy. Would this invalidate the *halitzah*? Tennenbaum replies that at the time of the ceremony the man was fit

---

[195] Vol. IV, ibid., no. 19

[196] Meg. 3a

[197] Based on Pes. 112a

[198] Orah Hayyim, no. 8

to be a judge and, in any event, the opinion was not intended seriously.

A soldier[199] was given the option of either taking an office job, in which case he would be obliged to work on the sabbath, or to have a job in the field, in which case he would not be able to wear *tefillin*. Which should he choose? Tennenbaum rules that it is better to choose the job in the field, since in the one instance the offence is positive, whereas in the other it is only a sin of omission.

In a Responsum dated 1888,[200] Tennenbaum considers the custom of the groom wearing a shroud at the wedding service. A groom refused to wear the shroud and the Rabbi wished to know whether, in view of this, he is allowed to officiate. Tennenbaum observes that he personally always refuses to officiate unless the groom wears the *kittel*, but he is appreciative of the special difficulties this Rabbi faces: namely, if he refuses to officiate, they can call on 'that one' (*ha-yadua*), presumably the local Reform Rabbi. Tennenbaum advises the Rabbi to explain to the family the idea behind the wearing of the *kittel*: that the couple will live in peace, love and harmony so that death alone will part them. If, in spite of this, the groom insists, the Rabbi should officiate, but make it clear that he is creating no precedent, and only agrees in order to forestall a worse offence.

Should a child be given the name of a person who died single?[201] Tennenbaum remarks that if the reason for the reluctance to give such a name is because the person died young, what difference is there between a bachelor and a married man who died young? He holds that in all such matters the common practice should be followed, and people do name their children after persons who died young. But if the parents are really apprehensive it should not be done.

It was the practice[202] for the manufacturer of coffins to send crosses to the retailers of these to be affixed to the coffins. In view of this, is a Jew permitted to be a retailer of coffins to Christians? Tennenbaum says that since the crosses come separately they may have been worshipped by Christians bowing to them. The correct

---

[199] Ibid., no. 56
[200] Yoreh Deah, no. 26
[201] Ibid., no. 70
[202] Ibid., no. 84

procedure is for the Jewish retailer to arrange for Christian workers to fashion a cross on the coffin and then, since no one has bowed to the cross, it is like an ornamental cross which it is permitted to sell.[203]

A Responsum[204] dated 1881 concerns a community of observant Jews. Since a man who profanes the sabbath in public is treated like a Gentile,[205] can such a person be admitted to membership of the congregation? Tennenbaum quotes the opinion of *Hatam Sofer* that the man who profanes the sabbath is to be excluded from the community, as a warning to others. But here, on the contrary, by accepting these people as members of the community they may be encouraged to give up their offence. In any event, there is a communal regulation that only a man who accepts the laws of the *Shulhan Arukh* can occupy any office in the community, so there is no danger of these men leading the community astray. However, care should be exercised since they may be of those who wish to destroy the Orthodox community from within.

Is it permitted[206] to erect an iron railing around a grave? Tennenbaum states that there are three possible objections. 1. It is copying the Gentiles, but this cannot apply where the intention is simply to give prominence to the grave. 2. It is disrespectful to the other dead in the cemetery, but in any event some tombstones are more impressive than others and it has never been suggested that all must be the same. 3. It is disrespectful to the living, who know that such a railing will not be placed around their graves But, if they do not object, it can be done.

Tennenbaum[207] disagrees with Moses Schick[208] that a *shohet* who served in a Neolog or *Status Quo* community can never again be permitted to serve in an Orthodox community. Since even the repentance of an apostate is accepted, if the *shohet* expresses his remorse he can serve in an Orthodox community.

Abraham Anakawa (b. 1810), Rabbi and Kabbalist, was born at Salé in Morocco where he later served as a Dayyan. His Responsa collection *Shemen Ha-Mor* was published in Leghorn in 1869 with

---

203 Cf. nos 114, 115 and 116
204 Yoreh Deah, no. 90
205 See pp. 246–7 above
206 Yoreh Deah, no. 138
207 Ibid., no. 142
208 See pp. 229–31 above

the aid of Sir Moses Montefiore, to whom the author expresses his indebtedness on the title-page.

A Responsum (no. 1) of Anakawa deals with a boy who is being trained to wear *tzitzit* and *tefillin*. Over which should he recite *shehehiyanu* ('Who has kept us alive')—the benediction recited when performing a religious precept for the first time? Anakawa rules that the benediction should be over the *tzitzit*. Apart from the purely legal considerations, Anakawa states: 'It appears from numerous passages in the holy *Zohar* that *tzitzit* always takes precedence over *tefillin*. This is reasonable, since the *mitzvah* of *tzitzit*, it is well known, is equal in weight to all the other *mitzvot*. All man's limbs and sinews are enveloped in its spirituality so that it is right for it to be given precedence.'

A curious Responsum (no. 3) deals with the widely held belief that holy men could use the words of the *Book of Creation* to create things by magic. The Talmud[209] tells of Rabbis who created a calf in this way on the eve of the sabbath. It was also believed that demons could be driven out by means of certain incantations. Hence the question put to Anakawa:

> I have been asked regarding those who engage in the science of letter combinations [*tziruf*] and who by this means, as is well known, can bring some material thing into being. Is it permitted to create a man and so forth on the sabbath through moving one's mouth while reading the *Book of Creation*, even though it results in the creation of a physical entity? Similarly, is it permitted for those who utter incantations in order to drive out an evil spirit to do this on the sabbath, or does it constitute a sabbath desecration?

Anakawa rules that both are permitted on the sabbath. He remarks that it is in any event illegal to drive out an evil spirit by magical means, but it is permitted where the life of the person afflicted is at stake, just as any other prohibition of the Torah can be set aside in order to save life. From this it follows that it is also permitted on the sabbath. As for creating through the *Book of Creation*, it is automatic and, as such, not a sabbath desecration. We believe, says Anakawa, that whenever the Torah is studied,

---

[209] Sanh. 65–6

new heavens are created, and yet it is a religious duty to study the Torah on the sabbath. It is illogical to draw a distinction between heavenly halls, which are purely spiritual, and physical things created through the *Book of Creation*, since the latter is also a legitimate subject of study. This Responsum should be compared with those of the Haham Zevi[210] and his son Jacob Emden.[211]

It was the custom (no. 44) in some places when a circumcision took place to burn incense in honour of the prophet Elijah, who is present at every circumcision. Does this offend against the prohibition of offering incense outside the Temple? Anakawa suggests a rationalistic interpretation of the custom. Jews used to live in filthy dwellings, and the incense was burned, in anticipation of Elijah's coming, to remove any unpleasant smells in honour of the visitor. This is certainly permitted and should not be abandoned, even though they now live in more salubrious surroundings.

Finally, a Responsum (no. 50) contains a number of rulings based on the decisions of earlier authorities: that a man who is no scholar but behaves and dresses as if he were should be placed under the ban; that it is forbidden to insult members of a charitable society, just as it is forbidden to insult a scholar; that it is forbidden to be strict on a matter where the sages of a town have given a lenient ruling; that if a man swears that such-and-such is true just as God is true, he requires to do penance for daring to compare any of God's creatures to the Creator.

Hayyim Sofer (1821–86) was Rabbi of the Orthodox community in Pest in Hungary. He was a pupil of Moses Sofer (though no relation), and of Meir Eisenstadt. His Responsa collection *Mahane Hayyim* was published in Pressburg in 1862.

A Gentile (no. 7), interested in Judaism and with the prospect of embracing the Jewish faith, asked a Jew to teach him. The Rabbis say that it is forbidden to teach the Torah to Gentiles, but is it permitted in this case? Sofer argues that if it is forbidden to teach the Torah to Gentiles even in such circumstances, how did Gentiles ever manage to become converted to Judaism since they would never know what Judaism has to offer? Sofer permit its

[210] Pp. 170-1 above   [211] P. 173 above

and advances two further reasons. First, it is forbidden to teach the Torah to a Gentile only where the intricacies of the law are at issue, but he may be taught the simple laws of Judaism. Second, the prohibition applies only to the Oral Law, but it is permitted to teach him the whole of the Pentateuch from the beginning of Genesis to the end of Deuteronomy.

A woman (no. 11) on her death-bed called her only son to her side and confessed to him that she is sure he is not the son of her husband but the result of an affair she had, so that the son is a *mamzer*. This son was a scribe, and he wished to know whether his mother's testimony has the result of invalidating any scrolls or *tefillin* he had written. Sofer discusses whether the mother's testimony is to be relied on and whether, in any event, a scroll written by a *mamzer* is invalid. The *Shulhan Arukh*[212] rules that some authorities declare it to be invalid, and various reasons are given. Sofer comes to the conclusion that the mother's testimony is not sufficient to make the son a *mamzer*.

A scholar (no. 18) wished to do penance and, as part of the penance, wished to avoid having marital relations for a period of time. Is he allowed to do this or is it wrong of him to do penance at the expense of his marital duty? Sofer argues that he has an obligation to his wife which prevents him from adopting this form of penance. He refers to the Responsum on penance of Ezekiel Landau,[213] who similarly states that abstinence from marital relations should not be resorted to as a form of penance, because the husband owes it to his wife.

Marcus Horowitz (1844–1910) was Rabbi of the Orthodox Community in Frankfort. Part II of his Responsa collection *Matteh Levi* was published by his son in Frankfort in 1932, and a number of these have theological interest.

A Responsum[214] dated 1888 concerns a man who was not circumcised. Can he be called to the Torah? Horowitz rules that the community should not honour him with an *aliyah* but, if he purchases an *aliyah* himself, he should be called. The Rabbi should, of course, seek to persuade him to fulfil the great *mitzvah* which devolves on him.

[212] YD 227   [213] See pp. 175–7 above   [214] Orah Hayyim, no. 4

A Responsum[215] was addressed to Dr Rosenthal, Rabbi of Cologne, in 1905 and concerns a man who had been converted to Christianity but has now returned to the Jewish fold. According to the rule of Moses Isserles in the Yoreh Deah (268), such a man has to have immersion and to accept upon himself anew all the obligations of Judaism. This man keeps the dietary laws and the sabbath but has not undergone immersion. Can he be called to the Torah? Horowitz first quotes the authorities on immersion and argues that in this case the immersion is merely a token one to demonstrate remorse. Thus, it is relevant only at the time of the man's return to Judaism, and there is no point in having it done long afterwards. The general principle is always to encourage converts to return to the Jewish fold. Since the man is observant, he must not be ostracised and must be treated as a full Jew. He can be called to the Torah.

An earlier Responsum[216] (1897) to David Zevi Hoffmann refers to the use of an organ in the synagogue service. Horowitz states that he yields to no one in contending that the use of an organ is strictly forbidden on the sabbath and on festivals, but he cannot bring himself to state categorically that it is forbidden also on weekdays. Since we know that an organ was used in the ancient community of Prague, it is impossible to argue that its use involves the prohibition on copying Gentile worship. If this prohibition is to be invoked, it should apply *a fortiori* to the wearing of canonicals by Rabbis, clearly copied from the church. The truth is that the prohibition does not apply where there are sound reasons for the practice. None the less, Hoffmann's suggestion that the organ be forbidden because the Reformers have adopted it has much to commend it. For this reason Horowitz is reluctant to permit it, but does not feel that an Orthodox Rabbi should make such an issue of it that he risks losing his post.

A Responsum[217] dated 1889 is addressed to Lipmann Printz and deals with the question whether women who have given birth should recite the *ha-gomel* benediction. Horowitz says that it is not the custom for them to recite the benediction and gives a theological reason for the custom. The benediction expresses the

worshipper's thanks for his deliverance and he refers to himself
as a sinner. God is thanked for saving sinners from harm. But
since child-bearing is a religious duty, God protects women
who give birth as of right, not in His grace because they are
sinners.

A Responsum[218] dated 1891 considers whether Jews are permitted to contribute towards the building of a church. Horowitz
first quotes the authorities who discuss the status of Christianity
according to Jewish law, and quotes many who rule that Christianity is not idolatry. Consequently, it is not only permitted but is a
sanctification of God's name. It is well known, he says, that Sir
Moses Montefiore sanctified God's name in this way by building
a church in Ramsgate. But it is forbidden if members of the
church are Jewish converts. Horowitz remarks at the end of this
Responsum:

> Because of all that has been said, we reach the following conclusion.
> It is obvious that there is no prohibition whatsoever; so you are
> quite right in saying that, in fact, it is meritorious, namely, that it is a
> *mitzvah* as sanctifying God's name . . . Let all the peoples on earth
> observe that we Jews are faithful, ready to suffer martyrdom for the
> sanctification of God's name by testifying that He is One and His
> name One. For this we are prepared to give up all our possessions
> and all we hold precious for the sake of our religion. For we all
> acknowledge that this duty of suffering martyrdom for the sake of
> God's unity is only binding upon us, not on any other people. We
> all acknowledge that whoever is not a Jew can become one of
> the saints and great men of the nations of the world and a son
> of the World to Come if he keeps the Noahide laws given to all
> mankind.

Abraham Bornstein of Sochaczew (1839–1910) was a son-in-
law of the famous Hasidic master Menahem Mendel of Kotzk
and himself a Hasidic master as well as an outstanding Talmudist.
His Responsa collection *Avne Nezer* is still authoritative.

A Responsum (no. 28) addressed to the Hasidic master Phineas
Elijah of Pilz in 1880 refers to a Reader in the synagogue suspected
of fornication. Bornstein refuses to disqualify the man without
knowing the full circumstances, and argues that a mere rumour is

[218] Yoreh Deah, no. 28

not sufficient to disqualify. He advises the community to provide the Reader with a sum of money to invest in business and this will keep his mind off sex.

A Responsum dated 1899 (no. 30) concerns two Readers in the town of Blashki, both of whom had pleasant voices but not as pleasant as those of two other God-fearing Readers who were not of such good family. Which set of two should be chosen to lead the prayers on Rosh Ha-Shanah and Yom Kippur? The particular flaws in their background were that the father of one was a *shohet* who had been disqualified by Rabbis who disapproved of the types of knives he used, while the brother of the other had been converted to Christianity. Bornstein rules that the two with more pleasant voices should be chosen. The disqualification of the father of the one is weak in any event, since customs regarding the types of knives differ from community to community. It is not the fault of the other man that his brother was converted, and he is to be disqualified only if he could have prevented it. Even the merits of a man do not accrue to the members of his family, so how can the sins of a man bring discredit on them?

Judah Aszod (1794–1866) was Rabbi of Punaszerdahely in Hungary. His collection *Yehudah Yaaleh* contains the following theological Responsa.

A Responsum (no. 140) to Moses Samuel Jelinek of Vienna deals with a *kohen* who fell in love with a wealthy woman who had had *halitzah* and was so forbidden to him, but whom he was determined to marry, come what may. There are many missionaries in Vienna only too eager to win Jewish souls, so that there is great danger that if he is not allowed to marry the woman he will become converted to Christianity in order to be able to marry her. Is it permitted to overlook the prohibition, which is only Rabbinic, in order to save souls? Furthermore, there is no certainty that those who claim nowadays to be *kohanim* are really such. Aszod protests vehemently at the very thought of permitting it. Most authorities rely on the presumption that those who claim to be *kohanim* are such. If we disregard Rabbinic law on such grounds, the whole Rabbinic system will fall apart. Isserles[219] rules that the court

[219] YD 334: 1

should not fail to impose the ban where it is deserved, even though the man so punished may be tempted to leave the Jewish fold. Even the *Ture Zahav* who rules otherwise does only so in connection with the ban, which is for an offence already committed. But God forbid that a man be permitted to sin because he threatens to become converted if permission is not given. Aszod advises that the man be spoken to kindly and that one should assure him that if he gives up the woman God will bless him.

A Responsum (no. 248) addressed to Solomon Hass, Rabbi of Dressnitz and author of *Kerem Shelomo*, takes up one or two points raised in that work. Aszod, for instance, advances a reason of his own why the Mishnah begins with the letter *mem* and concludes with the same letter. Rabbi Judah the Prince, who compiled the Mishnah, was gifted with the holy spirit and there is no doubt that this letter was used intentionally. It is necessary to begin every undertaking with a mention of God's name. Maimonides at the beginning of his great Code uses words the initial letters of which form the Tetragrammaton. Now the Kabbalists remark that the form of the letter *mem* resembles the two letters *kaf* and *vav*. The numerical value of these two letters is twenty-six, the same as that of the Tetragrammaton. Hass's work also refers to the story of Korah. Aszod here, too, suggests an interpretation of his own. God told Moses and Aaron to remove themselves from the community before the community was annihilated (Num. 17 : 10). The word translated as 'remove' is *heromu*, which Aszod connects with *terumah*, the offering given to the priest. According to the Rabbis, this was one-fortieth of the crop. Now the number of Israelites was 600,000, of which one-fortieth is 15,000. Actually there died 14,700 (verse 14) but this verse continues: 'aside from those who died on account of Korah'. The men who died with Korah were 250 (16 : 35) and together with Korah himself and his family the total was 300. Together with the 14,700, this totals 15,000. Aszod concludes:

> May God forgive us, but I believe that in this there has been re-
> vealed to me one of the secrets of the Torah and it is a marvel to
> anyone who understands. Even though it is not my habit to reply in
> Responsa on matters such as this which belong to things high above

the world, yet in your honour I have made a slight exception in response to your wish.

Finally, a Responsum (no. 256) addressed to Aszod's pupil, Moses Baer Shen of Kremz, contains a number of questions among which is the following. A Jew who threatened to convert to Christianity was bought off by the community two or three times. He has now gone to the priest's house and declares that, unless the community pays him a sum of money that he specifies, he will allow himself to be converted. What should be done? Aszod agrees with the questioner that the community should refuse to allow itself to be blackmailed further.

Abraham Palaggi (1809–99), Rabbi of Izmir, was the author of the Responsa collection *Va-Yaan Avraham* published in Izmir in 1884.

Palaggi discusses[220] whether it is permitted to take snuff in the cemetery. He quotes the Talmud[221] that it is forbidden to do anything in the cemetery the dead cannot do, because it is as if one were mocking them.

Once a year[222] the Consul visits the Rothschild hospital in the Jewish community of Izmir and on such occasions it is necessary to have the flag flying, but there is a cross on the flag. Palaggi permits it on the grounds that the cross on the flag is not an object of worship. None the less, he says, Jews outside the holy land cannot escape a certain inappropriateness in these matters and 'they serve idols in purity'.

In another Responsum,[223] Palaggi discusses the Talmudic ruling[224] that frowns on the study of Greek wisdom. Is it permitted to study secular subjects in the toilet? He quotes various authorities on this and reports that in the toilet of Judah Bibash (1780–1852), Rabbi of Corfu, later in Hebron, sheets were pasted on the walls containing extracts from the sciences of the Gentiles which he would read there.

If a man[225] promises to give some money to charity, does it shield him from harm from the time of his promise or only when he actually gives it? Palaggi says that such matters belong to

---

[220] Orah Hayyim, no. 3   [221] Ber. 18a   [222] Yoreh Deah, no. 9
[223] Ibid., no. 18   [224] Men. 99   [225] Yoreh Deah, no. 20

God's secrets but, so far as we can judge, he is shielded from the time he makes the promise. He should, however, do his utmost to give the money as soon as he can.

Is the duty[226] of visiting the sick binding on a woman? Palaggi quotes the Talmud[227] that one who visits the sick has his years increased, and the other passage in the Talmud:[228] 'Do only men need to live long and not women?'

Another Responsum[229] concerns a woman who takes snuff, but her husband objects. Palaggi rules that the husband cannot compel his wife to give it up. In the course of this Responsum, he remarks that it is wrong to dismiss a Reader in the synagogue from his post because he has bad breath.

Finally, Palaggi[230] discusses whether it is permitted to insult a man who is indifferent to the insult. Even if it is permitted, he argues, such a man belongs to the sect of scoffers who, the Rabbis declare,[231] will not see the face of the Shekhinah.

Solomon Kluger (1785–1896), Rabbi of Brody in Galicia, served in that capacity for nigh on fifty years. Here are a number of his theological Responsa.

In one (no. 16), addressed to Aaron Samuel Aszod of Nicholsberg, the question is discussed whether a woman who openly profanes the sabbath is to be treated as if she were a Gentile. Kluger rules that she is to be so treated. Even the Samaritans were treated as Gentiles,[232] and an apostate is worse than a Samaritan!

In a Responsum (no. 31) addressed to Levi Isaac of Roman, Kluger states that it is forbidden to sell a *terefa* chicken to an apostate and he remarks: God forgive the Rabbi who ruled otherwise.

Table-rapping is considered in a Responsum (no. 48) addressed to David Meir Frisch of Brezen. Kluger states that it is categorically forbidden as a kind of magical practice. He adds that he is puzzled by the psychology of such folk. They neglect many Rabbinic laws on the grounds that they are contrary to reason, and yet practise such an unreasonable and irrational thing as table-rapping. The

[226] Ibid., no. 25   [227] Ned. 40a   [228] Kidd. 34
[229] Even Ha-Ezer, no. 22   [230] Hoshen Mishpat, no. 18
[231] Sot. 42a   [232] Hull. 6a

Belzer Rebbe declared, he says, that it is a kind of *kelipah*, the Kabbalistic name for the demonic. In that case why does he not protest? Kluger replies that he has two reasons for his silence. 1. There are more serious sins about which he has to protest—e.g. the profanation of the sabbath. 2. His enemies who take delight in distorting his words will say that he has permitted it.

A Responsum (no. 87) to Jonah Ashkenazi of Pressworsk considers whether it is permitted to learn German in order to be able to pass the government examination for candidates for the Rabbinate. Kluger says that he finds it hard to reply to this question. It is hateful to him, so how can he recommend it to others? The study of this language leads almost inevitably to heresy. In former ages, sin was only in deed. Nowadays, it is not unusual to find men who keep the laws while having heresy lurking in their hearts. He quotes the Rabbinic saying:[233] 'Love work and hate lordship (*rabbanut*); and seek no intimacy with the ruling power.' He continues:

> It can be seen that the spirit of the Lord was in the Rabbis. They gazed by means of the holy spirit into those times when it was impossible to obtain a Rabbinical position without seeking intimacy with the ruling powers in order to win their favour by studying their sciences. Consequently, the Rabbi says: 'Hate the Rabbinical office and seek no intimacy with the ruling powers.' I advise you to refrain from it. Is the hand of the Lord powerless to help you to earn a living by other means? I have informed you of my views. More there is no need to add.

Another Responsum (no. 207) deals with the practice 'in the West' of erecting a mausoleum over the graves of famous saints. They are now beginning to do this in these lands. Is it permitted? Kluger permits it. There is no disgrace in the process to the earlier saints for this reason. In former times there were so many saints that there was no need to mark the grave of a saint. Not so nowadays. Consequently, on the contrary, the fact that it is done and the grave of a saint distinguished, reminds us of how many great saints there were in former times.

It is said (no. 214) that, as a cure for epilepsy, the patient's body

---

[233] Avot I: 10

should be touched with the hand of a corpse. Is it permitted to a *kohen* who may not come into contact with a corpse? Kluger quotes Maimonides[234] that it is not permitted to heal a person by means that involve a prohibition unless the cure is a natural one.

Another Responsum (no. 231) concerns the grave of the Hasidic master R. Aaron of Tchernobil. Is it true that *kohanim* may enter there because the remains of a Zaddik do not contaminate? Kluger refers to the Talmud.[235] Joseph Karo,[236] he says, quotes all the opinions. But the Talmud[237] says that R. Banaah used to mark the graves of the saints with white paint so that *kohanim* should not trespass there, which shows clearly that it is forbidden.

Kluger considers (no. 232) whether the mourning rites should be carried out for a son who has embraced Christianity. Kluger quotes the authorities who deal with this question, and comes to the conclusion that if the purpose is to express grief in public it is allowed.

Finally, Kluger considers a curious question (no. 234). It was believed that, at every circumcision, Elijah is present. Now, according to the Talmud,[238] Elijah is a *kohen*. May, therefore, a circumcision take place if there is a corpse in the adjoining room? Kluger replies that Elijah has to keep the laws only when he appears on earth in the form of a human being. At a circumcision he is 'the angel of the covenant'. He appears as an angel, and an angel is not obliged to keep the Torah.

---

[234] Commentary to Mishnah *Yoma*   [235] BM 114 and Tos.
[236] YD 373   [237] BB 58a   [238] BM 104

CHAPTER XI

The Twentieth Century

The twentieth-century Responsa deal extensively with modern inventions so far as these involve questions of law—e.g. the use of electricity on the sabbath and festivals; reliance on fingerprints as evidence; autopsies; heart transplants; artificial insemination; the use of the pill for purposes of contraception; travel by aeroplane; and even space travel by Jewish astronauts. But this century is not a period of new theological discussion among the Orthodox writers of Responsa, although a large number of twentieth-century Responsa do deal directly or indirectly with theological topics, among which the following may be recorded.

The Hasidic master Hayyim Eleazar Spira (1872–1937), Rabbi of Munkacs in Hungary, was the author of the Responsa collection *Minhat Eleazar*. He was an astonishingly well informed Talmudist with an acute historical sense, though he is recognised as a religious extremist.

In a Responsum,[1] Spira vehemently attacks the view put forward in the work *Besamim Rosh* by Saul Berlin[2] that there is no legal obligation of martyrdom after the destruction of the Temple, since martyrdom obviously belongs to matters of life and death (*dine nefashot*); just as there can be no capital punishment after the cessation of the Sanhedrin, there can be no decisions regarding

[1] Part III, Yoreh Deah, no. 46
[2] See pp. 347–52 below; *Besamim Rosh*, no. 301

martyrdom. Spira refers to Mordecai Banet and Moses Sofer, who proved that Berlin had forged the work. The cessation of the Sanhedrin resulted only in the abolition of the death penalty for criminals. Where and when a man must suffer martyrdom has nothing whatever to do with the Sanhedrin. It is a religious question entirely, applicable nowadays just like the similar question, also a matter of life and death, when and where a sick person may eat on Yom Kippur. For that matter, there is a risk to health in the study of the Torah which, as the Rabbis observe, weakens a man. Should we argue that because there is no Sanhedrin to decide whether or not the risk may be taken in each particular instance, no one should study the Torah? The implication of Saul Berlin's perverse argument is that the Torah is binding only during the time when the Sanhedrin functions. Berlin was, in fact, says Spira, one of those Rabbis, of admittedly great Talmudic learning, who were caught in the trap set by Mendelssohn's circle in Berlin, and his sole purpose was to undermine Judaism under the cloak of Rabbinic learning. Spira adds an interesting note. All his life he was a fierce anti-Zionist. He notes that in this Responsum Saul Berlin adds that Jews, in fact, did suffer martyrdom, although there was no legal obligation for them so to do, because they saw their lives as having no significance among the nations outside the Jewish fold. This, says Spira, seems on the face of it to be an admirable sentiment, but is the most dangerous of all in reality. It implies that there is no divine command for Jews to suffer martyrdom, but that they did so in the Middle Ages solely in order to preserve the separateness and distinctiveness of the Jewish people, thus substituting a profound religious motivation of the highest order with nationalism, 'as the Zionists do in our day'.

During the third year of World War I (in 1917), Spira was asked to give his consent to a proclamation by the Rabbis that the whole Jewish community of Hungary should engage in a public fast. He[3] is opposed to the suggestion. First, there are many people whose health will suffer if they fast, as they would if all the Rabbis urged them to. But more important, it appears from the Scriptures, the Talmud, the *Zohar* and other holy books, that this

[3] Part IV, no. 4

war is part of the 'birth-pangs of the Messiah'. We should bestir ourselves, therefore, to pray for the coming of the Messiah. If a public fast is proclaimed, the masses are bound to construe it as the need to pray for peace when the Jews, too, will be able to sink back into the comparative ease of exile—when, in fact, it is for the exile of the Shekhinah that we should mourn. Since the war is a prelude to the redemption, by praying for its cessation we imply that we do not wish to be redeemed!

In a very erudite Responsum,[4] Spira proves that the *Shulhan Arukh* ruling[5] that a son is forbidden by the fifth commandment from disagreeing with his father does not apply to debates in Jewish law. He quotes numerous instances from the Rabbinic literature in which the Talmudic Rabbis disagree with the legal opinions of their fathers.

Spira attacks[6] two rulings on the sabbath laws given by Patremoli's work *Tzapihat Bi-Devash*. In one section (no. 23), the author forbids the study of the Torah with deep application on the sabbath, on the grounds that this disturbs the 'sabbath delight' (*oneg shabbat*); and yet in another section (no. 26) permits funeral orations to be delivered on the sabbath. The truth is that the very opposite is correct. The study of the Torah, the Jew's greatest joy, is not only permitted with deep concentration on the sabbath but is itself the finest expression of 'sabbath delight', whereas funeral orations are certainly forbidden because they cause feelings of gloom and sadness.

Hayyim Isaac Jeruchem (1865–1943), Rabbi of Sambor ('Alstadt') in Galicia, Talmudist, Kabbalist and Hasid, wrote many hundreds of Responsa, but only a comparative few have been published in *Birkat Hayyim*, edited, and with a biographical sketch, by his son.

A Responsum (no. 3) of theological interest, dated 1930, is addressed to Mordecai Shalom Joseph Friedmann, the Zaddik of Sadegora. The leaders of the congregation obtained a valuable curtain made for the Ark in the synagogue, the work of a skilled craftsman. This curtain was used in a large synagogue for sixty years until the destruction of the synagogue during World War I.

4 Part IV, no. 6 5 YD 240: 2 6 Part IV, no. 45

But when the curtain was examined more closely it was found that the Ten Commandments, woven into its fabric, differed in order from the traditional, namely: 'I am the Lord thy God', 'Thou shalt not take the name of the Lord in vain', 'Remember the sabbath day', 'Thou shalt not kill' on the right-hand tablet; 'Thou shalt not commit adultery', 'Thou shalt not steal', 'Thou shalt not bear false witness', 'Thou shalt not covet' (twice) on the second, left-hand, tablet. 'Thou shalt have no other gods' is not found at all. It is possible that the changed order was due simply to the carelessness or ignorance of the craftsman, but it is also possible that it was made for a heretical sect 'like the Karaites'. Two questions were put to Jeruchem. First, is it permitted to use this curtain in the synagogue? Second, assuming that it is forbidden, may the curtain be sold to a museum?

Jeruchem rules that it does seem as if the curtain follows heretical views. True, Ibn Ezra in his commentary to the Decalogue in Deuteronomy does count 'Thou shalt not covet' as two commandments, but that is because he holds that 'I am the Lord thy God' is not a 'commandment' but a general introduction to the Decalogue. No Jewish view holds that 'Thou shalt have no other gods' be omitted from the Decalogue. And even Ibn Ezra, in his commentary to the Decalogue in Exodus, refuses to count 'Thou shalt not covet' as two. The Ten Commandments should be removed from the curtain, and then there is no objection to using the curtain in the synagogue.

For reasons that will become obvious as Jeruchem develops his argument, a Responsum (no. 8) dated 1905[7] is headed with a verse from the portion of the week: 'Lo, it is a people that shall dwell alone, and shall not be reckoned among the nations' (Num. 23 : 9). The Rabbi to whom the Responsum is addressed, and whose name is omitted for obvious reasons, had written a letter to Jeruchem in which he had given the date, 1904, according to the Christian calendar. Jeruchem rebukes him for this. No Jew should use the Christian date. In business letters we are compelled to do it for the sake of convenience, but there it is a pure conven-

---

[7] All the dates are, of course, in the Jewish reckoning but the English version is given for the sake of convenience

tion. But in a private letter to a fellow-Jew, God forbid that we should do it. Even of the use of the Christian date in business correspondence, though permitted, Jeruchem says that to it the Rabbinic saying[8] can be applied: 'Jews who live outside the holy land serve idols, though in pure innocence.'

In a Responsum (no. 20) dated 1930 to Israel Weltz of Budapest, Jeruchem considers, among other questions, whether it is permitted to listen to church music and church services over the radio. He rules that it is forbidden.

Responsum no. 27 is also addressed to Israel Weltz, and concerns a Jew who registered as having no religion in order to avoid having to contribute to the tax levied by the government on Jews to cater for special Jewish communal purposes. He now wishes to return to the Jewish fold. Does he require a token reconversion as does the apostate who reverts to his religion? A similar question had been discussed by other Respondents.[9] Jeruchem rules that no token reconversion is required in this case.

A Responsum (no. 42) is in reply to a Jew residing in London who ate *terefa* food while he was in a concentration camp under the Nazis, and now wishes to do penance. Jeruchem first observes that it appears from the letter addressed to him that most of the inmates were compelled to eat *terefa* in order to survive, and for this no penance is required. Even in those instances where it could have been avoided without detriment to health, no penance is required, since a prisoner in a concentration camp cannot be held responsible for what he does in his confused state of mind and, in any event, the terrible sufferings he had undergone in the camp have certainly purged his sins. None the less, the Jewish heart is grieved that forbidden food has entered the Jewish stomach. Consequently, the man should fast on Mondays and Thursdays for forty days.

Judah Grünwald (1845-1920) served for twenty-two years as Rabbi of Sotmar in Hungary, where he headed a large Yeshivah. His Responsa collection *Zikhron Yehudah* was published posthumously.

[8] AZ 8a; see p. 284 above   [9] See p. 280 above

Eliezer Deutsch of Bonyhad requested Grünwald, together with other Rabbis, to support him in his struggle against an attempt to have the preliminary Psalms in the liturgy (*pesuke de-zimra*) recited quietly, instead of with a loud voice as is the custom. Grünwald[10] unhesitatingly supports Deutsch. The Psalmist speaks of raising the voice in jubilant praise of God. Mistaken notions of decorum should not be allowed to prevent Jews from following the established custom of shouting aloud for joy unto the Lord. Those who wish to change the custom are guilty of departing from the practices of Israel. 'We must only follow the customs of our fathers which are vital and are established for ever.' The Responsum is dated 1902.

In another Responsum[11] on prayer, Grünwald considers the confession recited on Yom Kippur Katan: 'That which Thou hast forbidden I have permitted and that which Thou hast permitted I have forbidden, but my intention was not to provoke Thee.' In some versions, this latter phrase is given in brackets. Grünwald says the author, when he omitted these words (if he really did so) probably wanted to leave room for the man who knows that he did intend to provoke God, whereas, in the normal version, the sinner declares that he sinned for personal gain or pleasure, not in order to provoke God. Consequently, if a man knows that he did intend to provoke God, he should omit the words: 'my intention was not to provoke Thee' from his confession, but if his heart tells him that he did not intend to provoke God, he should recite them. Repentance, concludes Grünwald, is acceptable even for sins where the intention was to provoke God.

In a Responsum[12] dated 1911, Grünwald considers the case of a community in which the scrolls of the Torah were destroyed in a fire. The members of the community asked him to give them a penance. Grünwald replies that from now onwards they should resolve to pay greater respect to the Torah by refraining from conversation during the reading of the Torah and by greater concentration on the words being read. On the eve of the sabbath, the scroll from which it is intended to read on the morrow should be carefully examined so that no irreverence will be paid to the

[10] Orah Hayyim, no. 69   [11] Ibid., no. 12   [12] Ibid., no. 44

scroll through having to return it to the Ark, should there be an error in the writing. The community should pay an expert scribe to go from house to house to see if the *mezuzot* are fit for use. Best of all, they should demonstrate their love of the Torah by seeing to it that their children are educated in the ways of the Torah.

Grünwald was opposed to Zionism, and there is an anti-Zionist Responsum in the collection.[13] In the original collection there was also a Responsum against the Aggudat Yisrael, but this was later removed from the book.[14] The anti-Zionist Responsum is dated 1902. Grünwald first declares that it is obvious that no faithful Jew can be anything other than a great lover of Zion. We all weep daily for Zion and pray for her restoration. But political Zionism presents two dangers to the Jewish people. First, there is the danger of it awakening anti-Semitism. Ezra and Nehemiah did not go up to rebuild the community in the holy land until the rulers had given them permission. At that time, 'the bestirring came from above'—a Zoharic expression—but in our days the Zionists wish to 'bestir from below', without any sign from Heaven, and by so doing they place in jeopardy the whole Jewish community in the Diaspora. Second, political Zionism is a danger to the Jewish soul. The Zionists are irreligious and encourage 'Reform' (this word is in quotes in the original). Our hope is for God, not the Zionists, to rebuild Jerusalem.

Few Talmudists have had such an astonishing grasp of the whole Rabbinic literature as Joseph Rozin (1858-1936), Rabbi in Dvinsk in Latvia, known, after his birthplace, as the genius (*illui*) of Rogadshov. His Responsa collection, *Tzafenat Paneah*, is unusual both in the extremely cryptic style and in its entire reliance on early medieval scholars, ignoring the later authorities.

Responsum no. 3 concerns the purely theoretical question, based on the Midrash, that during their travels through the wilderness the Israelites were fed with manna which had the property of enabling them to taste in it any flavour they desired. Would they have been permitted to taste in the manna some forbidden food and so enjoy the taste, if not the substance, of

[13] Ibid., no. 187   [14] See *Encyclopedia Judaica*, vol. 7, p. 950

forbidden food? Rozin refers to the discussion in the Talmud,[15] and *Rashi*'s commentary to the passage, from which it appears that it is impossible for a donkey to come down from Heaven but, if it did, its meat would be permitted.

Another Responsum (no. 5) discusses a programme for the study of the Torah.[16] Rozin remarks that to understand the Talmud adequately it is necessary to work hard at the task. The student who wishes to study, for example, the Order *Nashim*, should first study tractate *Yevamot* with the commentaries of Asher b. Jehiel and the Tosafists. He should then study tractate *Kiddushin* with these commentaries and repeat it all, this time with an attempt to grasp all the legal principles involved. He should proceed to study *Gittin* and *Sotah* in the same way, then *Nedarim* and *Nazir*, then *Ketubot*, *Baba Metzia* and *Baba Batra*, all with a determined effort to master the legal principles involved in the Talmudic debates. In a second Responsum (no. 6) on the same subject, Rozin repeats his advice, adding that the Mishnah should be studied with the commentary of Maimonides, 'which illumines the eyes'. The student should then follow the advice of the Rabbis to pray that God make him successful in his studies.

In a Responsum (no. 69) on Zionism, Rozin quotes *Rashi*[17] who observes that Zion is outside Jerusalem. The Zionists chose the right name for their movement because there is not the slightest trace of religion in this group and they are truly outside the Jerusalem of the Jewish spirit. Rozin says that he feels obliged to join other Rabbis in protesting against the movement, lest his silence be construed as assent.

David Hoffmann (1843–1921), a pupil of Moses Schick, was a critical scholar as well as a traditional Talmudist. He served as Rector of the Rabbinical Seminary in Berlin and was acknowledged as the leading Halakhist of German Jewry. His Responsa collection *Melammed Le-Hoil* won wide acceptance even outside Germany.

One of Hoffmann's Responsa[18] deals with the arguments a Rabbi should advance against people in his congregation who

---

[15] Sanh. 59b   [16] Cf. Bacharach's view, pp. 163–5 above
[17] Yom. 77b   [18] Part I, no. 12

wish to introduce certain Reforms into the synagogue service. 1. They wish to give up the recital of the silent Amidah to rely on the recitation by the Reader. Hoffmann, after discussing the legality of such a procedure, declares that it is forbidden. The Rabbi should put forward the following argument. The Biblical model of how we should recite our prayers is provided by Hannah, of whom it is said: 'Now Hannah, she spoke in her heart; only her lips moved, but her voice could not be heard' (I Sam. 1 : 13). The proper manner of concentrating on the prayers is to pray silently. True, for our sins, we do not in any event concentrate as we should, but it is surely wrong to abolish the silent prayer and so prevent those who wish to concentrate from so doing. In his silent prayer each person can add petitions of his own in an intimate, personal way, which he cannot do when the Reader prays on his behalf. Why should we be reduced to the status of Pharaoh, who could not pray on his own behalf but had to ask Moses to intercede for him (Exod. 8 : 4)? It should be every Jew's pride to be able to recite the prayers for himself and not be reduced to the status of the unlearned on whose behalf the Reader's prayers were introduced. Is it reasonable to depart from the custom of our fathers merely to save four or five minutes' time? 2. They wish to introduce the custom that the kohanim forgo their right to be called up first to the reading of the Torah in order to give others an opportunity to be called up. Hoffmann sees no objection to this, provided the kohanim are called up first on some occasion. 3. They wish to abolish the priestly blessing. The Rabbi should point out what a marvellous blessing this is. Even the Gentiles, who use the priestly blessing in their services, acknowledge its high value. Anyone who wishes to abolish the priestly blessing must be an unbeliever in God and His Torah, in which the blessing is ordained. The Rabbi should do his utmost to encourage the kohanim to recite the blessing with a pleasant melody, and with decorum. But if the congregation is adamant, the Rabbi should not make it an issue. If the Rabbi resigns because of it, the only result will be that a Reformist Rabbi will be appointed in his stead. An Orthodox Rabbi should resign from his post in protest only if the congregation insists on introducing such Reforms that are extremely serious: the use of an organ in the synagogue, for instance, or a choir of female voices, or the omission of prayers for the coming of the Messiah.

Hoffmann[19] discusses whether it is permitted to smoke in the synagogue. After considering the views of various authorities, he observes that Christians would not dream of smoking in church and, if Jews treat the synagogue with any less reverence, there is a profanation of God's name.

A Rabbi turned to Hoffmann for advice.[20] His congregants insist on introducing an organ into the synagogue service. He knows that he cannot prevent it but wishes to consult Hoffmann on whether it is permitted to use the organ only during the week —e.g. at weddings or on the king's birthday. There is a good chance of their accepting such a compromise and, at least, it will mean that the organ will not be used on the sabbath and festivals. If he resigns, the only result will be that a Reformer is appointed who will allow more serious innovations. Hoffmann first refers to the protest of the Rabbis in the tract *Elleh Divre Ha-Berit*[21] against the use of the organ. From this it appears that while all the Rabbis agree in forbidding an organ on the sabbath and the festivals, they are divided on whether it should be permitted during the week. Hoffmann is extremely reluctant to permit it even on weekdays, but remarks that if, under pressure, a pupil of his was obliged to allow the organ to be used on weekdays, he would not therefore revoke the Rabbinic ordination he had given.

In another Responsum[22] on Reform, Hoffmann declares it to be forbidden to sell a synagogue if there is a likelihood that the purchasers will turn it into a Reform synagogue. On the change of use of a synagogue,[23] Hoffmann permits a building that was once a Protestant chapel and has since been used as a hospital, to be converted into a synagogue.

Like other Rabbis in the nineteenth and twentieth centuries,[24] Hoffmann discusses[25] whether Jews who profane the sabbath openly can help to make up the quorum for prayer. He quotes ˙

[19] Part I, no. 15   [20] Part I, no. 16   [21] See p. 233 above
[22] Part I, no. 17   [23] Part I, no. 20
[24] See pp. 246–7 above   [25] Part I, no. 20

various authorities who argue that nowadays Jews who profane the sabbath do so because they are frequently unaware of the seriousness of the offence. They have the status of 'children brought up among the heathen', who are not to be blamed for their transgressions and are to be considered as Jews. However, Hoffmann adds, it is obviously preferable if a man can arrange to recite his prayers together with a congregation of observant Jews.

Hoffmann considers[26] a problem that could have arisen only in the confused times Orthodox Jewry had to face in early twentieth-century Germany. An observant young man, though he attended a business school on the sabbath, refrained from writing there. When this came to the ears of the young man's father, he ordered him to write. The boy's mother, afraid of the quarrels that might result in the home from the boy's refusal, threatened to commit suicide unless the boy agreed to obey his father and write on the sabbath. Since the sabbath could be profaned in order to save life, would this be construed as life-saving so that the boy was allowed to write? Hoffmann replies in the negative. By no stretch of the imagination can this be construed as the kind of life-saving for which the sabbath must be profaned. If it were, unbelievers could destroy Judaism by threatening to commit suicide unless their near relatives gave up the practices of the Torah. Judaism does not ask us to yield to such blackmail.

A question was put to Hoffmann[27] whether it is permitted to suspend amulets in the room of a woman about to give birth to a child. Even those who do not believe in the efficacy of amulets must acknowledge that they have a helpful psychological effect on those who believe in them. Consequently, says Hoffmann, the rule[28] applies: 'Whatever is for the purpose of healing is not forbidden because of the ways of the Amorites.'

In another Responsum,[29] Hoffmann deals with the case, noted earlier, of a Jew who registered himself as one who had no religion. In the case of a convert to Christianity, the *Shulhan Arukh*[30] rules that a token reconversion to Judaism is required when he returns to the Jewish fold. Is the same required of this

26 Part I, no. 61   27 Part II, no. 63   28 Sabb. 67a; see pp. 76–7 above
29 Part II, no. 84   30 YD 268, end

man who left the Jewish fold but did not convert to another faith? Hoffmann rules that the man must be treated as a convert to another faith and the token reconversion is required. To rule otherwise would be to encourage people to register themselves as having no religion in order to escape the payment of the special government tax for Jewish communal purposes.

Hoffmann[31] discusses whether the coffin of the famous Rabbi Azriel Hildersheimer of Berlin was permitted to be brought into the synagogue for the funeral oration to be delivered there. He quotes the authorities who forbid the bringing of a coffin into a synagogue for this purpose. It was done, they say, for the great Gaon of Vilna, but that was because he was 'unique in his generation'. Hoffmann writes:

> In our case, there is no doubt whatever that it is permitted to bring the coffin of our teacher, may I be an atonement for him, into the synagogue for he, too, was unique in this orphaned generation. He had everything—holiness, purity, brilliance and wide learning. Day and night he toiled, meditating in the Torah, carrying out the precepts and performing deeds of benevolence. He ran as swiftly as a hind and was as strong as a lion in his efforts on behalf of the poor in the holy land and of other unfortunates. He spent his efforts in battling for our faith against all its foes, all for no financial gain or profit and with no attempt at winning a reputation, for he was an extremely modest man, treating every scholar with the highest regard as if he was his teacher. He had many other good qualities, too numerous to record. Consequently, in honour of the Torah and of divine worship and charity it is right and proper to bring his coffin into the synagogue and to deliver there the funeral oration.

One of three questions to which Hoffmann replies[32] in another Responsum is whether a Jew is allowed to donate money towards the building of a church. Hoffmann replies, unlike Horowitz considered in the previous chapter, that even those authorities who see no objection to Christians having the faith they have adopted (since, for them, such a faith is not idolatry), agree that for the Jew the Christian faith is idolatry. How, then, can a Jew be in some way responsible for what for him is idolatrous worship? If there is no other way, he should simply give his donation

---

[31] Part II, no. 106   [32] Part II, no. 148

without specifying that it is for the building of the church.

One of the most prominent and authoritative Hungarian Rabbis of the early twentieth century was Moses b. Amram Grünwald of Huszt (1853–1910), author of the Responsa collection *Arugot Ha-Bosem*.

The very first Responsum is addressed to a pupil whose name is not given, evidently to avoid embarrassing him, who asked whether it is better to go to bed early in order to rise early for prayer or to stay up late into the night studying the Torah, even though as a result he will fail to be up early enough to pray together with the congregation. Grünwald quotes Talmudic passages in which study of the Torah at night is highly praised but, he says, the Rabbis do not refer to a man staying up but to one who goes to sleep early and rises up in the middle of the night to study. None the less, it is well known that many pious Jews do stay up to study the Torah during the first half of the night. They no doubt argue that this is preferable for, if one were to rely on rising from one's bed, sleep may get the upper hand. God alone knows whether they are sincere. Yet since all depends on habits formed in youth, a young scholar should train himself to rise in the middle of the night 'on fire with enthusiasm for the Torah'. He refers his questioner to the work *Reshit Hokhmah* (*Kedushah* 7), where the sixteenth-century Kabbalist Elijah de Vidas collected all the Zoharic passages in praise of rising at night to study the Torah. As for the objection, how can it be meritorious to rise at 'midnight', since 'midnight' differs from place to place; the answer is that it is with our 'midnight' that God is concerned, since on high there is no time!

A Responsum (no. 14) of Grünwald is in reply to the letter of Eliezer Deutsch of Bonyhad—the same question, in fact, as that addressed to Judah Grünwald[33] (no relation) by the same Rabbi. Grünwald replies that Deutsch does not require his support. He is obviously in the right. The Psalms must be recited as a joyful shout to the Lord. In any event, even if some people do recite the Psalms softly, this is no excuse for drawing up a regulation that all must recite them silently.

[33] P. 293 above

Another Responsum (no. 15) is addressed to the Bet Din of Munkacs and replies to the question whether a Reader who has served in a Neolog or *Status Quo* congregation may serve in this capacity in an Orthodox synagogue. Grünwald rules unreservedly that he cannot, and that all the Orthodox Rabbis, including Moses Schick, have agreed that such a man be banned from serving as a Reader. It is similar to the case of the priests who served in the temple of Onias and who were thereby disqualified from serving in the Temple at Jerusalem, even when they repented.[34]

In a Responsum on Reform (no. 31), Grünwald deals with the case of a Reform Temple in which, after an enlargement, the Bimah had been placed back in the middle, not at the end as in Reform Temples.[35] Otherwise, however, the synagogue is like any other Reform Temple. Is it permitted to pray there? Grünwald says that the place still resembles the pattern of the German Reform Temple in the following respects: 1. The Reader wears canonicals 'as do the Gentile priests'; he has a choir to assist him and he pronounces the words in a foreign way. 2. They do not call people up to the reading of the Torah by their Hebrew names, but the beadle distributes cards beforehand containing the number of the portion to which each is to be called. 3. They conduct the wedding service in the synagogue and the preacher delivers there an address to the young couple, 'like the Gentiles'. 4. They have used a compass to discover the true eastern direction and have altered the position of the Ark accordingly, thus insulting all the saints in days of old who prayed facing the direction the Ark had in former times. In fact, even if they changed the whole synagogue into an Orthodox synagogue it would still be forbidden to pray there, just as it is forbidden ever to use a grave that has been dug on the sabbath. How can one pray in a place the very walls of which cry out because of the desecration of the religion that has there been perpetrated? There is a synagogue in Pest, called the Maimonides Synagogue, built entirely in the traditional pattern yet, since a few Reform innovations are accepted there, no God-fearing person will enter to pray there.

Judah Grünwald turned to his namesake (no. 38) to ask his

[34] See pp. 30-1 above   [35] See pp. 227-8 above

advice as to whether he should accept the position of Rabbi in town A. Grünwald states that he is extremely reluctant to reply, since the question has already been put to the foremost Hasidic masters, who are divided on the matter. When they are divided, how dare he presume to decide? Whichever decision is taken, some good people will lose a fine Rabbi; so how can he offer advice? The Kabbalists, he says, declare that if a man feels strongly impelled to perform a certain *mitzvah* he should know that he was sent into the world to carry it out. This is a matter that can be decided only by Judah Grünwald himself.

Grünwald was asked (no. 39) whether it is permitted to go to the circus so as to be able to recite the benediction over observing strange creatures. Some have argued that it is a *mitzvah*. Grünwald quotes the Talmudic passage[36] in which it is said that it is forbidden to attend the circus and, in any event, the things one sees there are an enticement to lewdness.

A Responsum (no. 62) deals with the Hasidic practice[37] of not allowing the Reader of prayers in the synagogue to wear garments made of wool. Does it apply even to an occasional Reader, such as when a mourner leads the prayers at the end of the service? The question came from Ohelje, the town of Moses Teitelbaum, who had strictly forbidden it. All the more so, remarks Grünwald, in our day, when so many of the old customs are under heavy attack.

The ruling given in the *Shulhan Arukh*[38] is that an infant should not be suckled by a Gentile nurse who eats food forbidden to Jews, because this has the effect of contaminating the child's soul. Grünwald was asked (no. 138) whether it applies to a Christian nurse who had eaten leaven at Easter, if it coincides with Passover? Grünwald replies that it is forbidden. Although the leaven is not forbidden food in itself, but only because it is Passover, yet it still has the effect of contaminating the child's soul, just as we find that wherever possible a pregnant woman should not eat on Yom Kippur. Although women are exempt from the study of the Torah, this rule applies to infant girls as well as boys.

Rabbi Simon Pollack (no. 211) asked Grünwald whether it is

---

[36] AZ 18b [37] See pp. 214–15 above [38] YD 81: 7

permitted on Yom Kippur to recite a general prayer for all the departed, or must a special prayer be recited for each. Grünwald expresses his surprise at the question. Pollack is an ordained Rabbi, and in these matters each Rabbi is entitled to do as he seees fit, since the whole question is mentioned neither in the Talmud nor in the Codes. True, it can be argued that the impious dead may suffer in comparison with the pious if they are all embraced by the same prayer, yet against this there has to be set the prohibition of burdening the congregation with lengthy, unnecessary prayers. In addition, boys and girls whose parents are still alive tradition- ally leave the synagogue when these prayers are recited. It is un- wise to keep them strolling about outside the synagogue for too long a period, because they will be encouraged to flirt with one another.

A Responsum (no. 213) to Jacob Rubin, Rabbi of Cracow, and his Bet Din, concerns the attempt of Dr Meir Jung to establish in Cracow a modern Rabbinical Seminary in which secular, as well as Rabbinic, subjects would be taught. Grünwald strongly opposes the establishment of such a school. If the Torah enjoins us to protect our bodies from harm, how much more does it en- join us to protest at the harm caused to the souls of our children. Experience shows that it is not possible to combine Rabbinic learning with secular studies. To plant these studies in the vineyard of the Lord is to sow mixed seeds in a vineyard. According to the Torah, a vineyard containing mixed seeds must be destroyed by fire.

Grünwald was asked (no. 213) whether it is permitted to trans- late the laws of *niddah* (separation from a menstruant) into the vernacular on behalf of women who do not know Hebrew. The danger is that the 'enlightened ones' (Maskillim) may construe it as Rabbinic approval of their fondness for secular studies and the learning of foreign languages. Grünwald observes that all the woes of Israel began from the day the Torah was translated into Greek. The Jews then began to take the words of the Bible liter- ally, as they appeared in the translation, and began to neglect, as a consequence, the interpretations of the Oral Law as found in the Rabbinic literature. It should, therefore, really be forbidden to translate these laws but, since they are so important, it is in fact permitted.

In another Responsum (no. 214) on translation, Grünwald discusses whether it is permitted to translate Jacob Ibn Habib's *Ein Yaakov*, an anthology of the Rabbinic Aggadah, into German. He quotes a letter of Hayyim Halberstam[39] forbidding it on the grounds that the Aggadot of the Rabbis are frequently absurd if they are taken literally, which was never intended, but which cannot be avoided in a translation.

Menahem Manish Babad (1865–1938), Rabbi of Tarnapol, enjoyed great authority in the Galician Jewish community and beyond. Babad, a Hasid of the dynasty of Belz, wrote the Responsa collection *Havatzelet Ha-Sharon*.

A Responsum[40] dated 1926 and addressed to Abraham Mordecai Ashkenazi discusses a problem faced not infrequently by Rabbis in modern times. A Jewish man married a Gentile woman and had a son by her. The man is in no way an observant Jew but wishes to have his son circumcised and given a Jewish name in order to pacify his parents. Is such a thing permitted? Babad quotes the Talmudic rule[41] that the court can accept a Gentile minor as a convert, but the reason given for the rule is that it can safely be assumed that when the child grows up he will give his assent to the conversion because it is advantageous spiritually to be a Jew. There will be no such advantage in our case, since the child will be brought up as a Gentile. It can be argued, on the other hand, that no harm is done by converting the child, since the Talmud goes on to state that the minor who has been converted can revoke it when he grows up if it is not pleasing to him then. Consequently, if the child, in fact, keeps the Torah when he grows up it is, indeed, a valid conversion retrospectively. If he does not keep the Torah when he grows up, he will thereby demonstrate that he does not consider it an advantage to be a Jew and the conversion will be automatically revoked. Yet there is the danger that others may look upon him as a Jew and he will be allowed to marry a Jewish girl. Babad concludes: 'However, it is extremely hard for me to accept responsibility on such a matter

---

[39] See pp. 263–4 above   [40] Yoreh Deah, no. 75   [41] Ket. 11a

as this since, God forbid, it may result in debarring a soul from finding security under the wings of the Shekhinah. Therefore I would want them to consult our Master, the holy man of Belz, long may he live, and they should do as he advises.'

A Responsum[42] addressed to Rabbi Meir of Zhabaraz discusses the recent custom introduced in that town of placing the tombstone at the foot of the grave, instead of at the head as in former times. Babad quotes a saying attributed to Ibn Adret that not even six hundred thousand signs and wonders can succeed in persuading us to reject any custom observed by the old women in Israel. This applies especially to such matters as death and burial. There is also a sound reason for having the stone at the head of the grave, that prayers can be recited near to the spot where the head of the corpse lies. Furthermore, just as the washing of the corpse begins with the head, so too, out of respect for this, the most important part of the body, the stone should be at the head. All this is attested to by the famous Kabbalists. Babad is astonished that they should have been responsible for such an alteration. He would suspect them of heresy did he not know personally the pious Rabbi who introduced the change. The Rabbi did it when his son died and he himself died soon afterwards. Babad says that he is inclined to believe that the Rabbi brought death upon himself before his time by departing from the established custom. He advises the townsfolk to remove the tombstones of the Rabbi and his son from the foot to the head of the graves. There can be no doubt that these two pious men in Paradise will be pleased that this is done.

Babad deals[43] with whether it is permitted to build a communal bathhouse with bricks which come from a church. Babad rules that it is permitted but, if possible, a Gentile craftsman should erase the crosses on the bricks since it is an unworthy thing to have crosses on a Jewish communal building.

Another Galician Rabbi of note was Abraham Menahem Steinberg (1847–1928), Rabbi of Brody, author of the Responsa collection *Mahaze Avraham*.

A Responsum[44] dated 1908 and addressed to Mordecai Meshul-

---

[42] Yoreh Deah, no. 94   [43] Orah Hayyim, no. 12   [44] Vol. I, no. 27

Iam Kepler is in reply to the question whether a disused bathhouse can be converted into a synagogue. Steinberg quotes a Responsum of Joseph Saul Nathanson of Lemberg[45] in which it is ruled that it is permitted to use a former Lutheran chapel as a synagogue. Steinberg also remarks that he was once asked whether a former brothel can be used as a synagogue. Steinberg observes that nowhere in the Talmud or the Codes is it stated that such a thing is forbidden. Yet, for all that, it should not be permitted, since the average person will find it extremely odd that a brothel can be converted into a synagogue. Even things permitted by law must be rejected if they seem extremely offensive to the moral sense and cause the masses to view aspects of Judaism with distaste.

In another Responsum[46] on the building of a synagogue, dated 1914 and addressed to Rabbi Judah Schwartz of Hungary, Steinberg considers whether it is permitted to build a synagogue with a transept like a church. Steinberg says that it is, of course, allowed to have an extension to the synagogue, but if it is done in such a way as to resemble the cruciform pattern of church architecture it is forbidden.

The question of whether those who profane the sabbath can help to form the quorum for public prayer is discussed by Steinberg[47] in a Responsum dated 1926 addressed to Solomon Friedmann of Lemberg. A private *minyan* was arranged there in which persons who profaned the sabbath or shaved with a razor were not called up to the reading of the Torah. Steinberg quotes those authorities who argue that 'nowadays', when people no longer appreciate the seriousness of the offence, the profaners of the sabbath are not to be treated as if they were Gentiles. He admits that we cannot rigorously apply the law disqualifying such persons and so cause strife in the community. But what objection can there be to strictness in this matter being exercised in a private *minyan*? Nevertheless, here, too, Steinberg warns that it should not be the cause of communal disharmony.

The question of cremation occupied many Orthodox Rabbis.[48] Rabbi Dr Meir Lerner of Altona wrote to a number of prominent

[45] See p. 252 above
[47] Vol. II, Orah Hayyim, no. 7
[46] Vol. I, no. 31; see p. 217 above
[48] See pp. 260–1 above

Rabbis to ask for support in his struggle against cremation. He wished the Rabbis to declare that he was correct in his ruling that the ashes of a cremated corpse must not be buried in the Jewish cemetery. In a Responsum[49] to Lerner dated 1904, Steinberg agrees with him. For the dead to be buried is a positive precept as stated in the Talmud.[50] Anyone who lays down in his will that his body should be cremated offends against the Torah. In addition, he demonstrates that he has no belief in the resurrection of the dead. Steinberg continues:

> Consequently, all who bear the Jewish name should take care never to walk in the ways of those unbelievers and must never depart from the custom of our forefathers who, from the day the holy Torah was given, buried their dead in the soil, as did our holy patriarchs and all the righteous and upright from the earliest times down to the present.

Strictly speaking, he can see no objection to burying the ashes in the cemetery, but if the younger generation sees that the Rabbis refuse to allow this, this will certainly help to put a stop to the practice. In the next Responsum,[51] Steinberg's son also sides with Lerner.

Steinberg forbids[52] the holding of a wedding service in the synagogue, since to do this is to copy Gentile forms of worship.[53] Although Isserles in his notes to the *Shulhan Arukh*[54] seems to speak of a wedding taking place in the synagogue, the text is corrupt and what Isserles really means is that it takes place in a special communal hall, as Israel Lipshütz has pointed out in his commentary to the Mishnah *Tiferet Yisrael*.[55] Steinberg notes that the Reformers are fond of quoting this passage in Isserles, but they are greatly in error.

An outstanding Eastern European authority was Hayyim Mordecai Roller (d. 1946), Rabbi of Tirgu Neamit in Romania. His Responsa collection is entitled *Beer Hayyim Mordekhai*.

Roller discusses[56] whether the author of a heretical work can be appointed as a teacher to Jewish children. He fails utterly to see

[49] Vol. II, Yoreh Deah, no. 38   [50] Sanh. 46a   [51] Vol. II, Yoreh Deah, no. 39
[52] Vol. II, no. 42   [53] See pp. 219–20 above   [54] YD 391: 3
[55] Introduction to Moed, Semahot   [56] Part I, no. 38

how anyone can imagine that it is permitted. The Talmud[57] states that while R. Meir studied under the heretic Aher, such is only permitted to a great man like R. Meir who is capable of exercising judgment and discrimination. For a heretic to be allowed to teach children is to allow their tender souls to be poisoned. A God-fearing man will allow his children to be taught only by a teacher who will cause the light of the Torah to illumine their souls, instructing them in the way that is good and upright in the eyes of God and man.

Rabbi Jacob Moses Katz asked Roller[58] whether it is permitted to raise the money required in order to repair the scrolls of the Torah by holding a ball. Roller curtly dismisses the question, quoting the prohibition of bringing the 'hire of a harlot' into God's house (Deut. 23 : 19), which, Isserles[59] rules, applies also to a synagogue, and to any other religious purpose. It is enough, says Roller, that nowadays Rabbi do not have the power to prevent mixed dancing. But how can they permit for the sake of the Torah something which contradicts the Torah?

Roller was asked[60] by Shalom Cohen, a Rabbi in Bessarabia, whether he should relinquish his post because his spiritual needs remain unsatisfied where he is. The Talmud[61] advises a man to leave his town if his material needs are inadequately catered for there; would it apply to spiritual inadequacy as well? Roller advises against the move. Even though the Rabbi cannot advance spiritually as much there as he would be able to elsewhere, God does not demand more of man than the best of which he is capable in the particular circumstances in which he finds himself. No man should think of giving up his means of earning a living, since some degree of financial security is essential if the Torah is to be studied as it should be.

In a Responsum[62] to Hayyim Rabinowitz, Rabbi of Jassy, Roller discusses the case of a teacher about whom there is strong circumstantial evidence that he smoked a cigar on the sabbath. Roller finds it hard to give a decision. On the one hand, circumstantial evidence is not accepted in Jewish law but, on the other,

[57] Hag. 15a   [58] Part I, no. 50   [59] OH 153: 21
[60] Part II, no. 10   [61] BM 95b   [62] Part II, no. 61

there is danger to the souls of the children. Rabinowitz will know himself how to decide after carefully weighing up the pros and cons.

Another Responsum,[63] addressed to Roller's relative Isaac Greenberg, deals with the case of the heirs of a brothel-keeper who wished to donate a large sum of money in his memory to an old people's home. Is it permitted or forbidden, because of the Deuteronomic law which forbids the bringing of the hire of a harlot to the house of the Lord? Roller refuses to render a decision for a town which has its own Rabbi, but he is prepared to discuss the law theoretically. Although Isserles, as above, forbids the use of the hire of a harlot for a synagogue, the prohibition does not apply to charitable purposes. In any event the actual money that is being donated is not itself the hire of a harlot. On the other hand, it might be decided to refuse the money on the grounds that, if their aim is to strengthen Judaism, the court is empowered to act in a way that would otherwise be illegal.[64] The matter should be referred to the town Rabbi, and communal strife must be avoided.

In a Responsum[65] addressed to his father on the building of the Temple in the Messianic age, Roller quotes authorities[66] that the Temple of the future will not be built by human hands but will drop down from Heaven.[67]

Roller discusses[68] the statement in the *Zohar*[69] that one should study some 'foolish matters' before engaging in the study of the Torah. The meaning cannot be that one should introduce a humorous note before studying, as Rabbah is said to have done,[70] because this would not be called 'foolish matters'. Nor can the *Zohar* be speaking of heretical works because it is strictly forbidden to read these. The *Zohar* refers to the study of the natural sciences which are called 'foolish matters' in relation to the Torah.

Roller, too, in a Responsum[71] addressed to Alter Schapiro, Rabbi of Tchernowitz, deals with the question whether the ashes of a cremated corpse may be buried in the Jewish cemetery.[72]

---

[63] Part III, no. 64   [64] Sanh. 46a   [65] Part II, no. 72   [66] *Zohar* I, 28a and 114a
[67] Cf. part III, end of no. 72   [68] Part III, no. 23   [69] III, 47b
[70] Sabb. 30b   [71] Part III, no. 32   [72] See pp. 306–7 above

The particular case was that of a man who died while on a visit to Italy and requested in his will that he be cremated. His heirs now wish to bring back the ashes to be buried in Tchernowitz in the Jewish cemetery. There is no objection according to the strict law, but the court has emergency powers,[73] and it may be necessary to invoke these in order to stop the practice. This man, after all, behaved like the wicked Titus who ordered his remains to be cremated so that God would not be able to punish him.[74] The ashes should be buried, but outside the fence of the cemetery.

Daniel Sternfeld of Tchernowitz asked Roller[75] to write in support of the proposed establishment there of a rota of people prepared to stay up all night with the sick. Roller warmly praises the idea, quoting at length from the work on benevolence by the famous Lithuanian teacher, the Hafetz Hayyim, entitled *Ahavat Hesed*.

On the question of a wedding service in the synagogue,[76] Roller[77] strictly forbids it, and observes that all the authorities are opposed to this innovation.

In Responsum[78] addressed to Daniel Sternfeld of Tchernowitz, Roller bitterly attacks a book called *Ketav Yosher Divre Emet*, in which the author argues that nowadays it is permitted for married women to have their heads uncovered, since the Talmud forbids it only because in those times it was considered an example of loose conduct, but it is so no longer. Roller says that the author behaves exactly like the Reformers who also argue that the laws should be changed in response to the *Zeitgeist*. There is no need to refute the argument in detail. It is all nonsense and we are warned against engaging in debates with apostates. In this generation, observes Roller, everything is topsy-turvy. The women uncover their head and expose their hair, whereas the men, by removing their beards, remove the hair that is man's glory. Not a single letter of the Torah must ever be changed because of the *Zeitgeist*.

Judah Laib Zirelson (1860-1941) was a prominent leader of Russian Jewry, a founder of the Aggudat Yisrael movement and

73 Sanh. 46a	74 Sot. 57b	75 Part III, no. 36
76 See pp. 219–20 above	77 Part III, no. 43	78 Part III, no. 52

310

the Chief Rabbi of Bessarabia. His Responsa collection *Gevul Yehudah* contains a number of theological interest.

Zirelson was asked (no. 2) why it is the custom when praying for a sick person to refer to him by his mother's name, not his father's—e.g. Isaac ben Sarah. Zirelson quotes the Talmud[79] saying of Abaye that his mother told him that, in magical incantations, the mother's name is used. Since incantations generally involve a prayer, it can be surmised that those responsible for the prayers introduced the idea of referring to the mother rather than the father. Zirelson suggests a possible reason for it. According to Jewish law it can be assumed that a man claiming to be the father of a child really is the child's father, but that is because in the majority of cases this is true.[80] Since it is only a very high degree of probability, there may be cases where the child was not in fact begotten by the man claiming to be his father and, when speaking to God, no degree of possible falsehood can be tolerated. Consequently, it was ordained that in every case the mother's name be mentioned. Furthermore, in public prayer, since no falsehood is allowed, where it is known that a child is not the child of the man claiming to be his father, he will perforce have to be referred to as the child of his mother, which will cause him considerable embarrassment. The rule was therefore introduced to call every child by his mother's name. Zirelson notes that the Rabbis were often concerned to avoid causing anyone public embarrassment.[81]

Responsum no. 7 deals with the custom that those who see a scroll of the Torah fall to the ground must fast. Does this also apply to one who saw the scroll on the ground but did not witness the actual fall? Zirelson refers to the Talmudic passage[82] in which it is said that the unlearned are punished because they speak slightingly of the Ark in which the Torah is deposited, by referring to it as a 'cupboard'. How much more is it a token of lack of care and respect if a scroll is allowed to fall, and this applies to the whole congregation which permitted a careless man to handle the scroll. But it could not possibly apply to one who was not there

---

[79] Sabb. 66b, cf. Gitt. 69
[80] See Hull. 11b
[81] Taan. 26b; Pes. 82a
[82] Sabb. 32a

at the time but only came later to find the scroll on the ground.

Zirelson also considers (no. 30) the case of a man who was reflecting on the ban (*herem*) the Jewish community used to impose on offenders, and fell asleep while so doing. He had a dream in which he saw someone being placed under the ban. Does that person require the ban to be lifted by ten men as the Talmud suggests?[83] Zirelson rules, on the basis of the remarks of the *Ture Zahav*,[84] that it does not apply where a man had been thinking of the ban before he fell asleep. The Talmud holds that a ban in a dream may be a visitation from Heaven, but this does not apply to the man who brought it on himself by thinking of it beforehand. He quotes the similar distinction made by the Hasidic master Menahem Mendel of Lubavitch in the name of his grandfather, R. Shneor Zalman of Liady (d. 1813). The Talmud[85] says that one who has a seminal emission on Yom Kippur should be anxious all the year. This applies only to a saintly man, in which case it is a visitation from Heaven. It does not apply to an ordinary man of whom it can be assumed that it was caused by the thoughts he had before falling asleep.

Mordecai Joseph Breisch (b. 1896) of Zurich is the author of the Responsa collection *Helkat Yaakov*.

Breisch considers (no. 153) whether a Jew is permitted to offer his prayers in a house surmounted by a cross. Although he quotes some authorities who hold that the symbols of a faith other than Judaism prevent the ascent of the prayers, he does permit it in an emergency.

In Responsum no. 93, Breisch discusses a problem formulated as: 'A certain person belonging to the progressives lost his father. The father, an observant Jew who even wore daily the *tefillin* of Rabbenu Tam, stated in his will to his son: "I absolve you from your obligation to say Kaddish in the morning." The implication is that the father did not wish to impose on his son the burden of having to attend synagogue services early in the morning and thereby be late for his business. The question is whether the son is obliged, or at least permitted, to carry out the wishes of his parent (i.e. that he should not say the Kaddish in the morning).'

[83] Ned. 8a   [84] OH 288: 3   [85] Yom. 88a

Breisch points to the authorities[86] who rule that if a father orders his son not to say Kaddish for him, he should be obeyed. This is on the basis of the Talmudic statement[87] that if burial is for the purpose of atonement for sin, then one who declares that he does not wish to be buried should be obeyed, since he does not want atonement. Since the purpose of the Kaddish is quite clearly that of atonement, the father should be obeyed. However, Breisch rules that in our case the son is not absolved. For one thing, the father did not actually order him to desist from saying Kaddish. The question of obeying parents does not, therefore, enter into it. The father merely absolved his son, and here it can be argued that 'with regard to these lofty matters concerning the soul's elevation in the world of truth, who knows whether the father will not wish to go back on his absolution?' Furthermore, in our case, the father's statement was not based on any aversion he had from Kaddish being said for him. He did wish his son to say Kaddish for him in the evening. His intention was solely to make it easy for his Reform son, and this included attendance at prayer in the morning, from which it does not lie in his power to absolve the son. Nowadays, concludes Breisch, the Kaddish frequently provides a strong link with Judaism and, through it, sons are led to lead a more intensive Jewish life. He adds the prayer: 'May the Lord heal the breaches of His people Israel and draw the hearts of the children of Israel near to His service.'

Another question concerning prayer discussed by Breisch (no. 114) is whether it is proper to recite memorial prayers under the *huppah*, at a wedding service, for the repose of the souls of the parents of bride or bridegroom. Breisch remarks that customs differ. In the district he comes from, Belz, it was not customary to recite these prayers. However, the famous founder of the Hasidic dynasty of Belz, R. Shalom, used to say that the departed parents of the young couple are given permission in the world of truth to go down to earth to partake of the festivities, and the custom may be based on this idea.

Jehiel Jacob Weinberg (1885–1966) was a leading Talmudist and religious thinker. He acquired a secular education and eventually

---

[86] *Pithe Teshuvah* to YD 344: 1   [87] Sanh. 46b

lectured at, and later became the head of, the Orthodox Rabbinical Seminary in Berlin. His Responsa collection is entitled *Seride Esh*.

Weinberg has an interesting Responsum[88] on the theological significance of sabbath observance. He argues that the Biblical references to God creating in six days and resting on the seventh as the basis of sabbath observance are not to be taken to mean that the sabbath is a kind of re-enactment of God's cessation from creative activity on this day. Sabbath observance was not ordained as an instance of *Imitatio Dei*. Weinberg quotes Maimonides:[89] 'For this reason we are ordered by the law to exalt this day, in order that the principle of the creation of the world in time be established and universally known'—i.e. the sabbath is the day on which God is hailed as Creator. Weinberg concludes: 'To sum up, the meaning is not that we must rest because God rested on this day, but that God blessed and hallowed this day so that we might testify that the world was created in the six days of creation.'

In another Responsum,[90] Weinberg discusses the case of a man who gave a lift to a friend who was killed in an accident to the car. Is the car-owner obliged to undergo the *teshuvat ha-mishkal* of the *Rokeah*?[91] Weinberg follows various predecessors in stating that 'nowadays' we do not have the strength to engage in mortification of the flesh as an atonement for sin. The man should redeem his sin by giving a sum of money to the victim's heirs if they are poor, otherwise he should donate the money to the Shaare Zedek Hospital in Jerusalem.

Eliezer Waldenberg (b. 1917) was a Jerusalem Rabbi of note, author of the Responsa collection *Tzitz Eliezer*.

Waldenberg considers[92] whether it is permitted to pray for the death of an incurable who is in terrible agony. Relevant to the discussion is the Talmudic tale of the housemaid of Rabbi Judah the Prince who, when her master was very sick, prayed: 'The immortals desire Rabbi, and the mortals desire Rabbi; may it be the will of God that the mortals may overpower the immortals.' But when she saw that Rabbi was suffering so much, she prayed:

---

88 Vol. II, no. 20   89 *Guide of the Perplexed*, II, 31
90 Vol. II, no. 38   91 See pp. 101–2 above
92 Vol. V, *Ramat Rahel*, chapter 5, and vol. VII, no. 49. Cf. the Responsum of Hayyim Palaggi in Freehof, *A Treasury of Responsa*, pp. 220–2

'May it be the will of God that the immortals may overpower the mortals.'[93] It would seem from this that it is permitted to pray for the death of an incurable who suffers great pain and, in fact, the passage is quoted by the fourteenth-century authority, the *Ran*, in his commentary to tractate Nedarim[94] as proof not only that it is permitted but that it is obligatory. Waldenberg argues from the silence of the other commentators and the Codes that they would disagree with the *Ran*, either because they follow the Rabbis and not the maidservant, who did pray for Rabbi to live, or because Rabbi was so saintly that there was clearly no need for him to undergo further sufferings on earth to atone for his sins. After quoting other authorities who have discussed the question, Waldenberg comes to the conclusion that it is not permitted to pray for the death of the incurable even if he endures great suffering, and those who do permit it do so only for strangers, not for the relatives of the sick person who may be governed by motives of self-interest, such as the unconscious desire to be rid of the burden.

Isaac Nissim (b. 1896) was, from 1955 to 1972, the Rishon Le-Tzion, Sephardi Chief Rabbi of Israel. His collection, *Yen Ha-Tov*, contains the following Responsa of theological interest.

Nissim discusses[95] the opening paragraph of the *Shulhan Arukh* in which Isserles states the ideal that God should always be in the mind. The statement is based on the passage in Maimonides' *Guide of the Perplexed*.[96] Nissim notes that Maimonides declares that only a few rare souls can attain to this stage. For the average person it is sufficient if God is in the mind at the time of prayer and then, by stages, the approximation of the higher ideal might be reached.

Nissim's son, Rahamim Bezalel, asked him[97] why we say in our prayers: 'The God of Abraham, the God of Isaac, and the God of Jacob' and not: 'The God of Abraham, Isaac and Jacob'. Furthermore, why is the name 'Jacob' used and not the superior name 'Israel'? Nissim first observes that the 'Men of the Great Synagogue', who composed this prayer, did so under the influence

[93] Ket. 104a   [94] Ned. 40a   [95] Orah Hayyim, no. 1
[96] III, 51   [97] Orah Hayyim, no. 34

of the holy spirit, so that there are profound mysteries behind every word. There is no doubt a mystical reason for the repetition of the word 'God' and for the preference for the name 'Jacob'. 'But', says Nissim, 'we have no concern with mystery.' Nissim suggests, as the simple reason, that the Biblical pattern is followed as in Exodus 3 : 6 and 3 : 15. He refers to the Responsum[98] of Meir Eisenstadt on the same subject.

Nissim considers[99] the saying of Isaac Luria that one should not give alms at night, because it is a time of severe judgments. The meaning can be only that the giving of alms to the charity-collector is not enjoined before the evening prayer, as it is before the morning and afternoon prayers. But there is no doubt that there is an obligation to give alms to the needy at any time of the day or night.

In another Responsum[100] on the Kabbalah, Nissim discusses the Kabbalistic rule that one should not read the Bible at night be-cause the 'Written Torah' belongs to the 'World of Action' and so does the night, and both these belong to the 'side of judgment'. Nissim observes that this applies only to one who can study the 'Oral Torah'. The man who is capable of reading only the Bible should do so at night, too, rather than waste the time by sitting idle. In any event, it is permitted on the sabbaths and festivals when the divine mercy is bestirred.

A Responsum[101] considers the case of a scholar who was ap-pointed town Rabbi. Another and greater scholar who had been passed over claimed that the man who had been appointed had used his family influence to secure the position, and he quoted the Rabbinic saying: 'As soon as a man is appointed to the position of community leader here on earth he becomes a wicked person in the eyes of Heaven.' The Rabbi felt deeply aggrieved but, thanks to the arbitration of the community, both parties were eventually pacified. Two questions were addressed to Nissim. First, where is this supposed Rabbinic saying to be found? Second, what punish-ment should be meted out to one who quotes the saying with reference to a Rabbi? Nissim replies that the saying is not found

98 See pp. 186–7 above   99 Orah Hayyim, no. 53
100 Ibid., no. 54   101 Yoreh Deah, no. 16

in the Talmud but is quoted as a Rabbinic saying by Maimonides in his commentary to the first chapter of Avot. It would seem that Maimonides had a different reading from our present text in Sanhedrin 103b. Nissim points out that in a number of Talmudic passages the opposite view is expressed: that a man's sins are pardoned when he is appointed leader of the community. Nissim suggests that Maimonides is thinking of the man who usurps authority, not of the man democratically elected.

Isaac Jacob Weiss (b. 1902), head of the Bet Din in Manchester, England, and later of the Bet Din of the *Edah Haredit* in Jerusalem, was a prolific writer of Responsa. His collection *Minhat Yitzhak* contains a number of theological interest.

An unusual Responsum[102] concerns the right of religious leaders to interfere with the freedom of the press. Some years before, Weiss and some of his colleagues protested against mixed dancing in the halls of Anglo-Jewish synagogues. An editorial in the London *Jewish Chronicle* strongly denounced the intervention of the Rabbis, and Weiss held that the protest, especially in the form it took, made the editor guilty of insulting *talmide hakhamim*. His Responsum considers the fine which should be imposed on the editor. He first argues that the editor must apologise, and that the apology must be given the same prominence in the paper as the original attack. Strictly speaking, the editor deserves to be placed under the ban but, unfortunately, this cannot be done, nowadays, because of the law of the land. However, the editor should be 'driven out of the synagogue' until he recants. As for the fine, the *Tur*,[103] following a passage in the Jerusalem Talmud which refers to a 'pound of gold', rules that one who insults a scholar must pay a fine of 30 denars of gold. Although many authorities rule that nowadays there are no *talmide hakhamim* so far as this fine is concerned, in our case the fine must be imposed, since the insult was not only to the persons of the scholars but to the Torah they were bent on applying in preaching against mixed dancing.

Weiss was formerly Rabbi of Grosswardein in Romania. Immediately after the Holocaust, before it was known who had

[102] Vol. III, no. 112   [103] HM 500

died and who had remained alive, he was asked[104] whether the memorial prayers should be recited for those who did not return home and could be assumed to be dead. Weiss quotes the differing opinions among the authorities, including the opinion that a man unjustly murdered by a tyrannical regime does not need to have the Kaddish recited for him, since his death is an atonement for all his sins. Weiss concludes that, on balance, the memorial prayers should be recited only when it is known for certain that the person for whom they are said is dead.

A Responsum[105] dated Manchester 1958 and addressed to Aaron Westheim in Paris concerns those who profane the sabbath in public. Are they to be treated as Gentiles, or is the argument accepted[106] that nowadays they are unaware of the seriousness of the offence? Weiss quotes the authorities who incline towards leniency but himself favours a strict attitude.

A year later, Weiss advises[107] Alexander Carlebach, Rabbi of Belfast, whether a Jew who has married out of the faith may be counted for the *minyan*, the quorum for public prayer. He rules that he is to be treated as a Gentile. He refers to Judah Grünwald who discusses the question and arrives at a similar conclusion.[108] He also refers to the Responsum of Zevi Ashkenazi (no. 38) and expresses his surprise that Grünwald was unaware of this Responsum.

Two Responsa,[109] both dated Manchester 1961 and addressed to Rabbi Michael Fisher of London, discuss the penance to be imposed on a doctor who by mistake gave a patient an injection of poison from which he died. Weiss and Fisher both refer to the ruling of *Tashbetz*[110] on the question. The *Shulhan Arukh* rules[111] that a doctor who kills his patient through an error in treatment is guilty of accidental homicide and is obliged to suffer exile to one of the refuge cities, in the Temple period when these laws applied. Consequently, the doctor has to do penance.

In the course of a Responsum[112] addressed to Rabbi Halberstam of Brooklyn, Weiss objects to the translation of the Rabbinic

---

[104] Vol. I, no. 133   [105] Vol. III, no. 26: 4   [106] See pp. 246–7 above
[107] Vol. III, no. 63   [108] See pp. 292–4 above   [109] Vol. III, nos 104 and 105
[110] See pp. 88–94 above [111] YD 366   [112] Vol. IV, no. 30

Aggadah into European languages. He quotes the Responsum on this subject[113] by Joseph Hayyim of Baghdad.

In 1966 Rabbi Gedaliah Hoffmann of Beersheba asked whether it is permitted to tell the time by a clock on a church spire. Weiss remarks[114] that the question is discussed in a Responsum of Hayyim Eleazar Spira of Munkacs[115] who permits it, according to the strict law, since the clock was only put there for the convenience of the public, not for the purposes of Christian worship. None the less, Spira says that if possible it should be avoided. Weiss notes that in any event there is no definite prohibition anywhere of looking at an 'idol'. The Talmud[116] rules that the prohibition on having benefit from something does not apply to looking at it, although some authorities do extend the prohibition in this way. In any event, the clock is not an object of worship.

A Responsum dated 1965[117] to Rabbi Teitelbaum of Brooklyn concerns a boy of seventeen who studies in a Yeshivah but whose father orders him to go to college in the evenings to study secular subjects. Is the boy obliged to obey his father? Weiss agrees with Teitelbaum that the boy should not obey his father. Even if a father orders his son to offend against a Rabbinic law the son must disregard his father's orders, therefore he must disregard even more the order to study secular subjects, where there is not only the question of the high duty of Torah study to be taken into account but the positive offence of studying secular sciences. Studying at a college leads to religious laxness and an acquaintance with heretical books.[118]

Rabbi S. A. Eckstein of Ottawa, an Orthodox Rabbi, in 1967 was sent an invitation to be present at the consecration of a new Conservative synagogue in Ottawa, but declined. He wishes to know whether he made the right decision. Weiss says[119] that he has no doubt whatever that he was right, and quotes from the Zohar:[120] 'They come from the side of those who said: "Come, let us build a city and make to us a name" (Gen. 11 : 4). These men build synagogues and houses of learning, and place in them

---

[113] See pp. 263–4 above [114] Vol. IV, no. 87 [115] *Minhat Eleazar*, vol. II, no. 73
[116] Pes. 26a [117] Vol. V, no. 79 [118] See p. 234 above
[119] Vol. V, no. 98 [120] I, 25b

Torah scrolls with rich adornments, but do it not for the sake of God but only to make a name for themselves.' If an individual sins it is one thing, but these men cause the public to sin. Consequently, it is obvious that according to the law the verse applies: 'Unto their assembly let my glory not be united' (Gen. 49 : 6).

Moses Feinstein (b. 1895) was a recognised authority and head of the *Mesivta Tiferet Yerushalayim* in New York. His Responsa collection *Iggerot Moshe* discusses theological as well as Halakhic questions.

A Responsum dated 1963[121] replies to a question formulated as: 'Is there any advantage in, or prohibition against, taking out an insurance policy, since, God forbid, it may appear to suggest a lack of trust in God in whose power it lies to make a man rich enough to leave a large sum to his heirs?' Feinstein declares categorically that it is permitted to take out an insurance policy. Basically, there is no difference between this and any other business undertaking. The Rabbis declare that it is forbidden to rely on miracles,[122] as when they say that it is a 'vain prayer' to ask God to change the sex of an embryo in its mother's womb. Trust in God means a conviction that all is from God, but God's blessing only follows on man's efforts: 'In the sweat of thy face shalt thou eat bread' (Gen. 3 : 19). Feinstein quotes Maimonides' ruling[123] that it constitutes a profanation of the divine name for a man to live on charity and do no work in order to study the Torah. Onkelos, paraphrasing the verse: 'But thou shalt remember the Lord thy God for it is He that giveth thee power to get wealth' (Deut. 8 : 18), says: 'It is He that giveth thee counsel to purchase property.' This means that God has given man the skills by means of which he might earn a living. Since God has revealed this new device of insurance in our generation, it should be seen as His 'counsel' to us. Feinstein adds that trust here consists in relying on God that the premiums will be paid—i.e. man will earn enough to pay them. The same applies, he concludes, to insurance against fire and theft and to car insurance. 'This is appreciated by God-fearing men who do take out insurance policies.'

[121] Orah Hayyim, no. 111   [122] Ber. 60a   [123] *Yad*, Talmud Torah 3: 10

Feinstein considers[124] whether, according to the Torah, a Gentile has an obligation to pray to God. Feinstein notes that prayer is not one of the seven precepts of 'the sons of Noah'. There is, therefore, no obligation for a Gentile to pray, but, if he does, he carries out a *mitzvah*. Does not the prophet say: 'For My house shall be called a house of prayer for all the peoples' (Isa. 56 : 7)? Moreover, it can be argued that when the Gentile is in need he has as much obligation as a Jew to bring his needs before God. That it is not counted among the seven Noahide laws should occasion no surprise. It is surely implied in belief in God, which is similarly not counted among the seven, but is obviously the root and foundation of them all.

In a startling Responsum,[125] Feinstein discusses the question of grace recited at a UJA banquet and the like by a Reform or Conservative Rabbi. Is it permitted to answer 'Amen' after a benediction recited by a heretic? Feinstein declares that since 'most of these Rabbis' do not believe in God (*sic*) and in His Torah, the benediction is a mere verbal form and 'Amen' should not be recited after it. Maimonides[126] rules that a scroll written by a heretic possesses no sanctity.

Ben Zion Uziel (1880–1953), the Rishon Le-Tzion, was an acknowledged Rabbinic authority. His Responsa collections *Mishpete Uziel* contain a number of theological discussions.

One of these Responsa[127] concerns the status of the *mamzer*, the issue of an adulterous union, who may not marry an ordinary Jewess. Suppose the natural parents of the *mamzer* repent of their sin and do so, moreover, out of the love of God. According to Rabbinic teaching, repentance out of love has the effect of converting the sin into merit. Consequently, the innocent child should no longer be considered to be the fruit of a sinful union. The sinners themselves now have their halo of merit and yet the poor child is still treated as a *mamzer*. Uziel replies that repentance, even out of love, does not have the effect of nullifying the sinful act, only of purifying the sinful soul. The psychological effect of sin is to make the sin increasingly attractive so that eventually the

[124] Orah Hayyim, no. 24
[126] *Yad*, Yesode Ha-Torah 6: 8

[125] Ibid., no. 56
[127] Even Ha-Ezer, no. 3

sinner persuades himself that it is not sinful at all. To rid the soul of this malady great effort is required and, if this is engaged in out of the love of God, the sin, the cause of the effort, is treated as merit. But it is in this sense only that the Rabbis speak of it as merit. Supposing, for example, a man had upset his stomach by eating forbidden food, it cannot seriously be suggested that if he repents out of love he will be automatically cured. The *mamzer's* taint is quasi-physical and not a punishment for the sins of his parents. The adulterous act automatically taints the soul of the child born as its result. The child is, indeed, innocent but the facts of life are such that the innocent do sometimes suffer for the sins of the guilty, as when the victim of a vicious assault is maimed for life. It is only by a miracle that the *mamzer* will become pure again in the Messianic age.[128]

Uziel discusses[129] the curious medieval belief in the incubus and succubus, demons who have sexual unions with human beings. The wife of a *kohen* declared that she had been raped by a demon. Is she forbidden to her husband as she would be had she been raped by a human being? Uziel quotes Meir of Lublin who rules that intercourse with a demon is not held to be intercourse within the terms of Jewish law.

The Rabbi of Beirut asked Uziel whether a daughter can say Kaddish for her parents.[130] He replies[131] that it goes without saying that the good deeds of a daughter bring merit to the souls of her departed parents, but Kaddish is in a different category. The main idea behind the Kaddish is that the son takes the place of his father in sanctifying the name of God in public worship. This can apply only to males who can form a *minyan*. It is somewhat surprising that Uziel fails to see that, if his logic is correct, a son should not say the Kaddish for his mother.

Uziel engages[132] in a fierce attack on suggested liturgical reforms in a certain community. He first argues that it is generally forbidden to depart from established custom and then turns to attacking the suggested reforms point by point. It was suggested

---

[128] Kidd. 72b   [129] Even Ha-Ezer, no. 11
[130] See p. 168 above for Bacharach's views
[131] *Mishpete Uziel, Tinyana* to Orah Hayyim, no. 13
[132] *Tinyana,* Supplements, no. 5

that, when the Torah is read in the synagogue, some portions should also be translated into English. Uziel considers this to be a profanation, comparable to the offering in the Temple of animals that have not been sanctified. Even the Targum of Onkelos in Aramaic, though sanctified in Israel, is not read during the synagogue service. Uziel also attacks the suggestion that fewer than one hundred notes be sounded on the *shofar* on Rosh Ha-Shanah. It is an ancient custom and must not be abolished. Similarly, while it is right and proper to have English translations of the prayers, these must remain in the prayer-book, not recited, as was suggested, on Yom Kippur. As for the suggestion that the recital of the afternoon prayer before a wedding should be abolished, this custom also has a sound foundation. Although marriage is a religious duty and hence the wedding service is too, it cannot be compared to the higher duty of public prayer. That is why it was ordained that the higher duty be carried out first. Interestingly enough, in his very defence of traditional practices, Uziel does not protest against having the wedding service in the synagogue.[133]

Uziel discusses[134] the case of a husband and wife from Bombay who visited Switzerland, where the husband died. The wife had him cremated so that she could have the ashes taken to Bombay, there to erect over them a magnificent tombstone. Is it permitted to bury the ashes in the Jewish cemetery? Uziel is uncompromising in his reply. This sinful woman did a thing unheard of in Israel. The ashes must not be buried in the Jewish cemetery and so give the impression that the community condones her offence. The cemetery is a sacred place, because of the belief in the resurrection of the dead which this woman denied.

Zevi Ezekiel Michaelson (1863–1942) was Rabbi of Plonsk and later a member of the Rabbinical Court in Warsaw. His collection *Tirosh Ve-Yitzhar* contains many Responsa of a theological nature. Michaelson's collection is very unusual in that it not only considers legal questions but gives numerous interpretations of the non-legal passages in the Talmud, interspersed with Hasidic tales and maxims of the great Rabbis. Much of this material is homiletical and pilpulistic, but some of it has theological implications.

The Hungarian Rabbi Gerson Stern was asked to officiate at the dedication of a new synagogue and requested Michaelson (no. 23) to provide him with some ideas for the occasion. Michaelson records an idea based on the Talmudic saying[135] that people live long even in Babylon (although long life is promised only to those who reside in the holy land) because they go frequently to the synagogue. There is an ancient tradition that all the synagogues in the Diaspora will be transported to the holy land when the Messiah comes, so that, even now, the synagogue has the same life-giving properties as the holy land.

In a Responsum dated 1896, Michaelson (no. 67) discusses what is to be done when a scroll of the Torah falls accidentally to the ground. He says that it is the custom for those who witness it to fast and, if they are too weak to fast, to 'redeem' it by giving alms. He, however, feels obliged to note that this custom has no basis in the classical sources. He admits that the custom should be followed, but is surprised that people who are so particular about the honour of the Torah should still show scant respect for the Rabbis who study the Torah and teach it.

The author of a work on the importance of wearing a beard asked Michaelson for his opinion in 1906. Michaelson (no. 68) quotes a number of authorities who hold that it is wrong to go clean-shaven and that a beard is an adornment for the devout Jew. He refers to the Responsum[136] of Joseph Ergas on the subject. Michaelson calls the beard the Jew's 'coat of arms', his proud mark of distinction.

Michaelson replies (no. 72) to a question put to him by his relative concerning a statement in the will of their grandfather, Samuel Elijah of Bilgoraj, that all his male descendants must pray in the Ashkenazi version and never change over to the Sephardi version as used by the Hasidim. Are they bound to adhere to these instructions, and what is the general position on the question of changing one's liturgical adherence? This kind of question was discussed in previous Responsa.[137] Michaelson comes to the conclusion that it is permitted to change the version and that, in such

---

[135] Ber. 8a   [136] See pp. 184-5 above   [137] See pp. 214-15 above

instances, the will of their grandfather cannot be considered to have binding force.

A Responsum (no. 100) dated 1935 contains the opinion of a number of Rabbis on a man's request in his will that he be buried in both his prayer-shawls: should it be heeded? In the course of his discussion, Michaelson remarks that the question came up when the Hasidic master Judah Laib of Gur, the *Sefat Emet*, died. At that time Abraham of Sochatchov gave a ruling, but it has not come down to us. He also ruled that it was forbidden for *Kohanim* to come into contact with the corpse (cf. no. 70). The famous Hasidic master, R. Menahem Mendel of Kotzk, protested vehemently against the suggestion that the corpse of a Zaddik does not contaminate. Michaelson also refers to another problem. Solomon in his dream did not ask for wealth or honour but for an understanding heart. But since it all happened in a dream, why should Solomon have been praised and rewarded for what, after all, was an unconscious choice? Michaelson gives the reply of Abraham Mordecai, Rabbi of Gur, and son and successor of the *Sefat Emet*, that the ancients in their dreams occupied a higher stage than we do in our waking life (cf. no. 209).

Michaelson agrees (no. 102) with Dr Meir Lerner that it is forbidden to bury in the Jewish cemetery the ashes of one who has been cremated.

A Responsum (no. 123) discusses, among other topics, whether the *mitzvot* will still be practised in the Messianic age.[138] Michaelson quotes some of the thinkers who deal with this question.[139] Among the further points he makes are: the Talmud tells us[140] that the Messiah will 'smell out' the guilty, but this is opposed to the law of the Torah that guilt can only be established by the testimony of two witnesses. Michaelson also refers to the 'commentaries' who ask: since death will be no more, will the *mitzvah* of levirate marriage perforce be abolished? Maimonides[141] argues that the whole sacrificial system was only a concession to the primitive ideas of the people. From this it would seem to follow that the sacrificial system will not be restored in the Messianic

[138] See pp. 63–4 above
[140] Sanh. 93
[139] See pp. 117–18 above
[141] *Guide of the Perplexed*, III, 23

age, as Albo[142] protests. But the truth is that while Maimonides gives this rationalist explanation of the sacrifices, he himself[143] rules that the sacrificial system will be restored in the Messianic age.

Finally, Michaelson has a Responsum (no. 143) on the problem of the sufferings of the righteous. He says that the only adequate response is to say that the human mind is incapable of grasping the mysterious ways of God, of whose wisdom there is no searching.

Abraham Isaac Kook (1865–1935), first Chief Rabbi of Palestine, mystic and religious philosopher, naturally touches on theological themes in his two volumes of Responsa, *Daat Kohen* and *Ezrat Kohen*.

Kook considers[144] the case of a *shohet* whose children profane the sabbath. He argues that it is a profanation of God's name if the responsible post of *shohet* is given to such a man, but this applies only if the children are still at his table. A man cannot be held responsible for his children once they lead independent lives.

A Responsum[145] dated Jerusalem 1925 and addressed to Menahem Mendel, *shohet* in Beersheba, concerns the Muslim authorities who allow *shehitah* to be carried out only if the *shohet* faces east and acknowledges Allah. Is it permitted? Kook rules that if possible it should be avoided, but otherwise it is permitted since Muslims worship God alone and are not idolators.

Kook discusses[146] the complaint registered against a Rabbi that he is not too careful in rendering decisions and that he first consults the books. But the *Ture Zahav* rules[147] that one who renders decisions in Jewish law is not obliged to carry all the laws in his head, and that it is perfectly in order for him to consult the sources. Even such a giant as Ezekiel Landau remarks in his Introduction to his Responsa collection *Noda Biyudah* that he consulted the sources.

In 1926 Kook addressed a Responsum[148] to Abraham Neumann

---

[142] *Ikkarim*, III, 14   [143] *Yad*, Maaseh Ha-Korbanot 2: 14
[144] *Daat Kohen*, no. 7   [145] Ibid., no. 10
[146] Ibid., no. 16   [147] YD 1: 5   [148] *Daat Kohen*, no. 66

the artist. Is there any objection in Jewish law to an artist painting
the portrait of a God-fearing man? Kook replies:

> I have the honour of informing you that there are pious folk who
> refused to have their portrait painted or to be photographed. There
> is some support for their attitude in the Codes, and it goes without
> saying that there is something in it as an attitude of special piety.
> Nevertheless, according to the plain law, as it has been accepted by
> the Jewish people who follow the *Shulhan Arukh*, it is permitted.
> This practice has, in fact, spread even among the God-fearing when
> there is some need for it—for example, in order to make the Torah
> and Judaism attractive, or for some other reason. Yet it is proper that
> the portrait should not be of the whole body (i.e. with the legs), but
> only the upper part of the body. Here is contained man's chief
> dignity and the heart in which his spiritual nature is given expression.
> And, after all, it is this aspect that is the true aim of all good artist
> and craftsmen.

A Responsum[149] from Jaffa dated 1912 is addressed to Hayyim
Pollack. Is it permitted to attend a seance? Kook discusses the
attitude of the Codes on 'inquiring of the dead'.[150] He states that
he cannot declare categorically that it is forbidden, but it is certainly not worth while to attempt to strengthen one's faith in this
way. It is better to be whole with God. The holy nation should
cleave only to the living God.

In a Responsum[151] from Jerusalem, Kook discusses in 1933
whether it is permitted to give charity to sinners. He argues that
it is, and adds: 'Generally speaking, it is nowadays essential to
draw down mercy on all Israel. Because of all our troubles it can
be argued that even those who sin intentionally are as those who
sin unintentionally.'

A Responsum[152] to the Rabbi of Cape Town is dated Jerusalem,
1935, and deals with cremation,[153] which Kook categorically forbids. Even if burial were no more than an ancient custom it is
forbidden to depart from it, but the truth is that cremation is
forbidden not by custom, but by law. Burial, moreover, streng-
thens belief in the resurrection of the dead. To be sure, God can
restore the body from the ashes, as He will do in connection with

[149] Ibid., no. 69   [150] YD 179: 10   [151] *Daat Kohen*, no. 131
[152] Ibid., no. 197   [153] See pp. 260–1 above

the martyrs who have been burned, but whatever is done to strengthen belief in the resurrection is praiseworthy. It is forbidden to bury the ashes of those cremated in the Jewish cemetery. Kook has another Responsum on the same subject.[154]

Dr de Sola enquired in 1920 about the adornment of the cemetery. Kook concludes:[155]

> The general principle is that the Jewish way is not to spend too much on the imaginary honour of the dead, but Jews try, instead, to give a great deal in charity for the benefit of the living. However, that which is moderate and proper wherewith to show respect for the dead should be done, and it belongs to the principle of respect for human dignity. All Israel has followed this practice since time immemorial, to do everything in a fit and proper way as befits the holy nation which keeps its faith. God will resurrect the dead. May He show us His salvation speedily and in our days and very soon.

A Responsum[156] dated 1935 is to the community of Shiraj in Persia, rebuking them severely for allowing some men and women to burn incense to demons.

Also in 1935 in a Responsum[157] addressed to Moses Jurewitz of the Torah Va-Avodah movement in Pressburg, Kook states that mixed dancing is strictly forbidden according to Jewish law. This traditional view, he says, far from being disadvantageous to the Jewish woman, is intended, in fact, to pay her the greatest compliment, and has been a powerful force in promoting the Jewish male's regard and respect for his womenfolk.

Finally Kook[158] discusses the prohibition on studying the Bible at night. He says that this goes back to the Lurianic Kabbalah, but does not apply if the Bible is translated as well as studied in the original Hebrew. How stupid are those people, he says, who rather than study the Bible at night prefer to sit idle and do nothing.

---

[154] *Daat Kohen*, no. 198
[155] Ibid., no. 213
[156] Ibid., no. 230
[157] *Ezrat Kohen*, no. 30
[158] Ibid., no. 34

CHAPTER XII

Summary and Conclusions

The views of each of the respondents having been considered in isolation, an attempt is made in this final chapter to observe how certain themes appear frequently in the Responsa literature and how these are treated in various ways by the writers. Only the recurring themes are here examined (in alphabetical order).

THE AFTER-LIFE

Maimonides' spiritual conception of bliss in the Hereafter occasioned much debate, seeming to be completely at variance with the standard official Rabbinic view. Abraham Maimoni (pp. 53–4) is at pains to defend his father. Elijah Mizrahi (p. 106) puts forward the view that Maimonides does believe in the resurrection of the dead. David Ibn Abi Zimra (p. 126) similarly defends Maimonides' orthodoxy and adds that, in spite of the formulation in Maimonides' Code, this thinker does believe in Hell. Joseph Hayyim of Baghdad (pp. 266–7) is prepared to affirm that the Garden of Eden is located on earth. Joseph Saul Nathanson (pp. 253–4) gives a spiritual interpretation of the Rabbinic saying that every good man will inherit 310 worlds in the Hereafter.

During the nineteenth and twentieth centuries, the objection of

Orthodox Rabbis to cremation was based partly on their literal understanding of the doctrine of the resurrection. The point is made by Jacob Saul Elyashar (pp. 260-1), Hayyim Mordecai Roller (pp. 309-10), Ben Zion Uziel (p. 323), Z. E. Michaelson (p. 325) and A. I. Kook (pp. 327-8).

Hai Gaon (pp. 21-2) discusses at length whether a man can sell his share in Paradise, coming down heavily against the validity of such a sale. In the sixteenth century, Moses Alashkar (p. 133) quotes the Gaon and arrives at the same conclusion. This question is also considered as late as the nineteenth century by N. Z. J. Berlin (pp. 257-9), who similarly invalidates the sale with a keen analysis of what is involved in the belief in eternal bliss for the righteous. He appears to be unaware of the earlier discussions.

ANGELS

The Talmudic sources are somewhat obscure as to whether there is any offence in the invocation of angels in prayer. The Gaonim (pp. 10-11), following the established pattern in their academies, see no objection, and centuries later Samson Morpurgo (pp. 193-4) takes the same line. In the nineteenth century, however, Moses Sofer (pp. 215-16) is none too happy about the practice. In deference to the earlier authorities he cannot bring himself to forbid the invocation of angels, but states that he himself avoids reciting prayers of this kind.

APOSTATES

Throughout the ages, the status of the Jew who had been converted to Christianity or Islam was widely discussed, obviously as a severely practical question. The apostate cannot enjoy the privileges of a Jew but is treated as a Jew for some purposes by the Gaonim (pp. 26-7), Gershom of Mainz (pp. 30-2) and *Rashi* (pp. 33-4). Solomon Ibn Adret (pp. 75-6) holds that the apostate is not to be rejected entirely and should be encouraged to revert to the fold. Simeon Duran (p. 91) considers that no mourning rites for an apostate are to be carried out by his relatives. Benjamin Zeev of Arta (p. 136) refuses to allow the Kaddish to be recited for an apostate and rules that, when the apostate's son is called to the reading of the Torah, it should not be by his father's name. Isserles (p. 142) takes issue with this latter ruling. In the case of Uriel da Costa's mother, da Modena (p. 158) inclines to forbid burial in the Jewish cemetery to an apostate dying unrepentant.

The general attitude in all periods was to welcome back warmly the apostate who had returned to Judaism. Both Isserlein (p. 104) and Ibn Zimra (p. 130) hold that no severe penances are to be imposed on him. The Gaonim (pp. 26–7) are also insistent that he is to be made welcome. Eliezer b. Isaac (p. 36) argues, however, that if the apostate is a *kohen* he can never again recite the priestly blessing. Gershom (pp. 30–1) and *Rashi* (p. 34) rule otherwise, and their opinion was followed in the eighteenth century by Landau (pp. 178–9). Marcus Horowitz (p. 280) permits a relaxation of the laws governing the token reconversion of the repentant apostate where to insist on the strict letter of the law would act as a barrier to his return. Elijah Mizrahi (pp. 107–8) can see no objection to a repentant apostate serving as a Reader in the synagogue.

BIBLICAL DIFFICULTIES

The rationalists among the Respondents hold that difficult Biblical verses or passages should be interpreted in a non-literal fashion. Others refuse to depart from the literal meaning. Simeon Duran (p. 93) insists that the story of Noah's ark is to be taken literally and Isaac b. Sheshet Perfet (p. 16) that, contrary to Gersonides, Joshua really did cause the sun to stop. The Gaonim (p. 6) consider that the serpent really did converse with Eve. They also hold that the Witch of Endor (pp. 13–15) did succeed in raising Samuel from the dead. Samuel b. Hophni (pp. 13–15) alone in the Gaonic period was prepared to say that the Witch engaged in trickery. Abraham Maimoni (pp. 52–3) also argues that the

Witch only pretended to raise Samuel from the dead. He (p. 53) states, too, that the Biblical account of Solomon having many wives should not be read as Scriptural approval of the king's conduct. Isaac of Vienna (p. 56) is bothered by the moral difficulties in the Jacob narrative, which he interprets to mean that Jacob did not use subterfuge in order to get the better of Laban.

Solomon Ibn Adret (pp. 61–3) is at pains to deny that the account of the creation implies that God changed His mind. Against the Maimonidean view that all Scriptural references to angels appearing to men are to appearances in dreams, Solomon Duran (p. 96) is emphatic that the events of Balaam's ass, of Jacob wrestling with the angel, and of the three angels who appeared to Abraham, are all real events. Joseph Hayyim of Baghdad (pp. 264–5) naturally refuses to interpret the Biblical anthropomorphism literally, and gives a figurative meaning to the term 'the image of God'. Ibn Abi Zimra (pp. 111–13) attempts a rationalistic interpretation of why Adam sinned and why Mordecai put the life of the people in danger.

CHRISTIANITY AND ISLAM

According to Rabbinic teaching, a Gentile is obliged to keep the seven Noahide laws in order to qualify as one of 'the righteous of the nations of the world' and so be worthy of enjoying eternal bliss in the Hereafter. One of these laws is the prohibition of idolatry. Does a Christian or a Muslim offend against this law by virtue of his religion? In other words, are Christians and Muslims idolators, according to Jewish law? So far as Jews themselves are concerned, all the authorities agree that it is idolatry if a Jew adopts the Christian faith. Isserlein (p. 104) permits a Jew to bow in respect to a Christian priest wearing a cross because the Jew's intention is not to bow to the cross, an opinion repeated by Moses Alashkar (p. 133). Isserlein (p. 104) permits a Jew to pretend to be a Christian only in order to save his life, and even then, only if he gives no formal assent to the Christian faith. Maimonides (pp. 47–8) declares that by no stretch of the imagination can

Islam be considered an idolatrous faith, but Ibn Abi Zimra (p. 124) nevertheless insists that a Jew must be ready to suffer martyrdom rather than embrace Islam. This author (p. 125) is severely critical of the preacher who taught that the Israelites thought Moses to be divine. In the twentieth century, A. I. Kook repeats the ruling that Islam is not an idolatrous faith. Judah Ayash (pp. 198–9), on the other hand, holds that Gentiles do not keep the seven Noahide laws in their entirety.

From the eighteenth century onwards, the Respondents accept the view that Christianity is not idolatry so far as Gentiles are concerned. The age of enlightenment evidently caused the official teachers of Judaism to adopt a more tolerant attitude towards other faiths. This is particularly evident in Fleckeles (p. 207) and, though with reservations, in Nathanson (pp. 252–3). Marcus Horowitz (p. 281) goes so far as to consider the donation of a sum of money by a Jew towards the building of a church to be a sanctification of the divine name, a view unacceptable to David Hoffmann (pp. 299–300).

CONFESSION

The subject of confession is discussed in our sources against the background of Christian practice and in relation to the Rabbinic views on the subject as taught in the Talmud. Menahem Azariah da Fano (p. 147) advocates confession in a loud voice for the Reader in the synagogue, whose form of confession is stereotyped in any event, but not for private devotions where the sins are particularised; the confession should not be overheard by others. Meir Eisenstadt (pp. 188–9) similarly declares public confession of sin to be forbidden.

DESECRATION OF THE SABBATH

In the Talmud, the public desecration of the sabbath is treated as an act of idolatry, in that the sabbath testifies to God as Creator.

333

According to the strict law, one who desecrates the sabbath publicly is not to be treated as a Jew. He cannot help to form the quorum for prayer nor can he be called to the reading of the Torah. But after the emergence of the Jew into Western society in the early nineteenth century, some were to be found, otherwise closely identified with their fellow-Jews and Judaism, who did work on the sabbath. Is a relaxation of the older law possible, since these men engage in no act of public defiance? Ehrenfeld (p. 222) insists on applying the law in all its strictness. Solomon Kluger (p. 285) is similarly uncompromising. Jacob Ettlinger (pp. 246–7) tends to favour the more lenient attitude, as do Hoffmann (pp. 297–8) and Steinberg (p. 306). Jacob Hayyim (p. 269) is strict but urges tact, while Tennenbaum (p. 276), though strict, holds that the sabbath profaner should be allowed to join an Orthodox congregation. I. J. Weiss (p. 318) quotes the more lenient authorities but favours the strict attitude.

DREAMS

In both the Bible and the Talmud a belief is implied in the efficacy of dreams as divine communications. The Talmud also speaks of fasting and other methods of warding off the effects of a bad dream. But in the Middle Ages there were strong philosophical objections to the whole idea of dreams as omens of future events. Ibn Adret (pp. 69–70), in his struggle against philosophical inroads, defends not only the efficacy of the dream but, as the Talmud implies, that the interpretation of a dream can have its effect. But he has reservations (p. 67) about the duty to fast after having a bad dream, and his attitude is shared by Simeon Duran (pp. 91–2). Joseph Hayyim (p. 267) discusses whether penance is required for a sin committed in a dream and J. L. Zirelson (p. 312) whether a ban imposed in a dream is binding.

THE KABBALAH

Many of the legal experts accepted the Kabbalah as a theosophical system with a divine guarantee as to its authenticity. Solomon Ibn Adret (pp. 64–7), a disciple of the early Kabbalist Nahmanides, is a total devotee of the Kabbalah and refers to this science frequently, though, like his master in his famous Commentary to the Pentateuch, always by hint rather than overtly. Simeon Duran (pp. 88–91) is similarly an upholder of the complete truth of the Kabbalistic system. His son Solomon, however, is opposed to the Kabbalah (pp. 98–9), while Perfet (pp. 83–4) neither denies nor affirms its truth, claiming that he has never been initiated into these mysteries and is consequently incapable of rendering an adequate opinion. Sirkes (p. 152) declares the Kabbalah to be the foundation of the Torah, while his contemporary Leon da Modena (pp. 158–60) is opposed to it. Landau (pp. 177–81) is very uncertain, while his disciple Fleckeles (pp. 208–9) is entirely negative. Ibn Abi Zimra (p. 110) is a Kabbalist himself and, like Adret, frequently uses Kabbalistic ideas in his Responsa. Another Kabbalist, Ergas (pp. 181–5), adopts the same attitude. Bacharach (pp. 160–3) examines the whole subject very thoroughly, coming down eventually in favour of Kabbalistic studies, though with certain reservations. It is to be noted that even the opponents of the Kabbalah do not deny the existence of an ancient mystical tradition. This they could hardly do, since there are references to such a tradition in the Talmud. What they do question is the Kabbalists' claim that their science is to be identified with the ancient lore referred to in the Talmud. Joseph Hayyim (pp. 261–74), not content with using Kabbalistic ideas even in his legal Responsa, has a complete collection of purely Kabbalistic Responsa appended to his work.

A much-discussed question among believers in the Kabbalah was whether final authority in the matters of practice is vested in the Kabbalah or the Codes. They all give priority to the Codes, but hold that the Kabbalah should be followed when the Codes are silent on a particular topic. This is the position adopted by Elijah Mizrahi (pp. 105–6), Ibn Abi Zimra (p. 123), Solomon Luria (p. 139), Zevi Ashkenazi (p. 171) and his son Jacob Emden (pp. 172–3), and Solomon Morpurgo (p. 193).

SUMMARY AND CONCLUSIONS

MAGIC AND SUPERSTITION

The philosophical school was opposed to all magic and superstition but the weight of Talmudic authority came down heavily against a total rejection, since the Talmud does refer to magical practices as if it believed in their efficacy. On the other hand, the Talmud, too, forbids certain pagan practices as 'the ways of the Amorites'. A rationalist like Maimonides was opposed to magic, yet even he (pp. 44–5) accepts Bibliomancy. The Gaonim (pp. 18–28) believe in white magic, especially in the possibility of working magic by the use of various divine names. But they refuse to accept the more ridiculous accounts of holy men travelling great distances by the force of will or making themselves invisible. Ibn Adret (pp. 74–9) rejects obvious pagan practices, but otherwise defends magical practices against the philosophical critique. Interestingly enough, he relies on alleged experience, as well as authority. His argument is that we must refuse to be coerced by vast philosophical theories unsupported by empirical observation. If magic works, as he believes it does, no amount of philosophical argument against its efficacy is of much use. On demons, Ibn Abi Zimra, faithful to the Talmud, takes issue with Maimonides and Meiri who hold that these do not exist. Luria (pp. 138–9) even permits resort to witchcraft where there is danger to life, though his attitude is somewhat sceptical. Bacharach (pp. 166–7) accepts that certain magical acts can have curative value, as does Eisenstadt (p. 187), though he forbids these when performed on behalf of others. Moses Sofer (pp. 217–18) attempts a rationalistic explanation of a well established magical practice. Joseph Hayyim (p. 274) resorts to magical cures for irrational phobias. Abraham Ankawa (pp. 276–8) similarly rationalises a folk-belief, but is prepared to believe (p. 277) that holy men can create things by reading the Book of Creation. Uziel (p. 322) in a legal discussion accepts the belief in the existence of the incubus and succubus. A. I. Kook (p. 328) strictly forbids the burning of incense to demons.

Interest in paranormal phenomena is reflected in some of the nineteenth- and twentieth-century Responsa. Kluger (pp. 285–6) sternly forbids table-rapping, but A. I. Kook (p. 327) cannot declare categorically that attendance at a seance is forbidden by Jewish law. None the less, Kook frowns on such questionable methods of 'strengthening faith'. Ettlinger (pp. 245–6) sees no objection in having recourse to hypnotism for curative purposes. David Hoffmann (p. 298) permits the use of amulets for their beneficial psychological effects.

THE MESSIAH

Belief in the coming of the Messiah is a basic principle of the Jewish faith naturally accepted in totality by all the Respondents. Hai Gaon (pp. 22–4) follows Saadiah in giving a detailed account of the whole Messianic process. Centuries later, Roller (p. 309) can still state, on the basis of Midrashic passages, that in the Messianic age the Temple will drop down ready-made from Heaven. Spira (pp. 289–90) is opposed to a communal fast during World War I because it implies the desirability of peace in our present state of existence, whereas the devout Jew ought to long for the advent of the Messiah with all the sufferings that must precede it. Ibn Adret (pp. 63–4), Ibn Abi Zimra (pp. 117–18) and, in modern times, Z. E. Michaelson (pp. 325–6) all discuss at length whether any of the precepts of the Torah will be abolished in the Messianic age.

MYSTICISM

In addition to the general question of the Kabbalah, some of our authorities discuss specific questions concerning mystical experience. Hai Gaon (pp. 15–18) gives a vivid description of mystical states and defends (p. 15) the *Shiur Komah*, on the mystical measurements of God, as an authentic inspired production. Maimonides (p. 47), on the other hand, declares it to be spurious and dangerous to faith. Ibn Adret (pp. 57–9) discusses at length the mystical claims of Abraham Abulafia and is extremely sceptical of them. Moses Sofer (pp. 214–15) and Hayyim Halberstam (pp. 238–9) both discuss Hasidic modes of prayer, and Landau (pp. 177–8) attacks the Hasidim. Halberstam (p. 240) believes that even in his day it is possible for a great saint and scholar to be gifted with the holy spirit. In Berlin's (pp. 254–7) analysis of the different approaches to Judaism, due weight is given to the mystical approach.

PENANCES

Neither the Bible nor the Talmud knows of special penances to be imposed for certain sins, but the moralistic works describe these in great detail. Our authorities differ on the degree of severity to be observed when penances are imposed. Abraham b. Isaac of Narbonne (pp. 42–3) is strict in his penance for the crime of accidental homicide, as is Jacob Weil (p. 102). Meir of Rothenburg (pp. 55–6) refuses to allow penance to be performed for a murder, the purpose of which was to save the victims from apostasy. Isserles (p. 142) tends towards leniency in matters of penance, while Trani (pp. 150–1) and Meir of Lublin (pp. 152–4) are more severe. Judah Ayash (p. 200) is similarly strict, while Meir Eisenstadt (p. 189) favours forbearance. The later authorities, Landau (pp. 175–7), Moses Sofer (pp. 216–17), Halberstam (pp. 236–7), Nathanson (pp. 250–2) and J. J. Weinberg (p. 314), are especially lenient. Joseph Hayyim (pp. 269–70) says that no penance is to be imposed on a doctor whose patient dies, but I. J. Weiss (p. 318) holds that penance is necessary where the death of the patient is due to the doctor's negligence. Both Landau (pp. 175–7) and Hayyim Sofer (p. 279) rule against resort to sexual abstinence as a means of penance. Ibn Abi Zimra (pp. 129–30) considers whether penance is required for sins committed by a minor.

A connected question is how the courts should treat sinners who threaten that, if severely dealt with, they will leave the Jewish fold. Ibn Abi Zimra (pp. 115–16) and Bacharach (pp. 167–8) both argue against yielding to blackmail, but Morpurgo (pp. 196–7) is rather more cautious.

PRAYER

Benedictions are ordained by the Rabbis to be recited before the performance of some precepts, but not before others. An attempt to uncover the principles at work was made by Ibn Plat (pp. 41-2), followed by Ibn Adret (p. 75).

The moral standing of the Reader in the synagogue is considered in the Talmud, but there is discussion among our authors on the procedure in practice. Ibn Migash (pp. 39-40) disqualifies only a man with a current bad reputation, but not one whose reputation was bad in his youth. Elijah Mizrahi (pp. 107-8) refuses to rule out even a man who had worshipped idols in his youth from officiating as Reader, provided he has repented. Meir of Rothenburg (p. 54), far from disqualifying a cripple from acting as Reader, considers it to be especially meritorious if he does so, since it is 'the broken vessels' that God desires. In the nineteenth century Ettlinger (p. 245) expresses the opposite view. Asher b. Jehiel (pp. 81-2) stresses the importance of having a righteous man rather than an aristocrat as Reader.

Ibn Adret (pp. 71-2) urges inwardness in prayer but emphasises that the reference is to simple faith in the ideas of the prayers, not to philosophical subtleties. Maimonides (p. 45) understands the Talmudic rules, that the place of prayer must have windows and that there should be no barrier between the worshipper and the wall, to be aids to concentration. Halberstam (pp. 238-9) follows the Hasidic objection to a Cantor and choir, while da Fano (p. 147) holds that all bodily movements should be avoided during prayer, except for a gentle swaying during the recitation of God's praises. Reischer (pp. 190-1), Judah Grünwald (p. 293) and Amram Grünwald (p. 300) all advocate the raising of the voice while singing in praise of God.

Zirelson (p. 311) offers a rationalistic explanation of why the mother's rather than the father's name is mentioned when prayers are offered on behalf of the sick. Waldenberg (pp. 314-15) does not favour prayers for the death of an incurable. Feinstein (p. 321) believes that Gentiles as well as Jews have an obligation to offer prayers to God.

PROVIDENCE

The Gaonim (pp. 2–5) and Maimonides (pp. 48–9) react against Islamic fatalism to qualify considerably fatalistic ideas found in the Talmud. Ibn Adret (pp. 76–9) refuses to be browbeaten by philosophical notions of what is and is not possible in the realm of Nature. Perfet (pp. 86–7) discusses the old question of divine foreknowledge and human free will. Questions regarding providence are discussed by Simeon Duran (pp. 92–3) and his son Solomon (pp. 100–1). Ibn Abi Zimra (p. 127) adopts a more fatalistic attitude, limiting human freedom to the moral life but holding that whether, for instance, a man is to be rich or poor is predetermined. Ibn Habib (p. 145) is emphatic that vicarious suffering is never part of God's plan, while in the twentieth century Z. E. Michaelson (p. 326) considers why the righteous suffer. Deist philosophy and pantheism are discussed by Zevi Ashkenazi (pp. 169–70).

In connection with theories regarding providence are the debates on whether the world will one day have an end. Maimonides does not think it will, but Ibn Adret (pp. 59–61) opposes this on the grounds of Jewish tradition. Solomon Duran (p. 100) and Leon da Modena (pp. 155–6) both tend towards a belief that the world will have an end but are prepared to leave open matters of this kind, as they affect no dogma of Judaism. Breslau (pp. 202–3) believes that God's providence can work, especially through the casting of lots, and bases his view on the Bible. Feinstein (p. 320) sees no contradiction to faith and trust in God in a man taking out an insurance policy.

REINCARNATION

This belief is not found in the Talmud. Saadiah Gaon holds it to be thoroughly un-Jewish, but the belief features prominently in the Kabbalah. Ibn Abi Zimra (pp. 127–9) utilises the belief to solve a problem raised by his questioner. Ibn Habib (pp. 143–4) conveys the pros and cons of the question but does believe in reincarnation. He acknowledges, however, that the belief seems odd to ordinary folk and strongly advises against public preaching of the idea. Breslau (pp. 203–4) bases his understanding of the law of levirate marriage on this doctrine.

REFORM

The rise of the Reform movement in the nineteenth century naturally brought about a strong reaction on the part of the Orthodox. Hayyim Kittsee (pp. 210–12) has a fierce polemic against the members of the Brunswick Reform Conference. The Sofer family (pp. 213–25), and especially Moses Schick (pp. 225–36), engage in polemics against Reform, as does Chajes (pp. 247–50) though in a more restrained and objective manner. Schick (p. 234) goes so far as to disqualify for ever a Cantor who had once served in a Reform Temple, but his opinion is contested by Tennenbaum (p. 276). Hoffmann (pp. 297–8), Ehrenfeld (pp. 222–5) and Amram Grünwald (pp. 300–4) all oppose innovations in Jewish religious life as smacking of Reform, while Feinstein (p. 321) forbids even the response of 'Amen' after a benediction recited by a Reform or Conservative Rabbi. Weiss (pp. 319–20) supports an Orthodox Rabbi who refused to accept an invitation to the dedication ceremony of a Conservative synagogue.

THE TALMUDIC RABBIS

For all the Respondents, ultimate authority is vested in the Talmudic Rabbis. Their legal decisions and theological views depend on how they interpret the Talmud. The Talmud first came under fire from the Karaites in the Gaonic period, then from the philosophers, the enlightenment thinkers and from Reform Judaism. Certain broad lines of defence can be discerned among the Respondents.

The Gaonim (pp. 6–9) recognised that some Talmudic statements are hyperbolic, so that their meaning is distorted when they are taken literally. The Gaonim (p. 9) also acknowledged the mythical element in some of the Talmudic statements about God. They also put forward the view (p. 11) that only unanimous statements of the Talmudic Rabbis are binding, not the opinions of individual sages. Samuel b. Hophni (pp. 13–15) is prepared to go further still. In non-legal matters this teacher holds that even unanimous views of the Rabbis can be disregarded when they conflict with 'common sense'. Even so staunch an upholder of Rabbinic authority as Sherira Gaon (p. 27) can argue that the Rabbis had only the medical knowledge of their day, so that the remedies found in the Talmud are not to be followed unless authorised by a competent physician.

In later centuries, however, there is a marked tendency to see the Talmudic Rabbis as spiritual supermen, infallible in all their utterances. Thus, da Fano (pp. 146–7) feels obliged to give a mystical meaning to statements which the Talmud itself declares to be pure hyperbole. Ibn Habib (p. 146) defends as morally significant even the occasional obscenities to be found there. Bacharach (pp. 165–6) is moved to defend the harsh statements in which the Talmudic Rabbis denigrate one another, though, from the context, it is clear that his chief concern is to prevent these being used as precedents by contemporary scholars. Breslau (pp. 201–2) tries to read spiritual ideas into a strange Midrashic passage. Halberstam (p. 242) is absolutely uncompromising that one who does not believe in the Rabbis is a heretic and cannot serve as a witness in a Jewish court of law. Leon da Modena (pp. 156–7) alone favours a less categorical acceptance of all the Rabbis' sayings.

THE TORAH

In a sense, every word of the Responsa literature is about the Torah, but we are here concerned with specific theological questions regarding the concept of Torah as these appear in the Responsa. Maimonides (pp. 45–6), following Talmudic precedent, is anxious to avoid any suggestion that the Decalogue is somehow more important than the rest of the Torah. Every word of the Torah is a divine communication of ultimate significance. Ibn Abi Zimra (pp. 110–11) advances a similar argument against Maimonides himself. Maimonides' formulation of thirteen basic principles of the Jewish faith tends to suggest that these are more important than the 'light precepts', whereas, in fact, each precept, light or severe, is a 'principle'. Ibn Adret (pp. 64–6) is similarly opposed to the reductionism implied in the attempt of the philosophers to state 'reasons' for the precepts. Over and above the obvious reasons there are great mysteries belonging to 'the secrets of the Torah', and these still apply even when the obvious reason eludes us.

To safeguard the doctrine that the whole of the Torah is the very word of God given to Moses at Sinai, both Ibn Abi Zimra (pp. 121–2) and Moses Alashkar (pp. 131–3) refuse to accept literally the Rabbinic suggestions that the script we now use for the Torah was not the original script. Both Bacharach (pp. 163–5) and Joseph Rozin (p. 295) provide a detailed programme for the study of the Torah.

CONCLUSIONS

The result of our survey, it is hoped, has been to demonstrate that the great Respondents took their theology seriously, giving the same care and attention to questions of belief that they gave to their legal decisions. That theological questions feature far less prominently in this literature than legal topics is not because matters of belief were secondary, as is sometimes assumed, but because the basic beliefs of Judaism required little elaboration. Both for the Respondents and their questioners the beliefs were constant and certain. There was no ambiguity about the fundamentals of the Jewish religion and few doubts about their meaning which needed to be resolved by an appeal to decisive authority. When challenges were presented to such hitherto generally accepted theological propositions as that the Torah is divine and immutable and that the Talmudic Rabbis are the final authorities, the questioners did, indeed, turn to their teachers for reliable doctrine, support and encouragement to hold fast to the tradition.

Precisely because the Respondents were not called upon to state their own personal views but those of the tradition (so far as we can judge, the two were in any event identical), the appeal is always to formulations in the classical sources of Judaism. Although it had long been recognised that the Talmud uses the term 'Halakhah' only in the sense of a final decision of legal questions, yet, in the Responsa, the Halakhic methods of reasoning are employed even when theological questions are considered. One might almost speak of a theological Halakhah. In our historically-minded age it is permitted to question whether, in fact, for all their rigorous examination of the sources, the Respondents were quite so objective. It is not difficult to see how the climate of opinion in a particular age, even in a particular land, influenced theological decisions, but then this surely also applies to the Halakhic decisions. It is doubtful whether any teacher can ever rise entirely above his age to survey religious questions of great moment in the completely detached manner in which the angels are said to carry out their functions on earth.

In view of the sameness in method and outlook among the Respondents and their use of the same authorities, it is striking that there is, none the less, a rich variety of views in the theological answers they provide. One teacher can be so imbued with the spirit of rationalism as to deny, contrary to the plain meaning of the Biblical text and the comment of the Rabbis, that the Witch of Endor succeeded in raising Samuel from the dead. Another teacher throws up his hands in horror at the very thought. One teacher can attach the highest significance to *Shiur Komah* as a holy, inspired book. Another teacher can declare the work to be spurious and dangerous, worthy only to be destroyed. One teacher can accept the Kabbalah as the soul of the Torah, while another sees it as a system produced by deluded minds. One teacher can declare categorically that God is best served by 'broken vessels' so that it is even advisable for a cripple to be a Reader in the synagogue. Another and much later teacher can have serious doubts on the matter. One teacher can see only good in a Jew

344

giving his donation to a Christian church. To another, such an act is sacrilege. One teacher can accept as a Reader in the synagogue even a former apostate, while another can vehemently reject a Reader who had once served in a Reform Temple. Here it is true that theology did not become Halakhah. Digests and summaries abound of the legal decisions of the great luminaries, but no one has ever thought of providing a kind of *Shulhan Arukh*, a final code, of theological beliefs binding on all Jews.

For the tidy mind, there is loss in the lack of a final authoritative system of Jewish belief. But matters of belief in all their complexity demand the free response of the individual human personality, and neat schemes are simply not available. There is no real loss in this. On the contrary, freedom of conscience becomes possible within the system. As someone has said, no man need say that there is no room for him to lodge in Jerusalem.

Saul Berlin and the 'Besamim Rosh'

The Responsa collections considered hitherto in this volume are all by acknowledged Rabbinic authorities who were addressed by questioners anxious to discover the teachings of Judaism as understood by its official representatives, the outstanding Rabbinic authories. But reference must also be made to the notorious Responsa forgery, *Besamin Rosh*, undoubtedly of theological interest, though obviously of quite a different order from the other Responsa examined in this book.

The story has often been told of the publication of this curious work and the furore it raised. (On this subject see Solomon B. Freehof, *A Treasury of Responsa*, pp. 242–6; Reuben Margaliot, 'Rabbi Saul Berlin, the forger of the book *Besamin Rosh*', *Areshet*, 1944, pp. 411–18, with note by I. Rafael; J. Rubinstein, *Ha-Darom*, no. 16, Tishri 5723, pp. 144–6; Moshe Peli, *Hebrew Union College Annual*, vol. XLII, 1971, Heb. sec., pp. 1–23; M. Samet, *Kiryat Sefer*, vol. 43, 1967–8, pp. 429–41, and M. Wunder, ibid., vol. 44, 1968–9, pp. 307–8.) Saul Berlin (1740–94), son of Hirschel Levin, Rabbi of Berlin, was a Talmudist of distinction and Rabbi in Frankfort-on-Oder, but close to the 'enlightened' circle of Moses Mendelssohn. Berlin published in 1793, in the town from which his name is derived, the book *Besamim Rosh* (2nd ed., Cracow, 1881). Containing 392 (the numerical value of *Besamim*) Responsa, it purports to be a collection of hitherto unknown Responsa by the famous fourteenth-century authority Asher b. Jehiel, the *Rosh*, collected and arranged with notes by one Isaac di Molina. Berlin added notes of his own under the title *Kassa De-Harsana*, and claimed that he had discovered the manuscript of the *Besamim Rosh* in Italy. The book was published with an approbation by Berlin's father and by Ezekiel Landau of Prague. The latter states that he has made it a rule for the past five years not to give approbations to new works, but writes that the teachings of the *Rosh* require no support from him, while Berlin's own notes are capable of standing on their own merit. Landau remarks further that he has been very ill and finds it hard to write at any length, all of which suggests that, though unable to refuse entirely Berlin's request (Landau notes that they were related), he had considerable reservations which he is at no pains to hide.

No sooner was the work published than careful readers noted that some of the views of the '*Rosh*' bore an uncanny resemblance to the early 'Reformist' views then beginning to emerge in the town of Berlin. The book was attacked as a forgery by Wolf Landsberg in the pamphlet *Zeev Yitrof* and by Mordecai Banet (1731–1829), Chief Rabbi of Moravia (*Parashat Mordekhai*, 1889, no. 5) in a letter addressed to Berlin's father. Yet, oddly enough, though the book was viewed with suspicion by later authorities, it is sometimes quoted by later Rabbis as an authentic exposition of Jewish law, evidently on the grounds (for which there is no proof whatever) that some of the Responsa do go back to the *Rosh* and other early teachers.

The following are the theological questions touched on directly or indirectly in the *Besamim Rosh*.

No. 43

The '*Rosh*' is asked whether a benediction has to be recited over forbidden food. The reply given is that a benediction certainly has to be recited over the food if it is permitted to eat it—e.g. when a sick person eats food forbidden by Rabbinic law or a person whose life is in danger eats food forbidden by Biblical law. But one who eats food forbidden by Biblical law when he is not in danger must not recite the benediction. If, however, a healthy person eats to satiety food forbidden by Rabbinic law, he has a Biblical obligation to recite grace after meals, since he has eaten his fill, and the Rabbinic prohibition cannot absolve him from his Biblical obligation. The casuistic argument is obviously only a screen for the implied suggestion that Rabbinic law can be guilty of frustrating Biblical law, an argument popular in the 'enlightened' circles in Berlin. God is to be thanked for the food, even though the Rabbis forbid eating that food.

No. 94

The question here is what is to be done if a woman is unable to eat the bitter herbs on Passover without becoming ill from so doing. The answer given is that where a person will fall sick as a result of keeping the *mitzvot*, he has no obligation to keep them, since the ways of the Torah are 'ways of pleasantness' and the duty of safeguarding one's health takes precedence over all other *mitzvot*. To be sure, 'Jews are holy' and exert themselves to keep all the *mitzvot*, but they should not do so where health is at stake. True, the Rabbis allow a person to commit a transgression only where life is at stake, not mere danger to health, but there they refer to the negative precepts. Again it is true that, according to the Jerusalem Talmud, R. Johanan drank wine on Passover even though he became ill as a result, but that was because this sage went beyond the letter of the law and was especially strict with himself. This law of strictness must not, in fact, be applied at all times. Indeed, there are times when the sage, far from being especially strict, should be especially lenient with himself if his aim is to keep his mind healthy and lucid. The sage will know when and where to be lenient. There are many arguments in support of this contention, but the reader must not be burdened with them. Again, the 'Reformist' tendency is blatant. The *mitzvot* are for the benefit of God's creatures and where to carry them out results in unpleasantness, there is no obligation to keep them. The 'sensible' view of the early Maskilim is stated without any real attempt to cloak it.

No. 190

A student of the questioner put the question to him which he now submits to the '*Rosh*': why do we find Rabbis called 'Ishmael' and none called 'Esau'? The questioner, however, states that he suspects the student of a lack of seriousness, since whenever the Rabbinic Aggadah is studied this man adopts a supercilious attitude to the Rabbis. The '*Rosh*' advises that this student be expelled from the Yeshivah as a corrupting influence. As for the question itself, the Rabbinic Midrash observes that Ishmael repented towards the end of his life and so was not a wicked man, but in any event Ishmael is a fine name and there is no reason why it should not be given to a child, even though the Biblical character who bears this name was wicked. It is only when the name itself is ugly—like Esau—that the Rabbis objected to it being given to a child, since the name is indicative, too, of an ugly character. Thus, in one stroke Berlin manages to convey a number of typical 'enlightened' ideas: that the Rabbis are intolerant, the '*Rosh*' ordering a poor student to be expelled from the Yeshivah; that the Talmudic Rabbis were inconsistent in accepting the name Ishmael and rejecting the name Esau; that the Midrash distorts the plain meaning of the Biblical text and is not to be relied on for Ishmael's repentance; and that a name has really no significance.

No. 240

A scribe wrote the scroll of Esther. This same man, while drunk on Purim, quoted the heretical views of certain philosophers. Now the rule is that a scroll of the Torah written by an *epikoros* ('heretic') is unfit for use. Does this apply, too, to the Megillah, which is 'only a tale', and, moreover, does not contain God's name? The '*Rosh*' replies that there is no difference whatever between the Megillah and a Torah scroll. However, the mere fact that a man occasionally gives expression to his inner doubts does not make him an *epikoros*. Many of the 'great ones in Israel' sometimes gave expression to opinions it is forbidden to listen to, 'may God forgive them'. An *epikoros* is one who consciously rejects any of the laws, 'even the lightest of the words of the Sages', not a man who merely gives expressions to his reservations but does not act on them. Furthermore, if a man does become an *epikoros*, this does not cause something he had done beforehand to be invalidated. Disbelief does not work retroactively. Here, too, the 'Reformist' tendencies are barely concealed. Doubts are cast on the book of Esther, the study of philosophy is condoned, doubts in matters of faith are tolerated and are attributed to the 'great ones in Israel', while the '*Rosh*', the great representative of Rabbinic Judaism, is slyly held up to ridicule for making no distinction between the Torah and a 'mere tale' like the book of Esther. Moreover, there is the suggestion that the Rabbis are hypocrites, stressing only correct conduct and having no regard for the truth.

No. 251

This Responsum discusses the thirteen principles of the Jewish faith as laid down by Maimonides. The '*Rosh*' expresses his surprise that he, being ignorant of philosophy, is asked to give an opinion, since topics such as these can be dealt with adequately only by one versed in Greek philosophy. In any event he is afraid to disagree with Maimonides, who states categorically that anyone who does not accept these principles is a heretic. Nevertheless, since Maimonides admits that he has worked out these principles by his own reasoning and has no authentic tradition, it is permitted to question whether he had a right to do what he did and so add to the Torah. If these really are the basic principles of the Jewish faith, why are they not found in the Torah or in the Rabbinic literature? In defence of Maimonides it can be argued that each sage is not only allowed but obliged to work out for himself the basic principles of the Jewish faith. In our day, we have no central authority; so the matter must be left to the individual sage. The original principles of the faith have been forgotten through the bitterness of Israel's exile, so that even Maimonides could attempt to recover them only by the very generous use of ideas taken from Aristotelian philosophy.

Which principles are to be formulated as such depends on the spiritual climate of the age. For instance, during the period of David and Solomon there was no need for any belief in the coming of a Messiah but, on the other hand, at that time worship in the Temple was essential to the Jewish faith. Nowadays, the opposite is true. We must look forward to the coming of the Messiah, but worship in the Temple belongs only to the past. Consequently, where Maimonides erred was in drawing up his principles for all time and in such a precise way, leaving no room for flexibility. The only true principle of the Jewish faith is that God has made a covenant with His people. He desires our well-being and happiness since He loves His creatures. In that case it behoves us to reflect on why we have to endure such a long and arduous exile. If it ever happened that, for our sins, the precepts could be a cause of unhappiness to us, we would have no obligation to keep them. The reason we suffer is because we have failed to heed the law of God in that we ourselves have added stupid and superstitious practices, and we have distorted the true meaning of the precepts. Thus the 'Rosh' continues at length to convey the programme of early Reform as it was adopted in late eighteenth-century Berlin. Barely concealed here are all the trends that became so prominent in the early Reform movement: the Messianic age is not necessarily one in which the Temple will be rebuilt; theoretically there may come a time when the observance of the precepts may become detrimental to Israel's well-being and then it will have to be given up; the reason why the Jewish people fails to find the answer to its problems is because it has overlaid the essential Torah with base practices it has made up. All that is needed to give the game away is for the 'Rosh' to use the word 'enlightenment'. But the 'enlightened' who read this Responsum can have had no doubts as to its intention.

No. 301

This is the Responsum discussed, as noted earlier, by Rabbi Hayyim Lazar Spira of Munkacs. It is signed not by the 'Rosh' but by 'Jacob Ibn Makhir'. The Rabbinic rule is that martyrdom must be suffered rather than an offence be committed involving idolatory, adultery or murder. 'Jacob Ibn Makhir' argues that a decision by a Rabbi, that a Jew must suffer martyrdom where the law demands it, is a life and death decision. Once the Sanhedrin came to an end, no Rabbi and no court has the power to give such a decision involving life and death, any more than capital punishment can be carried out now that the Sanhedrin is no more. It is, of course, a historical fact that Jews did give their lives when faced with embracing Christianity, but they did this not because the law demanded it, but of their own accord. 'Jews are holy', and they preferred death to the loss of Jewish identity. True, murder is in a different category. Even nowadays it is forbidden for a man to save his life by murdering an innocent man. But there is no obligation for martyrdom in the case of idolatry and adultery. This is because doubts arise according to the circumstances in each case, and a decision is required by a competent Rabbi. But since the decision that martyrdom has to be suffered is, in fact, a death sentence, no Rabbi can render such a decision, capital punishment having ceased with the cessation of the Sanhedrin. Berlin, in his note in the *Kassa De-Harsana* to this Responsum, notes that the name 'Jacob Ibn Makhir' is not found anywhere except in the Responsa of Ibn Adret, no. 385. He gives the impression of doubting the authenticity of this Responsum, but the net result of it all is that doubts are raised whether even the most fundamental laws of the Torah are eternally binding.

No. 327

This Responsum discusses the question whether it is permitted to teach the Torah to Gentiles. Can it be argued that the Talmudic prohibition applies only to idolators, and the nations among whom we reside are not idolators? The reply given is that the prohibition is still in force even though there are many Gentile priests well versed in the Bible. But if a Jew is a professional teacher and he cannot escape from teaching the Torah to Gentiles, he is allowed to do so; otherwise enmity will be caused between the two communities. Even when the '*Rosh*' comes down in favour of strictness, considerable qualifications are somehow added.

It is unnecessary to give any further examples of Berlin's method. Practically every Responsum in the volume contains a thinly disguised attack on Rabbinic Judaism. The only odd thing about it all is that anyone could have been taken in by Berlin's claim that the *Besamim Rosh* was an authentic collection of Responsa by Asher b. Jehiel and other distinguished Rabbis of the past, who were among the staunchest upholders of the Rabbinic tradition.

Isaac Lampronti's 'Pahad Yitzhak'

The famous encyclopedia of Isaac Hezekiah b. Samuel Lampronti (1679–1756) entitled *Pahad Yitzhak* contains many Responsa of Italian Rabbis. Most of these are on purely legal topics, but a few are of theological interest. The work contains, among other things, an anthology of theological Responsa, and these are found in volumes 7 and 10. They are here recorded in the order in which they appear.

Vol. 7, 'tzedah', pp. 16b–21a

We have seen that the question of whether Jews may hunt animals for sport has been discussed in the Responsa of Ezekiel Landau (p. 181) and Samson Morpurgo (pp. 195–6). Lampronti begins by quoting the *Shulhan Arukh* (Orah Hayyim 316 : 2) that to hunt animals with hounds is to offend against 'nor sat in the seat of the scornful' (Ps. 1 : 1). He quotes a Responsum on the subject by Shabbetai b. Elisha, an Italian Rabbi. Shabbetai discusses the prohibition on hunting for sport under the heading of waste (*bal tashit*) of nature's resources. Shabbetai adds the prohibition of the 'seat of the scornful' and states, furthermore, that hunting is a Gentile practice and it is forbidden' to walk in their ways'. Before quoting Shabbetai's reply, Lampronti gives his own view on the same lines in a Responsum addressed to his pupil. He concludes that while hunting for food is permitted, this should not be done by killing the animal with a gun or with arrows. The animals should be caught in a net and then *shehitah* carried out.

Vol. 7, pp. 33b–58a

This anthology discusses all the pros and cons (see pp. 10–11 above) of reciting those prayers in which the angels are entreated to bring our prayers to God. Is it permitted to offer prayers through an intermediary? Lampronti quotes attacks on the works *Hadrat Kodesh* and Gedaliah b. Solomon's commentary to the *Sefer Ha-Ikkarim*, together with a counter-attack, entitled *Agudat Ezov*, and a Responsum by Samson Morpurgo.

Against the invocation of angels it is argued that Maimonides' fifth principle of the faith insists that only God is to be worshipped, and this includes the idea that only to Him must prayers be offered. Gentile writers, when describing the Jewish religion, call attention, especially, to this feature of Judaism, that it encourages a man to approach God direct, not through an intermediary. Pure monotheism must refuse to recognise any intermediaries between God and man. The angels were created to serve God. How, then, dare we accord them any status in worship? True, appeals are made by Moses to the dead patriarchs, but Moses does not really appeal to them but rather asks God to grant his request in the merit of the patriarchs. Nowhere in the Bible do we find a prayer to the patriarchs to intercede on our behalf. It is astonishing that folk who are so scrupulous in avoiding any practice based on Gentile forms of worship should see no objection to the Gentile habit of invoking intermediaries.

In favour of the invocation of angels it can be argued that Maimonides was unduly influenced by Greek philosophy. The popular view that it is right and proper to invoke angels in prayer is based on the sound tradition of God's people, and should not be lightly disregarded. There is not the slightest breach in pure monotheism in the invocation of angels, since the angels are enjoined to bring our prayers to God and we have a right to remind them of their duty; which is all we are doing when we ask them to bring our prayers to God.

This section of the *Pahad Yitzhak* is very lengthy and is, in fact, the most comprehensive treatment of the topic in Jewish literature.

Vol. 10, pp. 19a–20a

This Responsum, signed Michael Ravina (?) of Alexandria, is quoted from the work *Afar Yaakov*. The question concerns a quarrelsome person who was a notorious sinner. He used to blow the *shofar* in the synagogue on the festival of Rosh Ha-Shanah. Should he be removed from this office or do we argue that since he has the hitherto accepted right to blow the *shofar* and is, after all, a Jew, he should be allowed to continue? The Midrash (Lev. R. 16) declares that God does not desire the praises of the wicked. Furthermore, this man does not normally frequent the synagogue and is therefore one who separates himself from the ways of the community and, as such, according to Maimonides (*Yad*, Teshuvah 3), has no share in the World to Come, unlike other Israelites. How can such a person act as Israel's deputy in blowing the *shofar*? The reason the horn of a cow is not fit to be used as a *shofar* is that a prosecuting counsel cannot become a defender, the cow being a reminder of the sin of the golden calf. The same principle applies in this case. The Kabbalists wax eloquent on the awe-inspiring moment when the *shofar* is sounded on Rosh Ha-Shanah, but no mystical speculation is really required to invalidate the blowing of the *shofar* by such a base person. It goes without saying, however, that once the man repents of his sins he can continue to occupy his high office, since nothing stands in the way of sincere repentance.

Vol. 10, pp. 28a–b

This question was put to Avidad Sar Shalom Basila of Mantua. Solomon Ibn Adret argues that there will still be an obligation to keep the precepts of the Torah in the time of the resurrection, but his argument is far from conclusive. According to the opinion (see pp. 53–4 above) that the resurrection will be purely spiritual, it can certainly be argued that there will be no precepts to perform, but even those who understand the resurrection in a literal fashion hold that the bodies of the righteous alive at that time will be of a spiritually refined nature so that it does not follow that they will be obliged to keep the precepts. Lampronti replies that he is at a loss to understand why the questioner, who has as much access to the literature as he has, and is more learned than he, should bother to solicit his opinion. Before this question can be discussed, one would have to decide between Ibn Adret, who holds that the world will come to an end, and Maimonides, who holds that it will not (see pp. 59–61 above). On the whole, Lampronti favours the view that the precepts will still be binding in that time. If the sole reason for keeping the precepts were that which we can grasp in this life, there would, indeed, be a powerful argument against keeping them in the period of the resurrection. But the truth is that there are mystical, hidden reasons for the precepts and, because of these, the precepts have eternal validity. In reality, states Lampronti, he is not ashamed to confess his ignorance in such matters. He agrees with his questioner that forms of bliss in the Hereafter will be purely spiritual. He is perfectly correct when he says that the Gentiles call them 'spiritualizati'. As for the doctrine of the transmigration of souls (*gilgul*, see pp. 143–4 above), Lampronti states that there are difficulties involved in this belief.

Nevertheless, the Kabbalah has the decisive voice where reason can advance arguments for and against.

Vol. 10, pp. 100b–114b

This contains a Responsum of Samson Morpurgo that the Ashkenazim must continue to follow their custom of donning the *tefillin* on Hol Ha-Moed. Lampronti and other Italian Rabbis agree. We are obliged to follow ancient custom and it is strictly forbidden for Ashkenazim to depart from their tradition. To be sure, one must not attack the *Zohar* in which there is a strict injunction against wearing *tefillin* on Hol Ha-Moed. Morpurgo refers to the Responsum of Solomon Luria we have noted earlier (p. 139).

Vol. 10, pp. 175f.

Here Lampronti gives a fairly comprehensive list of Responsa in which the subject of penances for sin is considered.

Bibliography

Primary sources (other than Responsa)

The Holy Scriptures, Jewish Publications Society, Philadelphia, 1917
Mishnah, var. eds; English trans. H. Danby, Oxford, 1933
Babylonian Talmud, Romm, Vilna, various dates; English trans. ed. I.Epstein, Soncino Press, London, 1948–52
Jerusalem Talmud, Krotoschin, 1886
Tosefta, ed. M. S. Zuckermandel, Pasewalk, 1881
Midrash Rabbah, Romm, Vilna, various dates
Midrash Genesis Rabbah, ed. J. Theodor and H. Albeck, 3 vols, Berlin, 1912–29
Sifra, ed. I. H. Weiss, Vienna, 1862
Sifre, ed. M. Friedmann, Vienna, 1864
Mekhilta, ed. J. S. Lauterbach, Philadelphia, 1933
Pirke De-Rabbi Eliezer (PRE), Warsaw, 1852
Avot De-Rabbi Nathan (ARN), ed. S. Schechter, Vienna, 1887; English trans. Judah Goldin, *The Fathers According to Rabbi Nathan,* Yale University Press, 1955
Yalkut, 2 vols, Salonika, 1521–6
Zohar, Zhitomer, 1862
Zohar Hadash, Warsaw, 1870
Zohar Hadash, ed. J. L. Ashleg, 21 vols, Jerusalem, 1945–55
Maimonides, Moses, *Commentary to the Mishnah,* var. eds
——, *Yad Ha-Hazakah,* Amsterdam, 1702
——, *Guide of the Perplexed,* trans. S. Pines, Chicago, 1965
Ibn David, Abraham (*Raabad*), Strictures to Maimonides' *Yad, see* Maimonides
Ibn Ezra, Abraham, *Commentary on the Torah,* var. eds
Jacob ben Asher, *Tur,* Warsaw, 1882
Karo, Joseph, *Bet Yosef,* Commentary to *Tur, see* Jacob ben Asher
Shulhan Arukh, var. eds

Responsa (arranged by century in order discussed)

Kohelet Shelomo, ed. S. A. Wertheimer, Jerusalem, 1899
Teshuvot Ha-Gaonim, Lyck ed., 1864
Otzar Ha-Gaonim, ed. B. M. Lewin, 1928–62
Sheiltot De-Rav Ahai, var. eds
Rabbenu Gershom, ed. S. Eidelberg, New York, 1955
Rashi, ed. I. Elfenbein, New York, 1943
Hakhme Tzarefat Ve-Loter, ed. J. Mueller, Vienna, 1881
Tosaphists, ed. Irving A. Agus, New York, 1954
Joseph Ibn Migash, Warsaw, 1870
Sifran Shel Rishonim, ed. S. Asaf, Jerusalem, 1935
Maimonides, ed. Joshua Blau, 3 vols, Jerusalem, 1957–61
Raabad, ed. J. Kapah, Jerusalem, 1964
Abraham Maimoni, ed. A. H. Freimann, Jerusalem, 1937
Teshuvot Pesakim U-Minhagim, R. Meir of Rothenburg, ed. I. Z. Kahana,
    3 vols, Jerusalem, 1957–62
Or Zarua, Zhitomer, 1862
Hayyim Or Zarua, ed. J. Rosenberg, Jerusalem, 1960
Rashba, 3 vols, Bene Berak, 1958–9
Rosh, Zolkiew, 1803
Ribash, ed. I. H. Daiches, New York, 1964; photocopy of ed. n.p., n.d.
Tashbetz, Amsterdam, 1738–41
Rashbash, Jerusalem, 1968; photocopy of Leghorn ed. of 1742
Jacob Weil, Jerusalem, 1959
Terumat Ha-Deshen, Venice, 1519
Elijah Mizrahi, Jerusalem, 1937
Radbaz, [Newark], N.J., n.d.; photocopy of Warsaw ed. of 1862
Moses Alashkar, Jerusalem, 1959
Benjamin Zeev, 2 vols, Jerusalem, 1969
Maharashdam, Salonika, 1797–8
Rashal, Fuerth, 1768
Rama, Amsterdam, 1711
Levi b. Habib, Lemberg, 1865
Menahem Azariah da Fano, Dyhernfurth, 1788
Maharit, Lemberg, 1861
Bah [Joel Sirkes], Frankfort, 1697
Manhir Eine Hahkamim, Meir of Lublin, Metz, 1769
Leon da Modena, ed. S. Simonsohn, Jerusalem, 1956
Havvot Yair, Jair Hayyim Bacharach, Frankfort, 1699
Haham Zevi, Zevi Ashkenazi, Amsterdam, 1712
Sheelat Yaavetz, Jacob Emden, Altona, 1738, 1759
Noda Biyudah, Ezekiel Landau, Jerusalem, 1969; photocopy of Vilna ed., n.d.
Divre Yosef, Joseph Ergas, Leghorn, 1742
Panim Meirot, Meir Eisenstadt, Lemberg, 1899
Shevut Yaakov, Jacob Reischer, Halle, 1710
Shemesh Tzedakah, Samson Morpurgo, Venice, 1743
Shav Yaakov, Jacob Popers, Frankfort, 1741–2

Bet Yehudah, Judah Ayash, Leghorn, 1746

Pene Aryeh, Aryeh Laib of Breslau, Amsterdam, 1790

Teshuvah Me-Ahavah, Eleazar Fleckeles, Kassa, 1912

Otzar Hayyim, Hayyim Kittsee, Maramarosziget, 1913

Hatam Sofer, Moses Sofer, *Orah Hayyim*, Budapest, 1863; *Yoreh Deah*, Pressburg, 1841; *Hoshen Mishpat*, Pressburg, 1872

Ketav Sofer, Abraham Samuel Benjamin Wolf Sofer, *Yoreh Deah*, parts I and II, Pressburg, 1879, 1884; *Even Ha-Ezer*, Pressburg, 1888

Shevet Sofer, Simhah Bunem Sofer, Vienna, 1906

Hatan Sofer, Samuel Ehrenfeld, Paks, 1912

Maharam Schick, *Orah Hayyim*, Sotmar, 1904

Divre Hayyim, Hayyim Halberstam, Lemberg, 1875

Riba, Joel Ungar, Paks, 1889

Binyan Tzion, Jacob Ettlinger, Altona, 1868

Binyan Tzion Ha-Hadashot, Jacob Ettlinger, Vilna, 1878

Maharatz, Zevi Hirsch Chajes, Zolkiew, 1849

Shoel U-Meshiv, Joseph Saul Nathanson, 5 parts, Lemberg, 1865–90

Meshiv Davar, Naphtali Zevi Judah Berlin, Warsaw, 1894

Maaseh Ish, Jacob Saul Elyashar, Jerusalem, 1892

Rav Pealim, Joseph Hayyim of Baghdad, 4 parts, Jerusalem, 1961

Nahare Afarsemon, Jacob Tennenbaum, Paks, 1893

Shemen Ha-Mor, Abraham Anakawa, Leghorn, 1869

Mahane Hayyim, Hayyim Sofer, Pressburg, 1862

Matteh Levi, Marcus Horowitz, Frankfort, 1932

Avne Nezer, Abraham Bornstein, 2nd ed., Tel-Aviv, 1944

Yehudah Yaaleh, Judah Aszod, part II, Pressburg, 1860

Va-Yaan Avraham, Abraham Palaggi, Izmir, 1884

Tuv Taam Va-Daat, Solomon Kluger, 3rd Series, part II, Podgorze, 1900

Minhat Eleazar, Hayyim Eleazar Spira, Bene Berak, 1968 (photocopy of part III, Bratislava, 1922; part IV, Munkacs, 1930)

Birkat Hayyim, Hayyim Isaac Jeruchem, New York, 1956

Zikhron Yehudah, Judah Grünwald, part I, *Orah Hayyim*, Budapest, 1923, part II, *Yoreh Deah*, *Even Ha-Ezer*, *Hoshen Mishpat*, Ohelje, 1928

Tzafenat Paneah, Joseph Rozin, 3 parts, Warsaw, 1935–6

Melammed Le-Hoil, David Hoffmann, 3 parts, Frankfort, 1926–32

Arugot Ha-Bosem, Amram Grünwald, Szalyva, 1912

Havatzelet Ha-Sharon, Menahem Manish Babad, Bilgoraj, 1931

Mahaze Avraham, Abraham Steinberg, vol. I, Brody, 1927; vol. II, New York, 1964

Beer Hayyim Mordekhai, Hayyim Mordecai Roller, part I, Cluj, 1924; part II, Cluj, 1932; part III, Cluj, 1936

Gevul Yehudah, Judah Laib Zirelson, 2nd ed., Poltava, 1912

Helkat Yaakov, Mordecai Joseph Breisch, vol. II, London, 1959

Seride Esh, J. J. Weinberg, vol. II, Jerusalem, 1962; vol. III, Jerusalem, 1966

Tzitz Eliezer, Eliezer Waldenberg, vol. V, Jerusalem, 1957; vol. VII, Jerusalem 1963

Yen Ha-Tov, Isaac Nissim, Jerusalem, 1947

Minhat Yitzhak, Isaac Jacob Weiss, 5 parts, London–Jerusalem, 1969–72

Iggerot Moshe, Moses Feinstein, *Hoshen Mishpat* etc., New York, 1963
Mishpete Uziel, Ben Zion Uziel, *Even Ha-Ezer*, Jerusalem, 1964; *Orah Hayyim*,
   Jerusalem, 1947; *Yoreh Deah, Tinyana*, Jerusalem, 1952
Tirosh Ve-Yitzhar, Zevi Ezekiel Michaelson, Warsaw, 1936
Daat Kohen; Ezrat Kohen, A. I. Kook, Jerusalem, 1969
Besamim Rosh, Saul Berlin, 2nd ed., Cracow, 1881
Pahad Yitzhak, Isaac Lampronti, photocopy, 10 vols, Mekor, Jerusalem, 1970

Other works

Abba Mari Astruc, *Minhat Kenaot*, Pressburg, 1838
Abudraham, var. eds
Abulafia, Abraham, *Peliot Ha-Hokhmah*, Koretz, 1784
Agus, I. A., *Rabbi Meir of Rothenburg*, Philadelphia, 1947
Albo, Joseph, *Sefer Ha-Ikkarim*, ed. I. Husik, Philadelphia, 1926
Altmann, A., *Studies in Religious Philosophy and Mysticism*, London, 1969
Anatoli, Jacob, *Malmad Ha-Talmidim*, Lyck, 1866
Azkiri, Eleazar, *Sefer Haredim*, Jerusalem, 1958
Bahya Ibn Asher, *Commentary to the Pentateuch*, ed. B. Chavel, Jerusalem,
   1966
Bahya Ibn Pakudah, *Hovot Ha-Levavot (Duties of the Heart)*, var. eds; English
   trans., M. Mansoor, Bahya Ben Joseph Ibn Pakuda, *The Book of Direction to
   the Duties of the Heart*, London, 1973
Baron, S. W., *A Social and Religious History of the Jews*, Columbia University
   Press, 12 vols, 1952–67
Berger, A., 'The Messianic self-consciousness of Abraham Abulafia: a tentative
   evaluation', in *Essays on Jewish Life and Thought Presented in Honor of Salo
   Wittmayer Baron*, ed. J. L. Blau *et al.*, Columbia University Press, 1959,
   pp. 55–61
Berliner, B., 'Rabbi Solomon Luria on the prayer-book', *Jews' College Jubilee
   Volume*, London, 1906, pp. 123–39
Birnbaum, P. (ed.), *Karaite Studies*, New York, 1971
Burak, M. J., *The Hatam Sofer*, Toronto, 1967
Cordovero, Moses, *Pardes Rimmonim*, Jerusalem, 1962
Crescas, Hasdai, *Or Adonai*, Ferrara, 1556
De Rossi, Azariah, *Meor Einayyim*, Vilna, 1863–6
Eibushütz, J., *Bene Ahuvah*, Prague, 1819
Eleazar b. Judah of Worms, *Rokeah*, Fano, 1505
Elleh Divre Ha-Berit, Altona, 1819
Encyclopedia Judaica, 16 vols, Jerusalem, 1972
Encyclopedia Talmudit, Jerusalem, 1947–
Epstein, I., *The 'Responsa' of Rabbi Solomon ben Adreth of Barcelona (1235–1310)*,
   London, 1925
——, *The Responsa of Simon b. Zemah Duran*, London, 1925
Epstein, L., *Marriage Laws in the Bible and Talmud*, Harvard University Press,
   1942
Ergas, Joseph, *Shomer Emunim*, Jerusalem, 1965

Finesinger, S., 'The custom of looking at the fingernails at the outgoing of the sabbath', *Hebrew Union College Annual*, Cincinnati, vol. XII–XIII, 1938, pp. 347–65

Freehof, S. B., *A Treasury of Responsa*, Philadelphia, 1963

Gersonides, *Commentary to the Bible*, var. eds

——, *Milhamot Adonai*, Riva di Trento, 1560

Ginzberg, L., *The Legends of the Jews*, 7 vols, Philadelphia, 1913–38

Goldman, Israel M., *The Life and Times of Rabbi David Ibn Abi Zimra*, New York, 1970

Gordis, R., *The Biblical Text in the Making*, New York, 1971

Ha-Levi, Judah, *Kuzari*, var. eds

Heinemann, I., *Taame Ha-Mitzvot*, 2 vols, 2nd ed., Jerusalem, 1949

Hershman, A. M., *Rabbi Isaac ben Sheshet Perfet and His Times*, New York, 1943

Herskovitz, M., *Rabbi Zevi Hirsch Chajes*, Jerusalem, 1972

Jacobs, L., *Principles of the Jewish Faith*, London, 1964

——, *Jewish Law*, New York, 1968

——, *Hasidic Prayer*, London, 1972

Jewish Encyclopedia, 12 vols, New York, 1901

Karlinsky, H., 'The pig and "permission" to eat it in the future' (in Hebrew), *Shanah Be-Shanah*, Jerusalem, vol. II, 1971, pp. 243–54

Katz, E., *Ha-Hatam Sofer*, Jerusalem, 1960

Katz, J., 'Though he sinned, he remains an Israelite' (in Hebrew), *Tarbiz*, vol. 27 (January 1958; dedicated to G. Scholem), pp. 203–17

——, *Exclusiveness and Tolerance*, Oxford, 1961

Landsberg, W., *Zeev Yitrof*, Frankfort-on-Oder, 1793

Lipshutz, I., *Tiferet Yisrael*, Vilna, 1911

Luzzatto, M. H., *Mesillat Yesharim*, ed. M. M. Kaplan, Philadelphia, 1936

Mann, Jacob, *Texts and Studies in Jewish History and Literature*, 2 vols, rev. ed., New York, 1972

Margaliot, R., 'Rabbi Saul Berlin, the forger of the book *Besamim Rosh*' (in Hebrew), *Areshet*, Jerusalem, 1944, pp. 411–18

Margalioth, M. (ed.), *Encyclopedia Le-Gedole Yisrael*, Jerusalem, 1946

Medini, H. H., *Sede Hemed*, ed. A. I. Friedman, New York, 1962

Merkavah Shelemah, ed. S. Mussajov, Jerusalem, 1921

Montefiore, C. G. and Loewe, H. (eds), *A Rabbinic Anthology*, London, 1938

Nahmanides, *Commentary to the Pentateuch*, ed. B. Chavel, Jerusalem, 1960

——, *Collected Writings*, ed. B. Chavel, Jerusalem, 1963

——, *Iggerot Ha-Ramban*, Königsberg, n.d.

Patremoli, S., *Tzapihat Bi-Devash*, Salonika, 1848

Petuchowski, J. J., *The Theology of Haham David Nieto*, New York, 1954

Plaut, W. G., *The Rise of Reform Judaism*, New York, 1963

Rapoport Albert, A., 'Confession in the circle of R. Nahman of Bratslav', *Bulletin of the Institute of Jewish Studies*, vol. I, 1973, pp. 65–96

Reines, A. J., *Maimonides and Abravanel on Prophecy*, Cincinnati, 1970

Saadiah Gaon, *Book of Beliefs and Opinions*, trans. S. Rosenblatt, Yale University Press, 1955

Saracheck, J., *Faith and Reason*, New York, 1935
Scholem, G., *Major Trends in Jewish Mysticism*, 3rd ed., London, 1955
——, 'Shiur Komah', *Encyclopedia Judaica*, vol. 14, pp. 1417–19
——, *Jewish Gnosticism, Merkabah Mysticism and Talmudic Tradition*, New York, 1960
——, *On the Kabbalah and its Symbolism*, London, 1965
——, *Sabbatai Sevi*, London, 1973
Sevin, S., *Ha-Moadim Ba-Halakhah*, 2nd ed., Tel-Aviv, n.d.
Silver, D. J., *Maimonidean Criticism and the Maimonidean Controversy*, Leiden, 1965
Singer, S., *Authorised Daily Prayer Book*, new ed., London, 1962
Sofer, S., *Iggerot Soferim*, Vienna, 1929
——, *Hut Ha-Meshulash*, Jerusalem, 1963
Trachtenberg, J., *Jewish Magic and Superstition*, New York, 1970
Urbach, E. E., 'The traditions about Merkaba mysticism in the Tannaitic period', in *Studies in Mysticism and Religion Presented to G. Scholem*, ed. E. E. Urbach, R. J. Zwi Werblowsky and Ch. Wirszubski, Jerusalem, 1967, Hebrew section, pp. 1–28
——, *Hazal*, Jerusalem, 1969
Weinstock, I., *Be-Maagale Ha-Nigleh Ve-Ha-Nistar*, Jerusalem, 1969
Weiss, I. H., *Dor Dor Ve-Doreshav*, 5 vols, Berlin, 1928
Wiesenberg, E., 'Related prohibitions: swine breeding and the study of Greek', *Hebrew Union College Annual*, Cincinnati, vol. XXVII, 1926, pp. 213–33
Zimmels, H. J., *Magicians, Theologians and Doctors*, London, 1952
——, *Ashkenazim and Sephardim*, London, 1958
Zunz-Albeck, *Ha-Derashah Be-Yisrael*, Jerusalem, 1947

Index

363

Printed and bound by CPI Group (UK) Ltd, Croydon, CR0 4YY

13/04/2025

14656581-0003